When Edward Wagenknecht was six years old, he read *The Wizard of Oz* and made up his mind that he was going to be a writer. Later, he was importantly influenced by Agnes Repplier, but he learned his biographical method (psychography) from Gamaliel Bradford, who had in his turn been influenced by Sainte-Beuve. As a scholar, Dr. Wagenknecht was trained at the University of Chicago, in his native city, when John Matthews Manly was head of the Department of English. He considers the great Chaucer scholar, Edith Rickert, the greatest teacher he ever encountered.

Dr. Wagenknecht is the only man who has ever written standard histories of both the English and the American novel. He is the author of a definitive book on Longfellow and has edited Mrs. Longfellow's letters and journals. He is regarded as an authority on Dickens and Mark Twain. He has also edited numerous anthologies (one of which, *The Fireside Book of Christmas Stories*, was phenomenally successful), and has reviewed for almost all important American book reviewing media. For many years, he has been one of the core reviewers of the *Chicago Sunday Tribune Magazine of Books*. He is devoted to silent motion pictures and phonograph records of opera, *Lieder,* and drama, and is passionately fond of cats.

Dr. Wagenknecht lives in West Newton, Mass., with his wife and three sons, of whom the youngest was named after Walter de la Mare. Since 1947, he has been Professor of English at Boston University.

THE SEVEN WORLDS OF
THEODORE ROOSEVELT

By EDWARD WAGENKNECHT

BIOGRAPHICAL: *The Man Charles Dickens* (1929); *Geraldine Farrar, An Authorized Record of Her Career* (1929); *Jenny Lind* (1931); *Mark Twain, The Man and His Work* (1935); *Longfellow, A Full-Length Portrait* (1955); *Mrs. Longfellow: Selected Letters and Journals* (1956); *The Seven Worlds of Theodore Roosevelt* (1958)

CRITICAL: *Lillian Gish, An Interpretation* (1927); *Values in Literature* (1928); *A Guide to Bernard Shaw* (1929); *Utopia Americana* (1929); *Cavalcade of the English Novel* (1943); *Cavalcade of the American Novel* (1952); *A Preface to Literature* (1954)

ANTHOLOGICAL: *The College Survey of English Literature* (with others) (1942); *Six Novels of the Supernatural* (1944); *The Fireside Book of Christmas Stories* (1945); *The Story of Jesus in the World's Literature* (1946); *When I Was a Child* (1946); *The Fireside Book of Ghost Stories* (1947); *Abraham Lincoln, His Life, Work, and Character* (1947); *The Fireside Book of Romance* (1948); *Joan of Arc, An Anthology of History and Literature* (1948); *A Fireside Book of Yuletide Tales* (1948); *Murder by Gaslight* (1949); *The Collected Tales of Walter de la Mare* (1950); *An Introduction to Dickens* (1952); *Chaucer: Modern Essays in Criticism* (in preparation)

INTRODUCTORY: *The Chimes*, by Charles Dickens (Limited Editions Club, 1931); *Life on the Mississippi*, by Mark Twain (Limited Editions Club, 1944); *A Tale of Two Cities*, by Charles Dickens (Modern Library, 1950); *Great Expectations*, by Charles Dickens (Pocket Books, 1956)

Theodore Roosevelt

The Seven Worlds of

THEODORE ROOSEVELT

by

EDWARD WAGENKNECHT

LONGMANS, GREEN & CO.

NEW YORK · LONDON · TORONTO

1958

LONGMANS, GREEN AND CO.
119 WEST 40TH STREET, NEW YORK 18

LONGMANS, GREEN CO., LTD.
6 & 7 CLIFFORD STREET, LONDON W 1

LONGMANS, GREEN AND CO., INC.
20 CRANFIELD ROAD, TORONTO 16

THE SEVEN WORLDS OF THEODORE ROOSEVELT

COPYRIGHT © 1958

BY EDWARD WAGENKNECHT

PUBLISHED SIMULTANEOUSLY IN THE DOMINION OF CANADA BY
LONGMANS, GREEN AND CO., TORONTO

LIBRARY OF CONGRESS CATALOG CARD NUMBER 58–12762

PRINTED IN THE UNITED STATES OF AMERICA

The pages following are an extension of the copyright page:

Acknowledgment of the right to quote from the works listed here-inafter is gratefully made to the following publishers and copyright-owners:

APPLETON-CENTURY-CROFTS, INC. *James Ford Rhodes, American Historian,* by M. A. DeWolfe Howe; copyright, 1929, by D. Appleton and Company. *The Man Roosevelt, A Portrait Sketch,* by Francis E. Leupp; copyright, 1904, by D. Appleton and Company. *The Most Interesting American,* by Julian Street; copyright, 1915, by The Century Co. *A Backward Glance,* by Edith Wharton; copyright, 1934, by D. Appleton-Century Company, Inc. *Journal,* by Brand Whitlock; copyright, 1936, by Ella B. Whitlock.

BRANDT & BRANDT. From *Released for Publication,* Houghton Mifflin Company. Copyright © 1925 by Oscar K. Davis.

CHRISTIAN HERALD MAGAZINE. *Theodore Roosevelt, The Man As I Knew Him,* by Frederick C. Iglehart.

THE CROWELL-COLLIER PUBLISHING COMPANY. "My Predecessor," by William Howard Taft, *Collier's Weekly,* XLII, March 6, 1909, p. 25. "The Great Friend," by Sonya Levien, *Woman's Home Companion,* XLVI, October, 1919, pp. 7 +.

and Letters of John Muir, by William F. Badè. *The Life and Letters of John Burroughs*, by Clara Barrus. *Beveridge and the Progressive Era*, by Claude G. Bowers. *The Quick and the Dead*, by Gamaliel Bradford. *Under the Maples*, by John Burroughs. *Roosevelt, His Mind in Action*, by Lewis Einstein. *The Letters of Richard Watson Gilder*, edited by Rosamond Gilder. *Fallodon Papers*, by Viscount Grey of Fallodon. *The Letters and Friendships of Sir Cecil Spring Rice*, by Stephen Gwynn. *Roosevelt in the Bad Lands*, by Hermann Hagedorn. *Forty Years in the White House*, by Irwin Hood ("Ike") Hoover. *Moorfield Storey, Independent*, by M. A. De Wolfe Howe. *Charles W. Eliot*, by Henry James. *What Me Befell*, by J. J. Jusserand. *Richard Henry Dana, 1851–1931*, by Bliss Perry. *Under Four Administrations*, by Oscar S. Straus. *The Life of John Hay*, by William Roscoe Thayer. *Theodore Roosevelt, An Intimate Biography*, by William Roscoe Thayer. *Theodore Roosevelt, The Logic of His Career*, by Charles G. Washburn.

THE MACMILLAN COMPANY. *The Roosevelt Family of Sagamore Hill*, by Hermann Hagedorn; copyright, 1954, by Hermann Hagedorn. *Theodore Roosevelt, The Boy and the Man*, by James E. Morgan; copyright, 1907, by The Macmillan Company. *Theodore Roosevelt The Citizen*, by Jacob A. Riis; copyright, 1903, 1904 by The Outlook Company. *The Autobiography of William Allen White;* copyright, 1946, by The Macmillan Company.

A. C. McCLURG & CO. *From Rough Rider to President*, by Max Kullnick.

OXFORD UNIVERSITY PRESS. *A Hoosier Autobiography*, by William Dudley Foulke.

THE REVEREND ENSWORTH REISNER. *Roosevelt's Religion*, by Christian F. Reisner.

RINEHART & COMPANY, INC. *The Life and Times of William Howard Taft*, by Henry F. Pringle. Copyright, 1939, by Henry F. Pringle.

CHARLES SCRIBNER'S SONS. *The Works of Theodore Roosevelt*, 24 volumes, Memorial Edition, edited by Hermann Hagedorn (including *Theodore Roosevelt and His Times*, by Joseph Bucklin Bishop). *Letters from Theodore Roosevelt to Anna Roosevelt Cowles, 1870–1918. Letters to Kermit from Theodore Roosevelt, 1902–1908*, edited by Will Irwin. *Selections from the Correspondence of Theodore Roosevelt and Henry Cabot Lodge, 1884–1918. Crowded Hours, Reminiscences* of Alice Roosevelt Longworth. *My Brother Theodore Roosevelt*, by Corinne Roosevelt Robinson. *The Happy Hunting Grounds*, by Kermit Roosevelt. *Charles Joseph Bonaparte, A Biography*, by Joseph Bucklin Bishop. *The Americanization of Edward Bok, The Autobiography of a Dutch Boy Fifty Years After. Twice Thirty*, by Edward W. Bok. *The Letters of Henry James*, edited by Percy Lubbock. *Impressions of Great Naturalists*, by Henry Fairfield Osborn. *Nelson W. Aldrich, A Leader in Politics*, by Nathaniel W. Stephenson. *Our Times*, by Mark Sullivan.

MRS. WALTER STOKES. *Roosevelt, The Story of a Friendship, 1880–1919*, by Owen Wister; copyright, 1930, by The Macmillan Company.

HENRY G. VILLARD. *Fighting Years*, by Oswald Garrison Villard.

IVES WASHBURN, INC. *Roosevelt in the Rough*, by Jack Willis and Horace Smith.

To my cousin

THEODORE WAGENKNECHT

of Chicago and Downers Grove, who was named for the
Great Man

Foreword

This book is the writer's contribution to the centennial celebration of the birth of Theodore Roosevelt.

It could not have been written without the encouragement and cooperation of the Theodore Roosevelt Association and especially of Mr. Hermann Hagedorn, whose kindness went far beyond the line of duty or any "official" consideration.

Quotations from unpublished letters, etc., have been made by kind permission of Mr. William M. Cruikshank, literary executor of the Theodore Roosevelt Estate.

As with all the books I have written since I came to live in the Boston area, I am deeply indebted to the hospitality of the Harvard University Library, which in this instance indicates both Mr. William A. Jackson, Director of the Houghton Library, and Mr. Robert H. Haynes, who, in addition to his other functions, is curator of the Theodore Roosevelt Collection in the Widener Memorial Library.

I am grateful to Boston University for relieving me of all duties as Professor of English during the first term, 1957–58, so that it might be possible for me to finish this book in time for the centennial celebration, and to Mr. Ralph Lowell, who invited me to deliver a series of Lowell Lectures on Theodore Roosevelt, the substance of which, though in somewhat different form, is embodied in this volume.

Publishers and copyright owners have been generous in permitting me to quote from books by and about Theodore Roosevelt and from other relevant material. These acknowledgments are made on the copyright page. Page references are listed in the Notes.

My son, Walter Wagenknecht, has assisted me greatly in proofreading.

EDWARD WAGENKNECHT

May 15, 1958

Contents

The Facts of T.R.'s Life

Theodore Roosevelt, second of the name, was born in a brownstone house just east of Broadway, at 28 East 20th Street, New York City, on October 27, 1858. The name, which is pronounced rō'-zĕ-vĕlt, is Dutch and means field of roses. Besides the Dutch, he had Irish, Scottish, Welsh, English, French, and German ancestry. The Roosevelts were a mercantile family who had been on Manhattan Island since the middle of the seventeenth century. T.R.'s mother had been Martha Bulloch, of Roswell, Georgia, whose family was to be prominently engaged, on the Confederate side, in the Civil War.

A delicate child, T.R. was educated mainly by private tutors. Though he was no child prodigy, he early became a mighty reader and collector of zoological specimens. Travel in Europe and in Egypt broadened his horizon. In 1872 and 1873, with his older sister, Anna (later Mrs. W. S. Cowles), and his younger brother and sister, Elliott and Corinne (later Mrs. Douglas Robinson), he lived with a German family in Dresden.

In June, 1880, he graduated from Harvard University, and on October 27 of the same year he married Miss Alice Hathaway Lee, of Chestnut Hill, Massachusetts. After less than four years of very great happiness, Mrs. Roosevelt died, on February 14, 1884 (the same day as T.R.'s mother), after having given birth to a daughter, the "Princess Alice" of her father's White House years (Mrs. Nicholas Longworth). Meanwhile, in 1882, T.R. had published *The Naval War of 1812*, upon which he had begun work while still a student at Harvard.

T.R. began his career in politics as the youngest member of the New York State Assembly (1882–1884), being prominently and aggressively identified with the reform element. In June, 1884, he was a delegate to the Republican National Convention at Chicago, where he opposed James G. Blaine but refused to break with his party after Blaine had been nominated or to support Cleveland, as the "mugwumps" did. In November, 1886, he ran for mayor of

New York against the single-taxer, Henry George, and Abram S. Hewitt, Democrat, who was elected.

Meanwhile he had established himself as a ranchman in the Bad Lands of North Dakota, where he spent as much time as his other duties would permit up to his marriage to Miss Edith Kermit Carow, at London, on December 2, 1886. He brought his bride to "Sagamore Hill," the big new house he had built at Oyster Bay, New York, where they both lived the rest of their lives, and where their five children—Theodore Jr., Kermit, Ethel (Mrs. Richard Derby), Archie, and Quentin—were born.

During the eighties and nineties, before public life had completely claimed him, Roosevelt was very active as a writer. Among his titles were the biographies of *Thomas Hart Benton* (1887) and *Gouverneur Morris* (1888) in the "American Statesmen" series, and two of his best "hunting books," as they are generally considered—*Ranch Life and the Hunting-Trail* (1888) and *The Wilderness Hunter* (1893). More important than any of these was his major opus, *The Winning of the West* (1889–1896), the most Parkmanlike work in American literature outside the writings of Parkman himself.

From 1889 to 1895 T.R. served as United States civil service commissioner, from 1895 to 1897 as president of the Police Commission of the City of New York, and from 1897 to 1898 as assistant secretary of the Navy. Continuing to dramatize the fight for aggressive, sometimes flamboyant, righteousness, he impressed himself increasingly upon the consciousness of America. Appointed civil service commissioner by President Harrison, he was retained by President Cleveland. A sensationally fearless and efficient police commissioner, he attracted wide attention by enforcing the Sunday closing laws for saloons. In his Navy post, he urged intervention in Cuba and labored zealously to get the Navy ready.

In May, 1898, he resigned his post to become lieutenant colonel of the First United States Volunteer Cavalry in Cuba, popularly known as the "Rough Riders." His daredevil behavior at San Juan Hill and the daring and probably insubordinate energy he showed, after the fighting was over, in insisting that the authorities bring the army home out of a fever-ridden area increased his popularity notably, and in November, 1898, he was elected governor of New York. He worked with the "machine" whenever the "machine" would work with him, "consulting" the Republican "boss," Senator Thomas C. Platt, as he had promised to do, but always using his own judgment about following Platt's advice. The bitterest disagreements were over the taxation of corporation franchises and the appointment of an insurance commissioner. Though Roosevelt wanted a second term as governor, he was practically forced to accept the Republican nomination for vice-president in 1900 under William McKinley. This may have been partly because Senator Platt wanted to "kick him upstairs," but it was more because of the spontaneous enthusiasm of the country at large and especially of the West for the Spanish War hero and reform Governor.

T.R. took office as vice-president on March 4, 1901, but he was required to bore himself by presiding over the Senate for only one session. On September 14 President McKinley died of an assassin's bullet, and T.R. became the twenty-sixth (and youngest) President of the United States.

Carrying out McKinley's policies, as he had promised to do, T.R. supported trust legislation and reciprocity treaties, but there were no precedents to guide him in settling the disastrous coal strike of 1902. When the United States recognized the Republic of Panama, which had seceded from Colombia, in November, 1903, the way was open for the construction of the Panama Canal. An Alaskan boundary dispute with Great Britain was settled, and both Germany and England were warned off from Venezuela.

In November, 1904, T.R. was elected President of the United States in his own right, his plurality over his Democratic opponent, Judge Alton B. Parker, being the largest any candidate had ever enjoyed. Important legislation of the second term included the Hepburn Act for the regulation of railroad rates and the Food and Drug Act (both 1906). There were also important services to conservation. In 1905 he negotiated an end to the Russo-Japanese War; in 1907 he demonstrated American naval power by sending the fleet around the world. Though this was widely regarded as the most spectacular example of T.R.'s wielding the "Big Stick," he himself considered it a service to peace, expecting it to have a deterrent effect upon Japan, whose nerves were sore as the result of anti-Japanese legislation in California, of which legislation Roosevelt bitterly disapproved.

T.R. had been elected president only once, and it is an under-statement to say that he could have had another term for the asking. He had to fight hard to avoid it. It went, instead, to his secretary of war, William Howard Taft, and T.R. betook himself to Africa on a combined hunting and scientific expedition, which resulted in the largest and most carefully chosen array of African fauna ever collected. Mrs. Roosevelt met him at Khartum in March, 1910, and they proceeded on a triumphal progress across Europe. He spoke at the Sorbonne and the University of Berlin. In Christiania he accepted the Nobel Prize for his services in ending the Russo-Japanese War. At Oxford he delivered the Romanes Lecture. In London he served as the representative of the United States at the funeral of King Edward VII.

Nominally T.R. had been a contributing editor to *The Outlook* ever since leaving the White House. In June, 1910, he was back in New York to take up active duties. Here he received as tumultuous a welcome as has ever been accorded a private citizen, but the enthusiasm manifested did not deceive him. The Republican party was already splitting between the "insurgents" (enthusiasts for "progressive" legislation and the "Roosevelt policies") and the conservatives, or "standpatters," headed by President Taft. Roosevelt returned to politics in New York State in the summer of 1910, but he did not yield to the demand of his followers that he declare himself a presidential candidate until early in 1912. In June, at the Chicago convention, he was defeated for the nomination by President Taft, after a bitter battle over the seating of rival delegates. Declaring that the "standpatters" had "stolen" their delegates and run the "steam roller" over them, Roosevelt and his adherents proceeded to organize the Progressive (or Bull Moose) party, which nominated T.R. and Hiram Johnson. A campaign of almost unparalleled bitterness, during which, on October 14, Roosevelt was shot, at Milwaukee, by a fanatic, ended in November with the election of Woodrow Wilson, Democrat, as a minority president.

From early in Wilson's administration, T.R. opposed the President's Mexican policy and some aspects of his domestic policy as well. T.R. spent the winter of 1913–14 on his last great wilderness expedition, during which he explored the River of Doubt in central Brazil. After the beginning of World War I he grew increasingly critical of what he considered Wilson's failure to protect American rights and defend standards of international morality. In 1916 he liquidated the Progressive party by refusing to accept its nomination for president and energetically campaigned for the Republican nominee, Charles Evans Hughes, who lost by a nose. After the United States entered the war, T.R. waged a valiant fight to be permitted to raise and equip a division of volunteers for service in France. Wilson's refusal to grant this request was the bitterest disappointment of his life, as the death of his youngest son, Quentin, over the German lines, in July, 1918, was his greatest sorrow. Supporting the war, Roosevelt continued to oppose Wilson's conduct of the war, but there was no decisive endorsement of his views at the polls until, in November, 1918, the American people decisively rejected the President's plea for a Democratic Congress. All political observers seem to agree that only death could have prevented T.R.'s unanimous nomination and triumphant election in 1920. He had escaped death in South America by the narrowest margin and, though he had managed to drag himself back to Sagamore Hill, he was never to be well again. The year 1918 he spent in and out of hospital; on January 6, 1919, the nation gasped in shock and astonishment when banner headlines proclaimed that he had died in his sleep.

During the years of his fame Roosevelt had published many more books, including *Oliver Cromwell* and *The Strenuous Life* (both 1900); *African Game Trails* and *The New Nationalism* (both 1910); *An Autobiography* and *History as Literature, and Other Essays* (both 1913); *Through the Brazilian Wilderness* (1914) and *A Booklover's Holidays in the Open* (1916); and a number of books about World War I: *America and the World War* (1915), *Fear God and Take Your Own Part* (1916), *The Foes of Our Own Household* (1917), and *The Great Adventure* (1918).

Theodore Roosevelt lived one of the most crowded and varied lives of which we have any record, but his deeds alone do not explain the unrivaled purchase which he held over the imaginations of men from the turn of the century until his death. He himself was greater than anything he did. To make his personality live again, as far as paper and ink can do it, is the task to which this book is given.

THE SEVEN WORLDS OF
THEODORE ROOSEVELT

ONE

The World of Action

I. "Many-Voiced Roosevelt"

Theodore Roosevelt, said Henry Adams, "showed the singular primitive quality that belongs to ultimate matter—the quality that mediaeval theology assigned to God—he was pure act." In so far as a very complex man may be thus simplified, one might say of him that his ruling motive was to express himself, all that was in him, to do, to dominate, to create, to put himself to work in the world. But he differed from the mere conquerors whom in this aspect he resembled in two important particulars.

One of the most penetrating things he ever said about himself was his reference to "those who care intensely both for thought and for action." There are very few such men; Roosevelt was one of them. Long before he became president, he was conscious of moving in a number of different worlds. Indeed, the presidency itself was not big enough for him. "I am not always able as President to feel the entire absorption in the so-called political questions that come up, which I suppose a President ought to feel . . . because I do not regard them as being one-tenth or one-hundredth part as important as so many other questions in our life." Once, invalided with a bad ankle, he writes his son Kermit that he is now "engaged busily in doing nothing when I am not at my Presidential work!"

Such an attitude might easily have produced a chaotic, divided life. T.R. was saved from this by his strong, William Jamesian "horror of words that are not translated into deeds, of speech that does not result in action," by his conviction that ideals which do not get themselves acted out are mere emotional debauchery. Moreover, he always had to be convinced that what he was doing was right, that it squared with the plumb line of the eternities. But since, for all of Henry Adams, he was not God, this could not always be, and when it was not he was obliged to employ infinite ingenuity to convince himself and others that it was. This

1

precipitated many bitter controversies, some of which have endured to this day.

Experience teaches most human beings that the worst man in the world knows his duty a good deal better than the best man performs it. Roosevelt actually makes the amazing statement that "the difficulty is not in the doing but in the finding what the right course is." "Whatever I think it is right for me to do," he told O. K. Davis, "I do. . . . And when I make up my mind to do a thing, I act."

This sounds like boasting. With him it is not boasting but calm, objective statement of fact. He was of the stuff of which martyrs are made, yet he had none of the fanaticism commonly associated with martyrs. Indeed, he was not extremist enough for most of his critics but had a tireless gift for compromise and adjustment.

His was a self-directed career, so much so that some observers, not necessarily unfriendly ones, have found an element of histrionism in it. Thus "Ike" Hoover, the White House usher, who loved T.R., yet said bluntly that he "seemed to be forcing himself all the time; acting, as it were, and successfully." And Gamaliel Bradford, catching up one of T.R.'s own great phrases, felt that he was always "playing a game . . . forcing optimism, forcing enjoyment with the desperate instinctive appreciation that if he let the pretense drop for a moment, the whole scheme of things would vanish away."

Thus phrased, these judgments are not complimentary to Roosevelt. With a change of emphasis they may easily become so. As all the world knows, T.R. was a sickly child. His early diaries give the impression of a thoughtful, sensitive, but not unusually intelligent boy. He was already interested in science and, to a lesser degree, in history; he was unusually affectionate, and he had apparently developed a certain gift of leadership in the nursery; aside from these things, he gave little promise of the man we know. He is hurt when his mother makes fun of him, once, for some manifestation of affection, and he cries when the coming of an unexpected guest disturbs the "sociable evening" he had planned to spend with his family. But when his father tells him that, though he has the mind to support a useful and distinguished career, he cannot have it with his present frail and sickly body, he replies,

"I'll make my body," and he makes it something that supports him for sixty years through the strain of the world's chancelleries and the horrors of its jungles.

As he made his body he made his mind and his personality. He decided what he wanted to be; he chose his role, and he played it to the end. "There were all kinds of things of which I was afraid at first, ranging from grizzly bears to 'mean' horses and gunfighters; but by acting as if I was not afraid I gradually ceased to be afraid. Most men can have the same experience if they choose."

This was Roosevelt's first and greatest battle, and he bore its scars until the end. He was the actor who himself came to be the role that he played. But he did not differ from the rest of us because he was an actor. He differed because he chose a grander role and played it more heroically.

II. "The Strenuous Life"

When he was twenty-one T.R. promised himself that he would work up to the hilt until he was sixty. It turned out to be a life sentence. "I always believe in going hard at everything," he writes Kermit. "My experience is that it pays never to let up or grow slack and fall behind."

So he became the apostle of "The Strenuous Life." Even in peaceful times he operated under a sense of urgency. "We, here in America, hold in our hands the hope of the world, the fate of the coming years; and shame and disgrace will be ours if in our eyes the light of high resolve is dimmed, if we trail in the dust the golden hopes of men." He lived every moment with magnificent gusto, and he was never known to rest except when he slept. Moreover, he lived outwardly and inwardly with the same zest. "The capacity to be bored," he says, "whether treated as a sin or a misfortune is an awful handicap." He acted up to the hilt, and at the same time a part of him stood off and watched—and judged—the acting.

To be sure, Roosevelt himself insisted that the word "strenuous" did not quite express what he had in mind. He disliked the French translation of *The Strenuous Life—La Vie Intense—*and liked the Italian—*Vigor di Vita.* It was not tension that he was out for. As he conceived it, the strenuous life would take in Emerson as well as Lincoln; it might consist in writing poetry, or studying Indian songs, or investigating the labor problem or the condition of the poor. The important thing was to find something worth doing and do it with all your might. "Get action!" he cries. "Don't flinch! Don't foul! Hit the line hard!"

Roosevelt loved work, courted responsibility, responded with enthusiasm to the thought of having all his powers occupied. Less than a month before his death he wrote Philip Roosevelt: "The Doctors think I will be all right in the end. I hope so; but I am ahead of the game anyhow. Nobody ever packed more varieties of fun and interest in the sixty years!"

He refused to sympathize with men who had to work hard, even if their occupations were hazardous. At the same time, as we have seen, he insisted that it is not enough that a man should do his work; he must enjoy doing it. "Oh, *aren't* we having a good time!" he would cry. In the Barnes libel suit, a telegram was read which Roosevelt was alleged to have sent to Senator Platt after the franchise tax bill had been passed. It contained only the words "Three cheers." "I do not remember the telegram," said T.R., "but it sound characteristic."

From the smallest job to the greatest the note is the same. He is glad he became police commissioner, "for it is a man's work." And when he is asked whether he is not going to take a vacation, he replies, "Where do you suppose I could have as good a time as I am having right here in New York?" A little later the assistant secretary of the navy cries, "I have been very busy, much to my delight, for I perfectly revel in this work." And still later, "I am so glad to be Governor—that is, to be at work doing something which counts." Or, more naïvely and with even greater zest, "Heavens and earth how busy I am at the moment!" Naturally it was the presidency he enjoyed most of all. "Lord! but this is disheartening work sometimes. But I enjoy it!" And when he gets fed up with the Brownsville controversy he does not go off to play golf and forget it, as another president might do; instead, he produces a scholarly article on "The Ancient Irish Sagas." "I have had a great time as President," he writes as he prepares to leave the White House behind him. And the next September, in Africa, he declares that "no ex-President . . . ever enjoyed six months as I have enjoyed the six months now ending."

Archie Butt reports that having agreed to make a speech, T.R. would immediately proceed, perhaps while riding on horseback, to think out what he wanted to say, and that often he would have it written out in full within twenty-four hours of having accepted the invitation. Speechmaking was not the only thing in which he was forehanded. Having read Jacob Riis's account of tenement conditions in New York, he promptly took himself to Riis's office and not finding him in, left a message on his desk: "I have come to help." When in 1899 he saw the tenement house exhibition of the New York Charity Organization Society he summoned its members: "Tell me what you want me to do as governor and I will do it." And they did not themselves yet know what needed to be done!

When he went down to Panama to inspect the building of the canal he disregarded the comfortable schedule that had been made out for him and took on numerous extra chores including that of investigating the cost and condition of the yams being sold at the government commissary. He even rang bells more vigorously than other people, and when he sat in a rocking chair, as he dearly loved to do, he would energize it "in direct proportion to the intensity of his feelings," often rocking himself across the room. He danced and sang doggerel with a senator, gave interviews while being shaved in the White House, talking so vigorously the while that his visitors always caught their breath for fear the barber would cut his throat, taught poetry to his children while he was dressing for dinner, and drew maps for them with his umbrella in the dust of the street when they went out to walk together. It was a strain for him to stay out of a fight, not to go in, but he had great difficulty in sitting still long enough to have his portrait painted. He did with ease what other men make an effort to do. He had to work hard to rest.

There is a delightful photograph of him reading in his later years. He is holding the book with both hands, close to his heavily spectacled eyes, and frowning at it with an intensity of concentration which would surely have served to tear the heart out of Kant's *Critique of Pure Reason.* But the name on the book is *Penrod.* More amusing still is John Burroughs's story of what happened one evening when he and Mrs. Roosevelt were sitting with the President at their little rustic hideout in Virginia. "Suddenly Roosevelt's hand came down on the table with such a bang that it made us both jump, and Mrs. Roosevelt exclaimed, in a slightly nettled tone, 'Why, my dear, what *is* the matter?' He had killed a mosquito with a blow that would almost have demolished an African lion." And surely Gamaliel Bradford has the perfect comment: "He killed mosquitoes as if they were lions, and lions as if they were mosquitoes."

III. Man Speaking

Another manifestation of Roosevelt's inexhaustible energy was in his talk; "frank, vigorous," Joseph Bucklin Bishop calls it, "and marvellous in its range over human history, ancient, modern, and contemporaneous." To be sure, some people did not care for his conversation. John Singer Sargent did not, and Henry Adams was bored when Roosevelt talked history to him (as Adams says) as if he were a high school boy, but found him brilliant when he talked about San Juan Hill. Yet other equally brilliant persons capitulated without reservations.

I have heard Mr. Rudyard Kipling [wrote William Roscoe Thayer], tell how he used to drop in at the Cosmos Club at half past ten or so in the evening, and presently young Roosevelt would come in and pour out projects, discussions of men and politics, criticisms of books, in a swift and full-volumed stream, tremendously emphatic and enlivened by bursts of humor. "I curled up on the seat opposite," said Kipling, "and listened and wondered, until the universe seemed to be spinning round and Theodore was the spinner."

For a subject anything would do. Bradley Gilman once heard him hold forth on "greetings and farewells among primitive people." "Can you have me to dinner either Wednesday or Friday?" he writes Mrs. Lodge in 1906. "Would you be willing to have Bay and Bessie also? Then we could discuss the Hittite empire, the Pithe-canthropus, and Magyar love songs, and the exact relations of the Atli of the *Volsunga Saga* to the Etzel of the *Nibelungenlied*, and of both to Attila—with interludes by Cabot about the rate bill, Beveridge, and other matters of more vivid contemporary interest." Though this was not meant to be taken literally, T.R. was quite capable of holding forth upon all these subjects and more besides, and those who accuse him of working up learned discourses to impress the experts will have to explain why he often talked quite as well to a child as to a monarch or a savant.

Whatever the subject, there was no pedantry and no "side," for Roosevelt never talked about anything that did not interest him, and he was always spontaneous in his treatment of it. Once Speck von Sternberg's description of hunting the auroch in the Ural Mountains led to a consideration of the differences between that animal and the American bison, from which T.R. went on to describe how the kings of Babylonia and Assyria hunted the wild bull.

The great controversy about Roosevelt's talk is whether it was conversation or monologue. Here the reader can prove anything he wishes to prove, for there is plenty of testimony on both sides. Sometimes even his admirers call him a monologuist. Archie Butt even says Roosevelt could not help monopolizing a conversation: as soon as he opened his mouth, everybody else stopped talking to hear what he had to say! Mrs. Winthrop Chanler tells of an enjoyable occasion at Lodge's place at Nahant: "He always liked to talk from a rocking chair; so one was brought out on the piazza, and [we] . . . sat around him while he rocked vigorously and told one story after another, holding us enchanted, making us laugh till we cried and ached." In 1902, after a dinner at the White House, James Ford Rhodes had this conversation with John Hay:

RHODES: That was a nice conversational dinner we had at the White House last night, Mr. Secretary.

HAY: Conversational do you call it? How long were we at table?

RHODES: About two hours.

HAY: Well, Wellman talked a minute, Sir Martin one and a half minutes, you a minute, and I do not more than that, and Theodore talked all the rest of the time. Do you call that conversation?

But when Rhodes asked T.R., two years afterwards, if he remembered that dinner, he replied, "Very well indeed. Was not John Hay great that night!"

On the other hand, William Beebe, Sir Harry Johnston, Henry Cabot Lodge, and Robert Haven Schauffler all insist that Roosevelt was an excellent listener.

Though a brilliant, humorous, high-powered talker [writes Schauf-fler], he was more ear than mouth. On the slightest indicaton that one of his guests had anything to contribute, he would jam on all his verbal brakes, stop dead in the middle of a sentence and, seizing the other's arm —if accessible—in a powerful grip—urgently demand: "Yes, yes, what were you going to say?". . . He was perhaps the most creative listener I have ever encountered. If we all had such audiences, we would con-tinually excel ourselves.

It may be that these testimonies are less irreconcilable than they seem. Warrington Dawson says that Roosevelt was an excellent listener to people who knew what they were talking about. "Where they did not, he had no patience with them and did not pretend to it." His mental processes, too, were extraordinarily rapid, with the result that he often saw the point long before his interlocutor had arrived at it. For duller human beings, conversation with T.R. obviously had its perils. "Participation," writes William Beebe, "de-manded keen attention and responsibility in sustaining one's point of view, for he continually tossed the theme from one to another of us—themes which never faltered or fell to earth. I have never, either in European salons or among the best American minds, known conversation of equal brilliancy."

IV. Energy to Burn

All this, first and last, produced a good deal of noise, and in the early days of the Roosevelt presidency there were those in Wash-ington who thought the noise incompatible with the dignity of the White House. Richard Watson Gilder speaks of "that human vol-cano, roaring as only a human volcano can roar!—leading the laugh and singing and shouting, like a boy out of school, pounding the table with both noisy fists." T.R. was indeed an incorrigible table thumper, and backslapper, too, for that matter; he even tried to pound the table when he had a bullet in him.

For it was not only the amount that Roosevelt talked which impressed people. It was the incredible energy of his utterance. Possibly the exaggerated emphasis he employed was originally adopted to overcome a speech defect.

Each syllable [writes Julian Street] leaves his mouth a perfectly formed thing; his teeth snap shut between the syllables, biting them apart, and each important, each accented syllable is emphasized not merely vocally, but also with a sharp forward thrust of the head which seems to throw the word clattering into the air. When he utters the first personal pronoun it sounds like "I-y-e-e-e," with the final "e's" trailing off like the end of an echo.

Add to these things the flashing teeth and pince-nez, the clenched, shaken fist, the leveled forefinger, the sarcasm and the humor, and the squeaking, falsetto break in the voice which he used so tellingly for humorous emphasis, and there is no question but that you have a phenomenon. "He seems to *explode* his words," says one observer. Once, we are told, he frightened a child while he was speaking in a church. I am not sure that Roosevelt's manner frightened the examining counsel at the Barnes libel trial, but it had a very unfortunate effect upon him. For one thing, it caused him to forget that he was a gentleman: "You need not treat me as a mass meeting because I am not. . . . Now, if your Honor please, I ask that this witness be requested to testify without gesticulation, and in the ordinary and in the usual way of a witness. . . . I do not want to be eaten up right here and now."

Moreover, the difference between his public and private utterance was only a difference of degree. Dictating to his secretary or talking with his friends, he walked, he pounced, he sat on the edge of his desk and swung his leg or curled up on a sofa with his foot under him. Josephine Stricker says he often dictated a speech to her quite as emphatically as if he were delivering it to an audience.

V. Tonic

The effect of this energy upon other people varied with the individual. William Dean Howells says frankly that Roosevelt made him tired. John Burroughs felt dominated and ill at ease in his presence. "One felt," he says, "that the Deity of Judgment might come at any moment." And even Eleanor Alexander, who married T.R.'s eldest son, and who loved her father-in-law devotedly, has recorded with delicious humor her initiation into the turbulent life at Sagamore:

The Roosevelt family enjoyed life far too much to be willing to waste their time sleeping. Every night they stayed downstairs until midnight; then, talking at the tops of their voices, they trooped up the wide, un-

carpeted staircase, and went to their rooms. For a brief ten minutes all
was still; and, just as I was dropping off to sleep for the second time,
they remembered things they had forgotten to tell each other and rushed
shouting through the halls. I used to go to bed with cotton in my ears,
but it never did any good.

When they went out in search of a picnic spot they rowed for
hours through Long Island Sound, then chose what seemed to her a
supremely inappropriate place in the blazing sun. "Faces and necks
were burned to a crisp; hands were blistered." By the end of the
summer she had lost twenty-six pounds.

Some even found T.R.'s energy definitely pathological. There was
a rumor current among doctors at one time that his blood pressure
was normally over 200; actually, Dr. Richardson never found it
higher than 130. President Eliot went through almost every shade
of attraction and repulsion toward Roosevelt, but certainly his
description of the President's visit to Harvard in 1905, for the
twenty-fifth reunion of his class, gives the great educator a high
place among the unconscious humorists:

I showed him to his room. The first thing he did was to pull off his
coat, roll it up with his hands, and fling it across the bed so violently
that it sent a pillow to the floor beyond. The next thing he did was to take
a great pistol from his trousers pocket and slam it down on the dresser.
After a while he came rushing downstairs, as if his life depended on it,
and as I stood at the foot of the stairs I said, "Now you are taking
breakfast with me?" "Oh, no," came the reply, "I promised Bishop Lawrence I would breakfast with him—and good gracious! (clapping his right
hand to his side) I've forgotten my gun!" Now he knew that it was against
the law in Massachusetts to carry that pistol and yet he carried it. Very
lawless; a very lawless mind!

Roosevelt himself lends aid and comfort to those who find a
pathological element in his energy when, in *Ranch Life and the
Hunting-Trail,* he remarks that "black care rarely sits behind a
rider whose pace is fast enough." And he once wrote home to his
sister from the West that "unless I was bear-hunting all the time I
am afraid I should soon get as restless with this life as with the life
at home."

For a great many people, on the other hand, T.R. was all tonic.
His "mere presence" in a room made Margaret Deland "tingle with

life." During World War I, Julian Street used to go out to Sagamore Hill when he felt he needed a tonic, and in London a physician told Lawrence F. Abbott that, instead of drawing power out of him as his other patients did, T.R. poured power into him. Sonya Levien, who worked with him toward the end of his life when he was on the *Metropolitan,* felt all this very strongly. His multitudinous visitors crowded the whole *Metropolitan* staff out of their offices, but in spite of the discomforts the girl perceived that she was living in an atmosphere of "warmth, loyalty, and energy." So, too, in the most impressive poetic tribute that has been paid him, Father Wilbur sings of

> Many-voiced Roosevelt, whose unflagging force
> Our sluggish torpor stirs, our chill blood warms.

VI. The Tom Sawyer Strain

T.R.'s energy and enthusiasm suggest a youthful or boyish spirit, and he had a strong Tom Sawyer strain in him all his life. Hermann Hagedorn thinks he did not lose it finally until Quentin was killed. "I had to go," he himself said of his late and extremely injudicious trip to Brazil. "It was my last chance to be a boy."

Practically everybody who came in contact with Roosevelt was impressed by this element in him. "You must always remember," said his dear friend, Sir Cecil Spring Rice, "that the President is about six." Mark Twain raised it to fourteen. William James placed him in the *Sturm und Drang* period. Even Woodrow Wilson felt his youngness when he came to him at the end to beg to be allowed to go to France. "Yes," he told Tumulty, "he is a great big boy."

This characteristic appears in T.R.'s eager response to almost every aspect of experience, in the perfectly wonderful times he was always having. It shows in his love of uniforms and costumes, in the fact that when he played with the children he sometimes seemed more childlike than they did, so that Mrs. Roosevelt thought it unsafe to permit him to bring them from Sagamore to the White House without her in attendance. Even when he was rude he was rude as a boy is rude, and Lyman Abbott tells us that when *Outlook* editorial conferences grew boring "he would not be impatient or say a word, but would quietly take something out of his pocket and begin reading." So, too, he keeps important men waiting while he plays with children or fondles animals. Who but Roosevelt would have thought of telling Wilson that if he would only let him go to France he would never oppose him politically again? Even more characteristic is his signing bills of which he disapproved but did not feel able to veto with "T. Roosevelt" instead of his full name and showing his displeasure by writing the "T. Roosevelt" as badly and illegibly as possible!

Above everything else, however, Roosevelt's youngness of spirit shows in his enthusiasm for outdoor sports, but this does not mean that he went at sports in a frivolous spirit or that he did not try to think through all the problems involved. He believed in sport as a means of cultivating vigor of body, and he believed in vigor of body not only for its own sake but "as an aid to vigor of mind, and, above all, to vigor of character." But he most emphatically did not believe in it "if it is made an end instead of a means, and especially if it is permitted to become the serious business of life." Though he sometimes had his doubts about intercollegiate athletics and was very active around 1905 in the movement to reform football abuses, he opposed President Eliot's desire to abolish football at Harvard. International competitions he disapproved of as likely to develop bad feelings between nations.

Roosevelt did not himself care much for gymnasium work, though he used it at times. Ike Hoover says that at night he would sometimes go out alone and run about the base of the Washington Monument. Though he left his bride on his first honeymoon to climb the Matterhorn, he did not in general care for mountain climbing, finding the pleasure out of proportion to the fatigue. He enjoyed rowing—he once rowed his wife for sixteen miles—but disliked sailing, partly because his stomach could not take it and partly, I think, because it was too quiet. For the same reason, fishing was out. Toward the end of his life he discovered in devilfishing a type that was strenuous enough for him, but he would have liked it much better if he could have practiced it on dry land! Of horseback riding he never tired.[1]

[1] In 1911 he wrote Mrs. Theodore Roosevelt, Jr., that he had been "driving the motor to and from New York with great vigor, like Mr. Toad; but the wear on the motor was great, and Mother . . . suddenly led a vigorous revolt, and now I have lost my proud position as Mr. Toad and merely use the motor to go to the train."

Roosevelt never played either baseball or football himself; neither did he often witness baseball games. He could never get very excited about sitting still to watch other people perform. The thing that interested him most about Ty Cobb was that he neither drank nor smoked.

Boxing and wrestling T.R. both enjoyed and believed in. At one time he believed and stated that he had been lightweight champion at Harvard, but this was an error of memory, as he afterwards acknowledged. Wrestlers, boxers, and jujitsu experts thronged the White House during his occupancy; often the President was damaged; finally he lost an eye. But he was no weak opponent; Mike Donovan said he sometimes had to use all he had to defend himself. In 1904 when Robert Johnstone Moody and his brother called on T.R. he kept them in his office for three hours, wrestling, demonstrating jujitsu, and talking athletics, with a waiting room full of people wanting to see him.

Prize fighting was different. Commercialized sport in general could always safely be counted upon to rouse the Puritan in him. As governor of New York he urged repeal of the law under which prizefights were permitted. It was not only the betting that he objected to. He also deplored the "shameful and hysterical curiosity which is to be satisfied only by seeing men risk their lives, where the risking of the life is itself what really attracts the onlooker, and not the courage or address shown in a manly sport." After the Johnson-Jeffries bout in 1910, with its appeal to racial antagonism, he urged that prize fighting be stopped by law in every state in the Union.

Golf Roosevelt never played. He would not have cared for it anyway, but in his time it was too "undemocratic," too much of a "sissy" game for a public man. On these grounds he advised Taft against it. He himself, he added, would never be photographed in tennis clothes.

Nevertheless, he played tennis—very badly, he says.

His method of playing [writes Theodore Roosevelt, Jr.] was original, to say the least. He gripped the racquet half-way up the handle with his index finger pointed along the back. When he served he did not throw the ball into the air, but held it in his left hand and hit it from between his fingers. In spite of this, and in spite of his great weight, he played a surprisingly good game.

At the White House he played on a court enclosed with canvas twenty feet high, where on a hot day the temperature would go to ninety or above. In 1882 Roosevelt once played ninety-one games of tennis in a day, and as late as 1908 he played in February and followed the game with a three-hour walk. Archie Butt describes one game in the pouring rain "with water over the entire court and the balls so wet that they would not bounce." But when Laurence Murray played with him he stopped the game as the rain began. "Just the day and time for a long walk and run. We will go!" So they did, without raincoats or umbrellas, and into the wilderness of Rock Creek Park. "Tie your shoes on extra tight, or the muck will pull them off." Which it did, notwithstanding. "From here it is exactly four miles to the White House gate. We will now run every step of the way back!" Which they did.

Weather never bothered Roosevelt much anyway. Richard Welling tells how, in Harvard days, he kept him skating one day at Fresh Pond in zero weather into the third hour—"Isn't this perfectly bully?"—at the same time cautioning him to watch his toes and ears! And once in Washington he took Maurice Francis Egan to walk with him in the pouring rain—"Lovely weather"—then stopped a cab to draw a diagram in imaginary lines on the chest of the horse to show him how to stab a wolf, which was the last thing he wanted to know!

But it would not be well to end on this bloodthirsty note. One year at Sagamore there was a chipmunk with urgent business requiring him to travel back and forth over the tennis court while a game was in progress. It was always stopped to accommodate him.

VII. No Mollycoddles Need Apply

This brings us to the famous "point-to-point" walks at Oyster Bay and in Rock Creek Park, whose only rule was "over or through, never around." If a creek got in the way, you forded it. If there was a river, you swam it. If there was a rock, you scaled it, and if you came to a precipice you let yourself down over it. Once just as William Dudley Foulke was starting out for a ramble with the President and his party there was an explosion in a nearby quarry, "and rocks were seen flying like hailstones, some of them clear across the river, others splashing into the stream. The President's face was lit with glee. 'Aha!' he exclaimed. 'We are going right there!'" When he got home, Foulke bathed and lay down to take a short nap before dinner. He woke up at half past five the next morning.

Roosevelt used these stunts both because he enjoyed them and, apparently, because this seemed to him a good way to test the mettle of other men. On February 16, 1908, he wrote Kermit:

Yesterday afternoon Fitz Lee and John McIlhenny and I took Colonel Lyon, of Texas, for a walk down Rock Creek. The ice had just broken and the creek was a swollen flood, running like a millrace. We did the usual climbing stunts at the various rocks, and then swam the creek; and it was a good swim, in our winter clothes and with hobnail boots and the icy current running really fast. Colonel Lyon balked at the swim; or, rather, he would have swum all right, but I was afraid to let him when I found he was doubtful as to his ability to get over; for I did not want a guest to drown on one of my walks.

One marvels at the spineless acquiescence with which most of T.R.'s guests allowed him to dragoon them into these tortures. There was one honorable exception. "Come on, General," called the President. "You are not afraid to swim the canal, are you?" "No, I'm not afraid," replied Frederick Funston, comfortable upon the bank, "and I am not a damned fool either."

In the West Roosevelt took even more dangerous chances than at Rock Creek Park. He is said once to have killed a mountain lion, hanging over a cliff, head downwards, with his guide holding onto his feet. Once he had himself lowered two hundred feet over a cliff so that he could snap a picture from the desired angle. The picture taken, his companions found that they lacked the strength to pull him up. Roosevelt could perceive no problem: the thing to do, he said, was simply to cut the rope and let him fall sixty feet into the icy stream. His companions insisted that this was suicide. One of them returned to camp, accordingly, for additional rope. This enabled them to lower Roosevelt twenty-five feet more. (By this time he had been hanging two hours.) Since no more rope was available, there was nothing to do now but chance the fall. T.R. was pulled out of the water upon a raft, half conscious. "He was stiff and sore for several days, from the bruises across his chest and under his arms, but he did no moaning about it."

All this is quite in line with Roosevelt's contempt for people who refused to take chances. He detested brutality, the wanton or deliberate infliction of injury, yet he said he would disinherit a boy if he were to weigh the possibility of broken bones against the glory of playing football for Harvard. Certainly he took no particular care of his own bones; neither did he teach his sons to guard theirs. Fortunately for himself he had not married a nervous woman. For all that, the shock of one of his accidents cost her a miscarriage, which was a pretty high price to pay for manliness.

Looking at the matter from the high moral standpoint, I suppose one would have to say that no man should hesitate to risk life or limb when the issue at stake is more important than life or limb. But, by the same token, if a man belongs not to himself but to the community and to God (and this is the assumption upon which Roosevelt functioned) he has no more right to risk himself upon any other basis than he has to commit suicide. Theoretically Roosevelt would have granted this—indeed, he himself says as much—but in practice he usually found it impossible to resist a dare. Thus George Meyer jumps his horse over a three-foot stone wall and a four-foot hurdle; so Roosevelt, though much heavier, forces his reluctant mount to the same exertion—and barely makes it. "I could not let one of my Cabinet give me a lead and not follow."

He went up in a box-kite airplane. He went down in a primitive submarine, "chiefly because I did not like to have the officers and enlisted men think I wanted them to try things I was reluctant to try myself." This sounds very well. It even relates to one of his most attractive characteristics—his unwillingness to ask of anybody else what he was not willing to perform himself, but one may still believe that the real reason he went down was that he could not resist the adventure. "I am going to New Orleans," he writes Kermit, in time of epidemic. "I believe the danger is infinitesimal, and I do not think a President ought ever, by his action, to give any chance to timid people to use his example as an excuse for their own timidity." But is it "timid" to stay out of a fever-stricken area when you have no business there? and should all the "timid" people of the United States have braced themselves to rush in and dare the infection? Certainly there can be no doubt at all about bounding up a hill with his brother-in-law, Douglas Robinson, each trying to outdo the other, so that "two stout, elderly gentlemen reach the top, breathing so stertorously that they are both unable to speak." This is not bravery, but foolishness.

VIII. In the Wilderness

The great sport with which T.R.'s name will always be connected is big-game hunting. Here again, as with sport in general, he insists that it must not be allowed to take the place of more important things. He ransacks history for horrible examples: Pliny advised Trajan to keep the Greeks absorbed in athletics so that they should not be dangerous to Rome; Louis XVI lost his head because he paid more attention to hunting than to statecraft; even the Boers owed their defeat in part to an "inordinate and ridiculous love of sports." The eighteenth-century squire who hunted during a battle "should by rights have been slain offhand by the first trooper who reached him."

Roosevelt was also very sensitive about being considered a game butcher. "To make a very large bag, whether of deer, or prairie chicken, or ducks, or quail, or woodcock, or trout," he writes Henry van Dyke, "is something of which to be ashamed and not to boast of." As early as 1879 he had told Hal Minot, "I have not done much collecting this summer, for, as you know, I don't approve of too much slaughter." In 1908 he wrote William T. Hornaday: "Of course I take absolutely your view of hunting. Except for meat or scientific purposes, I now kill nothing, and the surroundings of the wilderness mean to me more than the game itself." A few years later he tells Frederick Selous that the ordinary sportsman "is merely a vigorous and unintelligent butcher." For some time he had been thoroughly convinced "that nothing has been better than to have the camera substituted for the rifle as the wilderness hunter's real weapon." When he goes to Africa he does not wish to be thought of as having gone off on a hunting trip. "I like to do a certain amount of hunting, but my real and main interest is the interest of a faunal naturalist." Coming out of Africa, he did not care if he never fired his rifle again.

Roosevelt loved animals, both wild and domestic. Even on the hunting field they were individuals to him. He always hated to shoot a cow, always took care not to frighten a doe away from her babies. "Killing driven game . . . is the very poorest kind of sport that can be called legitimate." Shooting a trapped bear is one of the things that are simply not done. "Crusting" (going out after the deer on snowshoes) is "simple butchery" and no "self-respecting man" would resort to it except for the necessity of having meat.[2]

In short, the hunter must play it straight. He must himself do the work and take the risk. There must be no sham. "Game heads and antlers which represent merely the owner's money make that owner look absurd; trophies, save in rare cases when they are gifts, should be proof of the owner's prowess." T.R. condemned the habit of wearing elks' teeth on watch chains as severely as he had condemned the killing of birds to decorate women's hats when he was governor of New York; in 1907 he made a personal appeal to the Grand Exalted Ruler of the B.P.O.E. In the West he got his friend Jack Willis out of the business of killing bear and mountain sheep for their pelts, offering if necessary to lend him money to set him up in another line of work. "You are a Christian at heart; why don't you become a Christian in your ways, instead of a ruthless butcher of defenseless animals?" "Killing game the way you are doing it is not just wrong; it is cowardly and contemptible and wicked. It ought to be a criminal act, besides, and it will be when the people wake up to the facts."

Roosevelt's services to conservation are well known; if he had done nothing else that was good during his presidency he would still have justified his office here. He showed this interest as early as 1887 when he became one of the founders of the Boone and Crockett Club; he showed it as governor; he showed it in 1911 when he supported the Bayne Bill in New York. Writing to Colonel William Wood in that year, T.R. quoted with approval the view of Alfred Russel Wallace that "the wanton and brutal destruction of living things and of forests" ranks "among the first of forbidden sins." This destruction, he continues, was especially characteristic of the nineteenth century. It "goes hand in hand with the sordid

[2] In November, 1908, the novelist and antivivisectionist, Elizabeth Stuart Phelps, wrote to Roosevelt. He replied that in his view vivisection should be "rigorously regulated; and even the best doctors go entirely askew in their opposition to this regulation. It is curious how very merciful men, who themselves do only what is necessary, will oppose legislation which is absolutely needed in order to restrain brutal and callous men."

selfishness which is responsible for so very much of the misery of
our civilization."

Even disregarding the scientific interest, it would not be fair to
equate Roosevelt's interest in hunting with an interest in slaughter.
The eloquent preface to *The Wilderness Hunter* is in order here:

For . . . [the hunter] is the joy of the horse well ridden and the rifle
well held; for him the long days of toil and hardship, resolutely endured,
and crowned at the end with triumph. In after-years there shall come forever to his mind the memory of endless prairies shimmering in the bright
sun; of vast snow-clad wastes lying desolate under gray skies; of the
melancholy marshes; of the rush of mighty rivers; of the breath of the
evergreen forest in summer; of the crooning of ice-armored pines at the
touch of the winds of winter; of cataracts roaring between hoary mountain
masses; of all the innumerable sights and sounds of the wilderness; of
its immensity and mystery; and of the silences that brood in its still
depths.

For all that, it is not possible to deny that Theodore Roosevelt
did know the pure lust of hunting, that he possessed it and was at
times possessed by it. As a child in Egypt he killed and preserved
between one and two hundred birds. In 1885 he writes of foxhunting
on Long Island; he always kept in the same field as the hounds,
he says, and was in second at the death, ahead of huntsman and
master. In 1893 he dreams of "killing peccaries with the spear,
whether on foot or on horseback, and with or without dogs," of
"shooting walrus and polar bear" in the Bering Sea, or traveling
on dog sled to the Barren Grounds in chase of the caribou and the
musk ox, and of shooting alligators "by torchlight in the everglades
of Florida or the bayous of Louisiana." When he killed a white
goat with Jack Willis, "the yell of delight he let loose could have
been heard for two miles in any country. . . . He rubbed his hands
together, in the way he had when he was greatly pleased with anything, and fairly danced around with joy." Similar stories are told
about his behavior when he got his buffalo and antelope.

Nor was this exuberance confined to his earlier years. Planning his
African trip in 1908, he writes Sir John L. Harrington; "By George!
I am as eager to go to Africa and to hunt on the Pibor, as a boy
who has been reading dime novels and wishes to go West and fight
Indians." From the hunting field itself he later wrote Robert Bacon:

"Two days ago, I saw one of the finest sights anyone can see: the Nandi warriors killed a lion with their spears, two of them being mauled." Father Zahm says that when the South American trip was first broached, the thing T.R. wanted most was to kill a jaguar.

Moreover, T.R. initiated his sons into the joys of hunting as early as possible. Ted killed his first buck before he was fourteen, his first moose at seventeen; Kermit had killed both lion and elephant before he was twenty. Kermit, indeed, began shooting so young that his father had to support the gun. And even little Quentin went out with Dr. Rixey at eleven and killed three rabbits, which he brought back to exhibit to Father, "very dirty and very triumphant, and Mother, feeling just as triumphant, brought him promptly over with his gun and his three rabbits to see me in the office." I must admit I am shocked at the statement about the jack rabbits in *Hunting Trips of a Ranchman.* Though they are "hardly worth powder," they "offer beautiful marks for target practice when they sit upon their haunches."

Roosevelt has his own reasoned justification for all this, as he has for everything he does. He argues that any bird or mammal thoroughly protected would drive man off the planet, and that if wild things were not hunted at all they would increase to such an extent that farmers would exterminate them completely. Therefore, "the encouragement of a proper hunting spirit, a proper love of sport . . . offers the best guaranty for the preservation of wild things." His persistent refusal to sentimentalize comes to his aid notably here. "Nature is ruthless, and where her sway is uncontested there is no peace save the peace of death; and the fecund stream of life, especially of life on the lower levels, flows like an immense torrent out of non-existence for but the briefest moment before the enormous majority of the beings composing it are engulfed in the jaws of death, and again go out into the shadow." If wildlife multiplies beyond the capacity of nature to support it, winter brings death "by the long-drawn agony of slow starvation," a far more cruel end than the hunter's bullet.

These views are certainly not logically indefensible, but I confess they still leave me unable to explain how a man who loved animals as much as Roosevelt did could still *enjoy* killing them.

IX. Courage

When a man has such a record as has been described here, it may seem that there is simply nothing to say about his courage except that it is inexhaustible. Certainly Roosevelt had courage, moral and physical both. When he took on New York's corrupt political bosses singlehanded at the beginning of his career, his enemies ridiculed him as a kid-gloved reformer; when he criticized Wilson's wartime policies at the end, they said he ought to be shot to death as a traitor. Neither reaction caused him to swerve for an instant from his chosen course. When he had something unpleasant to say he always chose to say it to the most unsympathetic audience: declared for gold in the pro-silver belt; publicly rebuked the governor of Arkansas, sitting on the platform beside him, because he had implicationally defended lynching; condemned the Egyptian rebels against British rule in an address at Cairo, though he had been warned that he would be shot if he brought up this question.

His physical courage he proved to everybody's satisfaction during his ranching days. He was anything but a quarrelsome man in the West. Inasmuch as in him lay he lived peaceably with all men. Yet he laid out a bully who insisted that "Four-Eyes" was going to "treat," drew a bead on a band of Indians and again on a drunken, treacherous guide, refused to share his bed in a frontier hotel with a drunkard disposed to shoot his way in and warned that if the door were forced he himself would fire, and went into the wilderness to capture a trio of boat thieves, guarding them with his rifle for ten days, part of the time singlehanded, and bring them back to the authorities. Having heard that "Jake" Maunders had threatened to kill him on sight, he went to his shack and asked him if he wanted to do it now (it turned out that Jake had been misquoted). When it seemed possible that the picturesque Marquis de Mores might challenge him to a duel, he exhibited fearlessness but avoided truculence, and the danger passed over.[3] Hardships, of course, were

[3] The best account of this somewhat controversial matter is in Carleton Putnam, *Theodore Roosevelt: The Formative Years*, Chapter XXX. T.R. never fought a duel but this was not the only occasion when he came within hailing distance of it; neither were the circumstances always so extenuating. When he was police commissioner there was some silly talk about pistols in a row

not even worth talking about. "The thermometer was twenty-six degrees below zero," he writes of one adventure, and "we had had no food for twelve hours. I became numbed, and before I was aware of it had frozen my face, one foot, both knees, and one hand. Luckily," he adds with unconscious humor, "I reached the ranch before serious damage was done."

In war and in exploration it was all the same. "We had a bully fight at Santiago, and though there was an immense amount that I did not enjoy, the charge itself was great fun. Frankly, it did not enter my head that I could get through without being hit, but I judged that even if hit the chances would be about three to one against my being killed; that has been the proportion of dead to wounded here." When he was urged that he might die in Africa, he replied that the fear of dying would not keep him from what he wanted to do. In 1912 he spoke for an hour and a half in Milwaukee with a bullet in his body.

Roosevelt had views about courage. For one thing, he denied that moral courage "stands higher than physical. Each is indispensable, and each is in the long run worthless without the other." Furthermore, he regarded cowardice, in a race or in an individual, as the unpardonable sin. Beers jumps him on this, with considerable vigor and reason.

Is this true? [he asks] Cowardice is a weakness, perhaps a disgraceful weakness: a defect of character which makes a man contemptible, just as foolishness does. But it is not a sin at all, and surely not an unpardonable one. Cruelty, treachery, and ingratitude are much worse traits, and selfishness is as bad.

Roosevelt's mind, I think, would have granted this, but one need only compare his inexhaustible charity toward the transgressions committed early and late by some of the "great big, goodhearted,

---

with Comptroller Fitch. Jack Willis says he once challenged a Chicago lawyer. This seems to have been A. L. Trude, who, in 1895, said T.R. killed only in traps, had a white goat slaughtered by a guide, then posed for his photograph with it, etc. There is an unpublished letter of March 20, 1879, in T.R.'s handwriting, signed by Otho (?) H. Williams, Jr., and addressed to a fellow Porcellian, Charles F. Sprague, demanding an apology for "disgraceful conduct." Sprague is reminded that if it is not forthcoming he knows "the alternative." Arrangements are referred to "Mr. Roosevelt, my second."

homicidal children" numbered among his Rough Riders with his harshness toward the very different shortcomings of more effete types to know where his natural bias lay.

Yet T.R. himself never claimed to be above fear; neither were his horrors confined to the wilderness. Writing home to his sister Anna from Cambridge in 1876, and expressing an almost feminine pleasure in his room and the domestic comforts assembled there, he adds that he does not think the washerwoman "always acts squarely on the subject of my white cravats. . . . She is a negress, about as large as Cornelius, and as I am rather afraid of her I have not yet ventured to remonstrate." I have already quoted his "There were all kinds of things of which I was afraid at first, ranging from grizzly bears to 'mean' horses and gunfighters; but by acting as if I was not afraid I gradually ceased to be afraid. Most men can have the same experience if they choose." Again the actor becomes what he plays, and again we strike the note of exhortation. (What I have done, you can do.)

On this basis, a psychoanalytically inclined biographer might well argue that Roosevelt's whole career was motivated by fear. Fear of revolution determined his attitude toward capital and labor. Fear of other nations determined his foreign policy. And so on. Some might even add that fear of not being able to stand up to life motivated his many deeds of personal daring. If this be true, it indicates a temperament that T.R. shared with many other men. Francis Parkman, the subject of one of his own great admirations, had it in a far more exaggerated and less commonsensical form, and the same thing appears in the typical Hemingway hero today. But those who believe that these words indicate a slur upon any such men have failed to take into account that this variety of cowardice is the only courage possible for a modern man of intelligence and imagination.

X. "Brother Ass"

If Roosevelt's courage was unquestionable, his health was not.

I was a sickly, delicate boy, suffered much from asthma, and frequently had to be taken away on trips to find a place where I could breathe. One of my memories is of my father walking up and down the room with me in his arms at night when I was a very small person, and of sitting up in bed gasping, with my father and mother trying to help me.

For years he could only sleep sitting up. As late as 1873, in Dresden, he had a "small" attack which caused him to blow "like an abridged edition of a hippopotamus," and his hand trembled "awfully" when he tried to write his father about it afterwards.

Out of this weakness he set to work to build the body which carried him through all the activities that have already been referred to and his serious work in the world besides. One of the surgeons who examined him in Chicago after he had been shot during the campaign of 1912 reported that he had "a phenomenal development of the chest. It is largely due to the fact that he is a physical marvel that he was not dangerously wounded. He is one of the most powerful men I have ever seen laid on an operating table. The bullet lodged in the massive muscles of the chest instead of penetrating the lung." A little later an official bulletin signed by Dr. J. B. Murphy and his associates declared: "We find him in a magnificent physical condition, due to his regular physical exercise, his habitual abstinence from tobacco and liquor."

Yet T.R. died, completely worn out, at sixty; worse still, he began complaining of the encroachments of age before he was forty! "He was never," said Bill Seward, his Maine guide, "what I considered a sturdy man. His energy and will carried him forward." Obviously this does not completely cover the case. What Dr. Murphy saw on the operating table was not a delusion, and it was a physical, not a psychic, phenomenon. Nevertheless, there was what, for want of a better word, we may call a psychic element in Roosevelt's strength. Mighty as his body became, it was always dominated by his spirit. And with such a man, who can tell where body ends and spirit begins? Moreover, there had been, on the physical side, a forcing process, and once health and strength had been attained, he often made utterly unreasonable demands upon them.

Late in his Harvard career Roosevelt was told by a Cambridge physician that he had a weak heart and must avoid all violent exercise. "Doctor," he replied, "I am going to do all the things you tell me not to do. If I've got to live the sort of life you have described, I don't care how short it is." In the West he "ate heart

medicine regularly." Once his heart gave out temporarily while he
was climbing in Rock Creek Park. His frightened companions pulled
him up the precipice he was trying to scale, and he lay stretched
out upon the ground for forty minutes until his strength came back
to him. Even in civil service days he was subject to heavy colds
running into bronchitis, and a pillow fight with the children might
bring back the asthma he was supposed to have got rid of finally
in Dakota.

Roosevelt always had to be careful of his throat while campaigning. Sometimes it gave out on him altogether. Sometimes,
when he was worried, he had trouble sleeping, but this bothered
him less than it bothers most people. If he could not sleep he could
always read; moreover, he had the idea that he needed only five
hours. Above all, there was the constant handicap of defective
eyesight, which he never realized until he got his first gun and
found other boys shooting at things he could not see at all.

One day they read aloud an advertisement in huge letters on a distant
billboard, and I then realized that something was the matter, for not
only was I unable to read the sign, but I could not even see the letters.
I spoke of this to my father, and soon afterward got my first pair of
spectacles, which literally opened an entirely new world to me. I had
no idea how beautiful the world was until I got those spectacles.

He "made" his body but he could not make himself a new pair
of eyes, and when he was grown he could not tell a white man
from an Indian without his glasses or recognize one of his own
children ten feet away. Finally, a boxing accident produced the
hemorrhage which deprived him of the sight of one eye altogether,
and then it was worse than before.

The doctors in 1912 made a great point of Roosevelt's clean living.
Tobacco he never used in his life. Sexual delinquency simply did
not exist so far as he was concerned. He was as close to being a
total abstainer as a man can come without actually being one. With
food, however, he seems to have been much less temperate.

"I eat too much," he himself tells Kermit, and his difficulties
with his weight would suggest this. "My waist is steadily increasing," he writes Lawrence Godkin in 1901, "although I make play-

mates of all the more robust members of my official family in the way of walking and riding."

It does not seem that he was a gourmet. He felt the need of meat in the hunting field and on the range, and he had a fondness for game and for some fancy foods like terrapin, but he could be quite happy with pork and beans, or with bread and milk. He liked apples, pears, oranges, pineapples, and peaches, and disliked bananas, alligator pears, and prunes. "The first fact is certainly not to my credit," he says; "although it is to my advantage; and the second at least does not show moral turpitude."

O. K. Davis calls T.R. "an eager and valiant trencherman." "I have seen him eat a whole chicken and drink four large glasses [of milk] at one meal, and chicken and milk were by no means the only things served." And Lloyd Griscom pictures him "stoking up prodigiously, as though he were a machine." He disliked the scanty breakfasts he was given on South American ranches before leaving for the hunt, and once he and Kermit were caught redhanded, by their host, eating the cold chicken they had found laid out in preparation for lunch and which they had been unable to resist. "As father said afterward, we felt and looked like two small boys caught stealing jam in the pantry." Yet meals seem to have been the one thing for which T.R. was not always punctual, and there are stories about how he sometimes forgot to eat for the interest of talking.

He drank considerable quantities of both coffee and tea, and since he was particular about his coffee, Mrs. Roosevelt provided him with a service of his own. T.R. Jr. says that his special coffee cup "was more in the nature of a bathtub." When, in the nineties, he often visited Richard Henry Dana III and his wife, Edith Longfellow, in Cambridge, Dana noticed that he always took between five and seven lumps of sugar in his coffee, "and I bethought me of the humming bird which lives on sweets, and is one of the most strenuously active of vertebrates." In 1911, however, Roosevelt says that he has used saccharine, not sugar, for many years.

Roosevelt was not often incapacitated by illness during his mature years, and even in Cuba and in Africa he succeeded in keeping well when most of the men around him were down sick. He did, however, pick up a fever in Cuba, which recurred afterwards, and he left his health finally behind him in South America on the most ill-advised and most heroic expedition of his life. He wrote some of his articles for *Scribner's Magazine* in the jungle when he had a temperature of 105!

His usual method of incapacitating himself, however, was through accidents, which followed with monotonous regularity through the years, and I do not propose to mention them all. "I cut my face and broke my left arm." He is writing about a fox hunt in 1885. "After that I fell behind, as with one hand I could not always make Frank take his fences the first time; however three or four miles farther on a turn in the line enabled me to catch up, and I was in at the death. . . . I looked pretty gay, with one arm dangling, and my face and clothes like the walls of a slaughter house." That night he went out to dinner; the next day he walked for three hours in the woods. "I am always willing to pay the piper when I have had a good dance," he tells the remonstrating Lodge; "and every now and then I like to drink the wine of life with brandy in it."

The last part of 1904 must have been a nightmare. In October his horse put a foot through a rotten plank on a bridge and somersaulted. Roosevelt landed on his head and skinned his forehead to the size of a small saucer. To his great delight, the newspapers missed this item, but he very narrowly escaped meningitis. In November he strained a leg while boxing with the boys and then strained it again jumping a fence on horseback, breaking a blood vessel and leaving "a huge black and purple place on the inside of my thigh literally as big as two dinner plates." This happy occasion he celebrated by visiting the St. Louis Exposition and walking through the grounds "without letting any of the reporters get any idea that I was at all lame." The climax came in December, when he not only wrenched the thigh for a third time but also received the blow that caused him finally to lose the sight of an eye.

Nor was this the end of his accidents. "We are thoroughly enjoying Ted being with us now," he writes his son Archie in 1908. "I play tennis with him and with various other people every morning. Today Phil drove a ball hard, and hit my eye, breaking the glass and cutting my eyebrow, and making me stagger for about two seconds. But none of the glass went into my eye, and after I ran up to the house and washed the blood off I could go on with the game. I suppose I shall have a black eye now." Two days after getting home from the Barnes libel suit at Syracuse in the spring of 1915 he tried to ride a new horse, "was thrown off and broke two ribs, so that at the moment, like King Agag," so he writes Mrs. Arthur Lee, "I 'walk delicately.'"

Not all Roosevelt's accidents were incident to his pursuit of sport. In 1905, in a collision in the Gulf of Mexico, he was thrown through the window of a lighthouse tender, taking all the glass with him "except a jagged rim round the very edge." But the worst accident of all occurred at Pittsfield, Massachusetts, in 1902, when the carriage in which he was riding was struck by a trolley car, killing the secret service man beside him and throwing the President himself forty feet. This produced an abscess of the bone which necessitated very painful treatment and kept him in a wheel chair through the difficult period of the coal strike negotiations. The injured leg gave T.R. trouble for the rest of his life, flaring up again so seriously in 1908 that for a time it looked as though there would have to be another operation.

With all this indomitable spirit in the face of injury and illness and all the zest of living that possessed Roosevelt, I find it a bit surprising that he should not only have yielded to the encroachments of age but even proclaimed himself old again and again before his time. I can only attribute this to the assumption that the exploits he had put himself through had taken a terrible toll of him. As early as 1895 he says, "I guess my riding and shooting days are pretty well over." In 1901 he is "a person who in age and bodily habit is growing to have an unpleasant resemblance to the late lamented Mr. Tracy Tupman." In 1903 he tells Ted that he is "falling behind physically. The last two or three years I have had a tendency to rheumatism, or gout, or something of the kind, which makes me very stiff." In 1906 he feels like "a worn-out and crippled old man!" At the time of his African trip he was "an elderly man with a varied past which includes rheumatism." In 1915, after hunting in Canada with the Lamberts, he wrote Kermit that he had "shot atrociously, and ran and walked so badly that I shall never again make an exhibition of myself by going on a hunting trip. I'm past it!"

Rheumatism was probably the principal villain. "It not only

cripples me a good deal," he wrote Selous in 1911, "so that I am unable to climb on or off a horse with any speed, but it also prevents my keeping in condition." He welcomed his sixtieth birthday because it gave him the right to be as old as he felt, and signed a letter to his sister Corinne, "Ever yours Methuselah's understudy."

To be sure, Roosevelt's actions often belied his words. He went to Africa, went (unfortunately) to South America. During World War I the family had difficulty in restraining him from going off on another Western hunting trip, and he was planning to go devilfishing when he died. Nevertheless, the thought of decline was in his mind, and the thought helped to foster the fact. He once told Jack Willis that he did not expect to live long, coming of a short-lived family. Since he failed to husband his resources, one might even in a sense say that he did not desire a long life. "It does not do to try to live too long," he told Archie Butt. He even told an *Outlook* editorial conference in 1912 that he thought the political campaign would break him physically. "I have always wanted to live until the last of my children should be twenty-one," he said to Dr. Richards in the last year of his life. "Tomorrow will be Quentin's birthday, and I suppose I may as well go."

Roosevelt's illness and accident in South America and his conduct with reference to them involve considerations which must be discussed elsewhere. They involved the final destruction of his health and would have made the last year of his life a year of horror for a man with less courage. The pains that plagued him and the operations he went through it would be sadistic to record here. He not only lost the hearing of his left ear but because of a resultant lack of balance he had to learn to walk all over again. At one point his doctor told him that he had only performed four such operations as T.R. was facing and that every patient had died. A week after he had had it, Roosevelt was working in bed. Threatened with the wheel chair, he said, "All right, I can live that way too!" But by that time he can hardly have cared very much. "I never did care a rap for being sick, at this time anyhow," he wrote James Bryce in May; "because when so many young men with all the glory of life before them are being killed, or maimed and shattered, the fate of a retired, elderly civilian seems to me singularly unimportant." The immediate cause of his death was "malignant endocarditis, and an embolism in the coronary arteries." [4]

[4] In *Teeth and Health* (Putnam, 1921), Thomas J. Ryan and Edwin F. Bowers claimed that T.R. "was attacked by rheumatic fever, following the death of a tooth pulp or nerve, which became abscessed more than twenty years before. The acute attack of the disease which originated in the root of a tooth finally found complete expression in a pulmonary embolism." This claim, which was also put forth in other forms, caused some controversy; see the letters to and by Dr. Alexander Lambert on the subject in the Widener Library. An abscessed tooth was at one time involved in Roosevelt's illness, but this was not the basic difficulty.

TWO

The World of Thought

I. "Man Thinking"

T.R.'s amazing energy and enthusiasm were quite as impressive in the intellectual sphere as in the world of physical activity.

His delicate health in childhood made his early education considerably less rigorous than it would otherwise have been, and he never went to public school. His college was Harvard. His work there has been studied in some detail by Wilhelm, Ranlett, and others, and it is not necessary to give the details here. Since he graduated *magna cum laude*, was elected to Phi Beta Kappa, and received an "honorable mention" in natural history, he may certainly be said to have acquitted himself well, but he was very independent in his intellectual tastes and interests and was never a "grind." He had little interest in the subjects assigned to him for "themes," and he declined to do an "honors" thesis, preferring instead to begin work on his first book, *The Naval War of 1812.* His interest in becoming a professional scientist declined when he found that he would be expected to work with microscopes in the laboratory instead of in the field like Audubon.

There were many famous men on the Harvard faculty in T.R.'s time, but he bothered to mention only one of them in his *Autobiography*. As a loyal son of Harvard he faithfully attended class reunions and served as overseer; there was even some talk of making him president when Eliot retired. In his *Autobiography*, however, he sums up his college years somewhat cursorily. "I thoroughly enjoyed Harvard, and I am sure it did me good, but only in the general effect, for there was very little in my actual studies which helped me in afterlife." On the whole, this does not seem unfair. In all essential matters Roosevelt appears to have "made" his mind as he "made" his body.

Of the range of T.R.'s knowledge at least there has never been any question, and no one can read through his collected works with-

out being impressed by his intimate familiarity with history, literature, and science, as shown in the abundant illustrations which he
cites at his ease from all these fields. It was the same with his
conversation. "Whether the subject of the moment was political
economy, the Greek drama, tropical fauna or flora, the Irish sagas,
protective coloration in nature, metaphysics, the technique of football, or postfuturist painting," writes Viscount Lee, "he was equally
at home with the experts and drew out the best that was in them."
It is true that extravagant claims have sometimes been made for him
in this aspect. "In one afternoon," said his son Archie, "I have heard
him speak to the foremost Bible student of the world, a prominent
ornithologist, a diplomat and a French general, all of whom agreed
that Father knew more about the subjects on which they had
specialized than they did." Of course he did not, really. But he
did know enough to converse intelligently with all of them, which
is much, and far more than they could have done with each other.
And their testimony, which, as we shall see, can be duplicated again
and again, is not absurd, for what Roosevelt knew he knew with
passion; it possessed him; once more it was a case of Emerson's
"Man Thinking." His knowledge was highly integrated, and he was
continually crossing boundaries, moving back and forth from one
area of human knowledge to another, reaching out for appropriate
illustrations and applications of the principles under consideration
into fields where no man could possibly have conducted explorations
for this particular purpose.

It should be understood that T.R. makes no extravagant claims
for himself in this aspect, nor, for that matter, in any other. "I am
not learned," he told Mme. Jusserand. "I know about some subjects
which have interested me and which I have studied. Between them
are immense gaps." All he ever claimed was zest, delight in the
play of the mind for its own sake. "Thank Heaven! . . . the fact
that information is valueless has never deterred me from enjoying it."

Others felt differently. "It is to be supposed, seeing Colonel
Roosevelt was human," said Vilhjalmur Stefansson, "that there must
have been some fields in which he was ill-informed, but none of
these came to my attention nor, so far as I know, to the attention of
any of my friends in the various spheres of scientific exploration."
Frank Chapman said, "The Colonel knows more about birds than I

do." "Certainly in this island," said Lord Charnwood, "where statesmanship has long been associated with scholarly attainments, no
statesman for centuries has had his width of intellectual range."
In 1917 Major Stepanek, meeting him in New York, found that he
knew all the facts about Czechoslovakia that had had to be labori-
ously explained to the officials in Washington. In South America,
Father Zahm was amazed "by his broad and exact knowledge not
only of the fauna of the countries we were about to visit, but also
of the political and social histories of their people as well." Even
in a field like the law, which bored him, he could on occasion come
up with astonishing points.

Roosevelt could always turn from affairs of state to intellectual
pursuits, and when the affairs of state intruded upon his study or
learned conversation he could do what needed to be done and then
take up his scholarship again from the point where he had dropped
it. A month after Wilson had defeated him for the presidency, he
addressed the American Historical Society at Boston on "History as
Literature." In November, 1916, immediately after the defeat of
Hughes, he read a paper before the National Institute of the
American Academy of Arts and Letters. If ever he was obsessed
with anything, T.R. might be said to have been obsessed with the
war during the last years of his life. Yet sick as he was, and almost
crushed with the grief of Quentin's death, his reading, his writing,
his study in science, in history, in literature continued unabated.
"Praise Heaven," he writes Professor Grace Macurdy, in January,
1918: "Praise Heaven there are still one or two writers left who
do not demand an immediately utilitarian purpose in their studies!"
The last spring of his life he sent *The Atlantic Monthly* a reply to
what he considered inaccuracies in William Charles Scully's paper
on the African ostrich.

T.R. understood the difficulties of the scholar's life in America,
and he lamented when scholars were forced into journalism for
economic reasons. He knew that, if civilization is to survive, money
must be spent on learning, science, and art, even when people
are hungry and utilitarian values go unsatisfied. He saw some
danger in overspecializing in the colleges; at one time he was
critical of Eliot's "Germanizing"; and, being what he was, he inevitably insisted that the colleges should turn out "men." But he never

forgot that they must also "put a premium upon the development of productive scholarship, of the creative mind, in any form of intellectual work." The life of the scholar must be made attractive, financially and otherwise, and it must also be made clear that a scholar who does not produce is not worth much. There must be no leveling down in education, and there must be no discrimination between the sexes.

II. "Frensshe-atte-Sagamore"

In linguistics Roosevelt's achievements, though unorthodox, were not inconsiderable. With Greek and Latin he did not get far. "I never got so that reading any Greek or Latin author in the original represented to me anything except dreary labor." He envied Spring Rice his ability to spend enchanted evenings with Homer; he rejoiced, too, when his sons went beyond his own accomplishments in this line. Latin literature always seemed to him "comparatively trivial"; to lump it with the "magnificent" Greek as "classic" was "grotesque."

With the modern languages he was much more at home, and he habitually read not only literature but philosophical, scientific, religious, and historical books in French and German, and sometimes in Italian as well. Perhaps French was the language with which he did best. He read it all the way from San Antonio to Tampa on his way to the Spanish-American War, and he seems to have been braver about speaking it than he was with other languages. When he attended a dinner for General Joffre, it flattered him to know he was the only person present who could converse with the distinguished guest in his own language. On his trip to the West Indies in 1916 he made two public addresses in French.

But the French he spoke was a wonder to hear—"Frensshe-atte-Sagamore," he himself calls it. "I speak French, I am sorry to say, as if it were a non-Aryan tongue, without tense or gender, although with agglutinative vividness and fluency." "The President," writes John Hay, "talked with great energy and perfect ease the most curious French I ever listened to. It was absolutely lawless as to grammar and occasionally bankrupt in substantives; but he had not the least difficulty in making himself understood, and one subject did not worry him more than another." He seems to have played up his transliteration of English idiom for humorous effect, and he was "pleased as pickles" with himself when his French proved too fluent for the Japanese ambassador.

He tried to converse in German with Hermann Knauer during his presidency but ran into trouble and excused himself, "for it has been thirty years since I have spoken any German to amount to anything, though I read German fairly well and delight in German books. When I was at Dresden, I understood your language very well and at one time knew the 'Nibelungenlied' by heart; but today, if I wished to repeat it, it would be more the 'Nibelungen Noth' for me." Yet he had no difficulty in following a German sermon in Dakota on a 1903 speaking tour, and when Pastor Wagner visited the White House he and T.R. spoke French, German, and English, and recited passages from German poems. Once Roosevelt held forth to Hamlin Garland on the differences between archaic French and modern French, quoting examples of both—"Don't you see how much stronger, how much manlier, the archaic French is?"—and then he switched to the *Nibelungenlied:* "I like the German rhythm—that rhythm—better than I do the French."

III. History, Science, and Imagination

In history and in science Roosevelt was not only a reader and a student but also a practitioner. His knowledge of history was very great. It is true that he had his blind spots. Like many men of his time, he had little understanding of mediaevalism and scholasticism, and he comes something of a cropper when he tries to brush away the influence of St. Thomas Aquinas. But he makes up for this, as it were, by his intimate knowledge of many out-of-the-way matters, about most of which Americans in general knew nothing at all. In Budapest, Count Apponyi said T.R. showed such familiarity with Hungarian history as he had never before encountered in a non-Hungarian.

He used his historical knowledge to illuminate the problems of the present, as when he sweeps away the nonsense about "old" and "new" nations or compares and contrasts ancient Greek and modern Japanese. When Bryan makes his famous remark about a million men springing to arms at need between sunrise and sunset, he immediately remembers that Pompey facing Caesar had said something very much like it. History can also be a refuge against the trials of the present:

When they drive me too nearly mad, I take refuge in Maspero and study the treaty between Rameses II and the Hittites, comparing it with Rameses' preposterous boastings over his previous victories, and feel that after all we are not so far behind the people who lived a few thousand years ago as I am sometimes tempted to think.

But Roosevelt was sensitive to the romance of the past as well as its lessons, for he never forgot that learning, like labor, like everything, must give delight.

As a man steams into the Mediterranean between the African coast and the "purple, painted headlands" of Spain, it is well for him if he can bring before his vision the galleys of the Greek and Carthaginian mercantile adventurers, and of the conquering Romans; the boats of the wolf-hearted Arabs; the long "snakes" of the Norse pirates, Odin's darlings; the stately and gorgeous war craft of Don John, the square-sailed ships of the fighting Dutch admirals, and the lofty three-deckers of Nelson, the greatest of all the masters of the sea.

He felt this sort of thing as a child in Egypt, before he could spell:

The temple that I enjoyed most was Karnak. . . . To wander among those great columns under the same moon that had looked down on them for thousands of years was awe-inspiring; it gave rise to thoughts of the ineffable, the unutterable; thoughts which you can not express, which can be not uttered, which can not be answered until after The Great Sleep.

He felt it as a world figure, when he lectured at the Sorbonne:

Strange and impressive associations rise in the mind of a man from the New World who speaks before this august body in this ancient institution of learning. Before his eyes pass the shadows of mighty kings and warlike nobles, of great masters of law and theology.

For Roosevelt the importance of the imagination in first-class historical writing was very great. This is the burden of one of his most brilliant productions, the American Historical Association lecture on "History as Literature." It is not that he undervalues accuracy. Without it you get "merely a splendid bit of serious romance-writing, like Carlyle's 'French Revolution.'" But it would be better to lose every Greek inscription than to give up "the chapter in which Thucydides tells of the Athenian failure before Syracuse." Rightly or wrongly, Shakespeare has determined what people believe about Richard III. "Keats forgot even the right name of the man who first saw the Pacific Ocean; yet it is his lines which leap to our minds when we think of the 'wild surmise' felt by the indomitable explorer-conqueror from Spain when the vast new sea burst on his vision." The historian has obligations which Keats and Shakespeare escape, but "unless he writes vividly he cannot write truthfully; for no amount of dull, painstaking detail will sum up the whole truth unless the genius is there to paint the truth."

Roosevelt is astonishingly the same Roosevelt in scientific as in historical studies. But the scientific interest began earlier; in childhood it was the ruling passion. In New York, in Egypt, and in Germany he killed and mounted specimens. With the cooperation of several young relatives he founded "The Roosevelt Museum of Natural History" in 1867; by the fall of 1870 they had a thousand specimens, a constitution, and reports! Some of these specimens still exist in our museums today.

As with history, the first appeal was to the imagination:

I was walking up Broadway, and as I passed the market to which I used sometimes to be sent before breakfast to get strawberries I suddenly saw a dead seal laid on a slab of wood. That seal filled me with every possible feeling of romance and adventure. I asked where it was killed, and was informed in the harbor. I had already begun to read some of Mayne Reid's books and other boys' books of adventure, and I felt that this seal brought all these adventures in realistic fashion before me. As long as that seal remained there I haunted the neighborhood of the market day after day.

But, being unlike most of us, he did not stop there:

I measured it, and I recall that, not having a tape measure, I had to do my best to get its girth with a folding pocket footrule, a difficult undertaking. I carefully made a record of the utterly useless measurements, and at once began to write a natural history of my own, on the strength of that seal.

All Roosevelt's most beautiful and eloquent writing—the forewords to *African Game Trails* ("I sing of Africa and its golden

joys") and *A Booklover's Holidays in the Open*, the panegyric to
the frontiersman in *Ranch Life and the Hunting-Trail*, and the wonderful descriptions of birdsong in *The Wilderness Hunter* vibrate
to this note of passionate nature love. He never sentimentalized
nature or denied that it was red in tooth and claw. The evolutionary
hypothesis he accepted early, though he was quicker than many
of his contemporaries to perceive that evolution is not necessarily
and exclusively Darwinian. Above all, he did not permit it to make
a materialist of him. "The tracing of an unbroken line of descent
from the protozoan to Plato does not in any way really explain
Plato's consciousness." Independent of all theories, nature's fascination held, and he did not need to go to Africa for it, nor even to
the "surging seas of grass" and "the lovely rivers rushing between
the pine clad mountains" in the Far West. For, when all was said
and done, nothing was lovelier than "glorious April mornings on
Long Island, when through the singing of robin and song-sparrow
comes the piercing cadence of the meadow-lark; and of the far
northland woods in June, fragrant with the breath of pine and
balsam-fir, where sweetheart sparrows sing from wet spruce thickets
and rapid brooks rush under the drenched and swaying alder
boughs."

In 1906 he went down to Panama to inspect the canal. "All my
old enthusiasm for natural history seemed to revive, and I would
have given a good deal to have stayed and tried to collect specimens." He was never afraid of getting science mixed up with politics.
"I would like to discuss our national unpreparedness," he writes
W. L. Abbott in 1914, "and also the zoölogy of mid-Africa and mid-
Asia." Once, when Dean Lewis called for him in Philadelphia to
take him to deliver a political address, he found him deep in a
scientific discussion. He waved Lewis to a chair. "I know you want
me to go with you, but sit down a moment; to hear something about
tree-toads will do you good."

T.R. is not generally accounted a patient man, but he could wait
almost any length of time to spy out nature's secrets. "I would
willingly stand for two days to catch a glimpse of a wild manatee."
And the length of time he did stand to see and hear his beloved
birds is amazing. Moreover, his patience in collecting data is
matched by the care and caution with which he generalizes on

what he has found, being always very scrupulous not to make sweeping statements or to travel further than the evidence in hand will take him.

It was this passion for accuracy which precipitated Roosevelt into the most amusing of all his minor controversies, the attack on the nature-fakers, and here, too, he was far more moderate in his statements than is generally supposed. Even about his principal target, the Reverend William J. Long, he said nothing anything like so intemperate as Long said about him. Neither did he deny that the imagination had the same rights in nature writing as in any other area; he simply insisted that the distinction between fact and fiction must be understood. He was no less cautious in his more orthodox scientific controversies with reputable authorities, on the classification of coyotes and mountain lions, for example, and the protective function of coloration, where the latest scientific opinion seems to be on his side.

But while T.R. was in the White House the dominant note, so far as the scientists and nature writers were concerned, was certainly not criticism but encouragement. "It was to help along things like this that I took this job," he told David Starr Jordan, and while this was, of course, a great oversimplification, it is still true that no president since Jefferson had ever encouraged literature and science as much as he did.

Roosevelt's love of birds and his knowledge of them has already been hinted at. Here again he himself is very modest in his claims. "I am very sorry to say," he writes Frank Chapman, "that I either have to be very familiar with a bird or else it has to possess very marked and striking characteristics or else I am apt to fail to recognize it." But his own observations belie him. In 1906 he wrote Burroughs himself from the White House:

That warbler I wrote you about yesterday was the Cape May warbler. As soon as I got hold of an ornithological book I identified it. I do not think I ever saw one before, for it is rather a rare bird—at least on Long Island, where most of my bird knowledge was picked up. It was a male, in the brilliant spring plumage; and the orange-brown cheeks, the brilliant yellow sides of the neck just behind the cheeks, and the brilliant yellow under parts with thick black streaks on the breast, made the bird unmistakable.

Cutright thinks he was more observant of birdsong than he was of the appearance of the birds, and this would seem to go along with his defective eyesight; he once wrote Estelle Hart that "I am ashamed to say I never particularly noticed [the color of] the bluejay's eyes." Yet one day he picked up a tiny bit of brown fluff in the White House grounds and astonished his sister by muttering, "Very early for a fox-sparrow." When she asked how he could possibly be sure that the fluff had come from this particular variety, he replied, "Well, you see I have really made a great study of sparrows." A leaflet prepared with Henry Davis Minot, *The Summer Birds of the Adirondacks in Franklin County* (1877) was not only his first published work but the pioneering study in the field. Two years later came another, *Notes on Some of the Birds of Oyster Bay*. At the White House he identified some fifty-seven varieties of birds from his own observations. When he met Major Edward B. Clark he placed him by remembering that ten years earlier he had written an article on the prothonotary warbler. As late as 1915 the Bird Club of Long Island was organized at Sagamore with T.R. as president. In the summer of 1918 he was acknowledging a letter from his eldest son in which mention was made of birds at the battlefront—"the skylarks singing during the shelling, &c"—and he wrote a review of a new book about pheasants the very last day of his life.

One of the most charming items in Rooseveltiana is Viscount Grey's account of the happy time they had together when T.R. visited England in 1910. Grey had already been told by James Bryce, then British ambassador in America, that Roosevelt was planning his trip so as to be in England in the spring "when the birds would be in full song and he could hear them." Grey and T.R. took their point of departure from Tichborne in Hampshire, and for some twenty-four hours they were "lost to the world." Wrote Grey:

I found, not only that he had a remarkable and abiding interest in birds, but a wonderful knowledge of them. Though I knew something about British birds, I should have been lost and confused among American birds, of which unhappily I know little or nothing. Colonel Roosevelt not only knew more about American birds than I did about British birds, but he knew about British birds also. What he had lacked was an opportunity of hearing their songs, and you cannot get a knowledge of the songs of birds in any other way than by listening to them.

Grey adds that T.R. "had one of the most perfectly trained ears for bird songs that I have ever known" and "keen feeling and taste" as well.

IV. Savant

Evaluations of Roosevelt's achievements both in science and in history are easy to come by. He did not hide his light under a bushel. "I claim to be a historian," he says in one passage. He says that his place in scientific writing is of the wheelbarrow variety, but he also says, "I have done something in geography and something in ornithology, and something in other lines. I want to put myself in a position where I can be rightfully recognized as a scientist." Even before he gets home from South America he is eager to lecture on his discoveries for the Royal Geographic Society, sick as he is.

From youth to age, Roosevelt wrote furiously on everything that interested him; there were even times when writing was his principal occupation. "In the days of my youth I was a literary man myself" —or so he somewhat wistfully described himself at a dinner given by the Periodical Publishers' Association at Washington in 1904. The wistfulness shows again in his question to Beebe, "Which book of mine do you like best?" and the diligence in the fact that he did not even stop writing during his honeymoon. "I should like to write some book that would really take rank in the very first class," he wrote in his youth, "but I suppose this is a mere dream." Looking forward, in police commissioner days, to the end of his public career, he writes Mrs. Storer: "I shall be the melancholy spectacle for the Bunnies of an idle father, writing books that do not sell!" After he had become president they did sell and in later years he earned large sums of money from his writing, but it never ceased to trouble him that his work had not made its way without the support of his political prestige.

For all that, he did not think he wrote well. He will only give himself credit for "a good instinct and a liking for simplicity and directness." "Writing is horribly hard work to me; and I make slow progress. My style is very rough and I do not like a certain lack of *sequitur* that I do not seem to be able to get rid of." Yet he not only does literary work but does it, as one might say, in a literary fashion. "Unless the spirit moves me on a subject I cannot possibly write about it; that is, I do not like to write to order, as it were." In 1917 he writes gratefully to Brander Matthews, "I am very glad you think I write better than, or at least not so badly as, I used to write."

In 1912 Roosevelt told William Allen White that he thought about the best writing he ever did was in *African Game Trails*. This was not a settled view, however. Once he says that the scientific book of which he is proudest is the one on the life histories of African mammals, which he did with Edmund Heller. Again, he gives the palm to *The Wildernes Hunter*. Once he calls *The Winning of the West* "of all my axes the one best worth grinding," and once he pairs this work with *Hunting Trips of a Ranchman*. Charles G. Washburn says that Roosevelt thought Chapter IX of the *Autobiography* his best piece of writing. But he is never unreasonable, and he gave his publishers and editors less trouble than the veriest tyro. "I do not know whether I have made a good job of the *Cromwell* or not," he writes Charles Scribner. "I am inclined to think I have, but I do not suppose an author can ever tell about his own work."

Literary skill is less important for the scientist than it is for the historian, and so high an authority as C. Hart Merriam called T.R. "the world's authority on the big game mammals of North America." When the National Museum had for dissection a specimen of a prematurely born mammal which nobody on the staff could identify, they sent it up to the White House, and Roosevelt identified it at once and furnished information concerning it. One night at Merriam's, where some five thousand skulls were assembled, "he astonished everyone—including several eminent naturalists—by picking up skull after skull and mentioning the scientific name of the genus to which each belonged." Heller once mentioned to him "a very obscure species of mouse, discovered a number of years before in the northern part of British Columbia. He supposed that none but a specialist would know about this rodent. When he mentioned it, however, Roosevelt immediately began to tell him all about it. He was perfectly familiar with the little animal."

Roosevelt took his historical writing very seriously, knowing that he must be free to say as a historian much that he could not say as a public man. *The Naval War of 1812* is hardly more than the work of a boy, yet it is so fair and so soundly researched that, for all its American patriotism, it won its author the privilege of contributing to the definitive British history of the Royal Navy. The biographies of Thomas Hart Benton and Gouverneur Morris were done hastily, almost carelessly, for the "American Statesman" series, the *Benton* being finished in Dakota, far from libraries, after an SOS appeal to Lodge for aid which must strike the modern researcher as more than a little comic. Yet even here there are virtues. "Mr. Roosevelt does understand the West," wrote W. P. Trent, "and so he did justice to Benton," and Raymond Miller even suggests that his book may have influenced the work of Turner. The *Oliver Cromwell,* much later, does not contribute anything new, but as an essay in historical interpretation, in the wake of Roosevelt's beloved Macaulay, it has its points.

The important work, of course, is the gigantic fragment, *The Winning of the West;* this is distinctly of the school of Francis Parkman, to whom it is dedicated. It is not so good as Parkman, but Parkman made the writing of history his lifework; Roosevelt produced his *magnum opus* during breathing spaces in a very active career. He did not exhaust available source material, but he did open up new areas of it, unknown to most of the writers of his day; his vision was penetrating and his method of procedure sound. *The Winning of the West* is generally remembered for its brilliant descriptions of Border fighting; actually it gives much more than this. The author does not confine himself to political history; he shows philosophical grasp, power of generalization, and the ability to describe the workings of vast historical forces. The first chapter, a survey of the expansion of the English-speaking peoples, is much in the manner of John Fiske. Even the Border forays are not described for their own sake; the incidents presented are representative. Neither does Roosevelt permit his American patriotism to run away with him. He understands the British case in the Revolution and states it fairly; he understands, too, the weaknesses of the colonial soldiers and "debunks" their easy victories over the Indians. Even Washington is given a share in the responsibility for St. Clair's defeat. As for the frontiersmen themselves, even though his heart may be with them, he does not gloss over the fact that they were in some aspects a degenerate lot.

V. "Mere Literature"

"A man of force," wrote Brand Whitlock of T.R., "but wholly without spiritual perception. I suppose he never read intelligently, for instance, any poem, unless it were some ballad like John Gilpin's ride: he reads only for information, not for pleasure."

This is one of the most beautiful illustrations available of the truth of the old saying that ignorance never settled a question. "Books," says T.R., "are the greatest of companions." He even felt that American flowers suffer in comparison with European flowers for lack of literary associations. Reading was a passion, a "disease," a "dissipation," as he himself says, "which I have sometimes to try to avoid." Even the physical aspects of fine bookmaking enthralled him; when he came to Boston in 1907 he saved time for a trip to Houghton, Mifflin and Company to see some of their Riverside Press Editions, designed by Bruce Rogers. He loved the French ambassador Jusserand because he could talk about Shakespeare and Shakespearean scholarship to him. "Well," he cried to Edith Wharton, "I *am* glad to welcome to the White House some one to whom I can quote 'The Hunting of the Snark' without being asked what I mean!"

Quentin told his gang that Father read every book received at the Congressional Library "right off." He did not, but he managed to read most of the books that interested him, and many friends have testified that however new the volume they recommended to him he had always read it already. "His range of reading is amazing," wrote H. G. Wells; "he seems to be echoing with all the thought of the time, he has receptivity to the pitch of genius." John Hay said he knew of only one person who had read the great Nicolay and Hay history of Lincoln straight through, "and he is the busiest man in America, the President of the United States." Marconi was amazed by his knowledge in the specialized field of Italian history and literature. "That man actually cited book after book that I've never heard of, much less read. He's going to keep me busy for some time just following his Italian reading."

An unpublished 1904 letter to Mrs. Grant La Farge makes an interesting commentary on the range and extent of T.R.'s reading:

I am afraid I shall be of no use in giving you information about new books. I read very much at haphazard, and I am rather more apt to read old books than new ones—although the old books I read are not necessarily in the least what would be called classics. Have you read Hadley's Freedom and Responsibility? I have been delighted with it, as also with Trevelyan's History of our Revolution, and with his son's England in the Age of Wickcliffe. There are a couple of very good volumes on Gloucester life by Connolly, called, respectively, Out of Gloucester, and The Seiners, which would amuse and interest you for an evening; also a rather slender but interesting Boer story by Viljoen, called Under the Vierkleur, which I have just read. Mrs. Dewey presented me The Memoirs of the Baroness Bode, which are also light but good. Part of my reading this winter, which, as you know, is undertaken purely for recreation and not in the least for improvement, has consisted in an interleaved English and Italian Dante by Carlyle, an interleaved French and old French Song of Roland, and what is to my mind an interesting new book on the origin of the Indo-Europeans by an Italian, Michelis. I have also been interested in the Frenchman Bérard's suggestive, although rather wild, volumes on the Odyssey and the Phoenicians. I have read quite a number of books on Japan, including that Japanese novel, Prince Genji, written in the time of King Alfred, and also, of course, the Forty-seven Ronins, and the very interesting sketch of 'Bushido,' the Samurai ethical creed, by a Japanese. As for the books that I have ordinarily read, I really would not be able to tell you what they were. They have included various histories of Napoleon, Gustavus Adolphus, Charles XII, and Frederick the Great, but none that I regard as of more than passing worth. When I sit down to read I find I am apt to take either old favorites or perfectly light but nice books like Mrs. Wiggs of the Cabbage Patch.

There is a postscript:

At the moment I am reading St. Simon's 'Memoires' and some Celtic translations by Kuno Meyer.

Even in childhood Roosevelt had the fortunate capacity of complete absorption in his reading. His cousin, Emlen Roosevelt, says that the only way to get his attention when he was reading was to strike him on the back. "Once when we got into a discussion and became rather loud," writes Archie Butt, "and then got to laughing I suggested that we would disturb the President. Mrs. Roosevelt said it made no difference to him, that he would not hear us; and so we paid no attention to him after that if he was reading. Doctor Rixey and I carried on a conversation about him once in chairs next to his and he did not even hear us, not even when we mentioned his name."

Roosevelt read, too, with incredible speed. "In thirty years' observation of exchange-readers in newspaper offices," says Francis Leupp, "I have never seen anything to approach his celerity." There are stories of his leafing through the pages of a book or a report so rapidly that it would not seem he could possibly have read it and then, when he was questioned, offering to undergo an examination on what he had read.

Such a man would get a good deal of reading done under any circumstances; Roosevelt lost no available moment. "He always carried a book with him to the Executive Office," says William Howard Taft, "and although there were but few intervals during the business hours, he made the most of them in his reading." He even kept a book near the front door, so that if he had to wait for Mrs. Roosevelt a few minutes when they were going out together he could occupy the time.

Since reading was no effort for Roosevelt, he could read under impossible conditions. In 1910 he failed to appear on time at an important dinner which was being given for him on board a train between Khartum and Cairo.

I searched the train for him [writes Lawrence Abbott] and finally discovered him in one of the white enamelled lavatories with its door half open where, standing under an electric light, he was busily engaged in reading, while he braced himself in the angle of the two walls against the swaying motion of the train, oblivious to time and surroundings. The book in which he was absorbed was Lecky's "History of Rationalism in Europe." He had chosen this peculiar reading room both because the white enamel reflected a brilliant light and he was pretty sure of uninterrupted quiet.

I have never met, in literature or in life, a more amusing anomaly than that he should have taken *Anna Karenina* and Matthew Arnold with him on the expedition to capture the boat thieves in Dakota; on the way home he borrowed from the prisoners their copy of *The History of the James Brothers!*

Sometimes, in Africa, he read his famous "Pigskin Library" [1] "resting under a tree at noon, perhaps beside the carcass of a beast I had killed, or else while waiting for camp to be pitched; and in either case it might be impossible to get water for washing. In consequence the books were stained with blood, sweat, gun-oil, dust, and ashes; ordinary bindings either vanished or became loathsome, whereas pigskin merely grew to look as a well-used saddle looks." Sometimes when he got in from the field, he wrote his sister, he could not settle down to write his hunting articles until he had first spent an hour or two reading. But even this was nothing compared to his achievements in South America, where Kermit would find him propped against a tree reading Gibbon or *The Oxford Book of French Verse* when he was too sick to hold himself up without help.

VI. The Bible

The four pre-eminent books in the world, said T.R., are the Bible, Homer, Shakespeare, and Dante. Of these the first spoke to him most powerfully, and he made it speak, on occasion, with equal power, to his fellow Americans.

Roosevelt's two most famous quotations from the Scriptures were both battle references; the first concerned Armageddon, and the second extended and reapplied Deborah's curse upon Meroz. "We stand at Armageddon, and we battle for the Lord"—this was the end of the great speech he delivered to his Republican followers at the Auditorium Theater in Chicago, on June 17, 1912, just before the steam roller ran over them. Yet it was the Curse of Meroz which really, during World War I, sent Americans scurrying to their Bibles. "Curse ye Meroz, said the angel of the Lord, curse ye bitterly the inhabitants thereof; because they came not to the help of the Lord, to the help of the Lord against the mighty." It was Wilson's America, of course, that was Meroz, before the battle of the interventionists had been won.

[1] For a list of the books contained in the "Pigskin Library" and T.R.'s comments thereupon, see the article thus titled in his *Literary Essays*, "Memorial Edition," Vol. XIV.

This, however, was a somewhat specialized use of Scripture. In 1901, when a Sunday-School superintendent asked Roosevelt for a favorite quotation, he referred him to Romans 12:11—"Not slothful in business; fervent in spirit; serving the Lord." "Perhaps my favorite texts," he wrote in 1913, "are those at the end of the first chapter and the beginning of the second chapter of James." In *The Foes of Our Own Household* he called on Isaiah, Amos, Matthew, James, and Micah to express his sense of what religion requires of us. But it is Micah 6:8 which seems most characteristic of Roosevelt: "He hath shewed thee, O man, what is good; and what doth the Lord require of thee, but to do justly, and to love mercy, and to walk humbly with thy God?" This was the passage he chose to comment upon in the message to American soldiers which was inserted into the New Testaments given them in World War I.

T.R.'s quotations from the Scriptures are not particularly numerous, less so, perhaps, than the fame of the few great ones might suggest. But the language of the Scriptures was often enough upon his lips to demonstrate his thorough familiarity with them. He did not always verify his quotations, for he often quoted loosely; sometimes he even misquoted.

He was willing to have his administration judged by the saying, "By their fruits shall ye know them." After a Congressional victory he cries, "We have certainly smitten Ammon hip and thigh." "Surely you know that all the people whose opinion is best worth having . . ." he writes E. F. Ware in 1904, "know you have been the best Pension Commissioner we have ever had. . . . Now don't be annoyed a bit. Let the heathen rage, and the people imagine a vain thing." Tammany's return to power was like the dog returning to his vomit, and his only comment on the Progressive defeat in the Congressional elections of 1914 was to quote II Timothy 4:3–4.

In wartime he was more in the mood of the Old Testament prophet. "To my fellow Americans I preach the sword of the Lord and of Gideon." In the summer of 1915 he read President Wilson a lesson out of Ezekiel, and when, the next November, the President himself cited the same passage, T.R. gave himself credit for having made him aware of it! During this period he gets his best material out of the Old Testament, but he does manage to press the New into service when Wilson, in his relationship to Belgium, becomes the Levite in the parable of the Good Samaritan, who passed by on the other side. By implication, Wilson is Pilate also, "the arch-typical neutral of all time," and the pacifists in general become Pharisees, who "made broad their phylacteries and uttered long prayers in public, but did not lift a finger to lighten the load of the oppressed." Not even Roosevelt could ignore what he calls "the supposed teaching of the New Testament against war," but his attempt to break down this delusion is one of his weakest performances, for it impels him absurdly to overstress the driving of the money-changers out of the Temple (which was certainly neither war nor a step toward war), and to interpet literally St. Luke's obviously figurative "He that hath no sword, let him sell his garment, and buy one."

VII. The Classics

The conventional nineteenth-century allusions to the classics annoyed Roosevelt—"cheap pseudoclassicism," he calls it. Yet he seems to have known both classical literatures better than many "well-read" men do nowadays. He was fond of Polybius and Tacitus but not of Livy. In 1903 he writes Lodge that he has been reading Aristotle and Plutarch. In *The Strenuous Life* he cites the letters of Pliny the Younger and quotes from two "wonderful old Greeks," Aristotle and Plato; the quotation from Plato is tagged in a footnote signed with his initials, "Translated freely and condensed." There is a "Note" in *The Winning of the West* in which he recalls from memory a story out of Herodotus. He discusses Lucretius in a 1904 letter to John Morley, which shows the conventional reverence for Virgil and an awareness of Lucretius' own philosophical significance but which largely ignores his poetic quality.

As in other areas of his reading, T.R. often finds parallels between the classics and modern life. The sybarites of his own time make him feel as if he were living in the satires of Juvenal, and Tolstoy's amoral description of human conduct without commentary or interpretation reminds him of Thucydides.

The Greek dramatists seem to have been rather a special case. When he inspected W. R. Nelson's library at Kansas City he made a special point of looking for the Greek plays. In 1911 he wrote Gilbert Murray praising his translation of Greek plays and also his history of the Greek epic. But here, more than with much literature closer to him in spirit, we are conscious of Roosevelt's ever-present tendency to moral judgments. "What extraordinary people the Greeks were!" he exclaims after reading the *Electra* in 1906. "I do not know whether most to admire the wonderful power and artistic beauty of the play, or to shrink from the revolting nature of the theme."

The most interesting thing, however, is the conditions under which Roosevelt managed to do some of his classical reading. He read both Thucydides and Josephus during the 1900 convention and the *Anabasis* on a Western trip in 1903. Dean Lewis found him reading Herodotus during the 1912 convention while the band was playing and the crowd outside shouting "We want Teddy!" During his South American trip, however, the classics would seem to have failed T.R. He took Marcus Aurelius and Sophocles with him, "but when he tried to read them during the descent of the Rio da Dúvida," says Kermit, "they only served to fill him with indignation at their futility. Some translations of Greek plays . . . met with but little better success."

VII. The Glory of Albion

Naturally most of Roosevelt's literature was English and American. He speaks of *Beowulf* along with other epic material in his lecture on "History as Literature," and there is a reference to the Welsh *Mabinogion* in *African Game Trails*. His serious interest in Chaucer, dating from 1892, was motivated by his friendship with Professor Thomas R. Lounsbury, of Yale. Here he had, in the first place, to get over the shock of the *fabliau* material, which required effort for a man with his loathing of obscenity. He made the effort, however, and became a very respectable Chaucerian for a layman.

Though Mrs. Roosevelt was devoted to them, the Elizabethans meant little to T.R. Spenser he could not read at all and, oddly enough, in spite of the high rank he gives him, he seems to have had trouble with Shakespeare. *Macbeth* was his favorite play of Shakespeare's; he cared little for *Hamlet*. There are very few quotations from Shakespeare, though he was fond of Lady Macbeth's scornful reference to letting "I dare not" wait upon "I would." He built a whole speech around Jack Cade in the 1896 campaign, but the play from which he was most inclined to quote was *1 Henry IV*, with which he once devastatingly "put down" Lord Kitchener.[2]

In later life, however, there was a certain shift in T.R.'s attitude toward Shakespeare. When he was preparing to go to Africa he told Archie Butt that, though he did not care for Shakespeare, he was taking him along because he could get all of him in three pocket volumes containing "a lot of compressed thought." This was a fortunate decision, for it enabled him later to write home to the Lodges:

> You will both be amused to hear that at last, when fifty years old, I have come into my inheritance in Shakespeare. I never before really cared for more than one or two of his plays; but for some inexplicable reason the sealed book was suddenly opened to me on this trip. . . . I still balk at three or four of Shakespeare's plays; but most of them I have read or am reading over and over again.

Though he was very fond of Dryden's St. Cecilia ode, seventeenth-century poetry, for T.R., was largely Milton. His Cromwell sonnet serves as an appropriate epigraph for Roosevelt's book on that statesman, where Milton is viewed, conventionally, as "with but one exception the greatest poet of the English tongue, a man whose political and social ideas were at least two centuries in advance of his time." *Paradise Lost* was, in his eyes, priceless; a million pounds would not have been too much to give for it, though he does say, in a letter to David Gray, that it is only the first two books for which he greatly cares.

Roosevelt took in Milton's prose as well as his poems, and his views being what they were, he naturally found much to praise.

Having passed Milton, we jump through a few insignificant eighteenth-century references to the nineteenth century. In 1906 Roosevelt was much interested "in the project to buy and preserve as a memorial the house in Rome in which Keats died." Once he cites the "Ode on a Grecian Urn," along with Poe's "To Helen," as illustrating the meaning of genius. One night at college, after a couple of hours' boxing and wrestling, Roosevelt and two friends finished the evening "by reading aloud from Tennyson and we became so interested in 'In Memoriam' that it was past one o'clock

[2] Cf. *Letters*, VII, 405.

when we separated." "Ulysses" furnished an epigraph for *The Strenuous Life*. But he cared less for *The Idylls of the King*, "with their amiable curates-in-mail," which he thought compared unfavorably with Malory.

Browning was more important. Morison calls him T.R.'s favorite poet. He would seem at least to have challenged him more than the others. Mr. Hagedorn even thinks that a passage in "The Flight of the Duchess" may have influenced T.R.'s early determination to rebuild his body.

There is a good deal of Browning which I am wholly unable to read [so he wrote Martha Baker Dunn in 1902], but he has just exactly the quality you attribute to him, and those poems which I can read appeal to me as very few poems do. I don't care a rap what the inner meaning of "Childe Roland" is; What I care for is the lift, the thrill the poem gives; the look of the desolate country, the dauntless bearing of the Knight, and the strange thoughts and sights and the squat blind tower itself. I used to ranch in the Bad Lands, and I always thought of the hills which lay like giants at a hunting when I saw the great buttes grow shadowy and awful in the dusk. I am very fond of "Prospice"—what can a poet do better than sound the praises of a good fighter and a good lover? I wish you had quoted "Love among the Ruins." That has always been one of my favorites. Now I shall take up "Rabbi Ben Ezra," at which I have always shied hitherto.

He also enjoyed Matthew Arnold. "I suppose it shows an unhealthy and morbid temperament on my part," he writes Spring Rice, "and yet I have always been very fond of his poetry; I owe to his books many a pleasant evening by the camp fire." For all his wholesomeness and strenuousness, he was not quite proof against the seduction of FitzGerald and Omar Khayyám. I do not know how much he read Meredith, but he sent him an eightieth-birthday letter, praising him for "the sound of trumpet and horn" in his work. William Morris, who composed "in that odd tongue which he presumably considered an archaic variant of English," Roosevelt found slightly absurd, but he seems to have read him with some enjoyment. Swinburne, however, was the great surprise. I should have expected T.R. to turn from him with loathing. And there are poems, like the one in praise of Nell Gwyn, which he found it too much to take. Nevertheless, he was entranced by Swinburne's melody. He once told Kermit "that he had particularly enjoyed Swinburne and Shelley in ranching days in the Bad Lands, because they were so totally foreign to the life and the country—and supplied an excellent antidote to the daily round."

Among contemporary British poets, only Kipling and Masefield seem to have meant much to Roosevelt, and he even told Kermit once that he did not care for most of Masefield but exempted a few short poems "which thoroughly give the feeling of the West Indies." Of Kipling he never achieved an unprejudiced judgment, not only because Kipling was the bard of the kind of imperialism he believed in but also, in the beginning, because he was angered by Kipling's attitude toward America. In March, 1894, having entertained him and Mrs. Kipling at dinner, he described him as "an underbred little fellow" but "a genius" and "very entertaining." His wife was "fearful." According to his own account, T.R. gave Kipling "a very rough handling" on this occasion over his criticisms of the United States. Meeting Kipling again the following March, T.R. found his reactions fundamentally unchanged. In April he abruptly surrendered. "I have come round to your way of looking at Kipling," he wrote Brander Matthews. "When one knows him it seems preposterous to mind anything he says about the United States." To his sister he adds that Kipling "has been exceptionally well behaved since our rough-and-tumble the first night." In 1889 he calls Kipling's verse "rather poor poetry, but good sense from the expansionist standpoint," but taking his fiction into consideration he couples him in importance with Tolstoy.

Bunyan is the earliest English writer of fiction cited by Roosevelt, and *The Pilgrim's Progress* was always a very live book at Sagamore Hill. From it he took (and misapplied) the famous figure of the Man with the Muck-Rake, and he himself was widely compared to Valiant-for-Truth and Mr. Greatheart when he died.

The eighteenth century is again passed over lightly. One of T.R.'s strangest contrarieties was that he cared little for the desert island portion of *Robinson Crusoe* and greatly enjoyed the rest of it which nobody else cares for at all. He must have known his *Tom Jones* pretty well, since he speaks of Squire Western in his *New York* and was fond of referring to political alliances "between Blifil and Black

George," but I have found nothing to indicate what he thought of Fielding critically. A letter to one of his sons cites *Roderick Random,* though he is not sure that he does not mean *Humphry Clinker* (he didn't), as illustrating the terrible conditions in the British Navy of the eighteenth century. Like Mark Twain, he could not read Jane Austen. Unlike him, he adored Scott, whom he coupled with Macaulay as the two nineteenth-century writers he liked best. To A.L.A. libraries during World War I he presented a large number of copies of *The Antiquary, Guy Mannering,* and Dickens's *Our Mutual Friend.* All these, he said, teach "both manliness and decency," and *The Antiquary* and *Guy Mannering* are "best for soldiers." Latter-day criticism of Scott moved Roosevelt not at all. "Scott is one of the very big men who furnish endless entertainment for the innumerable small men of querulous disposition, each of whom seeks to establish credit for himself by trying to pick a flaw in the big man's great work."

The presence in T.R.'s *Letters to His Children* of two rather savagely anti-Dickensian utterances, in which the novelist is called a cad and a sentimentalist and berated for his attitude toward America, has misled a good many readers into supposing that Roosevelt did not like Dickens. On the contrary, he read him devotedly, and quotes from him far more often than from any other writer. "Like the fat boy in *Pickwick,*" he writes Elihu Root, "I wish to make your blood run cold!" "For Heaven's sake," he implores Philander C. Knox, "take care of yourself. I don't say for *my* sake; because, as you know, I always remember Messrs. Pickwick and Winkle!" His friend Spring Rice is a regular old Mrs. Gummidge when he starts worrying over T.R.'s African trip; one of the African porters carries an umbrella "tied much like Mrs. Gamp's"; and the egregious Ezra Tipple, the Pope-baiting Methodist of Rome, recalls Dickens's most obnoxious dissenters. A reference in a letter to a "young man named Alger" amuses him by recalling a "young man of the name of Guppy." The taxidermist who taught him in his youth had a shop rather like that of Mr. Venus in *Our Mutual Friend,* and when Archie began growing out of his clothes he reminded him of Smike. What is more, T.R. often seemed to himself like Dickens characters. "Like Mr. Tracy Tupman, I am both old and fat (and stiff to boot)." He took pains to keep King Charles's head out of his writings. He also speaks of "my Micawber-like temperament," but that was before he turned President Wilson into Micawber, on account of an alleged similarity between their epistolary styles! Wilson is Podsnap, too, refusing to recognize unpleasant facts; his postmaster, Burleson, is Silas Wegg; and the pacifists are Mrs. Jellyby. Godkin is a "beef-witted Chadband," and H. H. D. Pierce "a fat-headed Turveydrop."

Even when we come to *Martin Chuzzlewit* itself, Roosevelt did not deny the reality of the types Dickens castigated. "Hannibal Chollop was no mere creature of fancy; on the contrary, his name was legion, and he flourished rankly in every town throughout the Mississippi Valley." T.R. did object to the careless assumption that all Americans were like those described in *Chuzzlewit;* that, he says, would be like judging all Englishmen by Pecksniff, Bumble, and Bill Sykes.

But all the same I would like to have *Martin Chuzzlewit* studied as a tract in America. Hearst and Pulitzer are Jefferson Brick and Colonel Diver, in a somewhat fuller state of development; while Senator Carmack of Tennessee, Congressman John Sharp Williams of Mississippi and Governor Vardaman of Mississippi, not to speak of Senator Tillman of South Carolina, are Hannibal Chollop and Elijah Pogram over again.

T.R. loved Thackeray also and could read *Vanity Fair, Pendennis,* and *The Newcomes* again and again. Like many of us, he had a weakness for Rawdon Crawley. His own wedding in London "made me feel as if I were living in one of Thackeray's novels," as, many years later, Ted's escapades at Harvard reminded him of Pendennis!

I have been surprised to find little or nothing on George Eliot, the Brontës, or Thomas Hardy, but there are several references to Trollope. Marryat he read in childhood; he cites him in *The Naval War of 1812* as a source of information concerning the old Navy. There was a rascal in the state legislature who reminded him of a character in Lever. Surtees he loved, especially Soapy Sponge, though he manifests the common tendency to roll up all Victorian illustrators into one and call the result "Cruikshank"; in this case the right name is John Leech. He was very fond of Emily Eden's *The Semi-Attached Couple* long before its modern revival. He praises *Treasure Island* and often refers to *Dr. Jekyll and Mr. Hyde*. He even enjoyed Rider Haggard's *She*, though he has more to say about Haggard's more serious, utilitarian writing. He enjoyed Wells's early books but was very impatient of his sexual heresies and, later, what he calls his inaccuracy in scientific and historical writing. He had great admiration for the short stories of W. W. Jacobs. Conrad's quality he recognized as early as 1903. But basically he is old-fashioned in his attitude toward fiction: by 1906 he is complaining that he is not finding many new novels that he likes and that he is obliged to go back and read the old ones over again.

Bacon is the earliest nonfiction British prose writer to whom I have found Roosevelt referring. The seventeenth century is represented by Pepys (and, of course, Milton), the eighteenth by Dr. Johnson and Lord Chesterfield. There is an unpublished letter thanking J. C. Shaffer for the gift of Lamb's letters—"you could not have presented me with a book that I would value more." He was a good Borrovian, too, and quoted Borrow importantly in *Fear God and Take Your Own Part*. He read Matthew Arnold as critic as well as poet. Huxley was of some importance for his scientific thinking. He calls Herbert Spencer "a great philosopher, at least half of whose philosophy is wrong." There are references to William Ernest Henley, Frederic Harrison (with whom Roosevelt corresponded), and Andrew Lang. He admired G. K. Chesterton and did not consider it at all a compliment to him that he should be compared to Bernard Shaw, with whom Roosevelt had no sympathy whatever.

The two greatest English historians, for T.R., were Gibbon and Macaulay. He mistrusted Froude and found Freeman dull. Macaulay was, of course, one of his great heroes; he even thinks better of Brooks Adams for admiring him. Roosevelt loved Macaulay for his "eminently sane and healthy mind," his "wholesome spirit and his knowledge of practical affairs." "Of all the authors I know I believe I should first choose him as the man whose writings will most help a man of action who desires to be both efficient and decent, to keep straight and yet be of some account in the world."

Carlyle was a different story. Roosevelt knew that he could speak at times "like an inspired seer"; he appreciated, too, his ability to paint vivid pictures; but it is significant that when he praises his account of the French Revolution he couples him not with other historians but with two novelists—Dickens and Dumas. Indeed, he calls the book a "splendid bit of serious romance-writing." But what really roused T.R.'s wrath was the capricious morality of *Frederick the Great*. "He pretended to discern morality where no vestige of it existed. He tortured the facts to support his views. The 'morality' he praised had no connection with morality as understood in the New Testament. It was the kind of archaic morality observed by the Danites in their dealings with the people of Laish."

IX. The Americans

In American literature Roosevelt embraced the known and the unknown, the standard writers whom everybody reads and the writers who were his own particular pet discoveries. In *Hunting Trips of a Ranchman* he speaks of Irving, Hawthorne, Cooper, and Lowell as the "standbys, I suppose no man, East or West, would willingly be long without," but he quickly adds "for lighter reading . . . dreamy Ik Marvel, Burroughs's breezy pages, and the quaint pathetic character-sketches of the Southern writers—Cable, Craddock, Macon, Joel Chandler Harris, and sweet Sherwood Bonner."

He considered Poe the foremost American writer, an interesting item for those who have the general idea that T.R. could not understand or appreciate any temperament which differed from his own. Hawthorne he placed next in merit but professed not to enjoy. Poe and Hawthorne were the only two writers he put on his roll of American worthies in his address to the N.E.A. in 1905—"Washington and Lincoln, Grant and Farragut, Hawthorne and Poe, Fulton and Morse, St. Gaudens and MacMonnies." When he was in Dakota he thought the Bad Lands looked the way Poe sounded!

But the American poet Roosevelt loved best, far and away, was Longfellow. Indeed, he is one of Longfellow's greatest admirers, and he fights for him against detractors every inch of the way. He even disliked *The Oxford Book of English Verse* for what he considered its poor selection from Longfellow.

His favorite Longfellow poem was the masterly but not very characteristic "Saga of King Olaf." He praises the Cambridge poet, too, for his Civil War patriotism, not completely resisting the temptation all of us feel to make our favorite writers as much as possible like ourselves:

It was the gentlest of our poets who wrote:
        "Be bolde! Be bolde! and everywhere, Be bolde";
        Be not too bold! Yet better the excess
        Than the defect; better the more than less.
Longfellow's love of peace was profound; but he was a man, and a wise man, and he knew that cowardice does not promote peace, and that even the great evil of war may be a less evil than cringing to iniquity.

None of this means that he did not relish Longfellow also as the gentle poet of the domestic affections. When Simon Wolf and others asked him to make a protest in behalf of persecuted Russian Jews he thought of Longfellow's poem, "The Jewish Cemetery at Newport."

Next in his affections came Lowell, from whom he quotes more often than he does from Longfellow and who furnishes an epigraph for *The Winning of the West*. This is natural, for Lowell was much more than Longfellow the poet of public affairs. Unlike Longfellow, however, he does come in for some adverse criticism:

I have all of Lowell with me [he writes George Otto Trevelyan from Africa]; I care more and more for his Biglow Papers, especially the second series; I like his literary essays; but what a real mugwump he gradually became, as he let his fastidiousness, his love of ease and luxury, and his shrinking from the necessary roughness of contact with the world, grow upon him! I think his sudden painting of Dante as a mugwump is deliciously funny. I suppose that his character was not really strong, and that he was permanently injured by association with the Charles Eliot Norton type, and above all by following that impossible creature, Godkin.

Emerson, Roosevelt met, as a child, in Egypt of all places! He made no record of his impressions, but his sister Corinne recollected with pleasure "the lovely smile, somewhat vacant, it is true, but very gentle, with which he received the little children of his fellow countryman." T.R.'s references to Emerson are not numerous, but they all show high regard for him. In 1912 he told William Watson that he thought Emerson "a deeper man" than Blake.

About Whittier he says less, but when he declined, with regrets, an invitation to be present at Amesbury at the hundredth anniversary celebration of his birth, he wrote: "It seems to me that all good Americans should feel a peculiar pride in Whittier, exactly because he combined the power of expression and the great gift of poetry, with a flaming zeal for righteousness which made him a leader in matters of the spirit no less than of the intellect." "I only think of Holmes's poetry in connection with his prose," he wrote in 1901. "But it seems to me that we rate him rather low because he laughed instead of wept. I think that to lose his writings from literature would be a greater loss than to lose the writings of Montaigne."

Only Whitman, among the standard, major poets of the American flowering, was more or less left out. It is strange that Father Wilbur should have felt that when Roosevelt's "soul ellipse" is "rightly drawn,"

Whitman and Nietzsche are thy focal points.

T.R. was not insensible to Whitman's power. In his remarkable essay, "Dante and the Bowery," he declares that "Of all the poets of the nineteenth century, Walt Whitman was the only one who dared use the Bowery—that is, use anything that was striking and vividly typical of the humanity around him—as Dante used the ordinary humanity of his day." But even here he enters a caveat, for he goes on: "and even Whitman was not quite natural in doing so, for he always felt that he was defying the conventions and prejudices of his neighbors, and his self-consciousness made him a little defiant." In his 1916 address before the American Academy and the National Institute of Arts and Letters he called Whitman "a warped, although a rugged, genius of American poetry."

Of the minor American poems of the past Roosevelt's favorite, unquestionably, was "The Battle-Hymn of the Republic," which he wanted to have made our national anthem. He admired Julia Ward Howe tremendously "because in the vital matters fundamentally affecting the life of the Republic, she was as good a citizen of the Republic as Washington and Lincoln themselves," and dedicated *Fear God and Take Your Own Part* to her memory. To Maud Howe Elliott, a loyal Bull Mooser in 1912, he wrote in 1910: "There was not a man or woman in America for whom I felt the same kind of devotion that I felt for your mother."

Many of the poets of his own time were, of course, personally known to Roosevelt, and his estimate of their work was affected by his response to their personalities. This was true of John Hay, who wrote a noble sonnet about Roosevelt, and, in a measure, of Richard Watson Gilder. He encouraged Madison Cawein and Bliss Carman and not unnaturally took an interest in John Lomax's collection of cowboy songs and ballads. He "loved" Josephine Preston Peabody's *Harvest Moon*, though he told her she ought to have gone further in pointing out America's duty to Belgium. When Robert Haven Schauffler's "Scum o' the Earth" appeared in the *Atlantic,* he not only invited Schauffler to lunch but invited the magazine editors to meet him.

Between the invitation and the luncheon [wrote Schauffler], he had actually bought all my books and had read them aloud to his wife. Several times in the course of the meal, he held up the general conversation, to fill me with embarrassment and unholy pride as he made the editors a little address about one or other of these slightly known volumes. And I saw he had read them more carefully than any of the reviewers.

He also cared greatly for the poetry of George Cabot Lodge, son of his closest friend, and when "Bay's" poems were collected, after his tragically early death, it was T.R. who wrote an introduction for them. In it he said, "Of all the men with whom I have been intimately thrown he was the man to whom I would apply the rare name of genius." Though posterity has chosen to forget Lodge, along with Trumbull Stickney and the great William Vaughn Moody, this idea was not absurd, for it was shared by John Hay, Edith Wharton, and even Henry Adams.

When the "New Poetry," as Harriet Monroe and her followers liked to call it, came along just before World War I, Roosevelt was an interested part of the audience. I am not surprised at his interest in Frost and Lindsay, but the generous hearing he gave Edgar Lee Masters is more unexpected. I wonder if he knew how Masters had castigated him in *The New Star Chamber and Other Essays*, published by a forgotten publisher in Chicago in 1904, long before Spoon River had been explored.

Roosevelt's greatest contribution to American poetry was the way he managed to keep Edwin Arlington Robinson alive during the years when he was almost literally starving. Casting aside temporarily the role of a modern civil-service-reformer president and taking on that of a Medicean Maecenas (to the tune of $2,000 a year), he put Robinson in the Treasury Department in New York on the distinct understanding "that I expect you to think poetry first and Treasury second." What could an unknown, struggling, "minor" writer think upon receiving unheralded such a letter as this from the President of the United States? "I have enjoyed your poems . . . so much that I must write to tell you so. Will you permit me to ask what you are doing and how you are getting along? I wish I could see you." Even in those days Robinson was nobody's man but his own. When he declined the first job offered to him—that of an immigrant inspector in Mexico or at Montreal—the President wrote almost humbly: "Will you let me know what kind of a place it is that you could accept? . . . I may not be able to give you the place you desire, but I shall try." Roosevelt persuaded his own publishers, Scribners, to take Robinson over. He "boomed" *The Children of the Night* in *The Outlook*. Later he accepted the dedication of *The Town Down the River* and used an epigraph from Robinson in *A Booklover's Holidays in the Open*.[3]

Roosevelt probably mentions more American fictionists than poets and probably, in general, says less about them. In the nineties, at least, he thought our short stories better than our novels. That he should have been a Cooper enthusiast is not surprising, though he complains that Cooper romanticizes the life of the sailor. Melville's books were less familiar than Cooper's in T.R.'s time, but he knew them, though modern enthusiasts may be disappointed to find him

[3] Roosevelt did not like all Robinson's poems equally well. An unpublished letter of July 20, 1908, to David Gray, indicates special fondness for "Richard Cory," "The House on the Hill," and "Luke Havergal," though he is not sure he understands the last. He did not like *Captain Craig*. The most amusing aspect of the whole Roosevelt-Robinson encounter was the reaction of the learned literary critics to the President's invasion of the dovecotes. *The Critic* suspected that if T.R. had "kept *au courant* with the flood of American minor verse," he would have thought twice "before applying the word 'genius' to Mr. Robinson." The New York *Evening Post* regretted seeing "a person high in authority turn from his course to puff a book mediocre in character." It is interesting to remember that Roosevelt once conceived the idea of editing two poetic anthologies, one of hymns, etc., and the other of "profane" literature; also that in 1915 Mrs. Roosevelt got him to write some Christmas-stocking poems. He says, "my cave-man efforts were received with rapture."

coupling *Moby-Dick* with *Omoo*. In 1900 he expressed great pleasure that Frederick De Berard had included *Moby-Dick* in his list of sea stories. He knew Brockden Brown, Longstreet, and J. P. Kennedy, too, among the early writers, and he reviewed W. P. Trent's book on Simms appreciatively. Being of mixed Northern and Southern blood, he pondered carefully the justice or injustice of *Uncle Tom's Cabin*, and as late as 1914 he took nicknames from this book for himself and his political associates.

Mark Twain was the one American writer whose vastness of personality and whose Americanism might be compared with T.R.'s own, and one would expect Roosevelt to respond to him warmly. So he did. Like everybody else, he loved *Tom Sawyer* and *Huckleberry Finn*, but he placed *Pudd'nhead Wilson* higher than most readers do. He seems, however, to have missed the significance of *A Connecticut Yankee*, failing to perceive, as Parrington did so much later, that Mark Twain's criticisms of the sixth century still had their relevance in the twentieth.

It is interesting to compare what T.R. says of Mark Twain with Mark Twain's own furious denunciatons of him in *Mark Twain in Eruption* and elsewhere. Mark Twain did not dislike T.R. personally, but he regarded him as a dangerous political influence. He also detested his hunting. The President, he declared, had "tunneled so many subways under the Constitution that the transportation facilities through that document are only rivaled, not surpassed, by those enjoyed by the City of New York." When in 1908 T.R. dared, as Mark Twain conceived it, to name his successor, the great humorist thought that the Republic was dead.

Some of the most devastating things Mark Twain wrote about Theodore Roosevelt were private and not published during his lifetime, but the President was not unaware of Mark's violent anti-imperialism. He must surely have read the sensational attack on General Funston, whom T.R. admired, when it appeared in *The North American Review* in 1902. And indeed there is a 1901 letter in which T.R. calls both Godkin and Mark Twain "prize idiots" for their attitude toward current problems. But he does not seem to have permitted these differences of opinion to anger him toward Mark Twain, and he certainly did not allow them to cause him to change his mind about Mark's genius. In *The Strenuous Life* he even, extravagantly, calls him "a great philosopher." In 1905 he wrote George Harvey, expressing his regret at being unable to attend the Seventieth Birthday Dinner: "He is one of the citizens whom all Americans should delight to honor. . . . May he live long, and year by year may he add to the sum of admirable work that he has done."

Bret Harte probably seemed to stand closer to Mark Twain's throne in T.R.'s early days at least than he does now. Roosevelt has no very detailed critical comment on his work, but he must have read him diligently, for he quotes from him and refers to him a reasonable number of times, and he takes an epigraph from one of his poems for *The Rough Riders*.

In the nineties the realism of William Dean Howells seemed a little gray to T.R., as it did to many Americans, and he speaks of him as "taking a jaundiced view of life." Later he thought much more favorably of Howells. "I was a very young man when I began to read Mr. Howells's books," he wrote Edward J. Wheeler in 1917, "and they not only gave me the greatest pleasure, as works of literature, but they helped me a little in striving to be a decent citizen." He also approved the unsentimental conclusion of *The Rise of Silas Lapham*, praising Howells's opposition to self-sacrifice for sacrifice' sake.

His reaction to Henry James was much more violent—"a miserable little snob." James's internationalism and his residence abroad awakened all T.R.'s prejudices. James and T.R. met at least three times—in 1882, 1905, and 1914—and T.R. seems to have enjoyed these meetings.

For his part, James did not like Roosevelt much more than Mark Twain did. When T.R. succeeded to the presidency, James called him "a dangerous and ominous Jingo—of whom the most hopeful thing to say is that he may be rationalized by this sudden real responsibility." In 1912 he told Dr. J. William White that he could not even bear to think about Roosevelt, "the mere monstrous embodiment of unprecedented and resounding Noise." When, at World War I, T.R. took his strong pro-Ally stand, James could not but approve, but he must still stipulate, "Mr. Roosevelt is far from being dear to me."

Roosevelt loved Joel Chandler Harris, both as a writer and as a man. He had heard and loved some of the plantation tales in his own family before Harris set them down. But he did not confine himself to Uncle Remus, for in his view Harris was "not only a great writer but a great moral teacher," and he thought such tales as "Free Joe" even better than the Uncle Remus stories.

T.R. once met Stephen Crane, but I have found no comment on his work. Though he objected to Ambrose Bierce's pessimism, he thought some of the *Tales of Soldiers and Civilians* extremely good. He loved Frank R. Stockton and as early as 1913 considered him a neglected writer. Richard Harding Davis he at first disliked personally as an "everlasting cad," but he changed his mind about him when they were in Cuba together and thereafter thought highly of him until the end. After Davis died, T.R. called him "as good an American as ever lived." He had his reservations about Hamlin Garland at first also, considering him something of a crank. Later he and Garland were very close to each other, and he furnished a foreword for *They of the High Trails.* But he damned *The Octopus,* by Frank Norris, with faint praise because he was revolted by what he considered its extremism.

He was very faithful about following the work of friends and acquaintances. He read and commented upon the stories of John Fox, Jr., while they were being serialized, and he wrote Owen Wister and William Allen White detailed commentaries on a number of their books. "I really think you have done for the plainsmen and mountainmen, the soldiers, frontiersmen and Indians," he tells Wister, "what nobody else but Bret Harte and Kipling could have done, and neither of them have sufficient knowledge to enable them do it even had they wished." In his latter days T.R. rated Wister "the foremost American man of letters," though this did not prevent him from criticizing him where he thought he went wrong. He admired Winston Churchill more than most readers do nowadays and sought his acquaintance because of his interest in his novels. Robert Grant's *Unleavened Bread* he thought "a melancholy, indeed a painful, book, but . . . the strongest study of American life that has been written for many years."

Roosevelt was an indefatigable writer of fan letters to authors whose work he enjoyed. Once he offered to advance Moffat, Yard & Company the money to make an advance to Ellen Velvin on her

Wild Creatures Afield, "just so as to allow her to live while she is finishing it." "I think she is really trying to do good work, and I hear that she is very poor." Mary E. Wilkins Freeman, Charles Egbert Craddock, James Branch Cabell, Elsie Singmaster, and Stanley Waterloo are among the writers who received his warm, enthusiastic letters. Waterloo's *The Story of Ab* he liked so well that he wrote to the author even before he had finished reading it. He loved Elsie Singmaster's *Gettysburg* stories as "sermons teaching what is best and loftiest in the American spirit," and he was also very fond of her *Emmeline.* "Come down to Washington," he writes Martha Baker Dunn in 1905, "and see if you do not like us!"

It will be seen that T.R. often enjoyed what is generally called "popular" fiction; thus he was very fond of Kathleen Norris's *Mother* and Edna Ferber's Emma McChesney stories; he also liked Gouverneur Morris's novels and the stories of Richard Washburn Child. "I wonder if you feel that I am hopelessly sentimental," he wrote Miss Ferber in 1913, "because my only objection to the last twelve pages is that I would have liked somehow to see not only the boy marry, but poor Emma McChesney at last have the chance herself to marry somebody decent with whom she was in love!" When his friend Edward Bok was editor of the *Ladies' Home Journal* Roosevelt sometimes read and evaluated stories for him, and in 1914 he, Ida M. Tarbell, and Mark Sullivan judged a short-story contest for *Collier's.*[4]

Among American nonfiction books, Roosevelt naturally had a special interest in history and in nature writing. He asked for complete sets of Prescott and Motley for his twenty-first birthday; possibly he already had Parkman. In any case, he considered Parkman the greatest American historian; like Motley and Prescott, he had achieved the combination of accuracy and vividness which T.R. valued in historical writing, and, unlike them, he had devoted himself to an American subject. In 1888 T.R. sought and obtained permission to dedicate *The Winning of the West* to Parkman.

T.R. endorsed Henry Adams, though with some reservations. It seemed to him that in *The Law of Civilization and Decay* Brooks Adams had drawn false parallels between his America and the

[4] See *Collier's,* LIV, Oct. 3, 1914, p. 10, for his report.

great civilizations of the past. "Like the Roman Empire in the Second Century—like the Greek dominions in the Third Century before Christ—our civilization shows very unhealthy symptoms; but they are entirely different symptoms, and the conditions are not only different, but in many important respects directly opposite to those which formerly obtained."

Frederick Jackson Turner's paper on "The Significance of the Frontier in American History" came out just in time for T.R. to make good use of it in the third volume of *The Winning of the West*. Alfred Thayer Mahan's study of *The Influence of Sea Power upon History* importantly affected his own thinking. He told W. P. Trent that his *Southern Statesmen of the Old Regime* had compelled him to revise his opinion of Jefferson Davis and other Southern leaders, and in 1890 he called Grant's *Memoirs* "the greatest piece of literary work which has been done in America, or indeed anywhere, of recent years." Later he lauded Wister's book on Grant as "the very best short biography which has been written of any prominent American." He also enjoyed many other American historical works: H. O. Taylor's *The Mediaeval Mind,* William E. Dodd's *Statesmen of the Old South,* Benjamin Ide Wheeler's *Alexander the Great,* inevitably Henry Cabot Lodge's *George Washington,* and, much less inevitably but quite enthusiastically, despite his dislike for its mugwump author, Carl Schurz's *Abraham Lincoln.*

Among naturalists and nature writers from Audubon to Dallas Lore Sharp, I recall few whom Roosevelt did not know. Among modern Americans John Burroughs was undoubtedly his favorite. When he puts Thoreau second to Burroughs, Thoreau's special admirers must surely find it outrageous, but Roosevelt was no Thorovian; like Robert Louis Stevenson, he found the man of Concord somewhat anemic; he admits too that he never quite shook off the influence of Lowell's vicious caricature of Thoreau.

Among the older American essayists, Roosevelt praised George William Curtis; later he read "David Grayson," Brander Matthews, and Samuel McChord Crothers. Two of Crothers's books he took to Africa with him in the "Pigskin Library."

From the most distinguished essayist of her time, Agnes Repplier, Roosevelt foolishly shied away after having been offended by her treatment of Civil War poetry in her essay on "The Praises of War."

Professor Morison and his colleagues fall into the trap with him when they permit themselves in one of their footnotes to speak of Miss Repplier's "pacifism." She was about as good a pacifist as T.R. himself, and during the war he discovered it, and met her, and came at last greatly to admire her.

But of all the nonfiction writers of his own time in America, the one T.R. relished most was the great Finley Peter Dunne. And it says something for him that he should have done so, for "Mr. Dooley" renamed *The Rough Riders* "Alone in Cubia," nor did he ever spare Roosevelt even after they had become friends. "I regret to state that my family and intimate friends are delighted with your review of my book," T.R. wrote. "Now I think you owe me one; and I shall exact that when you next come east to pay me a visit. I have long wanted the chance of making your acquaintance." To Lodge he added, "How he does get at any joint in the harness." Dunne did not cure Roosevelt of his expansionism, but he came closer than anybody else to persuading him that the expansionist doctrine was in some aspects vulnerable.

Since Roosevelt was a public man, it may seem a little surprising that the one thing he should have been temperate in reading was newspapers. It is true that one observer has reported that he would come into the breakfast room of his hotel in Assembly days with all the newspapers he could get, that he would go through them while breakfasting and conversing, with incredible speed, and drop each paper, as he finished it, on the floor, unfolded, until, at the end of the meal, there was, on either side of him, a pile of loose papers as high as the table. If this was his early habit, it was soon outgrown. He loathed the Hearst and Pulitzer press, "that hideous yellow journalism," he calls it, "which makes a cult of the mendacious, the sensational, and the inane, and which, throughout its wide but vapid field, does as much to vulgarize and degrade the popular taste, to weaken the popular character, and to dull the edge of the popular conscience, as any influence under which the country can suffer." But this was not all. He hated the *Sun*. He hated the *Evening Post*. Sometimes he even hated the *Times*. "I have such an utter contempt for American newspapers," he writes in 1913, "that it is difficult for me to make up my mind to read any newspaper." Ike Hoover extends T.R.'s indifference to newspapers to the whole Roosevelt family. After a visit to the White House in 1908, James Ford Rhodes recorded that Roosevelt read hardly anything except *The Outlook* and *The Spectator*. In a sense this is misleading, for, to a certain extent at least, the papers were read for him and his attention called to items which his readers thought he should see.

The ban on newspapers certainly did not extend to magazines, not even popular magazines. Here again there are often sharp comments. His attitude toward *The Atlantic Monthly*, for example, depended upon what its policy at the moment happened to be; "I never see the *Atlantic*," he boasts in 1917. Yet he contributed to it, early and late, as he did to *The Century*, of which he complains in 1893 that it "seems to have a rooted aversion to anything literary," and to many others as well. He was a contributing editor of *The Outlook* from 1909 to 1914, when, after the Progressive debacle, his name had such a depressing effect upon the circulation lists, especially in New England, that there was nothing for it but to let him go.[5] From then until the end of his life he wrote for the *Metropolitan* and the Kansas City *Star*. In 1906–1907 the *Ladies' Home Journal* had a department called "The President," which constituted a kind of semiofficial expression of his views; in 1916–1917 he himself wrote, and published anonymously in the *Journal*, a department called "Men," in which he discussed such problems as how a father should behave the first time a young man came to call on his daughter. I know of no more cogent testimony to the sincerity of his interest in the family and its problems, and I can think of no other president who would have been capable of this.

According to O. K. Davis, T.R.'s method of reading magazines, on trains at least, was somewhat unusual:

The Colonel always had a great deal of reading matter with him, which he supplemented along the way by buying all the new magazines.

[5] A letter of Dec. 4, 1914, apparently to Lawrence Abbott, says that, in accordance with their telephone conversation, T.R. will dispose elsewhere of "my articles of a militant anti-Administration type and the like. . . . After March 1st our engagement will close; I have made arrangements with the Metropolitan; but from time to time I shall be able if you desire it, to send you some literary article of the type you have deemed appropriate for these closing three months—the type of articles included in my volume on History as Literature." (Quoted in undated catalogue, American Autograph Shop, Vol. III, No. 4.)

The character of the magazine did not seem to make any difference to him. . . . I have seen him again and again read a magazine from cover to cover, everything in it, special articles, poetry, stories, and all. And as he read it he would tear out the finished page and throw it to the floor, just as he did the pages of manuscript when delivering a speech.

Ike Hoover is surely wrong in denying him mystery stories, for we know of his interest in Arsène Lupin, and Kermit tells us that he could bury himself with equal ease "in an exhaustive treatise on the *History of the Mongols* or in the *Hound of the Baskervilles*." He also liked books about people cast away on desert islands. To these he added "my substitute for trashy novels" (he should have said, "my addition" to them), hunting books; the "short and simple annals of the rich," he sarcastically calls them. Some of these were current publications; others were old and rare; and he was anything but uncritical in his attitude toward them. It was natural, too, in view of his own experiences in the Dakotas, that he should have been addicted to "westerns," among them the work of Alfred Henry Lewis, Emerson Hough, and, of course, in one of his aspects, Owen Wister.

X. Tolstoy and Others

Roosevelt's knowledge of foreign literature was necessarily more "spotty" than his knowledge of literature in English, but the range was still wide. Except for *The Song of Roland,* he did not think he cared much for French poetry, complaining that it does not sing. (Kermit says that he did not care much for French novels either.) Nor, having "a robustly Occidental mind," did he respond very deeply to such Oriental literature as came his way, nor even to *The Arabian Nights.* Yet when, in South America, he was driven to *The Oxford Book of French Verse,* for want of something better, he found himself developing a taste for Villon, Ronsard, and others. Among modern French writers, he was very fond of Mistral, who also greatly admired him.

The remarkable thing is the number of different areas in which T.R. finds favorites. He skips from Körner to Topelius to *Jörn Uhl* to "the Bard of the Dimbovitza," from Carmen Sylva to the Italian modernist Fogazzaro to the modern French Catholic Henry Bor-

deaux. A Swedish bishop visiting America in 1901 went back home
to tell the King of President Roosevelt's astonishing familiarity with
Tegnér; Baron Rosen, listening to his conversation with the Ru-
manian minister, was "struck" by his evident familiarity with Ru-
manian literature. An unnamed lady guest at the White House,
having by chance read an Icelandic book, and hoping for once to
have an advantage over him, asked, "Mr. President, are you
interested in Icelandic literature?" "With a bounce in his chair he
turned an eager countenance upon me and said, 'Am I not!' and
then proceeded to tell me not only my one lonely Icelandic book
but dozens of others that I had never heard of."

We should expect Icelandic literature to appeal to Roosevelt;
he once told Stefansson that he placed old Norse literature next
after the classical in excellence and enjoyed it more. The *Nibelungenlied* was as familiar as *Roland* but not more so; he knew *Aucassin
and Nicolette* and *Reinecke Fuchs,* and he quotes Goethe's *Faust*
in the original as an epigraph to *The Strenuous Life.* He wrote Kuno
Meyer that he cared most for the second part of the *Nibelungenlied*
—the story of Kriemhild's revenge. "Of course it is not such great
poetry as Homer, but the fighting is very much better, and to my
mind the heroes are far more manly." His article on the Irish sagas
is illustrated by many references to other saga and epic materials.
In 1905 T.R. told an audience at Holy Cross College, in Worcester,
Massachusetts, that we were about to experience a revival of interest
in Celtic literature comparable to the earlier awakening of interest
in Scandinavian matters. "I wish," he said, "to see American institutions of learning take the lead in that awakening." In 1912 he
accepted with great pleasure an honorary presidency of the Gaelic
Literature Association. Perhaps it was this interest that carried over
into his enthusiasm for modern Irish literature and particularly for
Lady Gregory and her group. When the Irish Players came over
in 1911, Roosevelt's interest in the drama for once grew keen, and
he calmly bestowed upon them the leadership of world theater.

Roosevelt considered himself "a fairly good Dumas man," but
he did not care greatly for Balzac. He was very fond of Sienkiewicz's
picture of the war of the Poles against the Turks and Tartars in
Fire and Sword and *Pan Michael,* but he did not like *Quo Vadis?*
because the nonresistance of the Christians made him angry. He

went "all out" for one modern French "uplift" book, *The Simple Life,* whose author, the Reverend Charles Wagner, was introduced by the President when he lectured in Washington.

The two European writers whom Roosevelt referred to most often are Dante and Tolstoy. Though he claimed no special knowledge of Dante, his reverence for the Italian was very great. In "Dante and the Bowery" he celebrated the realistic side of Dante's genius. In 1912 he told both Robert Grant and James Ford Rhodes that he would have been like the cleric who made the great refusal if he had declined to run. During World War I he cited Dante's scorn for the neutrals who served neither God nor his enemies.

Tolstoy challenged Roosevelt by his greatness as a novelist and repelled him by his pacifism and his unhealthy attitude toward sex, especially in *The Kreutzer Sonata.* After reading *Anna Karenina* in 1886, T.R. wrote his sister Mrs. Robinson:

I took Anna Karénine along on the trip and have read it through with very great interest. I hardly know whether to call it a very bad book or not. There were two entirely distinct stories in it; the connection between Levine's story and Anna's is of the slightest, and need not have existed at all. Levine's and Kitty's history is not only very powerfully and naturally told, but is also perfectly healthy. Anna's most certainly is not, though of great and sad interest; she is portrayed as being a prey to the most violent passion, and subject to melancholia, and her reasoning power is so unbalanced that she could not possibly be described otherwise than as in a certain sense insane. Her character is curiously contradictory; bad as she was however she was not to me nearly as repulsive as her brother Stiva; Vronsky had some excellent points. I like poor Dolly—but she should have been less a patient Griselda with her husband. You know how I abominate the Griselda type.

In an *Outlook* essay of 1909, T.R. argued

that Tolstoy is a great writer, a great novelist; that the unconscious influence of his novels is probably, on the whole, good, even disregarding their standing as works of art; that even as a professional moralist and philosophical adviser of mankind in religious matters he has some excellent theories and on some points develops a noble and elevating teaching; but that taken as a whole, and if generally diffused, his moral and philosophical teachings . . . would have an influence for bad. . . .

In the "revolting" *Kreutzer Sonata* he finds a "moral perversion" which could appeal only to decadents and could only have come "from a man who, however high he may stand in certain respects, has in him certain dreadful qualities of the moral pervert."

In *The Strenuous Life* Roosevelt tried to tie up the two aspects of Tolstoy's thinking of which he disapproved. "The same quality that makes the debauchee and the devotee alternate in certain decadent families, the hysterical development which leads to violent emotional reaction in a morbid nature from vice to virtue, also leads to the creation of Tolstoy's 'Kreutzer Sonata' on the one hand, and of his unhealthy peace-mysticism on the other." Yet when he lectured at Berlin on "The World Movement" in 1910 he was still generous enough to say that, though "it would be a bad thing indeed to accept Tolstoy as a guide in social and moral matters . . . it would also be a bad thing not to have Tolstoy, not to profit by the lofty side of his teachings."

XI. The World of *Alice*

Living as he did with children about him, it was inevitable that T.R. should also give much attention to children's books. I doubt that he would have abandoned such literature altogether even if he had been childless. Writing to Mrs. James T. Leavitt in 1907, he thanks her for a volume which it was "just dear" of her to send him: "there is nothing I enjoy so much as a good boy's book." Roosevelt did not shy from robust tales of adventure in this area, but even when he was a child himself he was intelligent enough to perceive that there was no reason why boys should not enjoy Miss Alcott's stories as much as girls did. Kipling's *Stalky & Co.* he condemns as roundly as he praises *Captains Courageous,* "for there is hardly a single form of meanness which it does not extol, or of school mismanagement which it does not seem to applaud." When a little boy named Randolph Howard wrote to him about his interest in *Peck's Bad Boy,* Roosevelt was not pleased. "I am not very fond of Peck's Bad Boy myself," he replied. "I want every boy to be manly and able to fight for his own rights and those of his country, but I want him to be gentle and upright also."

The mental diet of the Roosevelt children was not confined to juvenile productions, for their parents aimed to introduce them to the best literature just as soon as they were able to assimilate it, with Scott and the Bible always high on the list of favorites. But they had the standard fairy tales, including those of Knatchbull-Hugessen, so unjustly neglected nowadays, and the traditional nursery rhymes, besides such modern good ones as those of Laura E. Richards. There is a delightful letter to Mrs. Robinson: "Darling Corinne: Inasmuch as we are to have Cocky Locky, Henny Penny and Goosey Poosey at lunch, why omit Foxy Loxy? I am anxious to see Dr. R—— and I do hope you will ask him to lunch on Thursday also."

Roosevelt had his doubts about the utilitarianism of Maria Edgeworth and *Sanford and Merton*, but this did not prevent him from talking about "Little Rosamond's day of misfortunes" when things went wrong with him. Devotees of *Alice* are a higher order than the Knights of the Garter, and none among them has loved the book more than Theodore Roosevelt. He quotes *Alice* on every possible and impossible occasion, and once he signed a letter to Corinne, "Your extravagant and irrelevant but affectionate brother, the White Knight." If he loved any other writer in this field as much as he loved Lewis Carroll, it must have been Kenneth Grahame, and indeed his affection for *The Wind in the Willows* hardly knew any bounds.

Mrs. Roosevelt was the usual reader to the children, with T.R. taking over on special occasions, as when she was absent and he was acting as "vice-mother." Once he read John Hay's "Jim Bludso," which made a great impression and inspired many questions from Quentin "including one as to whether the colored boy did not find sitting on the valve very hot." But T.R. was more famous for telling stories than for reading them. Even as a child he did this, making up yarns which *The Jungle Book* afterwards recalled to his sister's mind. Later he was given to both ghost stories and wolf stories, though, for that matter, he liked to read ghost stories to himself as well as tell them to the children, having a preference for ghosts of the gory variety, like F. Marion Crawford's in "The Upper Berth" and some of the ghosts of M. R. James. He did not care for the psychological ghosts of Henry James. The "scary" tales were most effective on camping trips when the children lay around the fire at night, wrapped in their blankets.

The smallest of us lay within reach of father where we could touch him if the story became too vivid for our nerves and we needed the reassuring feel of his clothes to bring us back to reality. There was, however, a delicious danger in being too near him. In stories in which the "haunt" seized his victim, father generally illustrated the action by making a grab at the nearest child.

XII. The Gentle Art of Quotation

Roosevelt was a less allusive writer and speaker than I should expect so bookish a man to be, though he had a few favorite quotations which he used repeatedly. At one time I thought that the reason for this must be that his verbal memory did not equal his wonderful memory for facts. But there are difficulties in the way of this explanation. Some have even believed that Roosevelt had what we call a photographic memory. Astonished by the intimate knowledge of Chinese affairs he showed upon greeting a China delegation, President Penniman, of the University of Pennsylvania, asked him whether he had primed himself for the occasion. "No," he replied, "I have not read a book about China for some time . . . but I remembered a book that I had read some time ago, and as I talked the pages of the book came before my eyes, and it seemed as though I were able to read the things therein contained." According to Charles Willis Thompson, this applied even to his own speeches, written out in advance. He could see the page in his mind's eye and modify it in delivery. A number of contemporary writers testify that Roosevelt quoted from their writings extensively when he met them, sometimes quoting obscure passages which they themselves did not recognize. On the other hand, I find it very difficult to understand how a man with a photographic memory could have been such a bad speller as Roosevelt was. Words like "don't" he always spelled "do'n't," and about the only thing he seems to have been particular about was that he had a violent objection to the British spelling of words like "honor." Even his close friends might expect to find their names misspelled; I have found "Jane Adams," "Mrs. Humphrey Ward," "Elsie Singmeister," "Prof. J. R. Lounsbury" and "Lounsberry," and "Charles D. Elliott" (for President Eliot), also "the Hibbert's Journal" and "Houghton & Mifflin."

Theodore Roosevelt, Jr. recorded that his father would teach him the poems he loved, "by word of mouth, as the old minstrels taught," while dressing for dinner. When he rowed back from camping expeditions with his children he would chant a seafaring ballad, and John Loring says that when T.R. was in Africa he and Kermit would quote poetry to each other by the yard. Loring asked if Roosevelt had memorized these passages. "No," he replied, "they are works of which I am particularly fond, and I read them twice or three times a year." On the other hand, Archie Butt says that fond as he was of "The Battle-Hymn of the Republic," he always had to be prompted when he tried to repeat it.

This testimony may be less contradictory than it seems. Most of the poems Roosevelt habitually repeated aloud seem to have been of the ballad variety, with strongly marked rhythms and mnemonic devices. I have insisted against his detractors that he was interested in literature for literature's sake, but he may still have been more interested in content than he was in form. How fine his ear was for the subtler melodies of verse—or even prose—I do not know. He himself once declared, "I don't know that I have any real ear for rhythm at all. I don't even know enough to be able to tell why it is I like the prose of De Quincey and Poe, which always gives me a sense of color, and of music . . ."

XIII. Literature and Society

Roosevelt was quite clear that the fundamental purpose of literature was to give aesthetic pleasure, yet he frequently applies nonaesthetic standards of evaluation. Perhaps the idealistic basis upon which his judgments rest is best stated not in anything he says about literature but in his letter to the painter Simons, whose work he so greatly admired, and two of whose paintings still hang in the North Room at Sagamore Hill:

I agree absolutely with you that art, or at least the art for which I care, must present the ideal through the temperament and the interpretation of the painter. I do not greatly care for the reproduction of landscapes which in effect I see whenever I ride and walk. I wish the "light that never was on land or sea" in the pictures that I am to live with— and this light your paintings have. When I look at them I feel a lift in my soul; I feel my imagination stirred.

Mrs. Roosevelt, he indicates to both Owen Wister and Winston Churchill, might judge *Lady Baltimore* or *Coniston* purely from the aesthetic standpoint, but he himself cannot. Like Bernard Shaw, he felt that comedy is closer to life than tragedy and has greater social value. "Let in some sunlight, somehow," he urges Wister. "Leave your reader with the feeling that life, after all, does—go—on." He threw aside David Graham Phillips's novel, *The Plum Tree*, in disgust when he first attempted to read it, then gave it another try and changed his mind when he found elements of idealism in it.

The social usefulness of literature is stressed heavily in what he has to say about such writers as Sarah Orne Jewett, Mary E. Wilkins Freeman, Octave Thanet, and Myra Kelly. He wanted American literature to build upon the foundations of world literature, but he did not believe it could achieve its own purpose and make its distinctive contribution unless its writers were thoroughly steeped in the knowledge of their own country and their own day. In one early (1888) article, he gets his dislike of unpatriotic Americans, his dislike of French realism, and his adherence to moral wholesomeness all mixed up together. American writers who choose to live abroad are contemptuously dismissed—"not theirs the realism that gives us so excellent and true a type as, for instance, Silas Lapham—but men who apparently seek to supplement French realism, which consists in depicting the unspeakably nasty, by a realism of their own, the portrayal of the unutterably trivial."

This suggests, finally, the moral criterion in Roosevelt's judgment of books, which anybody who knows him would take for granted if it were not stated at all. "I am old-fashioned, or sentimental, or something, about books! Whenever I read one I want, in the first place, to enjoy myself, and, in the next place, to feel that I am a little better and not a little worse for having read it." Zola's characters are "hideous human swine." Rabelais and Boccaccio have their merits but finding them is like examining "a gold chain encrusted in the filth of a pigpen."

XIV. Sock and Buskin

One branch of literature, the acted play, appears to have meant little to Roosevelt. As a child in Dresden he saw a number of Shakespeare plays. There are a few references to theatergoing in Boston during his Harvard years, but the plays were inconsequential and his comments somewhat critical. In London he and his first wife saw *Patience*. In Washington we hear of his attending plays like *The Crisis, The Yankee Consul,* and Zangwill's *The Melting Pot,* which was dedicated to him, but his comments, when recorded, generally concern the social or political implications of the work.

Ike Hoover says it was hard work to get Roosevelt to go to the theater but that when he got there he enjoyed himself. Though Owen Wister speaks of his discussing the art of Henry Irving, John Drew is the only quality legitimate actor of his time to whom I have found an authentic tribute. There is, however, an unpublished letter to Maude Adams, declining perforce an invitation whose nature is not specified and looking forward to seeing her at lunch. He enjoyed the Ben Greet Players on the White House lawn in 1908. As for the actors of the past, in his reference to the Astor Place riot in *New York*, Macready appears only as "an obnoxious English actor," which is not very knowledgeable from any point of view and certainly not from that of theatrical history!

Roosevelt is reported to have loved *Peter Pan*, which I should expect in view of both his interest in Barrie and his love of fantasy in general. He knew Bayard Veiller from police commissioner days and in 1913 wrote to congratulate him upon his great success, *Within the Law*. There are also unpublished letters to George C. Tyler and David Belasco. He expressed interest in Harrigan and Hart and, later, Montgomery and Stone, with whom he was personally acquainted, as he was also with Hal Reid. An anonymous article in *The Theatre* [6] names Fritzi Scheff, Elsie Janis, Maxine Elliott, Nat Goodwin, and DeWolf Hopper among Roosevelt's favorites, but I do not know how much stock we can take in this. He did, however, once write Oliver Wendell Holmes the younger of the interest which his "worm-eaten heart" could take in light opera. He also enjoyed the magician Kellar, and during the war he had a scheme to use Harry Lauder to combat anti-British propaganda. In 1908 he sent a message of encouragement to the founders of the ill-fated New Theater, and in 1916 he signed a testimonial for the dean of American drama critics, William Winter.

[6] "When the President Goes to the Theatre," *The Theatre*, VIII (1908), 120 +.

The new art of the motion picture developed entirely during Roosevelt's lifetime but, except that he posed for the newsreels, it might almost just as well never have existed so far as he was concerned. In the beginning he did not even want to do that; when Lodge suggested his making a phonograph record in 1904 he inquired whether he was entirely sober. "Besides talking into the phonograph would you not like me to dance a little before a kinetoscope?" [7] In 1897 he reports having seen "the vitascope representation of the Corbett-Fitzsimmons fight." Unlike Woodrow Wilson, he did not comment on D. W. Griffith's *The Birth of a Nation* in 1915. Literally the only dramatic film I find any record of his having seen is *The Battle-Cry of Peace*, the powerful piece of preparedness propaganda put out by his Oyster Bay neighbor, J. Stuart Blackton, of the Vitagraph Company. Roosevelt was in on the planning of this almost from the beginning, and, though he refused to appear in it lest his appearance should cause the picture to be regarded as a plea for his nomination in 1916, he did persuade General Wood, Admiral Dewey, Secretary of War Garrison, and Lyman Abbott to do so. His interest, however, was far from aesthetic.

Bradley Gilman, who knew T.R. well, once tried to explain his indifference to the theater and the concert hall:

The pleasure from all these high arts is a pleasure that assumes passivity in the listener or observer. And Roosevelt got little joy from passive mental states. Further, in the case of the theater, I think that its stimulations, artistic though they might be, were distrusted by him. He was fiercely eager for what is genuine, without any pretence. And he could not, or would not, enough subordinate this craving for reality and sincerity to allow him to enjoy the simulations of the stage.

The vocabulary is ill chosen here, and the emphasis is wrong. The views expressed are not reconcilable with Roosevelt's taking so much pleasure as he did in poetry and fiction and in such fantasies as *The Wind in the Willows*. But Gilman is not completely mistaken,

[7] In 1912 T.R. recorded for the Victor Talking Machine Company *The Liberty of the People* (31872); *Mr. Roosevelt Pays His Respects to Penrose and Archbold* and *The "Abyssinian Treatment" of Standard Oil* (35249); *Why the Trusts and Bosses Oppose the Progressive Party* and *The Farmer and the Business Man* (35250).

for all that. The theater and the concert hall do immobilize the audience, as a reader, who may choose his own time and place to read, is not immobilized, and in a sense they require more passivity. The reader, of course, *is* the performer; he produces the play in the theater that he carries under his hat. As we have already seen, T.R. did not relish sport as spectacle either. "It must always be remembered that the mere spectators at any form of sport get little or no benefit from it save what is obtained from any other harmless diversion and that it is both unhealthy and slightly ridiculous for them to permit their taste to looking on at a sport . . . to develop into an absorbing passion." "Harmless diversion" and "slightly ridiculous" —how could you sweep the great arts of the stage aside more contemptuously? For all that, there is no puritanical revulsion against the arts but rather a William James-like sense of the dangers of stimulation without expression. Roosevelt is not often an unconscious humorist; he generally paid his own jokes the tribute of his own falsetto squeak of enjoyment. But one sentence from a letter to Ted at Harvard is the most ridiculous statement of its kind since the old church disciplines lumped "dancing, theater-going, and card-playing" together and condemned them all. "I am very glad," he writes, "that you have given up the theater and drinking, and also smoking anything except a pipe."

XV. "When Music Sounds . . ."

There were many musicals during the White House occupancy, but these reflected Mrs. Roosevelt's taste more than her husband's. Mrs. Laszlo's violin playing made it easier for him to sit still while her husband was painting his portrait. One summer night at Sagamore the colored servants started in to sing, and he and his daughter Ethel got up from their beds and went out to the veranda to listen.

In 1899 Roosevelt records that he admires the Wagnerian opera "in a perfectly dumb way," but when Robert Bacon asked him whether he wanted to go to the opera in Paris in 1910 he replied, "Personally, I should be very melancholy if I spent an evening at the Opera, but very probably Mrs. Roosevelt would like to go." There is one 1915 reference to "the victriola, or whatever that musical instrument is called," but this may be T.R.'s uncertain spelling rather than musical indifference.

The singer Hulda Lashanska was once quoted in the New York press as attributing considerable musical sensitiveness (though not technical knowledge of music) to T.R. Brahms, Schumann, and Chopin, she said, were his favorite composers. He is also reported as having entertained Engelbert Humperdinck, the great German composer of *Die Königskinder* and *Hänsel und Gretel,* and to have discussed music and German literature with him. Both Natalie Curtis and Blanche D. Abrams have testified to his interest in Indian music, but anthropology and public policy seem the important considerations here. He was never unaware of the social values of any of the arts, and he was always in favor of whatever would substitute "healthy pleasure for undesirable pleasure." He once attended a concert at the Third Street Music Settlement in New York.

Boys and girls [he said], do not envy your neighbors who may have many automobiles in their garages while you have your piano, your violin, or 'cello. Prepare yourself to earn the living wage, but do not forget to leave the casement open to let in "the light that never was on sea or land." Let the love for literature, painting, sculpture, architecture, and, above all, music enter into your lives.

In general, the simpler music served T.R. best. He was very fond of hymn singing and had so many favorite hymns that he had difficulty in naming them all—"How Firm a Foundation," "Ein feste Burg ist unser Gott," "Holy, Holy, Holy," "Christ Is Made the Sure Foundation," "Jerusalem the Golden," and "Abide With Me."

When the Arion Singing Society performed at the White House, he asked for "Dixie," "My Old Kentucky Home," and "Old Folks at Home." "Dixie," he said, was the best of all tunes, better even than "Garry Owen." I think the only singer mentioned in Roosevelt's writings is Louise Homer, whom he praises for having had a career without permitting it to interfere with her home life. David Bispham has recorded, however, that when he sang at the White House the audience demanded "Danny Deever" as an encore, though Mrs. Roosevelt had specifically asked him not to sing it. "Its conclusion brought the President upstanding to his feet, and with hands outstretched he came forward saying, 'By Jove, Mr. Bispham, that was bully! With such a song as that you could lead a nation into battle!' "

Since T.R. was told even in childhood that he resembled the cormorant in voice as well as appetite, it may seem absurd to consider him as a musical performer. Yet he loved to sing. In church he lifted up his voice in praise, singing the hymns, says Archie Butt, about an octave lower than the choir, but doing pretty well in the more difficult Gregorian chants. On the range, in Dakota, he hummed the same song over and over again, "but what the words were or the melody is a secret that belongs to the wind." To his children he crooned an old Dutch lullaby which was the only Dutch he knew.

Above all, he kept singing softly under his breath, in carriage or automobile, during his political campaigns. John J. Leary heard him humming "Garry Owen." E. A. Van Valkenburg says he sang "a Negro ditty." But, according to James Amos, he relied very heavily on "Nearer, My God, to Thee." "I had to laugh because it would be hard to imagine anything further from 'Nearer, My God, To Thee' than the tune Mr. Roosevelt was singing. I've heard him sing that tune scores of times, but never anything like the real tune and never the same way twice."

He danced occasionally, too, and his dancing seems to have been somewhat better than his singing. "Last evening, besides our own entire family party, all the Lodges, and their connections, came to dinner. We dined in the new State Dining-room and we drank the health of you and all the rest of both families that were absent. After dinner we cleared away the table and danced. Mother looked just as pretty as a picture and I had a lovely waltz with her. Mrs. Lodge and I danced the Virginia Reel." George Cherrie says T.R. "danced a hornpipe in true sailor fashion" on the way to South America. In 1909 he danced with Ethel at one of her parties in the White House and was touched and pleased and flattered to find that she thought he did it well.

XVI. The Graphic Arts

Roosevelt also shows considerable interest in the arts of architecture, painting, and sculpture. Officially it shows in such things as his eagerness to have the Smithsonian Institution accept the Freer bequest, in his appointment of a Fine Arts Council to advise the government on building, and in the way he enlisted Saint-Gaudens, Millet, and others to design new coins and medals. Glenn Brown has paid warm tribute to his services in supporting the architects who have made modern Washington a thing of beauty. "In our future architectural histories we must credit Roosevelt with saving the integrity and beauty of the White House and preserving the dignity of the Capitol." He also calls him the real founder of the National Gallery of Art.

Roosevelt once declared that "the most magnificent architecture that our race has ever been able to produce" was to be found in "the great Gothic cathedrals of the Middle Ages." Elsewhere he shows a tendency to let the Greek temple share this glory. In Italy in 1887 he found the "florid barbarism" of the Byzantine, as exemplified in Venice—"dashed with something stronger"—appealing to "some streak" in his nature, but it did not really shake his loyalty to the Gothic.

In the eighties Roosevelt had already got it settled that he admired Raphael, Michael Angelo, Murillo, Rembrandt, Greuze, and others, and that he detested Rubens. He did not greatly change his views thereafter; neither did his enthusiasm decline. What he looked forward to most eagerly in his tour of Europe, after emerging from the African jungles, was some time alone with Mrs. Roosevelt in the galleries.

He admired Turner, Washington Allston, and Frederic Remington, among later painters, and he took delight in the illustrators Howard Pyle and Maxfield Parrish. But his favorite modern painter was undoubtedly the Turneresque Bruseius Simons. Roosevelt probably never received a gift which he cherished more than Simons's "The Seats of the Mighty," which Arthur Lee presented to him.

Among sculptors, he admired, and took a patriotic pride in, Saint-Gaudens and Frederick MacMonnies. He encouraged John J. Boyle and Edward Kemeys, asking for an investigation when it seemed that Kemeys was not to be permitted to exhibit at the St. Louis Exposition. He also admired James Fraser's "The End of the Trail." His finest piece of art criticism is undoubtedly what he wrote about two creations of Saint-Gaudens:

In the figure on the Adams grave, and in the figure called "Silence" there was nothing to hamper the play of the artist's thought, and he produced two striking creations of pure imagination. The strange, shrouded, sitting woman, the draped woman who stands, impress the beholder with thoughts he cannot fathom, with the weird awe of un-earthly things; of that horizon ever surrounding mankind, where the shadowy and the unreal veil from view whatever there is beyond, whether of splendor or of gloom.

It should surprise nobody that Roosevelt often strikes the note of nationalism in art. "Why is it," he once asked Arnold Genthe, "that our young artists think they have to go to France and paint Brittany fishermen? Why don't they stay at home and paint Michigan lumbermen? They're just as picturesque and they're Americans." When he found Washington Allston described as "the American Raphael," he thought it "a piece of silly vulgarity," but when the writer went on to say that Allston made a great mistake in leaving London, where he might have succeeded Nathaniel West as presi-dent of the Academy, to return to America, he was furious. "He . . . fails to see that undoubtedly one of the reasons why Allston was a much greater painter than West was his possessing those traits of character which made him remain an American instead of becom-ing an Englishman, as West did."

The right feeling can be maintained in big things as well as in little, and it must become part of our inmost national life before we can add materially to the sum of world achievement. When that day comes, we shall understand why a huge, ornate Italian villa, or French château or make-believe castle, or, in short, any mere inappropriate copy of some building somewhere else, is a ridiculous feature in an American landscape, whereas many American farmhouses, and some American big houses, fit into the landscape and add to it; we shall use statues of such a typical American beast as the bison—which peculiarly lends itself to the purpose —to flank the approach to a building like the New York Public Library, instead of placing there, in the worst possible taste, a couple of lions which suggest a caricature of Trafalgar Square; we shall understand what a great artist like Saint Gaudens did for our coinage, and why he gave to the head of the American Liberty the noble and decorative eagle-plume-head-dress of an American horse Indian, instead of adopting, in servile style, the conventional and utterly inappropriate Phyrgian cap.

Less to have been expected from Roosevelt than these reactions was the extraordinary paper, "A Layman's Views of an Art Exhibition," which he published in *The Outlook* in 1911, after visiting the International Exhibition of Modern Art in New York. He is sure that "change may mean death and not life, and retrogression instead of development," sure, too, that Matisse has "pathological rather than artistic significance." Yet he is by no means obscurantist. "It is true, as the champions of these extremists say, that there can be no life without change, no development without change, and that to be afraid of what is different or unfamiliar is to be afraid of life." And he praises the exhibition as a whole because "there was not a touch of simpering, self-satisfied conventionality" to be found in it anywhere.

To name the pictures one would like to possess—and the bronzes and tanagras and plasters—would mean to make a catalogue of indefinite length. One of the most striking pictures was the "Terminal Yards"— the seeing eye was there, and the cunning hand. I should like to mention all the pictures of the president of the association, Arthur B. Davies. As first-class decorative work of an entirely new type, the very unexpected pictures of Sheriff Ben Chandler have a merit all their own. The "Arizona Desert," the "Canadian Night," the group of girls on the roof of a New York tenement-house, the studies in the Bronx Zoo, the "Heracles," the studies for the Utah monument, the little group called "Gossip," which has something of the quality of the famous fifteenth idyl of Theocritus, the "Pelf," with its grim suggestiveness—these and a hundred others are worthy of study, each of them; I am naming at random those which at the moment I happen to recall. I am not speaking of the acknowledged masters, of Whistler, Puvis de Chavannes, Monet; nor of John's marvelous children; nor of Cézanne's old woman with a rosary; nor of Redon's marvellous color-pieces—a worthy critic should speak of these. All I am trying to do is to point out why a layman is grateful to those who arranged this exhibition.

THREE

The World of Human Relations

I. "You May Write My Life across the Skies"

The interest in morality which we have seen breaking in upon Roosevelt's other interests even in the aesthetic field was completely genuine, and there was no pretense about it. The moralist's approach was inevitable for him; as he himself said, the White House was "a bully pulpit!"

The difference between this approach and the legal approach much more common in government was never better illustrated than when T.R., as governor of New York, sent one of his messages to Elihu Root for criticism.

In the article on "Modern Industrial Conditions" [said Root], you say "some of the wealth had been acquired by means which are utterly inconsistent with the highest rules of morality, and which yet under our present laws cannot be interfered with." I think that is a dangerous suggestion. It is not a function of law to enforce the rules of morality, and any attempt to do that would necessarily result in a statutory limitation on individual action and utter destruction of freedom, and be far more injurious than the evil which you are describing.

The point made, T.R. agreed with Root in the particular instance, but the experience effected no reformation in his thinking. "The Federal Government does scourge sin; it does bid sinners fear." Thus a message to Congress in 1908. And again: "All I asked, on behalf of the people of the United States, of Santo Domingo was that it should be good and happy." Even the Mikado must be "eldered" when the occasion arose, and during the Russo-Japanese peace negotiations T.R. implored him to have Japan "show her leadership in matters ethical no less than in matters military. The appeal is made to her in the name of all that is lofty and noble, and to this appeal I hope she will not be deaf."

Roosevelt's nature could not admit nor accept moral determinism.

He admitted, even affirmed, that many persons do wrong through force of circumstances. And there can be no excuse for not doing your utmost to make it easier for men to do right and harder for them to do wrong. But in the last analysis it is the character of the individual that counts, and this must be kept strong if the Republic is to endure. You do not make things better "by blinking the fact that sin is sin, and the stain indelible on earth; but you can . . . help those whom it is possible to raise."

T.R. was all for a "healthy" attitude toward sex, avoiding both libertinism and "platonism." He did not believe that thinking or talking a great deal about sex was healthy, but he thought that what talk there was should be absolutely truthful. If he could be brought back into our society today he would be so horrified by the change that has taken place in this area that he would be ashamed to look a woman in the face. He might even be ashamed to look a man in the face, since Owen Wister tells us that when he developed in his presence a current theory concerning the identity of creativity in art and sexual potency T.R. was acutely embarrassed. "He might almost have been a refined, nineteenth century lady, to whom I was making risqué remarks."

He could talk about sex, however, when the public welfare seemed to him to demand it, as his anti-race suicide crusade demonstrated. "If the best classes do not reproduce themselves the nation will of course go down; for the real question is encouraging the fit, and discouraging the unfit, to survive." On the negative side, he believed in sterilizing the criminal and the feeble-minded. He also regarded a husband who imposed unlimited childbearing upon a frail wife as a selfish brute, though he added a warning that "the human race cannot continue to exist if it wants to shield itself from every breeze." There are times, however, when he gets pretty emotional about it, as when he declares that "artificially keeping families small" involves "pre-natal infanticide . . . [and] abortion, with its pandering to self-indulgence, its shirking of duties, and its enervation of character." By some process of reasoning not entirely clear to me, he reached the conclusion that to make up for the sterile, the unmarried, and other classes the average family must aim at producing four children, five, he tells Ted, at the outside. Sometimes, however, he forgets this figure and praises families of twelve, fifteen, and sev-

enteen; once he told the governor of Nebraska that he was a better man than himself because he had nine children to Roosevelt's
six.[1]

Like his father before him, Roosevelt abhorred the double standard, and he proposed to abolish it by raising the man's standard,
not lowering the woman's. For "male sexual viciousness" and "the
flagrant man-swine" he had no toleration whatever. "I abhor the
creature who uses the expression that 'a man must be a man.'"
He abhorred "seeing life" also if you see "that part of life which it
is a thousandfold better should remain unseen!" Speech, moreover,
must be as clean as conduct. He tells us that during the whole time
he was with the Rough Riders "there was never a foul or indecent
word uttered at the officers' mess—I mean this literally; and there
was very little swearing." He was not a profane man himself, though
he could put more force than the vilest expletive could command
into a word like "creature" when he really wanted to lay a man out.
"It is the duty of regimental and particularly of company officers,"
so reads a presidential order of 1902, "to try by precept and example to point out to men under their control, and particularly to
the younger men, the inevitable misery and disaster which follow
upon intemperance and upon moral uncleanness and vicious living."

Practice matched precept. It is impossible that there can ever
have been a cleaner-living man than Theodore Roosevelt. When he
was police commissioner, his political enemies once had him shad-
owed at night, thinking to catch him off guard. "What!" he cried
when he heard of it, "going home to my babies?" In one important
crisis of his life his sexual idealism flared out in the occasional
naïveté which is one of his most endearing qualities. After his first
wife's death he wanted to marry Edith Carow. But before he
capitulated he walked the floor for three days, "pounding one fist
into the other palm, expostulating the while to himself: 'I have no

---

[1] T.R. once got himself into an embarrassing situation by condemning Bernard Shaw on birth control without having read him, quoting out of context a
sentence which he clearly had not understood. When Robert L. Wolf called
him on it, he admitted his fault and immediately ordered a copy of *Man and
Superman*, as Wolf had advised, but more than half his letter to Wolf (Sept. 7,
1917) was taken up with criticizing Shaw on the war. His second letter to
Wolf was hurried and evasive: "I am pressed beyond belief and have time
for but a word." See "Shaw vs. Roosevelt on Birth Control," *Physical Culture*,
LII, Sept. 1924, pp. 33–34 +.

constancy. I have no constancy.'" Such were the standards he set
for himself.

Roosevelt once told Henry White "that women interest him as a
rule very little." This seems an overstatement. He was in no sense
a "lady's man," but he was sensitive to the charms of women. This
shows in his kindly attitude toward the wives of young naval
officers, whose problems he understood and whose lot he wanted
to make as easy as possible. It shows in his attitude toward his
own daughters-in-law and toward many other young women with
whom he was brought into contact. His eagerness to get his own
children married was more like what we expect of a woman than
of a man.

Moreover, Roosevelt had reverence for women:

The birth pangs make all men the debtors of all women; and those
men have indeed touched the lowest abyss of brutality and depravity
who do not recognize something holy in the names of wife and mother.
No man, not even the soldier who does his duty, stands quite on the
level with the wife and mother who has done her duty.

On the specialized matter of the suffrage Roosevelt was always
rather lukewarm. He was never against it. In the early days his
attitude was rather, as he told Susan B. Anthony in 1898, that it
was not very important. Ten years later his position was essentially
unchanged. Equal rights did not, in his view, necessarily involve
identity of function. "I am unable to see that there has been any
special improvement in the position of women in those states of
the West that have adopted woman suffrage." He reiterates this
substantially in 1912, the very year that the Bull Moose platform
came out for woman suffrage. By 1917, however, he thought there
should be "an immediate addition to the Republican National Committee of one woman member for every suffrage state." The truth
seems to have been that, though Roosevelt's mind granted the
justice of votes for women, his emotions were never enlisted or his
imagination fired by it. He did not really like "modern" women.

But T.R. did not want women dominated by men either. German
women, he thought, were dominated too much; it lessened their
attractiveness. He told W. R. Nelson that it made him furious to
see "a husky man going along with his wife, letting her carry the

baby. I know that sort of a fellow is no good." Once, on a train, he himself took a fretful child from its tired mother, walked the floor with it until he had put it to sleep, and then returned it to her. "I have mighty little use for the man who is always declaiming in favor of an eight-hour-day for himself who does not think anything at all of having a sixteen-hour-day for his wife." In his eyes a man who thought of a wife who was doing her duty as an economic parasite was both a brute and a fool. She was as much the head of the house as he; she was as much entitled to education and self-realization as he; the money he earned was as much hers as his; and there was no more reason why she should obey him than he her. Indeed, Roosevelt goes further yet, for he considered the family more important even than the state, and in the family the woman should be supreme.

Yet women needed protection. At the time of the Russo-Japanese peace negotiations T.R. told Baron Kaneko that America and Japan must learn from each other, and that one of the things Japan must learn was how to treat women. He did not approve of women going to dangerous places even as missionaries, and when the war came he was as anxious to keep the women of his family out of France as to get the men into it.

Once at a luncheon he asked an expert on wolves whether the male wolf takes any interest in the female during pregnancy and parturition or assumes any responsibility for the care of the cubs. Out of fifteen years' experience the expert assured him that in many cases which had come under his personal observation the wolf had done both. T.R. banged the table in his exultation. "I'm glad to hear it," he cried. "I think better of him."

Sexual crimes sickened Roosevelt. Rape he thought worse than murder, and he opposed lynching as punishment for it, "not in the least" because of sympathy for the criminal—he has forfeited "the right to any sympathy of any kind whatsoever"—but because of "a very lively sense of the train of dreadful consequences which follows the course taken by the mob in exacting an inhuman vengeance for his inhuman crime." When raids were made on disorderly houses in his police commissioner days, the men were jailed along with the women. He wanted brothelkeepers imprisoned, not fined; the girls should be reclaimed if they were reclaimable; if not, they should be sent to institutions. He heartily praised Arthur Lee's bill which provided corporal punishment for white slavers in England, and he himself took great pleasure as president in announcing the adherence of this government to an international agreement for suppressing the traffic in girls.

He knew, too, that wayward girls can be reclaimed only by those who approach them lovingly and without recoiling from them. He even learned in time that so-called "shotgun" marriages are often not desirable. But he would hold a father quite as responsible financially for an illegitimate child as for one born in wedlock. And though he never believed that economic security can guarantee decency, he knew that lack of economic security can easily wreck it, and he held that "the corporation or individual capitalist paying a starvation wage to an employee, and especially to a woman employee, is guilty of iniquity, and is an enemy of morality, of religion, and of the state."

He asked one thing more—to get rid of sentimentality. When his devoted friend and admirer, Jacob Riis, went "mushy" on him by begging him to save the Brooklyn murderess Mrs. Place, he would not be seduced:

I have exactly the same feeling that you have about womanhood and about the burdens which nature has placed upon women and the duty of man to make them as light as possible. For instance, where a poor seduced girl kills her child to hide her shame, I would infinitely rather punish the man who seduced her than the poor creature who actually committed the murder. But there are some fiends among women, and I hardly think, old man, that we help womanhood, by helping these exceptions.

Theoretically T.R. found it no more difficult to conceive of a nonmonogamic than of a nonnationalistic social order. Even in the society in which we live, he admitted that exceptional people have, under exceptional circumstances, sometimes been able to disregard the marriage tie without moral injury. Nevertheless, the general rule must be that adultery ranks with treason. Divorce for frivolous motives shocked him, and he attacked the Reno divorce mill in Reno itself. Our chaotic marriage and divorce laws as a whole shocked him too, and he wanted them regularized under federal supervision. To excuse the breaking up of a home on the plea of "love" was in his eyes "one of the worst of fallacies." Man can control his passions and emotions. But he believed, too, that it is "mere foolishness" for the innocent party in a broken marriage "to refuse to get a divorce and marry again."

When people tried to tell Roosevelt smutty stories, he simply turned on his heel and walked off. (He once told Hamlin Garland that Lincoln's toleration of such stories grieved him sorely.) Once a toastmaster at a banquet had the supremely bad judgment to tell an off-color story in his presence. Roosevelt was visibly annoyed, and for a moment his companions feared that he would interrupt the speaker. Instead, he turned to his neighbor and began an animated conversation with him which continued throughout the toastmaster's address. When the speaker sat down, he pointedly refrained from congratulating him. He refused to receive Gorky when he came to America with his common-law wife. He discouraged Leopold of Belgium's coming to America ("dissolute old rake"), and when the Russian Grand Duke Boris, who had behaved disgracefully in America as well as in Europe, invited himself to lunch at Sagamore Hill, Roosevelt received him but Mrs. Roosevelt absented herself. When she was inquired after, the President offered neither explanation nor excuse.

In his early days the sinners Roosevelt met at least knew that they were sinners; before he died they were calling white black and black white. He was equal to this also. When John Reed told him he believed in free love, T.R. replied, for all the world like Lady Bracknell, that "A young man should believe in something." A young woman with a similar line of talk was similarly handled. Beaming upon her, he declared, "My dear lady, you and I are practically of one mind. The only difference between us is that I want all the married women to have children. You want only the unmarried ones to have them."

To end a serious matter on a light note, we might look at T.R.'s amusing encounter with the proprieties, one day in 1909, when an unknown girl, about sixteen years old, attached herself to him, Senator Lodge, and an orderly as they were riding in Rock Creek Park. For about four miles she rode beside the orderly, conversing eagerly with her much-embarrassed companion, who answered her many questions in monosyllables or not at all. All this the President regarded as "foolish and unseemly" but decided to ignore. As night began to fall, however, he "did not think it wise, or proper on any account, that this totally unknown young girl should continue to ride with three strange men after dark." Accordingly, he halted and spoke to her and told her that she must now take her departure. She might have her choice of routes, and they would take another one, but go she must. And the girl, not at all pleased, rode off into the gathering dusk.

The odd thing about the matter is that it does not seem to have occurred to Roosevelt that the youngster might well have been safer "with three strange men after dark" (one of them a distinguished senator, another the President of the United States) than if she were turned loose in the night all by herself!

II. The Demon Rum

Only two serious charges of immoral conduct were made against Roosevelt in the course of his career. The first may be stated in the words of George S. Newett, in the Ishpeming, Michigan, *Iron Ore*, October 12, 1912: "Roosevelt lies and curses in a most disgusting way; he gets drunk too, and that not infrequently, and all his intimate friends know about it."

T.R. had been waiting for this. Rumors of his drinking had been in circulation for a long time. In justice to himself and his children, and in decent respect for those whom his example might influence, he had made up his mind that the next time the statement was made by a responsible person, he would sue for libel.

In so far as there was any basis for these rumors, it may be sought in T.R.'s extreme animation and appearance of excitement in public, especially when speaking. As Henry Adams had put it, sarcastically, a decade earlier, "Theodore is never sober, only he is drunk with himself and not with rum."

The witnesses called having utterly refuted the charges, Newett withdrew them unconditionally, stated in effect that he had not known what he was talking about, and offered his apology. Whereupon T.R.:

In view of the statement of the defendant, I shall ask the court to instruct the jury that I desire only nominal damages. I did not go into this suit for money. I did not go into it with any vindictive purpose. I went into it, and, as the court has said, made my reputation an issue, because I wished, once for all, during my own lifetime, to deal with these slanders, fully, and comprehensively, so that never again will it be possible for any man, in good faith, to repeat them. I have achieved my purpose, and I am content.

Damages were assessed, accordingly, at six cents.

Here is T.R.'s own sworn testimony as to his drinking habits:

I have never been drunk or in the slightest degree under the influence of liquor. . . . I do not drink either whiskey or brandy, except as I shall hereafter say, except as I drink it under the direction of a doctor; I do not drink beer; I sometimes drink light wine. . . . I have never drunk a high-ball or a cocktail in my life. I have sometimes drunk mint juleps in the White House. There was a bed of mint there, and I may have drunk half a dozen mint juleps in a year, and certainly no more. At home, at dinner, I may partake of a glass or two glasses of white wine. At a public dinner, or a big dinner, if they have champagne I will take a glass or two glasses of champagne. . . . In the White House, I have drunk light wine, and not usually at all if we were alone; if there were guests I might drink a glass or two of light wine, and I might not drink anything; and in the White House I never touched brandy or whiskey except as I have described it in connection with the mint juleps or under the doctor's direction. . . . In Africa the expedition took with it a case of champagne, a case of whiskey and a bottle of brandy. I never touched a drop of either the champagne or the whiskey. . . . The only brandy I took was at the time of my two fever attacks. I drank in those two fever attacks, by direction of the doctor, about seven tablespoonfuls. . . . After the second fever attack I refused to take any more, and took tea. . . . Never, on any occasion, on any day, in the entire time that I was in the White House, had I ever touched a drop of anything prior to lunch, never under any circumstances. . . . If Mrs. Roosevelt and I were alone we had only tea or milk or water, whatever it was, at lunch. If there were any guests, there would usually be light wine on the table. . . . If we dined alone we had no wine and no liquor of any kind on our table. . . . [On campaign trips I sometimes took one or two goblets of milk before going to bed] with a teaspoon of brandy in each tumbler. . . . I don't believe that I ever went into a saloon in the western country except where it was at a little hotel, where the only two rooms would be a kitchen and a dining room. . . . I don't ever remember of drinking at a bar; certainly not for fifteen or twenty years. . . .

According to Ike Hoover, the President's mint juleps were always weaker than his guests', and James Amos says that at a banquet he would always prepare the President's glass with cracked ice clear to the brim, so that when it came to be filled up with champagne the amount it could hold would be very small. In his navy days, he once invited a group of naval officers to tea on board a flagship, and this time it was tea, though he served it in a punch bowl, with ice and mint! A similar mischievous sense of humor actuated him one day when "Tom" Platt came to Sagamore. Asked what he wanted to drink, Platt injudiciously replied, "I'll take whatever you do, Mr. President." "I always take tea," replied Roosevelt, and ordered Mr. Platt served a cup of tea. There was no drinking on the famous ride in January, 1909, undertaken by Roosevelt and his party to prove that his orders to army officers had not been too severe, but Mrs. Roosevelt gave each a mint julep when they got back. At the last meeting of the "Tennis Cabinet," when T.R. was presented with a bronze cougar, only sherry was served. In later years at least he forbade the carrying of liquor on his campaign trips, and he always regarded cardplaying by the newspapermen who accompanied him as a sign of mental deficiency, his attitude deepening to definite disapproval if they played for high stakes.

One of T.R.'s western friends, Lincoln Lang, says that when he was ranching "he could enjoy a glass of toddy now and again with his friends, in the pure spirit of sociability, as well as anybody." But, since he adds that he considers this one of the necessary attributes of the "real man," his testimony may be discounted somewhat. Another witness says that T.R. saved Lang himself from evil ways, and still another declares that, though T.R. "hobnobbed with any bow-legged puncher in camp, he drew the line sharply on their occasional festivities. Although the entire social life of the cowboy centered in the saloon, I never saw him take a drink or even smoke."

T.R. himself recorded that he was "higher with wine" the night he was initiated into the Porcellian than he ever had been before or would ever be again. David S. Barry says that he was under the influence of liquor at a dinner given by the Lotos Club of New York to the Gridiron Club of Washington while he was governor of New York, and apologized for his hiccuping on the ground that he had already attended two or three dinners that evening. The only other observer who records anything like this is Senator James E. Watson, who says T.R.'s champagne was "spiked" behind his back at "Uncle Joe" Cannon's birthday dinner, so that he was "in as convivial spirits as any of the rest of the gathering." [2] Archie Butt makes the amazing statement that Roosevelt, alone among those present, took a scotch and soda when he visited Taft at Beverly in June, 1910, saying that he needed rather than wanted it. If this is true, he must have been even more uneasy on that trying occasion than he is generally supposed to have been.

Being a veracious chronicler, I am finally under the necessity, which pains me deeply, to report that Roosevelt once enjoyed a "purple" night at a roadhouse in New Rochelle, one Sunday morning in the fall of 1917! This occurred because he insisted on giving breakfast to a group of newspapermen and an escort of policemen after a speech in Bridgeport, and the Post Road Inn was one of the few places open. T.R. ordered lobster and champagne for the company and himself drank part of one glass. Most of the time he spent talking.

But Roosevelt had to take up an attitude toward liquor as a public man as well as an individual. In 1886 he boasted that in three campaigns he had never paid for a drink nor entered a saloon. When he was starting out on his first campaign for the legislature, his sponsors took him to a prominent saloonkeeper to be looked over. The saloonkeeper told him that he regarded liquor licenses as too high. Roosevelt replied that in his judgment they were not high enough and that if he were elected he would do his best to get them increased, which he did. But his sponsors did not think it necessary to have him confer with any more saloonkeepers.

Even before he became police commissioner T.R. had urged labor to make war on the saloons "that yearly swallow so incredibly large

[2] About the Cannon dinner, T.R. wrote James H. Pound, Feb. 4, 1913: "I remember rather vaguely the Cannon dinner, for I went to many such dinners. Doubtless while at it I drank champagne. I certainly did not drink whiskey, and certainly made no such remark as Miller alleges, for the very excellent reason that I never during my whole stay in Washington, and as far as I remember during my whole life have drunk whiskey at a dinner there or anywhere else, and never said that I would ever take a little drink or a big drink of whiskey. It is a pure lie."

a proportion of the workers' salaries." Enforcing the Sunday closing law was the first striking act of his administration. At the outset he refused to say whether he thought it a good law or not. It was the law, and it was his business to enforce it. There was some significance, nevertheless, in the fact that he elected to close the saloons rather than the bakeries or the barbershops, both of which came under the same law, and as Sunday closing began to pay its dividends in a decreasing crime rate and greater prosperity and happier homes in the poorer districts, Roosevelt was more and more convinced that it was a good thing. If he had ever doubted it before, he knew then that liquor works more harm among the poor than any other cause, and that despite the presence of many decent people in it, the liquor business is tied up with criminality as no other business has ever been.

T.R. sometimes appointed drinking men to responsible posts but always with the stern warning that, unless they controlled themselves, they would fail in their work and be dismissed, which in some cases they were. John L. Sullivan was strengthened and encouraged in his own battle with the demon rum by T.R.'s faith in him, and supported in his activities as a temperance lecturer after he had won his personal fight.

Throughout most of his career Roosevelt favored regulation of the liquor traffic through local option and opposed national or state-wide prohibition on the ground that it was unenforceable and would do more harm than good to the temperance cause. In the legislature of 1884 he broke with his usual allies to oppose a prohibition measure. Though Roosevelt himself literally loathed beer, which he claimed to have tasted only once in his life, under duress, in Milwaukee, he was at this time making a distinction between the respectable beer drinker and "the habitual whisky-drinker," who "is a curse to himself, a curse to his family, and a curse to the community at large." In 1904, too, he opposed national legislation against the brewers, and in 1912 he opposed a prohibition plank in the Bull Moose platform.

By 1915, however, Roosevelt is calling prohibition the ultimate goal, and when the United States entered World War I he "urged that Congress should prohibit the manufacture or sale of liquor made from any edible grain." That same year he accepted Clarence

True Wilson's invitation to become an advisory member of the Methodist Board of Temperance, Prohibition, and Public Morals, and in 1918 he warned those who were urging him to run for governor of New York that if they took him it would be upon a platform favoring national prohibition by constitutional amendment.

III. The Ananias Club

In the course of his career T.R. put a good many people into the Ananias Club, and was in his turn nominated for the same organization by a number of admirers. This is the only other serious charge made against him in his private capacity.

It should be noted at the outset that he never had a reputation for furtiveness but rather for frankness to the point of rudeness. "He had manifest sincerity of purpose that disarmed suspicion," says Root. "He was incapable of deception, and thoughtless of it." Lyman Abbott called him "without any exception the most outspoken man I have ever known."

Even those who did not know T.R. intimately were frequently startled by his straightforward indiscretion. "He does not know how to hide anything," says Booker T. Washington. "In fact, he seems to think aloud." When Upton Sinclair was summoned to Washington after writing *The Jungle* to sit in on conferences, it seemed to him "that a President of the United States, talking in the presence of a wholly irresponsible and desperately determined young Socialist agitator, ought to exercise at least a little reserve and caution. But apparently that point of view had not occurred to Teddy."

When the Kaiser wanted T.R. to become involved in Morocco, he replied with a frank and detailed statement of his difficulties with Congress, "for they understand foreign affairs there with difficulty"! To King Edward VII he wrote in the same crisis as if he were gossiping with cronies at a club:

White speaks in the highest terms of your man Nicholson; between ourselves he grew to feel that neither the German nor the French representatives at Algeciras were really straightforward. On the other hand, I am bound to say that both their ambassadors here, Jusserand and Sternberg, were as straightforward as could be.

Even more indiscreet were his utterances to the British ambassador, Sir Mortimer Durand, whom he did not even like, but to whom he misrepresented himself as cruelly as his worst enemy could have done it: "If I had the power to dissolve parliament, and the will to override the Constitution, I should be tempted to do the same [as Cromwell did]." When Lloyd Griscom was in Tokyo he sent him by regular mail in White House envelopes letters containing the frankest criticism of Russia, "very awkward," says Griscom, "if his undiplomatic language had become public property." And when England was holding back on Russo-Japanese negotiations, he had the State Department cable Whitelaw Reid in London: "The President desires you to find out whether the English Government really does wish for peace or not."

With newspapermen, and sometimes with others, he used the somewhat specialized method of talking very freely and frankly on the implied understanding that nothing should be printed except what he had specifically authorized. Once he talked "in confidence" to George W. Smalley, for twenty minutes, "not a word for print." "I understand," said Smalley, "that what you have told me is not to be repeated. But may I say that from a talk I have had with a high official authority I draw such and such conclusions?" And T.R. replied, "That is why I sent for you."

Obviously this is a somewhat rough-and-ready method, and I am not prepared to say that nobody ever made a mistake or that nobody got hurt. I find it difficult to believe Villard's story that once T.R. came in to the correspondents waving two stories. "Here," he said, "is a story and here is the denial which you will print the next day." But it does seem clear that sometimes he "leaked out" information for the purpose of testing public opinion, and that if the reaction was unfavorable he would later declare that there was nothing in it.

However truthful T.R. may have been by instinct and habit, it is not possible to maintain that he saw himself and those who supported and opposed him calmly and dispassionately. He often saw darkly through a glass of prejudices and passions. He was not a scholar calmly evaluating the events of centuries past in an alien country; he was concerned with matters in which his whole being was enlisted and to which he had committed his life.

Roosevelt prepared records of many of his deeds for the attention of posterity. I believe that in general he came as close to telling the truth as a man can come in talking about himself. But he certainly left a great deal out, even to the extent of omitting the discussion of many controversial matters from his *Autobiography*. In his famous review of *The Foes of Our Own Household*,[3] Stuart Sherman demonstrated T.R.'s skill in selecting quotations from Washington and Lincoln, presented out of their verbal and historical context, to condemn Wilson's position and support his own.

Some of the charges against Roosevelt in these and other connections are considered elsewhere in this volume; some are too petty to consider; some it is impossible to consider for lack of evidence on either side. He certainly made statements about himself that were not accurate. He was never a lawyer. He was never lightweight champion at Harvard. His naval post did not come to him unsolicited. But it is not reasonable to suppose that he deliberately lied about these things. His support of Addicks in Delaware is difficult to explain; he seems to have made bad appointments in Pennsylvania to please Quay; in 1904, when there was a reform battle on in Pennsylvania, Wayne MacVeagh wrote that "the whole effective power of the Administration at Washington was against the reformers." He has been accused of protecting the Santa Fe Railway when it was charged with giving secret rebates, out of consideration for a Cabinet member, Paul Morton, but he met this charge head on, in public and in private.

People ask me in the name of "the square deal" to prosecute Morton [he wrote Beveridge]. I can only prosecute him on condition of prosecuting every official of every railroad running west of Chicago. As a matter of fact I should not be justified, with any evidence now before me, in prosecuting any of them; and the idea that I should single out the innocent man who is my friend and leave probably innocent men who are not my friends alone, is both foolish and wicked.

In 1903 T.R. gave newspapermen the statement that John D. Rockefeller had telegraphed a number of senators, "We are opposed to any antitrust legislation. Our counsel will see you. It must be stopped," or words to that effect. The resultant indignation got

[3] "Why Mr. Roosevelt and the Rest of Us Are at War," *Nation*, CV (1917), 532–37.

the President's legislation through. This was widely regarded as one of T.R.'s inventions, but in 1908 the Hearst Standard Oil revelations proved that he had not made it up. On the other hand, John D. Rockefeller certainly did not sign and send any such telegrams personally. "Probably Mr. Roosevelt knew that," says Ida M. Tarbell, "but somebody in the Standard was passing on such a word; and Mr. Rockefeller was the responsible head of the organization. His name did the work. Congress passed the bill in a hurry."

"Smart," sharp practice, surely, but quite in line with T.R.'s tendency toward personalizing and dramatizing. And drama and complete accuracy are rarely reconcilable.

T.R.'s claim not to have dictated the nomination of Taft in 1908, nor to have used patronage for that purpose, rests upon hairsplitting distinctions. "I appointed no man *for the purpose* of creating Taft sentiment; but . . . I have appointed men *in recognition* of the Taft sentiment already in existence." It is quite true that the G.O.P. in 1908 would much rather have nominated Roosevelt himself. But nobody can be so innocent as to suppose that they could have nominated anybody else except Taft without repudiating the President's leadership altogether. And T.R. himself wrote W. D. Foulke in 1912, "Taft never did anything for me. I made him President."

More interesting than any of these matters is Roosevelt's quarrel with the railroad tycoon, E. H. Harriman, which involves their correspondence during the 1904 campaign and the question of who asked whom for aid. Obviously it is impossible to find out what happened at a conference between two persons each of whom flatly contradicts the other's report. It is certain, however, that when T.R. released the relevant correspondence in April, 1907, he omitted his initial letter of June 29, 1904—"As soon as you come home I shall want to see you"—as well as the opening sentence of Harriman's reply—"I was very glad to receive your note of June 29 last while I was in Europe." It is certain that Harriman was interested in the fate of Frank Higgins, the G.O.P. gubernatorial nominee in New York, who ran 100,000 behind his ticket; it is also true that, after the White House interview, Harriman was instrumental in raising a fund of some $250,000. There was apparently no difference of opinion between Harriman and the President until December, when T.R. told the railroad magnate that he had changed his mind about making Chauncey M. Depew ambassador to France.

The worst that can be said against T.R. is that he did know that the outrageous statements he attributed to Harriman—that he "could buy Congress," the judiciary, etc.—and Roosevelt's consequent denunciation of Harriman as a man of "deep-seated corruption," an "undesirable citizen," and an "enemy of the Republic," rested upon the testimony of one man, James S. Sherman, and that they were categorically denied by Maxwell Evarts, who was also present when Harriman's statements were supposed to have been made. It is entirely possible that T.R. believed Sherman and disbelieved Evarts, but he did know that there was an element of doubt. Harriman's biographer, George Kennan, is quite just, furthermore, when he points out that, though Harriman had not in any way changed his fairly familiar business methods, he did not become in T.R.'s eye a monster of iniquity until after the President had quarreled with him. On the other hand, it should be recorded that James Hazen Hyde quoted Harriman damningly to Philip Jessup—"I control the New York Legislature"—and that in 1911 George Sheldon, treasurer of the Republican National Committee, wrote T.R. that the records showed that Odell, as chairman of the New York state committee, had asked Sheldon's predecessor, Bliss, for $250,000 to save the state ticket. Bliss explained the need to Harriman, who raised $160,000, Bliss raising $80,000 more. Sheldon stated that this money went direct to Odell, and never into the National Committee treasury at all.[4]

The Outlook believed at the time that no real question of varacity was involved in the quarrel between Roosevelt and Harriman. "The difference can be accounted for by a difference of interest and emphasis in their minds at the time, and a difference of recollection since." As T.R. himself expressed it, with reference to another mat-

[4] T.R. wrote William Dudley Foulke, Oct. 24, 1908: "The correspondence with Mr. Harriman has been made public. Any man who reads it must see that inasmuch as my final letter was to tell Mr. Harriman that what I had to say could be said just as well after election, it was a simple impossibility that it could have referred in any way to a campaign contribution." On Jan. 19, 1915, he pointed out, in a letter to William Z. Ripley, that Harriman had supported Sherman for vice-president two years after T.R. had condemned Harriman on Sherman's testimony.

ter, in a letter to John Brisben Walker, "You see, with the best intentions people may entirely disagree in their memories of what has passed between them." But this line of reasoning seems to apply better to another form of the story, agreeing with neither Roosevelt's account nor Harriman's. This is the story told by Oswald Garrison Villard in his autobiography.

During the 1904 campaign, according to Villard, T.R. became panicky and called a group of businessmen to Washington and persuaded them to contribute $250,000 to his campaign. One of them, Daniel S. Lamont, told the story to the Democratic candidate, Parker; this was the basis for the charges which Parker made late in the campaign, and which T.R. so indignantly denied.

Nothing more was done for four years. Then, during the 1912 campaign, Villard got the story from Thomas L. Manson, the banker, who claimed to have had it from the late Hamilton McK. Twombly. Villard wrote:

He then revealed that Roosevelt had sent word to Twombly, Harriman, Frick, Lamont, and others that he wished to see them at the White House and that it would be worth their while to come to see him. The group assembled at Twombly's magnificent home at Morristown, had dinner there, and were driven in automobiles to a private car which was sidetracked at the further end of the Pennsylvania terminal in Jersey City. No one was allowed to know who was in the party or what the purpose was except those who composed the group. The midnight train to Washington picked up the car and dropped it early the next morning some distance from the Washington station.

There the travelers were routed out and driven in automobiles to the White House which they reached at seven o'clock. They were taken in by the entrance opposite to the Treasury Department and were immediately ushered into the President's presence. They found him in a complete funk. He told them that unless a large sum of money was raised Parker would carry the election. He must have at least a quarter of a million and at once. He then promised this group, whom he had so bitterly attacked, whose business methods he had so correctly criticized, that if they gave him that money they would have nothing further to fear from him during his second term as President. He declared that it would be much worse for them if they allowed Parker to be elected if only because of Parker's stand on the tariff. They took his word, accepted his surrender, and gave him the money he desired.

Attempting to verify the story, Villard visited Henry Clay Frick for collaboration: "I did not have to tell him what Mr. Manson had said to me, and his narrative corroborated the former's at every point. He gave a graphic description of that early morning call at the White House and then said with astounding bluntness: 'He got down on his knees to us. We bought the son of a bitch and then he did not stay bought.'" But Frick would not be quoted without his attorney's approval, which, naturally, was not forthcoming.

This is such a wonderful "thriller" that it seems a shame to have to consider it from any other standpoint. It is not, of course, to be rejected out of hand simply because of its melodramatic atmosphere. But the failure of the story to harmonize with either Roosevelt's or Harriman's account is a more serious objection.

Though Roosevelt was never in any serious danger during the 1904 campaign, he thought he was, for he was always inclined to be pessimistic about elections. A priori, there is therefore nothing either dishonorable or improbable in the idea that he might make an appeal for funds. If such a meeting as Villard describes did take place, there would obviously be many shades of difference in the minds of the persons involved in it, and memory might well be expected to exaggerate these differences as time went on. But it is not conceivable that Roosevelt could offer to sell out his whole administration and himself for four more years in the White House, and if the great financiers who allegedly thought they were buying him were simple enough to accept any such pledge as Villard says he gave, then all of them put together were too stupid to run a peanut stand, to say nothing of the great enterprises they did successfully manage. "It would be *much worse* for them," says Roosevelt himself, "if they allowed Parker to be elected." If he made an appeal, it must have been made along this line.[5]

[5] A 1905 letter of Roosevelt's to Joseph Bucklin Bishop is mildly interesting in this connection: "I am in rather a quandary how to get at Frick. It is of course not a matter that I wish to write about, simply because there are a large number of people who would believe that my motive was to make a newspaper organ for myself; and I cannot ask Frick down here now because it would at once be believed that I was taking part in the Equitable squabble. Moreover, I do not know how he stands on the railroad rate matter, and whether my attitude in the matter has in any way changed his friendship for me. I have written to Knox to come on here and shall see if I can not communicate with Frick through Knox." This seems to refer to a report that the *Evening Post* might be for sale. On Feb. 22, 1908, T.R. wrote Frick himself a letter, presenting Peary, who was in search of funds for an arctic expedition.

IV. Charm

In all his activities except writing Roosevelt had to work closely with people. His thinking about human beings and his approaches to them were warm, trusting, and tender. He believed that "the poorest way to face life is to face it with a sneer." "It is an interesting country," he writes of Southern California in 1903, "and I think will produce a new type. . . . The missions interested me greatly, and of course the people most of all."

His theory of human nature was never sentimental, for he knew that there was "a very dreadful alloy of base metal" in the average man. That was why he never built too much upon present popularity; that, too, was why, charges having been made, he always thought they must be investigated, for "human nature is so queer that it is hard to say that anything is impossible." One of the most touching anecdotes in the whole vast domain of Rooseveltiana is the story of the unscrupulous, ambitious hostess who, in 1902, enticed him into her house in Charleston, skillfully baiting her trap with no distinguished Southern gentleman or lovely Southern lady but, as she said, with an old Negro, born in slavery, who wanted to shake the President's hand! Not even such experiences could disillusion Roosevelt permanently; neither could political defeat. "Probably we have erred," he wrote in 1914, "in thinking that even in this country men were a little better and a little more intelligent than they actually are. Nevertheless, although we have fallen, I believe as firmly as ever that the cause for which we stand will ultimately be victorious."

Fortunately not all the women who crossed his path were like the one in Charleston. When he visited Vienna in 1910 he smiled at Maria Jeritza, standing as a young girl in the crowd assembled to greet him. "And it was such a hearty, kindly smile, so full of good will and joy in life, so spontaneous and not from the lips alone" that not only did she smile "back at him with all my heart and soul" but long after she had become a famous singer she treasured that smile "as a delightful personal recollection, one of those charming, evanescent moments in life of which one has no material record, but whose memory stands out and is never forgotten." At the very end of his life he won the heart of another girl, Sonya Levien, at the *Metropolitan:*

He was one of us from the first to the last. He was not stingy with his friendship, but included us in his life and interests, and wanted to be included in ours. Before one knew it one would tell him all about one's self. With that insatiable curiosity found only in men of perpetual youth, he would draw us out, get an intimate vision of our background, our religion, our ideals and ambitions; and he always remembered correctly our names, our hobbies, and our families.

A great help in social relations was Roosevelt's undeniable charm and magnetism. Of course it did not always work. If he was intensely loved, he was also intensely hated. But those who hated him seldom knew him well. As Irvin S. Cobb put it, "You had to hate the Colonel a whole lot to keep from loving him."

Nobody has ever called T.R. a handsome man, and many of his admirers, like Miss Levien, did not know why they loved him. "I wonder," she writes, "how a man so thick-set, of rather abdominal contour, with eyes heavily spectacled, could have had so much an air of magic and wild romance about him, could give one so stirring an impression of adventure and chivalry." But the interesting and touching thing is Roosevelt's own response to all this. "No one could accuse *me* of having a charming personality." He thought he always had something to overcome before he could win men's hearts and envied Will Taft his advantage over him in this respect.

Of course the man Sonya Levien lost her heart to was very different physically from the Roosevelt of earlier years. Nobody, not even Dickens, can have changed much more in his outward seeming than did Theodore Roosevelt. The youngster who returned from Europe in 1870 was a "tall thin lad with bright eyes and legs like pipestems." The youth that Harvard knew wore "reddish, powder-puff side whiskers which no chaffing could make him cut." It is amazing to remember that in his legislature days he was called "Oscar Wilde" and "a blond young man with eye-glasses, English side-whiskers and a Dundreary drawl in his speech." But of all the amusing impressions which observers formed of him in the course of his career, surely the most amusing is that of his reluctant hunting guide, Jack Willis, who, upon first meeting him, thought that he looked like a rich brewer's son who had been raised on beer!

The flash of his glasses, William Allen White thought, gave him a "glint" which was missing when he took them off, "for his grayish blue eyes were the least ferocious feature in his face," and White goes on to develop the double aspect of T.R.'s personality—the "primitive—impetuous, imperious, splashing in a reservoir of vigor" —and its opposite—"sophisticated, not ever quite furtive, but often feline. There sometimes glanced obliquely from his face the shadow of some inner femininity deeply suppressed, some exquisitely well-bred but devious female ancestress who sometimes flicked catwise out of his subconsciousness." There is more journalism than science about this, but the idea that there was a strong feminine element in Roosevelt is not peculiar to White. Julian Street expresses something of the same thing when he compares Roosevelt in his later years to a friendly old lion, though it was not, if anything can be apart from that, the lion's felinity of which he was thinking particularly. When the end came, Archie cabled, "The Old Lion is dead," to his brothers in France. If we are going out for animal images, however, Roosevelt's figure and movements, the fierce friendliness of his countenance, and the mingled puzzlement and determination of his entire aspect suggest much more a bear than a lion.

There was one picture of himself in which Roosevelt took delight not because it looked like him but because it looked the way he would like to have his children think he had looked! While Sargent was painting his portrait he wrote enthusiastically to Kermit that it was "going to be great." In his later years he seems to have got very tired of being photographed and even more tired of being painted. When his college class wanted a painting of him for the Harvard Club of New York, he suggested that they copy the Sargent. This need not necessarily indicate modesty, however; he liked the Sargent, and he regarded portraits in general as "great lotteries." Once he told D. E. Thompson that none of his photographs were very good; once he canceled an appointment to have Stieglitz photograph him for *The Century* when he found that the photographer would require an hour or two; he could not, he said, possibly spare more than fifteen minutes. "Heavens and Earth!" he once wrote Brander Matthews, "what a frightful mouth I must have! Thanks to the comic papers, I am given the gift to see myself as others see me."

As to clothes, the usual view is that Roosevelt was quite indifferent. He always dressed for dinner, even when he and Mrs. Roosevelt were dining alone, and this not only in the White House but also at Sagamore, where he preferred knickers for daytime wear. He himself says that he usually wore the same tie until it was worn out. Both James Amos and Ike Hoover convey the impression that, though he was always well dressed, he wore what Mrs. Roosevelt set out for him and thought nothing about it.

These things had not always been true, however; I doubt that they were ever true without qualification. Look at the buckskin suit he wore in the West, and the way he had himself photographed in it; he was even photographed holding a bead on the boat thieves! In police commissioner days, he sported such attire as had never been seen in Mulberry Street—a pink shirt and, in summer, a black silk sash instead of a vest, with the tassels hanging down as far as the knee. It is said that when the Mikado sent him samurai armor, he tried it on and paraded up and down the White House corridors in it. Most of all, however, I love his speculations over the possibility of wearing the uniform of a colonel of cavalry on his European tour in 1910. Archie Butt assured him that he had the right and described the uniform to him—"brilliant with yellow plumes and gold lace: in fact the handsomest and most showy uniform we have ever had in the service." This made it almost irresistible, and he at once said that he would order one and wear it with patent leather boots. But Mrs. Roosevelt laughed at him: "Theodore, I would never a wear a uniform that I had not worn in the service, and if you insist upon this I will have a vivandière's costume made and follow you throughout Europe." I wonder how much it hurt him to give it up, and whether he was comforted by Whitelaw Reid's telling him that, since all the Europeans would be in uniform, he, in evening dress, would always find himself the most conspicuous person in the room.

It is difficult to discuss Roosevelt's charm without seeming to drool; nevertheless, this element cannot be omitted, for it was a very influential factor in his career. "He had the quality of vitalizing things," says Oscar Straus—"a situation or condition coming within his executive ken became so charged with life and imagination that men wanted to put their hands and minds to it." "His personality," said Richard Washburn Child, "so crowds the room

that the walls are worn thin and threaten to burst outward." And
he adds, "You go to the White House, you shake hands with Roosevelt and hear him talk—and then go home to wring the personality
out of your clothes." And William Allen White, again, paints on a
larger scale:

He sounded in my heart the first trumpet of the new time that was
to be. I went home from our first casual meeting . . . to tell Sallie of the
marvel of the meeting. I was afire with the splendor of the personality I
had met, and I walked up and down our little bedroom at the Normandie
trying to impart to her some of the marvel that I saw in this young
man. . . . I had never known such a man as he, and never shall again.
He overcame me. And in the hour or two we spent that day at lunch,
and in a walk down F Street, he poured into my heart such visions, such
ideals, such hopes, such a new attitude toward life and patriotism and the
meaning of things, as I had never dreamed men had.

He awakened courage like his own in others. Lewis Einstein tells
of the ambassador who came to a dangerous place in a mountain
valley near the Lake of Geneva. "He was alone at the time and
there was no reason why he should proceed any farther. . . . But
the feeling that Roosevelt under similar circumstances would have
gone ahead also made him persevere." And Bishop Lawrence, of
Massachusetts, lying on the operating table, waiting for an anesthe-
tic, looked up and saw his picture on the wall. "No one can wince,"
he told himself, "while Theodore is looking on."

This power long outlasted his presidency. After he had called
at the White House in 1910, Ike Hoover told Archie Butt it was
the only happy day anybody in attendance there had had in two
years, "and not one of us would exchange it for a hundred-dollar
bill." In 1913 Spring Rice writes from Washington: "Oh, T.R., how
I wish I could see you. I nearly wept at Rock Creek Park near the
rock! I could *hear* you—the flowers are indeed beautiful now."

In my faith in Theodore Roosevelt [wrote William Dudley Foulke], I
have seen no ground for change and continue to regard it as a supreme
achievement that I was able to win and to keep the warm and abiding
friendship of this great man. His sudden death seemed like an eclipse
darkening the world, and when, on the following day, returning from
Indianapolis, I saw upon my table two short notes, just received signed

with the dear familiar hand that could then write no more, it seemed that much of that which made life valuable had passed away.

This, it may be said, was magnetism, not charm. So it was, but the one is difficult without the other. Anyway, there can be no doubt that the charm was there. "I have never known another person so vital," says White, "nor another man so dear." "Camping with the President was a memorable experience," says John Muir. "I fairly fell in love with him." The years he spent with Roosevelt, Jacob Riis testified, were the happiest he ever had. "Then was life really worth living." Edith Wharton was surprised, in looking back over her contacts with him, to find how few they had been. "He had the rare gift of bridging over in an instant those long intervals between meetings that so often benumb even the best of friends, and he was so alive at all points, and so gifted with the rare faculty of living intensely and entirely in every moment as it passed, that each of those encounters glows in me like a tiny morsel of radium." Richard Henry Dana, too, found the charm as potent in 1917 as it had been in the nineties. Describing a casual meeting at the Harvard Club of New York, he writes, "In the chair next to him for half an hour I basked in the sunlight glow he shed about him." And even after 1912 Elihu Root cried out to a friend, "I care more for one button on Theodore Roosevelt's waistcoat, than for Taft's whole body."

Finally, Roosevelt's charm was often felt as potently by foes as by friends. Rudolf Eucken, coming "with a great prejudice" against him, went away "completely won" by his charm. Senator Spooner went to see him one day, "angry as a hornet," and came out "liking him again in spite of myself." James Ford Rhodes, estranged from him by the 1912 campaign, ran into him when he came to Boston to address the American Historical Association, immediately after his defeat, and capitulated all over again. "It was lucky that I did not meet him before election or I fear that I should have been won by his fascination." During the Barnes libel suit, C. W. Thompson found a reporter for an anti-Roosevelt paper walking up and down a hotel lobby and cursing. When asked what was wrong, he replied, "Roosevelt, damn him. I can't keep hating him if I get within twenty feet of him, and, damn it, I'm always forgetting and doing it accidentally. He's spoiling my story." But I do not know that anything is more impressive than the words of Woodrow Wilson, who might certainly have been excused for hating Roosevelt if any man could be. "I was . . . charmed by his personality," he told Tumulty. "There is a sweetness about him that is very compelling. You can't resist the man."

V. Among His Fellows

Roosevelt himself claimed the power "of coming to a consensus with my fellows." As long as he lived he rejoiced to bring different kinds of people together. John Carter Rose once remarked that he gave every man he had talked with for five minutes the impression that he liked him very much. "By George," replied T.R., "I don't believe I ever do talk with a man five minutes without liking him very much, unless I disliked him very much."

Sometimes, to be sure, he did that. He was not equally drawn to all sorts and conditions of men. He liked "Abraham Lincoln's 'plain people'. . . the folk who work hard on farm, in shop, or on the railroads, or who own little stores, little businesses which they manage themselves." He disliked and mistrusted capitalists, socialists, timid good men, and in general those who had led sheltered lives, and he did not always succeed in being fair to these groups. A good many of the intellectuals who attracted him on other grounds were comprehended here, and he often felt that the "plain people" had more idealism and common sense than those who had gone through Harvard and who read all the best periodicals. Even farmers and mechanics were for T.R. something of an acquired taste. The cowboy, on the other hand, appealed to him through his picturesqueness and the heroic quality of his life. He credited his stay in the West with teaching him what people are really like and how they think. In later years he liked to go to the Masonic lodge at Oyster Bay because he could sit on the benches while his cousin's gardener presided, and when he had his run-in with the Vatican officials at Rome what he dreaded was "lest good humble people who had been devoted to me, people like Sister Sebastian in Newark, and Mother St. Peter in Albany, who had regarded me as a special friend and champion, should be hurt and have their belief in me shaken."

Yet, though Roosevelt loved to talk to people who interested him, he was never, in the usual sense of the term, an intensely social being. He was no "joiner"; it is doubtful that he was even a good "mixer." It was his own opinion that, though he made acquaintances easily, he really cared for few people. "Huge banquets and such" were "horrid functions" in his eyes, and both he and Mrs. Roosevelt loathed staying in other people's houses. When he went to London he sought out "an old fogey hotel." For the more frivolous activities of organized society he felt only contempt, and he was often bored even by people whom he respected. Even of his cowboys he says, "I made no effort whatever for mere social association," and others confirm this. "With all of them I exchange civilities," thus he writes his sister of his shipboard companions in 1909, "which make them think they would like to know me better, which I'll see that they don't." I have been particularly impressed by the fact that in enumerating the advantages of having comfortable means he gives the climactic position to the advantage of having one's house stand apart, away from other houses.

For all that, Roosevelt had a social background, and he took it for granted even when he disparaged it, referring casually, for example, to "the men of leisure and cultivation, the men who are my social friends." At Harvard, where there were those who thought him a snob—"I really think I have as swell a turnout as any man"— he "made" the most exclusive of clubs, the Porcellian, and though Gilman suggests that he was too earnest to fit into it very well, he was delighted, in later years, when Ted was taken in, and "savage . . . in spite of my realizing how small such a thing bulks in a man's life" when it looked as though Kermit were going to be passed over. Certainly one letter to his sister from Cambridge is pure snob: "I most sincerely wish I knew something about the antecedents of my friends. On this very account I have avoided being very intimate with the New York fellows." Another letter, four years later, from Chicago, is not much better: "There are a great many very fine houses; but I should rather doubt the quality of the society." Both his daughters made formal debuts, though Alice's was considerably less fashionable than she wanted it to be! In the White House etiquette was stricter under the Roosevelts than it had ever been before, with much regard to protocol and the proprieties, as when an invitation to Senator Tillman was summarily withdrawn after he had participated in fisticuffs.

Roosevelt is reliably reported to have been a thoughtful and tactful host, often displaying a remarkable knowledge of his guests' interests and concerns. At formal receptions he showed great skill in keeping a line moving without giving anybody the feeling that he had been hurried away. But, for all that, he was never quite conventional. He did not keep himself in the background like the hostess in a French salon. Instead, as Owen Wister reports, even in the White House, "the host used to dash his opinions and challenges across the company much in the same manner that he served tennis balls in the court." And Edith Wharton and others have spoken of the tendency he sometimes manifested to isolate himself with some particular guest who could talk to him at length about some subject in which he was really interested.

But Roosevelt's tact manifested itself very strikingly upon larger stages than drawing rooms. His motto was "Speak softly and carry a big stick." It was the stick which caught the popular imagination, but to Roosevelt the soft speaking was equally important. From college days on, he was known as a restraining, peacemaking influence among his friends. As vice-president he leaned over backwards to avoid asking favors of his chief. Certainly nobody has ever been more tactful in dealing with foreign governments, more careful to save face for the people with whom he was negotiating, more scrupulous about not betraying confidences.

All this was well illustrated in the Russo-Japanese peace negotiations. When the envoys of the rival powers were entertained at luncheon, all questions of precedence were neatly avoided by serving the food buffet style with no places set. "The man who had been represented to us as impetuous to the point of rudeness," wrote one of the Russian advisers, "displayed a gentleness, a kindness, and a tactfulness mixed with self-control that only a truly great man can command."

For all Roosevelt's occasional violence of language, his close associates insist that he did not have a bad temper. Above all, he was never sulky, peevish, or ill-natured. When things went wrong, he not only carried his part of the load but as much of other people's as possible. "I have had companions—good, bad and indif-

THE WORLD OF HUMAN RELATIONS

ferent," writes George Cherrie, who was in South America with him. "Only one, Theodore Roosevelt, remains in my memory as the ideal camp mate." And, for all his combativeness, he always remembered that you cannot fight for everything you want, even when you are right; you have to choose what you are going to make a stand for and let the rest go. There are cases in which he overcame rudeness in others by opposing his own sweetness of temper to it. "What a place the Presidency is," he cries, "for learning to keep one's temper!"

He even humored the idiosyncrasies of his children, and that, too, in such a matter as letter writing.

Would you rather that I wrote a longish letter to both of you together [he wrote Belle and Kermit in 1915], or two shorter letters to the two of you separately? I don't think Belle will care but Kermit has as many unexpected individual preferences as his mother (which perhaps is one reason why he has always been so very sympathetic to me!), and he may suddenly violently object to my writing to both jointly and regard it as a symptom of infamous lack of interest on my part; or on the other hand he may think it on the whole a creditable and rather nice thing for me to do; and I wish to be guided by his judgment and preference in the matter.

For all that, he was a formidable man. There was so much of him, and it was so overwhelming, that he often seemed to be bringing up all the heavy artillery to keep order in a child's playground. "The strength of his convictions and the vivacity of his speech and manner," says Charles J. Bonaparte, "confused and frightened timid men or those who knew him slightly, and led them to think of and describe him as arbitrary and overbearing . . . but only one who wasn't afraid of him could fairly judge or really like him." Archie Butt admits that even his friendship was sometimes terrifying. "I have tried to do right and be honorable without thinking about it very much, but when I am with him I become stampeded for fear that I may do something that if he knew he would not approve."

Like many men of overwhelming force and power, Roosevelt seems often to have made a stronger impression than he had intended. His clash with Senator Foraker over the Brownsville matter at a Gridiron Club dinner is often rated a shocking performance; at least it seems to have made a good many people uncomfortable. But

T.R. wrote about it to Beveridge afterwards in the mildest terms. "Foraker ought not to have been called upon to speak: but as he was called upon, I do not blame him for the speech he made." He added that he "was inclined to make a Berserker speech" himself in reply, but apparently he felt that he had restrained himself![6]

VI. The Helping Hand

Roosevelt's acts of kindness and consideration, his gifts of time, money, and interest were multitudinous. He hated "to see humble people hurt if it can be helped." He also hated cruelty and coldness of heart. "It may be true that he travels farthest who travels alone; but the goal thus reached is not worth reaching." He often interceded for offenders, or gave them another chance, and when he could not give necessary financial assistance himself he sometimes secured it from wealthy friends.

William Allen White says that when he told him Governor Hadley had tuberculosis, T.R. "cried out for a moment, shocked and pained by the tragedy of it." He visited the part-Indian Senator Matthew S. Quay when he was on his deathbed, and Quay said he wished "he could crawl off like a wolf on a big, lone rock and die in the sun." T.R. was so touched by these words that he quoted them to Lincoln Steffens, and then became furiously angry because Steffens did not warm to them and to the man who had uttered them. No one, I think, could read the chapter on "Civic Helpfulness" in *The Strenuous Life,* nor the extraordinary message which Roosevelt sent to Congress concerning his trip to Panama in 1906, without being fully convinced of his genuine interest in the spiritual and material welfare of human beings. He inspected New York tenements when he was in the legislature, but he also inspected them with Dr. Chapman, quite unofficially, within a year of his death. His message to Congress in 1908 concerning employers' liability made general recommendations concerning the problem as a whole, and then went on to urge "a special bill . . . covering the case of Yardmaster Banton, who was injured nearly two years ago while doing his duty. He is now helpless to support his wife and his three little boys."

It is this thrilling humanity of Roosevelt's, this inability ever to

[6] Foraker's own account of the matter in his letter to his son (*Correspondence with President Roosevelt,* pp. 38–45) attributes no discourtesy to T.R. either.

lose the individual in the mass, that makes him such a sympathetic figure. "I couldn't sleep," he writes Maurice Francis Egan during the coal strike; "it is horrible to think that a great number of our people, mothers and little children, are starving with cold." And so, too, in quite different vein, to a woman who had written an interesting letter to his wife, "I like to think of you reading my letter of acceptance in the intervals of putting up the preserves." When, in police commissioner days, it was necessary to turn men off for drinking, he was not very sorry for them, "for men have got to pay the penalty for their misdeeds; but it was heartbreaking to see their wives and children suffer for the misdeeds of the men." In 1911 a thirteen-year-old Philadelphia girl appealed to Roosevelt after her father had been dismissed from the post office. Though he had no authority in the matter whatever, the ex-President not only answered her but enclosed a letter to the postmaster in which he respectfully asked for an investigation. On the day the *Lusitania* was sunk, while William Barnes's libel suit against him was being tried in Syracuse, and when he had no idea whether he would win or lose, he wrote two letters. One was to the New York Eye and Ear Infirmary in behalf of a woman, totally unknown to him personally, who needed an expensive eye operation, and whose total resources were $600, which Roosevelt did not want her to spend. He had already appealed for her to the Roosevelt Hospital and had got no help. Now he asked the Eye and Ear Infirmary for information concerning the cost of the operation and offered to pay half of whatever they charged her. The other letter was to Charles G. Washburn in Worcester, Massachusetts, asking him to investigate a plea from a woman in Athol.

Roosevelt felt a special interest in and responsibility for those who worked with him, whether they were his servants, the savages who trekked with him in his hunting expeditions, or the officers who served in his Cabinet. When an act had to be performed which he thought might be unpopular, he would always do it himself, instead of permitting the Cabinet officer in whose area it fell to do it for him. When the Russo-Japanese peace was unpopular in Tokyo, he even began worrying about whether Japanese etiquette would require the envoys who had negotiated it to commit suicide!

"The little courtesies counted with him quite as much as the greater ones," says Ike Hoover. "It was a common practice for him to go all over the house saying good bye on leaving or for a greeting upon returning from a trip." On Christmas and birthdays everybody had to have little gifts. He always remembered the names of the servants in his friends' households, too, and greeted them, at parting, often with a word in their own language. He was delighted when a maid was introduced to him as "Miss So-and-so," and once, having been presented to all the members of a party except the chauffeur, he said, "I have not met this gentleman." When he revisited Harvard as president, the woman who had washed for him when he was a student there insisted, against the advice of the police on guard, upon seeing him. She was called by her name and welcomed cordially. "It was very kind of you to come over to see me for old times' sake." Perhaps this was the same visit on which he astonished President Eliot by stepping out of the academic procession to greet "an epileptic defective known to many generations of students as John the Orangeman."

The newspapermen who accompanied Roosevelt on his tours tell the same story. "Of all the candidates I have ever travelled around with . . ." says Charles Willis Thompson, "Roosevelt was the most thoughtful and forehanded: he made our work several tons lighter." He was very solicitous, too, about injuries and illnesses, this in spite of his habit of completely ignoring such things in himself. The people who came to hear him were individuals in his eyes also, and he told Archie Butt that he once found himself waving frantically at a herd of sheep. Burroughs reports his leaving his lunch rather than let a group of children miss a greeting, and O. K. Davis writes of the Colorado woman who was standing in the rain, on the wrong side of the train, with a baby in her arms, waiting for him to go by. "He jumped to the rear platform and waved his hand to the woman. She saw him and with both hands lifted the baby up toward the Colonel. There she held him until the train had rolled far down the track and was almost out of sight."

When fire destroyed two houses at Oyster Bay, T.R. at once sent for the people concerned and offered to advance the money needed for rebuilding. When he played Santa Claus, as he did each Christmas at the Cove School, he planned it so that each child should write a letter to his teacher beforehand telling what he wanted

Santa to bring. "Then I walked over, through rain which turned to wet snow," thus he describes his Christmas of 1917 to Ted, "to give the nice Gillespie children their presents—these included a globe of goldfish for the smallest girl, which I had carried out in the train from New York with considerable agony."

VII. The Quality of Mercy

If Roosevelt was capable of such warmth as this to strangers, one would certainly expect him to be more than usually kind to his friends. He praised them generously, gave them appointments in the days of his power, and stood by them loyally in every way. Sometimes, as with Lodge, close, warm friendship survived serious differences of opinion in politics. To be sure, he would not make appointments which he considered unsuitable, for he had an obligation to the public as well as to his friends. "The public service of the country is not to be regarded as an asylum." Nor did he shrink from plain, kindly speaking when such refusals had to be explained. But as early in 1900 he had nominally lent, actually given away, thousands of dollars to friends in need whom he could not conscientiously give the appointments they had asked of him.

This consideration for others operated both in small matters and in great. The boxer whose blow caused him to lose the sight of an eye never learned what he had wrought. "To have told him would have only caused him to feel badly." When Jacob Riis, to his embarrassment, found himself wearing a decoration at a function where everybody else was plainly attired, Roosevelt made a point of telling him how glad he was he had put it on. When Jane Addams, on a public occasion, lost her hat, Roosevelt took off his hat also and rode bareheaded beside her. Once in the West he even drank and praised a glass of buttermilk, which was nauseous to him, rather than hurt the feelings of the pioneer woman who had offered it to him.

There is a general impression that Roosevelt was hard on his subordinates, and I do not doubt that he required zeal and industry and faithfulness. But it was a matter of principle with him not to wait for perfect tools but to do the job in hand with the best tools that were available. Sometimes his indulgences went very far indeed, as when, in police commissioner days, he kept a stenographer who couldn't spell, and himself corrected her letters for her, because her wages were an important factor in the support of her younger brothers and sisters. When the Spanish War came, he told both John Drew and Henry Cabot Lodge that they were too old to go, and had families to think of, but he did not apply this reasoning to himself. John Loring says that he gave only two positive orders in Africa. "One was when he forbade the whipping of porters for disobedience. . . . The other . . . [was when] I had attacked a lioness. . . . He forbade me to again attempt to shoot a lion with the small rifle that I had been using."

But I must not leave the impression that T.R. loved mercy only and ignored justice. He believed in helping a man when he stumbled; he also believed that it was useless to try to carry him when he could not or would not walk, and he accepted the stern law of life that those who cannot adjust themselves to the conditions of existence must perish from the earth they cumber. As for criminals, he believed that punishment had only two legitimate ends—to protect society and to rehabilitate the criminal. But "We are not playing 'puss in the corner' with criminals," and with the average term of "life imprisonment" running fourteen years, he did not think it safe to talk about abolishing capital punishment. He could express this attitude brutally at times, as when he tells Brand Whitlock, "I'll tell you where we differ. You think no one should be killed; I think the world would be a good deal better off, if some undesirable people were out of it!" But he also wanted to "make the discharged convict feel that he has paid his penalty and that now matters are even, and that he must have as good a chance as anyone else," and he found the unhappy necessity of frequently refusing petitions in behalf of condemned criminals a horrible part of his work as governor.

Above all, he had no sympathy whatever with the mushy sentimentalists who implored mercy for white slavers, peddlers of obscene literature, and other enemies of mankind. Once when a delegation called to plead with him, he pulled some of the peddler's wares out of his desk and thrust them upon them; once he shamed such a group by denouncing their futilities in the press.

It was not only with criminals that T.R. could face the moral distinctions of life. He met them with his own brother Elliott, to whom, early in life, he had been very close and who had exercised considerable influence upon him. In 1894, shortly after the death of Elliott's wife, he writes his sister Anna, "I do wish Corinne could get a little of my hard heart about Elliott; she can do, and ought to do, nothing for him. He can't be helped, and he must simply be let go his own gait. He is now laid up from a serious fall; while drunk he drove into a lamp post and went out on his head. Poor fellow! if only he could have died instead of Anna!" Little more than two weeks later, Elliott was up and about again and already drinking heavily; "he must break soon." The end came before the month was out. "There is one great comfort I already feel," wrote T.R. to Corinne; "I only need to have pleasant thoughts of Elliott now. He is just the gallant, generous, manly boy and young man whom everyone loved."

VIII. Judgments

Roosevelt's preoccupation with moral judgments often involved very picturesque, sometimes extremely amusing, denunciation. It would not be difficult to compile from his utterances what H. L. Mencken used to call a *Schimpflexicon*. Yet it may still be true, as E. A. Van Valkenburg claimed, that Roosevelt never cherished personal animosities. In *Hanna*, Thomas Beer records that being asked why he characterized a certain man as a fat spider, T.R. replied simply that that was his way of putting it. Few persons of volcanic ebullience are able to cherish animosity. In denunciation as in any art, an artist must cherish his materials.

He spread a wide net, and the most strangely assorted fish swam into it. Congressman J. Hamilton Lewis was a "pink-bearded monkey" and Bernard Shaw a "blue-rumped ape." George Creel was an "absolute liar," Maurice Low a "circumcised skunk," and Richmond P. Hobson a "blackguard and a cad." G. W. Smalley was a "copper-riveted idiot," John Wanamaker a liar with a "sloppy mind," Herbert W. Bowen a "disloyal, treacherous, and bumptious ass." Sir Mortimer Durand had a brain of about "eight-guinea-pig-power," Senator Tillman was "one of the foulest and rottenest demagogues in the whole country," and the Venezuelan leader, Castro, was an "unspeakably villainous little monkey." As late as 1911

Archbishop O'Connell was a scoundrel because he had been "an open champion of Spain when we were at war with her."

Some condemnations took in whole classes—"these Newport cads," the "small body of shrill eunuchs" who criticized T.R.'s Panama policy, or "those political and literary hermaphrodites," the mugwumps. He was particularly unreasonable about the mugwumps, whom he spoke of harshly for many years after his break with them in 1884—that "dishonest and lying scoundrel," Moorfield Storey; "dogs" like Carl Schurz; and John Jay Chapman, who could be considered honest only on the assumption that he was of unsound mind. In later years pacifists came in for similar abuse, especially if T.R. had thought well of them earlier. By 1910 Nicholas Murray Butler "has developed into an aggressive and violent ass along a number of different lines," completely belying the promise of his youth and early middle age. Jane Addams, the wisest woman in America, had been very close to him in 1912, but because she "and her kind" disagreed with him about the war, they had become poor, silly creatures by 1915, "a disgrace to the women of America." Even royalty was not exempt, and one of the most vivid passages in T.R.'s description of his European trip is his detailed description of Queen Wilhelmina as "excessively unattractive and commonplace, and . . . [so] conceited and bad-tempered" that she reminded him of "the puffed-up wife of some leading grocer" in an American country town.

As historian and man of affairs, Roosevelt often found it necessary to evaluate his predecessors as well as his contemporaries. James M. Cox reported on a long conversation between Columbus and Cincinnati during which T.R. "ran the list of our statesmen, found things in Washington to criticize; Jefferson, to him, was a demagogue; Jackson he called barbarian. Lincoln might have done things differently and McKinley had the fault of not saying no." The criticism of Washington and Lincoln cannot have been very severe. In spite of what Cox says about Jackson, the rugged quality of that old hero so appealed to T.R. that from time to time he would call him one of our three or four greatest presidents; he would have liked to do the Jackson volume in the "American Statesman" series. This was apparently an emotional reaction however, for T.R. was well aware of Jackson's shortcomings. "Andrew Jackson," he wrote W. E.

Chandler, "did some awful things and in many respects he was not more than half civilized, but he was a great deal of a man, for all that, and I have always had a certain sneaking admiration for him." [7]

One historical figure was still alive to defend himself against T.R.'s strictures; this was Jefferson Davis. He wrote a letter of protest, to which the twenty-six-year-old Roosevelt replied haughtily (in the third person!) that he saw no need of "any further communication whatever between himself and Mr. Davis." As late as 1905 he thought he had done right about this, but by 1908, if we may believe Archie Butt's report, he had changed his mind.

Of the "great" Americans of the past the one T.R. had the most trouble with was the very one whom in his breadth of interests he resembled more than any other predecessor, Thomas Jefferson. As early as 1896 Jefferson's accession was, in T.R.'s eyes, "a terrible blow to this nation." The next year he told W. P. Trent that he had given him a more favorable view of both Jefferson and Davis, but if there was a change of heart here it was certainly not permanent. The severest judgment of Jefferson is in the life of Thomas Hart Benton, where he is unscrupulous and untruthful, the father of nullification and therefore of secession. T.R. praised Jefferson for his services to science and Western expansion, but he thought him an incapable executive and a "slippery demagogue," a man who had imagination and sentimental aspiration but lacked courage and common sense.

On his more recent predecessors, Cleveland and McKinley, Roosevelt blew both hot and cold. He criticized Cleveland freely both as governor of New York and as president; for one thing, his foreign policy was cowardly. In 1884 he found reasons in "his public career, in the first place, and then private reasons as well"

[7] Controversy over his reference to Tom Paine, in his biography of Gouverneur Morris, as a "filthy little atheist" pursued Roosevelt to the last year of his life; in addition to the letters printed by Morison, there are interesting unpublished letters to M. M. Mangasarian (April 11, 1918) and W. N. Van der Weyde (April 19, 1918). Roosevelt still thought "that, with the substitution of deist for atheist," his statement was "substantially just and accurate," though in view of the time it had wasted for him in subsequent controversy with Paine's admirers, he regretted having made it! Van der Weyde continued writing him letters on the subject until, on Aug. 21, Roosevelt finally wrote him that he would discuss the subject no further. In *American Literature and Christian Doctrine* (1958), Professor Randall Stewart finds Paine "impervious to the whole realm of spiritual aesthetic values."

why he should not be elected president. At one time he thought Cleveland unfriendly to civil service, but he must have changed his mind about this in 1893 when the President retained him as commissioner. He warmly approved Cleveland's conduct in Illinois at the time of the Pullman strike, and he seems to have feared he might become the Democratic candidate in 1904. At McKinley's funeral he sought Cleveland out; he turned to him for help at the time of the coal strike; and he praised him generously when he died.

Roosevelt's most celebrated remark about McKinley was that he had the backbone of a chocolate éclair, probably because of McKinley's reluctance to fight Spain. It is amusing to turn from this to a letter written to John Hay in 1900, when Roosevelt was himself McKinley's vice-president: "I do not think I am wrong in my historic judgment of contemporary matters when I say that President McKinley's administration will rank next to Lincoln's during the whole nineteenth century in point of great work worthily done." This must have been written in a moment of great enthusiasm, for in April, 1901, he is complaining to the Storers that, while McKinley has on the whole been an excellent president, he looks at things too cold-bloodedly. As late as September 22, 1911, he wrote his son Ted that, with all his faults, Taft was still a better president than McKinley had been.

Younger men in politics were Roosevelt's allies, enemies, or potential rivals. Outside his own party, the most spectacular rival was William Jennings Bryan. Roosevelt fluctuates somewhat in his attitude toward Bryan but, except at the end, when, as Wilson's secretary of state, Bryan gets mixed up with his hatred for Wilsonism, he is not inclined to be intemperate, though he does feel a certain contempt for the Commoner's intellectual powers. His statement to Walter W. Strong—"Bryan is a good-hearted man of precisely the temperament best fitted to make a success as 'barker' for a patent medicine"—is late but it expresses a point of view which Roosevelt achieved early.

Toward John Peter Altgeld he was far more intemperate; for one thing, he seems to have considered him an abler man than Bryan and therefore more dangerous. I am surprised that he should have fallen in with the hysterical contemporary view of Altgeld as a dangerous radical and lover of anarchists. Actually Roosevelt and

Altgeld had a good deal in common: both believed in the capitalistic system, and both were convinced that capitalistic abuses must be sternly corrected if that system were to survive.[8] The intemperance, however, was not all on one side, for Altgeld himself remarked that "the jawbone of an ass is a respectable instrument compared with the jawbone of Teddy, which has neither tooth nor stinger, but simply a buzz at both ends and in the middle."

If William Randolph Hearst did not become a serious contender against Roosevelt in the political arena it was not for lack of trying. Roosevelt himself may well have saved us from having Hearst in the White House. When the publisher ran for governor of New York against Hughes in 1906 the vote was very close (749,002 to 691,105), and it is at least possible that the statement Roosevelt sent Root to make in his name at an important meeting may have influenced enough votes to decide the election. As it turned out, most of Roosevelt's denunciations were of Hearst as a journalist; some of these are censored in his *Letters*. "He is the most potent single influence for evil we have in our life," he wrote John St. Loe Strachey in 1906, and though he praised Hearst for his Standard Oil exposures, and even conferred with him about them, he did not believe that Hearst ever acted from disinterested motives; even when he was on the right side, he was arraying class against class and nation against nation to further his own career and build up his own profits. During the war he acquired new reason to hate "that unhung traitor," as he then called him, and in March, 1918, he warned Clemenceau that Hearst was "the most influential and malignant foe of the Allies, and the most powerful supporter and friend of the Germans in the United States."[9]

[8] Roosevelt was reported in the press (see Pringle, p. 164) as having declined to meet Altgeld in 1896 on the ground that he might "at any time be called upon to meet the man sword to sword on the field of battle." See *Letters*, I, 592, for Roosevelt's denial that he ever said this.

[9] Roosevelt also loathed the Pulitzer and James Gordon Bennett press; among editors of better reputation, he greatly disliked E. L. Godkin and Oswald Garrison Villard. With *The New Republic* he was at the outset in warm sympathy, for Herbert Croly was one of the few writers who, during his later life, had an important influence on him, and he considered Walter Lippmann "the most brilliant young man of his age in all the United States." But the war changed this; by 1918 the editors of *The New Republic* are "degenerates" and the paper itself "on an exact level morally with the Hearst papers; the difference is merely one of manner."

In his own party, the man Roosevelt feared at the outset was Mark Hanna, whom he considered a dangerous rival for the nomination of 1904. Roosevelt had no reason to love Hanna, who had called him a "damned cowboy" and a "madman" whom it was unsafe to place where there was only one life between him and the presidency. After McKinley's death, however, Hanna conducted himself in a completely straightforward fashion, and it does not seem possible that Roosevelt can have accepted the Hearst–F. Opper view of him as the conscienceless tool of Wall Street, an absurd and unjust misconception which persists, among many who should know better, to this day.

Since Roosevelt wanted to be elected in 1904, nobody can reasonably blame him for putting Roosevelt men instead of Hanna men in strategic positions whenever the opportunity came. But the final, decisive, head-on clash between the two men was cruel. It came in May, 1903, being precipitated by Hanna's co-senator and rival, Joseph B. Foraker, who asked the Ohio Convention to endorse Roosevelt for 1904. Hanna refused to go along. "The issue which has been forced upon me . . ." he wired the President in Seattle, "has come in a way which makes it necessary for me to oppose such a resolution. When you know all the facts I am sure you will approve my course." Roosevelt replied two days later with a telegram which he immediately gave to the press: "I have not asked any man for his support. I have had nothing whatever to do with raising this issue. Inasmuch as it has been raised of course those who favor my administration and my nomination will favor endorsing both and those who do not will oppose." This left Hanna with only a choice between breaking openly with the administration and eliminating himself as a candidate for 1904. He chose the latter course. As Roosevelt expressed it, "It simplified things all around, for in my judgment Hanna was the only formidable opponent so far as the nomination . . . [was] concerned." It was perhaps the master political stroke of his career; no wonder it gave him "a new and vivid interest in life." As it turned out, it was all unnecessary, for Hanna died on February 15, 1904; "a veritable tragedy," T.R. called it. During Hanna's last illness he and the President established almost affectionate relations.

Senator Foraker never had Hanna's stature in the party, but he

tried hard to secure it. He and Roosevelt were on at least outwardly agreeable terms until they clashed over railway legislation
and the Brownsville matter. "He is a very powerful and very vindictive man," wrote Roosevelt in 1906, "and he is one of the most
unblushing servers and beneficiaries of corporate wealth within or
without office that I have ever met." The Standard Oil scandals set
going by William Randolph Hearst drove Foraker from public life,
and Roosevelt urged Taft not to appear on the same platform with
him in 1908. Yet there are friendly letters from Roosevelt to Foraker
in 1912 and 1915, and when T.R. had occasion to refer to Foraker in
the Barnes libel trial he called him "a very powerful man in politics, a man with whom at times I disagreed most rabidly," but "a
man for whom I have always had a real liking" and "not the ordinary
type of boss at all." When Foraker's *Notes of a Busy Life* was published the next year, Roosevelt read it and at once wrote him of his
admiration for "your entire courage and straightforwardness (in the
railway rate legislation I respected you a thousand times more
than I did most of the men who voted for the bill)," then, more significantly, went on to say: "There is no use raking up the past now,
but there were some things told me against you, or in reference to
you, which (when I consider what I know now of my informants)
would have carried no weight with me at the time had I been as
well informed as at present." This is an interesting admission on
Roosevelt's part not only that he could be wrong but that he was
capable of being taken in by untrustworthy advisers. It gives
Foraker, I think, the distinction of being the only public man to
whom he ever apologized.

La Follette was a rival more worthy of Roosevelt's steel. But
though T.R. praised the progressive legislation that the Wisconsin
senator had put through in his own state, he never really liked him
or believed in him. As early as 1905 he judged him "a shifty self-
seeker," who, though "in favor of some excellent things," limited
his usefulness by setting out to make a personal reputation "by
screaming for something he knew perfectly well could not be had."
In 1907 he was more friendly toward him, but this friendliness did
not endure. Three years later, writing to Ted about his general approval of La Follette's policies, he adds, "He is, however, an extremist, and has that touch of fanaticism which makes a man at

times heedless of means in attaining his end." In 1912 the rivalry between the two men for Progressive leadership ended whatever chance for good relations there might otherwise have been.

La Follette was very likely justified in his anger against those of his followers who used his temporary breakdown at the publishers' banquet as an excuse for deserting him and switching their support to T.R., but there is no justice whatever in his complaints against Roosevelt himself. The ex-President had committed no crime against him save that of refusing to support him, and since he had never endorsed him, he was under no conceivable obligation to do this. On February 13, 1912, T.R. wrote Charles McCarthy in Wisconsin: "Indeed I thoroughly appreciate what it has meant to you to have Senator La Follette as a leader. He has done a very great deal, and he has done most of all in getting behind him an extraordinary set of workers." But the very next day he wrote Alford W. Cooley: "La Follette has done first rate work in Wisconsin, but he does not size up for the national field any more than Chase or Seward sized up for it." Whether T.R. was right or wrong, there is no inconsistency between these letters. He was quite sincere in both.

His opinion of La Follette after the Bull Moose campaign got under way was something else again; by December he thought the senator as mad as the would-be assassin who had shot him! During the war he became even more intemperate, and when La Follette opposed the armed neutrality bill, he became a "skunk" and a traitor who ought to be hanged if war should come.

Hay, Root, and Taft were less rivals of Roosevelt than colleagues and subordinates; Charles Evans Hughes was a leader of later emergence, whom Roosevelt respected but did not like. T.R. regarded Hughes as a man of courage and integrity, incapable of compromising with corruption, but he also thought him cold, conceited, selfish, and under the domination of the "mugwump press." When he was annoyed T.R. spoke of Hughes as "the bearded lady" or bearded iceberg who "withdraws into his whiskers." He also thought Hughes jealous of him and supported him for re-election as governor in 1908 quite without enthusiasm. In 1916 he wrote Julian Street that the Republican delegates at Chicago were for Hughes "for the excellent reason that he has avoided saying anything on any subject at the very time when it is criminal not to speak." After Hughes had been nominated, he supported and campaigned for him because "at his worst he will do better than Wilson, and there is always the chance he will do very well indeed."

Yet Hughes had originally been nominated for governor on Roosevelt's endorsement, and Roosevelt had applauded his investigation of the insurance companies. Differences between the two developed early in Hughes's first administration over the governor's determination to go his own way and T.R.'s feeling that he was disturbing party harmony. It is possible, as Hughes's biographer, Pusey, suggests, that "in some measure Roosevelt shared the bosses' concern about the rise of a popular and independent figure in his home state," but it is also true that Hughes gave Roosevelt the impression that his efforts to help were not welcome.

Many years later Hughes said he had not wanted the 1908 nomination because "the position of a successor to Theodore Roosevelt would not be an attractive one. I was sure that, although out of office, he would still desire to have a dominating influence and that he would have a large following which would make the way of his successor hard." Certainly Roosevelt did not want Hughes to have it, and he is generally credited with having kept Hughes's important speech of January 31, 1908, off the front page by sending his sensational "malefactors of great wealth" message to Congress on the same day. Twice during later years Hughes let T.R. down badly: once, when, having led him into the New York primary fight of 1910, he himself withdrew from it after Taft had offered him a seat on the Supreme Court; again, when T.R. wanted him as a witness in the Barnes libel suit and he could not remember about the point on which he was asked to testify.

Roosevelt never had a quarrel with John Hay, nor apparently gave him any suggestion during his lifetime that he thought he had any shortcomings either as a public servant or as a man. When Hay died he expressed his sense of loss feelingly. But after Hay's letters had been privately printed in 1909 he wrote Lodge one of his long for-the-record letters in which systematically, though without any apparent rancor, he strips Hay of the credit that had hitherto been allowed him as an outstanding secretary of state. Hay, Roosevelt now says, was ease-loving and morally timid, and shrank from everything rough or unpleasant. He was afraid of senators, congressmen, and other politicians to such an extent that he would make any appointment they asked of him and then relieve his feelings by denouncing the person to whom he had yielded. He could not be trusted to conduct negotiations with England because he admired her so intensely nor yet with Germany because he disliked her so much. All the "vital work" involved in the Panama negotiations was done without him; he was a handicap rather than a help in the Alaskan boundary dispute; in China he did nothing. As secretary of state he never initiated a policy nor helped greatly in carrying one out, though he was often useful in drawing up statements.

Tyler Dennett suggests that Roosevelt's *amour-propre* may have been wounded by certain passages in the Hay letters. This is possible, but Roosevelt could not, on this account alone, have completely revised his whole conception of Hay's services to his administration; what he has to say is far too specific for that. And Dennett himself supports T.R.'s later estimate of Hay's character when he writes about the secretary's emotional and personality difficulties: "Unhappiest of all was the fact that so often he lacked positive convictions as to what might be right and what might be wrong. Never, even to the end, was he able completely to unify his convictions and think his way through." The charge of anti-German prejudice is quite just, but T.R. seems to have given himself too much credit and Hay too little in describing how the administration handled the Kaiser's propositions concerning China.

Root was praised extravagantly by T.R. as "the greatest intellectual force in American public life since Lincoln." From him as from Taft his former chief was later estranged as a result of the battle of 1912. There was no public quarrel here, and there is no long record, as in Taft's case, of growing misunderstanding and estrangement. But as chairman of the convention Root engineered the "steam roller" that crushed Roosevelt's hopes, and to the victim this conduct seemed "infamous," as "rank" as Taft's and more "wanton," as bad as the things for which small-time politicians were sent to Sing Sing. He was still saying things like this in 1916, though by then there had been a partial coming together of the two men through their common opposition to Wilson.

T.R. himself had once argued that Root's corporation-lawyer background could never prevent him from doing his duty as president of the United States, for the lawyer serves his clients, and if Root were president, the people of the United States would be that. Perhaps he should have remembered that at the convention the Republican party was Root's client, and if the Republican party did not want Roosevelt, he simply had to be eliminated. For all that, Root might have left the job to somebody who did not have his own particular personal relations to T.R. If he had conducted himself in 1912 as Lodge did, Roosevelt would no more have broken with him than he broke with Lodge or Nicholas Longworth.[10]

IX. Taft, Friend and Enemy

There are cases in which Roosevelt has been accused of injustice to his subordinates. The most spectacular instance is the quarrel with the Bellamy Storers, in which the President charged that, as wife of his ambassador to Austria, Mrs. Storer had embarrassed him by pulling strings to get Archbishop Ireland made a cardinal. I believe that Roosevelt had in the past shown more interest in Archbishop Ireland's advancement than, at the time of the break, he could be persuaded to acknowledge, but the Storers were seriously at fault in leaving his long letter of December 11, 1905, unanswered. He did not write again, demanding an answer, until February 3, 1906, and when this letter too was greeted with stony silence, he waited until March 5 before he telegraphed demanding Storer's resignation as ambassador. Like Roosevelt, I do not see how he could have an ambassador who would not answer his letters,

[10] Though they had no political, and virtually no personal, contacts, it is interesting to note T.R.'s decided dislike of Winston Churchill, "a dreadful cad," as he calls him to Whitelaw Reid. This dislike he shared with Lodge, and they extended it to include Churchill's father. "Both," says T.R. "possess or possessed such levity, lack of sobriety, lack of permanent principle, and an inordinate thirst for that cheap form of admiration which is given to notoriety, as to make them poor public servants." Once he even puts them with Hearst, and once he distinguishes between Churchill and the American novelist of the same name by referring to the latter as "Winston Churchill the gentleman." Before T.R. went to Africa, Churchill sent him a special copy of his book, *My African Country*, which T.R. acknowledged cordially enough, but only because "I suppose I ought to write to him." Oddly enough, he sent the letter first to Whitelaw Reid to make sure it was "all right." At the beginning of World War I he sent Churchill a message, however, congratulating him on mobilizing the fleet.

and the conduct of the Storers afterwards in publishing Roosevelt's correspondence, etc., does not create faith in their good judgment.

Other cases involve people like Charlemagne Tower,[11] Herbert W. Bowen,[12] General Miles and Admiral Brownson, J. L. Bristow,[13] H. J. Hagerman and his father,[14] H. H. Kohlsaat, and even a society editor on a Washington paper, whom, according to the smug and venomous Annie Riley Hale, who wrote two disparaging books about Roosevelt, the President refused to have in the White House again after her reporting had displeased him and ultimately drove from her employment.[15] It is impossible for me to judge all these charges fairly with the evidence at my disposal. In the case of the society editor, I must say that I believe Roosevelt would have been quite capable of doing what Mrs. Hale charges if his sense of propriety had been sufficiently outraged, but this is purely a subjective judgment. My faith in Kohlsaat's accuracy is shaken by his statement that Roosevelt left his letter of March 15, 1912, unanswered and broke off communication with him. Actually T.R. answered the letter the day it was received, and his reply is printed in Morison's collection. As for the famous controversies with Admiral Brownson and General Miles, there is no doubt that both men were guilty of a breach of discipline (one of T.R.'s advisers

[11] Pringle thinks that T.R. sacrificed Tower in the controversy over the Kaiser and David Jayne Hill, but it should be pointed out that he did not send the stern letter of rebuke he had first prepared but instead dispatched a much briefer, milder communication. (See *Letters*, VI, 989–92; Pringle, *T.R.*, pp. 485–90.)

[12] Herbert W. Bowen, American minister to Venezuela, protested the actions of the asphalt interests. Unable to interest Francis B. Loomis in the State Department, he told the story to the New York *Herald;* he was called a liar and retired from the service. The case against Roosevelt in this connection is stated by John W. Bennett, *Roosevelt and the Republic*, pp. 185–91.

[13] J. L. Bristow, fourth assistant postmaster general and special commissioner to Panama told Charles G. Dawes in 1904 that T.R. "cast him ruthlessly aside after listening to the enemies against whom he had faithfully promised to protect him, when he appointed him to the work of running down some thieves." Bristow drew the conclusion that Roosevelt was insincere in his friendships, "subordinating all matters of personal loyalty or the rights of an individual . . . to his own ambitions and interests." He seems to have convinced Dawes, who wrote that Secretary Gage agreed with Bristow, and added, "I suspect Roosevelt makes a hard man to work under." (Charles G. Dawes, *A Journal of the McKinley Years*, pp. 405–6.)

[14] Annie Riley Hale, *Bull Moose Trails*, Chapter IV.

[15] Annie Riley Hale, *Rooseveltian Fact and Fable*, pp. 97–98.

thought Brownson should have been court-martialed); the only question is whether the punishment was too severe, and, in Miles's case, whether T.R. was consciously or unconsciously influenced by a dislike occasioned by past grievances.[16]

The great quarrel of Roosevelt's life was, of course, his quarrel with Taft. Taft was not Roosevelt's first choice as his successor; he would have preferred Root. But Root did not want the post; neither did T.R. believe that the West would accept a corporation lawyer. Pringle believes that T.R. had made up his mind in favor of Taft by the summer of 1905. "He has no more fear in dealing with the interests of great corporate wealth," wrote Roosevelt to George Otto Trevelyan in that year, "than he has in dealing with the leaders of the most powerful labor unions; and if either go wrong he has not the slightest hesitation in antagonizing them. To strength and courage, clear insight, and practical common sense, he adds a very noble and disinterested character."

He wrote and talked in the same vein to Taft himself. If T.R. is anywhere fulsome, if he ever gushes, it is here. "You blessed old trump, I have always said you would be the greatest President, bar only Washington and Lincoln, and I feel mighty inclined to strike out the exceptions!" And once, as if he were coaching a potential "Miss America," "Let the audience see you smile *always*, because I feel that your nature shines out so transparently when you do smile—you big, generous, high-minded fellow."

Where, then, and when and why did the estrangement begin? There is no suggestion of any difficulty before the election, though T.R. was disappointed that Taft did not put more fight into his campaign. Once he went over Taft's head in ordering a campaign contribution refused, and once he gave a letter of Taft's to the press without first securing the candidate's consent.

But if Roosevelt was not uneasy, other people were. As early as August 9, Moorfield Storey wrote Charles Francis Adams that, while publicly Taft stood committed to the Roosevelt policies,

[16] See Philip C. Jessup, *Elihu Root*, I, 245–50. Samuel Leland Powers, who witnessed T.R.'s rebuke of Miles, gives an account of it (*Portraits of Half a Century*, p. 171) which, though not in all respects agreeing with the official account by Joseph B. Bishop (*Theodore Roosevelt and His Time*, Chapter XVI), has T.R. behaving in a considerably less spectacular manner than he is sometimes given credit for.

"privately he allows it to be understood that he will not carry them out." It is certain that Roosevelt was deeply troubled when he learned that Taft was going to drop Cabinet officers whom he had had every reason to suppose he was planning to retain and to junk Roosevelt's Number One man in the diplomatic service, Henry White at Paris. By February, Henry Adams was wondering "if the new President is so bent on making a clean sweep of Roosevelt's men, why did we elect him expressly to carry on the Roosevelt regime?" Mrs. Taft had never been an influence for peace between the two men, and according to her own account in her autobiography, Mrs. Longworth was not at this time much better. When Mark Sullivan asked T.R. just before Inauguration Day how he thought Taft would make out, the retiring President replied, "He's all right; he means well and he'll do his best. But he's weak. They'll get around him. They'll lean against him."

Yet if T.R. was so thoroughly disillusioned as this so early in the game, it seems strange that he did not break with Taft sooner than he did. In Africa, in February, 1910, he received word that Gifford Pinchot had been dismissed, and along with it Pinchot's own sixteen-point indictment of the new President's policies, but he refused to express an opinion. Between Naples and Rome, H. N. Needham tried to draw him. "Instead of criticizing the President he said that he would take no man's testimony, not even that of his own sworn friends, but would judge for himself after a careful examination of Mr. Taft's record." From London, on June 8, he made a similarly noncommittal answer to a letter in which Taft himself had reviewed his first fifteen months in the White House.

Naturally Taft was not satisfied with a noncommittal answer, nor yet with Roosevelt's similar response to the letter with which he greeted him upon his return to America. Despite his announcement that he would have nothing to say about public affairs for sixty days, T.R. soon permitted Hughes to draw him into the New York primary fight, in which he suffered the first of the series of defeats which pursued him from here almost to the end of his life.

In the summer of 1910 the party stalwarts treated the ex-President with a shocking discourtesy, which there is no reason to suppose Taft disapproved of. At one point the President seems to have sent T.R. an implied ultimatum, in which he offered to cast out Cannon and Aldrich as his advisers in exchange for Roosevelt's endorsement; Roosevelt thought this letter "futile" and "silly" and wrote Lodge how he and Mrs. Roosevelt had laughed over it. T.R. had to make an all-out fight even for the chairmanship of the New York State convention, which he won by only 568 votes to 443. In spite of all this, as Mowry has demonstrated in convincing detail, he fought hard all through 1910 to hold insurgents and standpatters together, refusing to take up an extreme position on either side.

By fall he is saying privately that Taft has now proved his lack of leadership, but he thinks it absurd to suggest that he is not upright. This song runs through 1911. In June he writes one Fisher that he does not intend in any way to criticize his successor. In August he told Benjamin Ide Wheeler that Taft was stronger than he had been. "If two years ago he had acted as he has two years later . . . he would have won hands down." He adds that there is "a strong reaction against the Insurgents, because they have gone too wild and too far, and have split up every which way." A week later he wrote Alford W. Cooley that, though the insurgents had produced a number of first-rate state leaders, they had "no one who is big enough to size up to the nation scale." In September he rebuked William Kent for attacking the President. "You and Gifford are altogether crazy about Taft." Even as late as February 14, 1912, he declared that he had not "a shade of irritation" in his mind about the President.

Thereafter the change came quickly. By April 16 the Taft managers are behaving infamously, and Taft himself is conniving at it. By April 18 he is tied up with Lorimer and Penrose. On April 26 Taft took the initiative by attacking T.R. in a speech at Boston, after which T.R.'s letters speak of him as a "scoundrel," a "fool," and "a good bit of a blackguard." By May 28 the Taft forces were, in T.R.'s view, ready to "steal" the convention, and on June 4 Taft stands where the Copperheads stood in 1860.

What, now, of candidacy? The interesting thing is that the idea should have been in T.R.'s mind so early and the decision postponed so long. As early as June 21, 1909, he writes Henry White from Africa that his 1904 statement was not a promise that he would *never* run again. On March 4, 1910, he writes from Egypt that "at present it does not seem to me that it would be wise . . . for me to be a candidate." At the New York convention of 1910 he would not be a party to any endorsement which would limit his freedom of action in 1912.[17]

In January, 1911, he does not think there is one chance in a thousand that he will be nominated, but he will not refuse in advance, since, unlikely as the exigency appears, he must keep himself free to heed the call of duty. Late in June he wrote O. K. Davis that he was not sure he would not refuse the nomination even if it came to him unanimously, and in October he felt he had the right to expect every friend to do his utmost to prevent its being offered to him. In November and December he answered many letters from would-be supporters, thanking them for their confidence in him but indicating that he himself hoped he would not be nominated. Yet, though he refused to come to Nebraska to speak, he did not discourage an attempt to put his name on the primary ballot. Early in December he wrote Ted, "I am beginning to feel that I would welcome the nomination of either Taft or La Follette on the first ballot, just to prevent the chance of a stampede to me."

On January 16, 1912, he wrote a long letter to the publisher Frank Munsey, who was to be one of his great financial backers, saying that he was not ready to speak out nor did he believe that conditions required it. But "if the people should feel that I was the instrument to be used at this time, I should accept even although I knew that I should be broken and cast aside in the using." On January 23 he is still insisting that he does not want it "as far as I know my own soul"; on February 7 he writes Longworth that he is "pretty well convinced" that Taft will get it. At the same time he is making

[17] To Mrs. Theodore Roosevelt, Jr., T.R. wrote, on Nov. 27, 1910: "What I now most want is just what is forced on me; to stay here in my own home with your mother in law, to walk and ride with her, and in the evening sit with her before the great wood fire in the north room and hear the wind shrieking outside; to chop trees and read books, and feel that I am justified in not working. I don't want to be in Africa, or on the ranch, or in the army, or in the White House; I like to think of them all, now and then; but the place I wish to be is just where I am. I was in Washington the other day, and went to the White House (where the old employees greeted me with touching affection, and all, especially 'Hoovie' sent Ted their love); I thoroughly enjoyed seeing the White House, just as I enjoy seeing Harvard when I go back there; and it is the literal fact that I should feel almost as badly to go back to live in the White House and become President again as I should to go back to Harvard for a four years course."

statements to other correspondents which seem to imply, though they do not say, that he is in the race. On February 13 he told Longworth that he was going to speak out, and on February 21 he declared, "My hat is in the ring." Three days later he wrote the governors who had sent him an arranged letter imploring him to declare his candidacy, "I will accept the nomination for President if it is tendered to me."

On March 21 he wrote Arthur Lee in England that the odds were four to one against him. By June 28, six days after Taft had been nominated, Roosevelt's crisis psychology was fully developed. "I do not know whether we will be able to succeed in the great movement for social and industrial reform . . . but I do know that the alternative is a general smashup of our civilization; and succeed or fail, I hold it to be the duty of every decent man to fight to avoid such a smash."

During the troubled period in the relations between Taft and Roosevelt whose outlines we have here been tracing, they clashed over Taft's arbitration treaties and his public lands policy (both of which involved *Outlook* articles by Roosevelt), but the thing that seems really to have exacerbated the situation was the government's move against United States Steel, on October 27, 1911, partly for having violated the Sherman Act by purchasing, with Roosevelt's approval, the Tennessee Coal and Iron Company, "making me," as T.R. said to John Hays Hammond, "either a fool or a knave." This was the kind of criticism that T.R. could not endure, and since Taft had been a member of his Cabinet when the merger took place, he accused him of bad faith and called his action "small, mean, and foolish." His article on the subject in *The Outlook* [18] was one of the most important of his career; he himself said that it "was generally accepted as bringing me forward for the Presidential nomination." It helped rewin conservative support for him and convinced some industrialists that his attitude toward big business was less uncompromising than that of the administration. On January 14, 1912, Archie Butt lunched with Mrs. Robinson, and "found only a great sadness in her mind—no resentment, no bitterness, only a deep regret that things should have turned out as they have." He quotes

[18] "The Trusts, the People, and the Square Deal," *The Outlook*, XCIX (1911), 649–56.

her directly: "Oh, Major Butt, it is too late now. If it had not been for that Steel suit! I was talking with Theodore only last week, and he said that he could never forgive."

During this same period two meetings were arranged between Roosevelt and Taft. On the last day of June, 1910, T.R. called on the Tafts at their summer home at Beverly, Massachusetts. According to Mrs. Taft, this meeting was "remarkably pleasant and entertaining." "I was glad . . . to find the old spirit of sympathetic comradeship still paramount and myself evidently proved unwarrantably suspicious." She adds that T.R. told many stories of his adventures abroad and "with his keen appreciation of the ridiculous and his gift of description, gave us as merry an afternoon as we ever spent with him." But apparently there was no discussion of politics, and Taft himself afterwards told John Hays Hammond that he was disappointed nothing had been accomplished.

The other, more important meeting, at New Haven, on September 19, was a desperate and distressing failure. This time politics were discussed, but an unhappy controversy developed afterwards as to who had sought the meeting and who had asked aid from whom. Roosevelt, who had not expected success, felt that the encounter had confirmed his suspicions that intercourse with Taft was now impossible, and the President told Archie Butt that he and T.R. had come definitely to a parting of the ways.

After 1912 Taft and Roosevelt did not see each other again until April, 1915, when they were both honorary pallbearers at Professor Lounsbury's funeral. Here they shook hands, Taft taking the initiative, but there was no conversation. In October, 1916, they met again at the Union League Club in New York at a reception for Hughes. Both were now opposed to the Wilson policies, and this helped to draw them together. Yet when Taft heard a few days later that T.R. was going to campaign in Arizona, he said, "The farther he goes away the better." After the election he saw T.R. "planning again for 1920. . . . He is like an old man of the sea on the back of the Republican party."

Real reconciliation did not occur until the last year of Roosevelt's life. After T.R.'s very serious illness early in 1918 Taft wrote him a friendly letter, to which he replied in kind, answering Taft, he said, before he dealt with any other letters. Other correspondence followed; then in May, while T.R. was alone in the dining room of the Blackstone Hotel in Chicago, with no knowledge that Taft was in the city, the latter came up with his hand held out and cried, "Theodore, I am glad to see you." Whereupon the two sat together, and it was over. The Colonel communicated the news first to John J. Leary. "Jack," he said, "I don't mind telling you how delighted I am. I never felt happier over anything in my life."

There remains one question more, and like all the most interesting questions it cannot be definitely answered. Was the fight necessary? It accomplished nothing except a Democratic victory, which, from the point of view of both contestants, was an unmitigated calamity. T.R.'s letters make it perfectly clear that he knew in 1912 as well as anybody knows now that from the politic point of view the sensible thing to do would have been to allow Taft to be re-elected in 1912, to make, as T.R. viewed it, an even worse mess of things during his second administration, while T.R. held himself in reserve as very likely the unanimous choice of the party in 1916. Two considerations made it impossible for him to hold back: (1) Taft had given the country a reactionary administration, betraying T.R. and undoing, or attempting to undo, the achievements of his regime; (2) he had secured his renomination by dishonest means. Were these charges just?

On the first count, even such ardent Roosevelt supporters as Henry Howland, of *The Outlook*, have admitted that the Taft administration was not "barren of achievement. On the contrary, its record of achievement was substantial." In some areas, like the enforcement of the Sherman Act, it may even be reasonably argued that Taft was bolder than his predecessor.

This does not, in itself, cancel out the reactionary tendencies of the Taft administration. It may be argued that in so far as the Taft administration was progressive, it derived from the momentum inherited from its predecessor. How long this momentum would have continued without a change of leadership, and what four more years of Aldrich and Cannon might have achieved, it is difficult to say.

It should be noted, too, that dissatisfaction with the Taft administration did not originate with Roosevelt. Before he had expressed himself at all, others had spoken quite as bitterly as he was to speak at the height of the 1912 fight.

In the light of Taft's long and distinguished service both before and after his presidency, his memory needs no defending. But,
though he was not a bad president, he was a marvelously inept
one. He had never really wanted the office, and he never
learned how to play the political game. One suspects that his four
years in the White House were the uneasiest of his life, and Taft
was never at his best when he was uneasy or unhappy. Even when
he did the right things he said the wrong ones, or else he saved
his wisest judgments for his private letters and spoke clumsily in
his public utterances.

Taft has the reputation of being a more agreeable man than
Roosevelt, but men with an element of weakness in them are never
agreeable when they find themselves in a situation which accentu-
ates that weakness. As Root said, Taft was less "advisable" than
Roosevelt, and he had a strain of petulance which was at its worst in
the face of opposition. Certainly Roosevelt was somewhat aloof
and standoffish toward him after his return from abroad. There is
evidence that Taft was sensitive about this, and he did not help
matters by talking with occasional petty spitefulness about Roosevelt to his associates. Even publicly, it should be remembered, not
all the hard things that were said around 1912 emanated from
Roosevelt. His were only remembered longer because they were so
much funnier. Taft called T.R. fakir, juggler, green goods man, and
gold brick man. He was also "the most dangerous man we have had
in this country since its origin." "I look upon him as I look upon
a freak, almost in the zoological garden, a kind of animal not often
found." And if T.R. suffered from crisis-psychology, so did Taft.[19]
On February 12, 1912, just after the governors had sent their letter
to T.R., Taft spoke of "extremists" who would duplicate French
Revolutionary conditions among us, or "that babbling anarchy that
once characterized the South American Republics." These people
were not progressives, he declared, but only "political emotionalists
or neurotics." Even after the campaign was over, in January, 1913,
Taft declared at a Republican dinner in New York that the Re-

[19] So did others. On Feb. 25, 1912, Barrett Wendell "felt as if social revolution were near, probably inevitable." On Sept. 17 he wrote of T.R., "He is
capable, in the fervor of his self-confidence, of attempting to seize the government by force"!

publicans had won the election in the sense of having kept out of office a man and a party who would have established tyranny and perhaps even the confiscation of private property!

Some aspects of the convention must be dealt with elsewhere. In the sense that it thwarted the will of the majority of Republican voters, who had made it abundantly clear through the primaries that T.R. was their choice, it deserves to be called crooked. On the other hand, its defenders are justified in pointing out that the machine operated in 1912 as the machine always operates, and that Roosevelt's indictment was therefore directed against a system to which he had never objected until it began to work to his disadvantage. In 1908 he had even rejected a proposal to amend the manner in which Southern delegates were chosen, thus strengthening Taft's hand for 1912. It is also generally believed that Roosevelt and his followers played the political game to the extent of contesting for strategic purposes many seats concerning which there was no real question, though, as Pringle says, "whether thirty votes were stolen or seventy-two has no real bearing on the outcome," for the convention was in the hands of the Taft forces, and these men were prepared to disqualify as many Roosevelt delegates as might be necessary in order to ensure victory.[20]

X. A Man Named Wilson

But the man Roosevelt disliked most in this world was never William Howard Taft. He was Woodrow Wilson. "I despise the man and dislike his policies," he told John J. Leary, "to the point of hate."

There was no "quarrel" between Roosevelt and Wilson, for the simple reason that Wilson never replied to any of Roosevelt's criticisms nor gave any indication that he knew the criticism had been made. This amazing self-control on the President's part must have been infuriating to Roosevelt; certainly it gave Wilson a tremendous strategic advantage.

[20] T.R. himself never admitted any political manipulation at Chicago. "We did not make a single contest of the ordinary sort," he wrote Lemuel E. Quigg in 1913, "before the nominating convention—when I say 'we' I mean the responsible people who were for me and had seats on the National Committee. These men by my explicit request voted against us on every contest raised by Mr. McHarg or anyone else where there was a shade of doubt. We fought before the convention only contests where there was no more doubt than there was of our having carried California."

First contacts between Roosevelt and Wilson date back to the nineties. Pringle gives the impression that they were altogether untroubled. "That they never became close friends was due to circumstances rather than desire." I am not so sure of this. As early as 1896 Roosevelt objected to Wilson's notion "that what we needed was parliamentary responsibility in the English sense." This was "idle" because Wilson did not understand "the real conditions under which our government worked." Yet in 1902 he rejoiced in Wilson's elevation to the presidency of Princeton. "Woodrow Wilson is a perfect trump." Not only did he write Wilson a letter of congratulation, but he also told Grover Cleveland that he had long admired Wilson's "constructive statesmanship and administrative ability." In December of the same year Roosevelt wrote "as a decent American" to thank Wilson for his paper on American ideals in the *Atlantic* and to invite him to spend a night at the White House.

In 1908 Roosevelt is sufficiently "impatient" with Wilson's attitude on the control of corporations and other matters so that he has not bothered to read Wilson's new book, *Constitutional Government in the United States,* though when Lyman Abbott sends him a quotation from it he calls it "great." This may indicate that T.R. was angered by an interview with Wilson in the New York *Times,* on November 24, 1907, containing some rather scornful references to Roosevelt. Wilson protested that the *Times* had not presented his views accurately but he did not disavow the opinions expressed.

In 1911–1912 Roosevelt's attitude toward Wilson wavers. Though he doubts his sincerity, he considers him the ablest man in the Democratic camp. As late as February, 1913, he still thought it possible that "if he is big enough to master his party he may make a great record and rivet the attention of the country upon him."

In April Wilson angered T.R. when he attacked his corporation policy by publishing in *The World's Work* an article based on one of his campaign speeches. T.R. thought the article "based on deliberate misrepresentation . . . done not with frank directness but by innuendo and inference." (He answered in the October *Century.*) "It is the first time I have known a President of the United States," he wrote A. D. Swann, "after his election, to publish a wanton and misrepresentative attack on an enemy." In July he writes

Senator Bristow, "Personally I do not like Wilson and do not believe in him, and from any standpoint it is utter nonsense to hope to make anything out of a States Rights party." In a public address in July he can still speak of "our scholarly and well-intentioned President," but he also feels that "the 'New Freedom' means nothing whatever but the old license translated into terms of pleasant rhetoric." By September he is confessing "contemptuous dislike" of Wilson to Lodge. He is "a narrow and bitter partisan," he is intellectually dishonest, and though he has nerve in domestic politics, he is a "ridiculous creature" in international affairs. In June, 1914, he wrote Lyman Abbott that he now felt honor bound "to stand in strong opposition to the Administration" on both domestic and foreign policy, it having produced industrial depression, given over all attempt to remedy social evils, and abandoned "the interest and honor" of America altogether. The next month he writes even more severely to Henry L. Stoddard, "I regard Mr. Wilson's Administration as a menace to our national honor, and an obstacle to our social and economic well-being at home."

Roosevelt was, therefore, already committed to opposition to Wilson before the European War began. And though, to his later regret, he supported Wilson's neutrality policy at the beginning of the war, this was not because he had any confidence in him or in his secretary of state. On the first of August, with Europe trembling on the brink, T.R. sets down the President as "ridiculous and insincere," "a college president with an astute and shifty mind, a hypocritical ability to deceive plain people, unscrupulousness in handling machine leaders, and no real knowledge or wisdom concerning international affairs," while Bryan is "a professional yodeler, a human trombone," and "our own special prize idiot." By November Wilson is "a scholarly, acrid pacifist of much ability and few scruples." He has a wonderful command of language which he uses not to communicate his meaning but to conceal it, being fundamentally desirous to cover up his fatal lack of purpose. He is also timid, unscrupulous, cold-blooded, and selfish, playing for the Irish and German vote, and for glory as a peacemaker, which T.R. at this date is still ready to concede he may reasonably hope to win.

In 1915 matters grow steadily worse. In January, fearing that the ship purchase bill might lead to conflict with both England and

France, T.R. called Wilson just the kind of pacifist who might inadvertently stumble into war. Now he is no longer satisfied to accuse him of failing to support the Allies; he is secretly working for Germany! In June T.R. had a head-on clash with the administration over the criticism of public affairs he had made in a speech at Plattsburg.

From here on T.R.'s language grows more and more violent. Wilson is called "infernal skunk," "abject coward," "wretched creature," "astute, unprincipled, physically cowardly demagogue," and "utterly selfish, utterly treacherous, utterly insincere hypocrite," with a soul "rotten through and through." Even his literary style is that of a "Byzantine logothete" (the one brilliant phrase of the conflict). "Wilson, by the way," he writes his son Kermit, in 1916, "is, I really believe, the most wretched President we have ever had." From him with whom Wilson's badness had become an obsession, that "by the way" is a precious example of unconscious humor.

There was no abatement in T.R.'s bitterness even after the United States entered the war. "The President has played dirty and slippery politics as he always does, and as he has never been influenced by a real patriotic motive, there is no reason to expect anything else from him now." For a long time T.R. did not believe that Wilson intended to send troops at all; after it became clear that he would, he found everything shockingly mismanaged. Even in the spring of 1918 he thought Wilson still hoping for "peace without victory." Antiadministration papers which criticized the government were prosecuted; proadministration papers which obstructed the war were protected. Appealing for the election of a Democratic Congress, Wilson made loyalty to himself, not support of the war, the test of fitness for office.

It is a sad story whichever side of the controversy one happens to be on, and I do not believe that Roosevelt himself knew whether temperament, dispassionate conviction, or resentment of injustice weighed upon him most heavily. There was nothing upon which he prided himself more than the building of the Panama Canal. There was nothing else in which he had wrought quite so wisely and well. He had to believe that if he were to go on living with himself; he simply could not be dispassionate toward anyone who besmirched his greatest achievement. We know how strongly he felt upon the subject from the pains he took to defend himself in his long discussion of "The Panama Blackmail Treaty" in *Fear God and Take Your Own Part* and elsewhere. Once he discussed with Julian Street the propriety of an ex-president criticizing the President of the United States. "The most striking attack of this character I know of," he said, "was . . . made by a president upon an ex-president. I refer to the offer of twenty-five million dollars to Colombia by Mr. Wilson because of what I did, as President, about the Panama Canal." Yet nobody can be sure that he would not, in the long run, have taken up exactly the same attitude toward Wilson's foreign policy if this element had not been present. Personally I think he would.

XI. The Spirit of Puck

It will be seen that not even Roosevelt's bitterest partisanships were untouched by his humor. It is true that there are those who deny him humor. He was too intense, they say, too much in earnest, to be able to achieve the detachment, the relaxation of mind which the humorous attitude requires. Those who dislike him add that he was too egotistical and self-centered.

Inasmuch as the humorous attitude implies that there is nothing high or low in life that requires to be taken quite seriously, this is just. "There are some subjects, such as the character of a woman, as to which jesting is offensive." Yet there was a great deal of fun in him. He never went long without clowning, and he even enjoyed jokes on himself except when they involved the imputation of dishonor.

Sometimes his funmaking took the primitive form of pounding his friends, and once, at a public reception in the White House, he greeted a lady as "the wife of that reprobate" and held up a whole line while he held forth in affectionate denunciation of the shortcomings of her husband! It is amusing to learn that his humor was not understood in England. At Oxford a don, showing him pictures of ancient members of the college, switched suddenly to a plaque of an Assyrian monarch. Roosevelt quipped, "Ah! this graduate was obviously *very* early English," and the don, in embarrassment, changed the subject! When it was erroneously reported that, having examined a picture of Derby Day, he had remarked, "Tempora mutantur," *Punch* telegraphed for confirmation. Roosevelt telegraphed back:

Statement incorrect. In commenting on pictures I never use any language as modern as Latin. On the occasion in question my quotations were from cuneiform script, and the particular sentence referred to was the pre-Ninevite phrase "hully gee."

The receipients of this message were not quite sure whether it was confirmation or denial!

It is true that some of Roosevelt's jokes have an element of sarcasm in them and that a good many of them are concerned with himself. Thanking Herbert Parsons for a Christmas remembrance in 1911, he writes:

The diary you gave me was exactly what I wished. It will serve me to put down my appointments with Cataline, Clodius (both of whom are now in *The Outlook* office disguised as lady typewriters), that brutal embodiment of lawless passion, Dr. Lyman Abbott, and the various other "tools" through whom I intend to assault the liberties of the republic.

And when Scribners inadvertently advertised *Outdoor Pastimes of an American Hunter* as "Outdoor Pastimes of an American Homer," he made a whole drama out of it to Brander Matthews:

I am hurt and grieved at your evident jealousy of my poetic reputation. Evidently you have not read my notable review of the epic poems of Mr. Robinson, or you would appreciate that, even though I have not written poetry myself, I have yet shown such keen appreciation of the poetry of other great poets that I felt justified in securing the insertion of the advertisement. If you saw my review of Mr. Robinson's poems you may have noticed that I refrained from calling him "our American Homer." This was simply due to the fact that I hoped some discriminating friend would see where the epithet ought to go; less perhaps as an acknowledgment of what I have actually done, than as an inspiration and prophecy concerning the future.

The mischief expressed here found many other manifestations. At the beginning of the Spanish-American War, one Atlantic seaboard city frantically demanded protection against the Spaniards! The assistant secretary of the navy at once provided a Civil War monitor.

It was armed with one smoothbore gun about as effective as a cul-verin; it was manned by twenty-one Naval Militia, and it was towed by a tug. I sent it out there to that port and it completely satisfied them, completely satisfied those two statesmen and that city. It was quite unfit to deal with any foe of modern times, although it might possibly have dealt with the Spanish Armada, though I am not sure.

Similarly when the coal operators demanded an "eminent soci-ologist" on the arbitration board to settle the coal strike, but re-fused to accept any representative of organized labor, Roosevelt triumphantly solved the problem by appointing a labor man and calling him an eminent sociologist! And again the solution was accepted.

He loved to have third persons present at "private" conferences, especially when he suspected that he was going to be asked for something he had no right to give and no intention of giving. Once he had William Allen White, whom Senator Tom Platt had threat-ened to sue for libel, but whom he did not know by sight, present at an interview between T.R. and Platt, which he timed so that they left the White House only a few minutes apart, to set the re-porters speculating.

Once he walked in on a party of newspapermen burlesquing his speeches and himself proceeded to give a burlesque to end all bur-lesques. Once, again, he overheard Frederick Palmer mimicking him. "Do I do it as forcibly as that?" he asked. "Quite, Mr. Presi-dent." "I like to be forcible," he replied very forcibly. He was amused, not annoyed, when, in California, John Muir thoughtlessly handed him a letter from Charles S. Sargent containing disrespect-ful references to himself, and when a guest at a White House re-ception told him that his name would go down in history with Washington's, he is said to have inquired, "George or Booker?"

XII. The Vindictive and Magnanimous

One special question about Roosevelt in his human relationships is the question whether he was vindictive toward his enemies. It would not be necessary to raise this except that he himself insists upon it, "being personally of a slightly vindictive temperament, at least in extreme cases." At a Gridiron Club dinner, late in T.R.'s administration, Vice-President Fairbanks remarked that he had never thrown a line to trip an adversary. When Roosevelt's turn came to speak, he took up this remark as indicating a difference between Fairbanks and himself. "I have thrown a line to trip an adversary, and—I would do it again." Early in his career he declared, "There are a few whom I shall not be likely to forgive." And at the very end Leary records his saying that he wished he had been able to "take care" of all his enemies. Sir Esme Howard says that when the death of a certain senator was reported to him and he was reproached with not seeming sorry, he replied, "Of course I'm sorry. I'm sorry it's not Senator X."

Yet Joseph Bucklin Bishop, Lawrence F. Abbott, and William Allen White all deny that T.R. was vindictive. "He could denounce a man savagely," says Bishop, "and a few months later show a kindly feeling toward him. His anger was fierce but it soon burned itself out." Henry L. Stoddard, to be sure, tells of T.R.'s refusal to renew relations with a writer who had attacked him in a magazine article. "He has known me eight or ten years in an intimate way. If when he thus knew me he could make such charges, he proves himself to have a character I dare not trust in the future." But this was not animosity but simply a sad, resigned acceptance of the facts of the case.

Despite the utterances already quoted, Roosevelt's own basic theory was in accord with this. "The poorest of all emotions for any American citizen to feel is the emotion of hatred toward his fellows." Even wrongdoers should be opposed without hatred. "I do not believe in telling untruths over a man's grave, but I do feel that death wipes out all that is merely personal."

The fairest verdict on T.R. in this aspect, I think, is that, though he was far from achieving the selfless magnanimity of Lincoln, he was a good deal better than he claimed to be. There was plenty of fierceness in his make-up, but there was little brooding implacability. He made more enemies than most men do, and he was more often disappointed; in the course of his life he did at least a reasonable amount of forgiving. "Mr. Ryan was very strongly opposed to me and wished to beat me and I believe he was entirely sincere in his desire to do it." "Oh, when Mr. Payn came to me, I never had an ill will towards Mr. Payn and I don't blame him for having ill will towards me, not a bit." Despite all his difficulties with Secretary Alger, he praised him in his *Autobiography* for his conduct of the Spanish War. He also promoted Charles Humphrey, who, he thought, had treated him badly. "I am not going to allow people to say that I have refused to promote a good officer on account of my personal feeling. . . . If it had been another officer in my place at that time, I would never sign his commission."

He accepted only six cents damages from Newett, though he might very well have broken him. He also probably saved the life of his would-be assassin in Milwaukee by demanding that he be brought before him. His motives are obscure here, and he hardly seems to have thought of his assailant as a human being. "I would not have objected to the man's being killed at the very instant, but I did not deem it wise or proper that he should be killed before my eyes." Later he says that he has no feeling against him, though he has very strong feelings "against the people who, by their ceaseless and intemperate abuse, excited him to the action, and against the mushy people who would excuse him and all other criminals once the crime has been committed."

XIII. The Man and Himself

When a man has difficulties getting along with his fellow men, the usual difficulty is that his self is getting in the way. Most people probably feel that Theodore Roosevelt was a great egoist. Certainly if self-assertion makes an egoist, he was. He did not want to be vice-president because he did not think he could stand it "to preside at senatorial debates and be foreclosed from retorting when foolish ideas were advanced." In Washington he bounds in on a meeting of the Art Commission. "I have just come from fighting with my friends at the other end of the Avenue. I don't always like it much, but I *flatter* myself that *they* like it less!" This is the side of Roosevelt that John Burroughs ungenerously speaks of as the "strong dash of the bully" in him. Certainly it is what Henry Adams meant by his incomparably vivid and vicious figure, "The twelfth century still rages wildly here in the shape of a fiend with tusks and eyeglasses across the way."

His aggressiveness as police commissioner, when he roamed New York, Haroun-al-Raschid guise, catching corrupt and lazy policemen red-handed, is well remembered. A spoilsman votes no funds for the Civil Service Commission, and Roosevelt retaliates by holding no examinations in his district, so that none of his constituents can get jobs. When the Panama Canal Commission does not function effectively, he wants to do away with it and make Goethals single head; Congress refuses; Roosevelt, consequently, puts Goethals in as head of the commission and, by executive order, makes all the other commissioners subordinate to him. He orders the fleet round the world, and when Congress threatens to refuse to appropriate the necessary funds, he replies that there is enough money on hand to get the fleet to the Pacific, and so far as he is concerned it can stay there until Congress chooses to provide means to bring it back. While the agricultural bill is passing through the Senate in 1907, a Western senator tacks on an amendment providing that the President cannot create any more national forests in the Northwest. Roosevelt signs the bill, which is otherwise desirable, and just before it becomes law, he sets aside 16,000,000 acres.

These actions were dramatic in themselves. They were made more so by the way he performed them, by his vivid, often exaggerated, talk, and his unsurpassed gift for finding moral turpitude in his opponents. "Do you want any action about those Federal officials?" he asks Taft. "I will break their necks with the utmost cheerfulness if you say the word." The thought of the wicked forces arrayed against him was never far from his mind or his tongue: he spoke about them even in the supremely inappropriate context of the William Belden Noble Lecture at Harvard in 1910. In 1908 he involved the government in libel suits against the New York *World* and the Indianapolis *News,* in which he got upon some pretty shaky legal ground, and which came to nothing.

Roosevelt did not often, in the usual sense of the term, boast about his achievements. To be sure, there is the celebrated—and highly debatable—"I took Panama." But usually his self-evaluation preserves at the least the form of objectivity. "I served as president for seven years. I look back on those years with the feeling that my record was a credit to my country and will so stand in history." Again, he tells Joseph Ford, "I have never felt a shadow of doubt as to the wisdom of my policy, for after all, in its last analysis, my policy is nothing whatever but the policy of common honesty and common sense." And though criticism may make him angry it cannot make him flinch. "You need not be under any anxiety as to there being any revelations that can possibly do me any damage," he writes J. C. O'Laughlin, "either about this Steel Corporation matter, or about the Sugar Trust, or the Panama Canal, or anything else connected with my administration. They can investigate me until they are black in the face."

The tone does not change very much when he is speaking of himself more personally. "I obtained every chance I got by showing that I was better able and better fitted to do the job than anyone else was." In 1900 he declares, "I was nominated because . . . the great bulk of the party insisted upon having me, feeling that I was absolutely necessary in this crucial contest for what I regard as the salvation of the Nation." In 1907, when he is voluntarily relinquishing his office, he writes Frederic Harrison, "I have certain peculiar advantages of position and temperament which would enable me to continue to render service to the people." Still later he feels that "in time of crisis the labor people would be apt to turn to me as being the one man they could trust," while, on the other hand, "the very big moneyed interests will always feel more afraid of me than of anyone else . . . simply because they know I can and will do just exactly what I say."

Much, perhaps most, of this is demonstrably and incontrovertibly just. There are times, however, when T.R. gives himself credit which belongs to others. "This decision I caused to be annulled by the court that rendered it" represents a gross oversimplification both of the shift in the Supreme Court's attitude, during his administration, concerning the relations between the government and business and of the nature of our government itself. He once gave himself credit for a treaty with Great Britain which had been virtually negotiated before he came into office.

There are other expressions of T.R.'s self-esteem which are more indirect than these and therefore more significant and revelatory. "Speaking with the frankness of an open nature," for example, and "If I possessed a mean and timid soul . . ." He refused to help Richard Watson Gilder gather data about his early years because "they were absolutely commonplace. . . . It was not until I was sixteen that I began to show prowess or even ordinary capacity."

He is afraid to get too prominently into the 1916 campaign because if he does he will make Hughes a tail on his kite.

Perhaps the most striking expression and exhibition of T.R.'s self came after he was shot at Milwaukee during the campaign of 1912. "As I stood up I coughed and at once put my hand to my lips to see if there was any blood. There was none, so that as the bullet was in the chest I felt the chances were twenty to one that it was not fatal." And so, instead of going to the hospital, he proceeded to the hall, where he exhibited his blood-soaked shirt and the manuscript of his speech with a bullet hole through it and delivered his address, but almost lost his temper with the selfish fools who crowded up on the stage to try to shake hands with a wounded man after he had finished. This was one of the great heroic adventures of Roosevelt's life. But it was also a performance, not a singer's performance or an actor's but a bullfighter's or an aerialist's, for this man was staking his life. In *Antony and Cleopatra* Shakespeare used the release of intoxication to show what the triumvirs looked like off guard. Fate used Roosevelt's wound for a similar purpose, and there was a frank naïveté about his exhibitionism on this occasion that I think he never matched elsewhere. But not only because it was heroic but even more because it was boyish and innocent, one is so touched by it that it seems cruel to consider it in this aspect.

For himself, Roosevelt told his audience, he did not care a rap. "I have had an A-1 time in life and I am having it now." It was "a very natural thing that weak and vicious minds should be inflamed to acts of violence by the kind of awful mendacity and abuse that have been heaped upon me for the last three months by the papers in the interests of not only Mr. Debs but of Mr. Wilson and Mr. Taft." (When Roosevelt was his own man, he would never, surely, admit that abuse could hurt that much!) "I am all right—I am a little sore. Anybody has a right to be sore with a bullet in him. You would find that if I was in battle now I would be leading my men just the same. Just the same way I am going to make this speech."

It must have been a night to remember, not only for Roosevelt but for everybody who heard him. Charles E. Merriam, who had come up from Chicago to address the overflow meeting, has left a vivid account of it. When he learned that Roosevelt had been shot, Merriam assumed that he was going to greet the audience and withdraw. When he became convinced that T.R. intended to give his speech he returned to his own meeting, talked for twenty or twenty-five minutes, and returned to the main hall. T.R. was still speaking. "His voice, however, was much feebler than normal. He was swaying from side to side as if he might at any moment collapse or fall. They had stationed a man in front of him, one in back of him, and one on each side to catch him in case he should fall." Probably T.R. was in no condition to think of the strain to which he was subjecting his audience. Yet he seems to have watched and pondered everything.

When I began to speak [he remembered months afterwards], my heart beat rapidly for some ten minutes, but aside from that about all the real trouble I had was that on account of my broken rib I had to breathe quick and short, so that I could not speak as loudly as usual, nor use as long sentences without breathing. When I got to the railway car I shaved and took out the studs and buttons from my bloody shirt and put them in a clean shirt, as I thought I might be stiff next morning. This all tired me a little, and when I lay down in my bunk my heart was again beating fast enough, and my breath was short enough, to make me feel somewhat uncomfortable. But after a while I found that I could turn, if I did it very carefully, to my unwounded side, and then I fell asleep.

XIV. Pride and Humility

Before T.R. is set down as arrogant or overweening on the basis of the considerations hitherto presented, there are many other considerations to be weighed. Though he was the dominating figure of his time, he quite consistently maintained that he was not a genius or a great man.

I am just an ordinary man [he told O. K. Davis], without any special ability in any direction. In most things I am just about the average; in some of them a little under, rather than over. I am only an ordinary walker. I can't run. I am not a good swimmer, although I am a strong one. I probably ride better than I do anything else, but I am certainly not a remarkably good rider. I am not a good shot. . . . I never could be a good boxer, although I like to box and do keep at it, whenever I can. My eyesight prevents me from ever being a good tennis playeɪ, even if otherwise I could qualify. . . .

. . . I am not a brilliant writer. I have written a great deal, but I always have to work and slave over everything I write. The things that I have done . . . are all, with the possible exception of the Panama Canal, just such things as any ordinary man could have done. There is nothing brilliant or outstanding in my record, except, perhaps, this one thing. . . .

To be sure, this is not all self-disparagement. As we have seen, Roosevelt was reasonably satisfied with his achievements; if he encompassed them with the powers of an ordinary man, so much the more credit to him! So much more, too, does he become an inspiration and an example to his fellows, and of this aspect he was never unmindful. He himself believed that the commonplace things are most important in life; he also believed that the powers of the ordinary man could be developed much more than they generally are.

There are two kinds of success [he says]. One is the very rare kind that comes to the man who has the power to do what no one else has the power to do. That is genius. I am not discussing what form that genius takes; whether it is the genius of the man who can write a poem that no one else can write, "The Ode on a Grecian Urn," for example, or "Helen, thy beauty is to me"; or of a man who can do one hundred yards in nine and three-fifths seconds. . . . Only a very limited amount of the success of life comes to persons possessing genius. The average man who is successful—the average statesman, the average public servant, the average soldier, who wins what we call success—is not a genius. He is a man who has merely the ordinary qualities that he shares with his fellows, but who has developed those ordinary qualities to a more than ordinary degree.

Obviously Roosevelt was not a genius as Keats and Poe were geniuses. Neither was he such a genius as Sir Isaac Newton or Alexander Hamilton. However, he had a much higher degree of competence over a much wider area than any of these men. "The genius that Roosevelt possessed," said George Bird Grinnell, "consisted in this, that he never stopped doing his best." T.R. himself conceded to Julian Street, "If I have anything at all resembling genius it is the gift for leadership," but I think he underestimates his extraordinary rapidity of comprehension and performance and his outstanding executive ability.

When he occupied a subordinate position Roosevelt knew how to behave like a subordinate; when he was in command he was always ready to give credit to those who cooperated with him. Wood had no trouble with him as a subordinate in Cuba; once, having thoughtlessly breached discipline, he voluntarily reported himself "the damndest ass within ten miles of this camp." He would have been willing to go to France in 1917 as a junior officer. Roosevelt may be naïve in openly giving himself credit for great tact and patience in the Russo-Japanese peace negotiations, but there is no question that the ascription is just, and he showed the patience of a saint in the trying coal strike negotiations, accepting even rudeness and insult from the operators with his eye on the single-minded objective of achieving industrial peace.

He is always willing to share his spotlight with others also, or for that matter give it up to them alone and himself retire to the wings. The Kaiser can have the credit in the Morocco crisis—he can even have the credit for settling the Russo-Japanese War if he wants it—and if the Czar would like to be posted as having called the Second Hague Conference, that is quite all right with Roosevelt; he is only a little amused that anybody should be concerned about such things.

T.R. knew more doubt about himself and his actions than the general public ever suspected. "It is an awfully difficult thing to know just what to do. I am sometimes at my wits' end, but I do want you to know that I am painfully endeavoring to do what is right, after looking over the whole field." But he has no way to be *sure* that he is right, and when the fleet has started around the world he is not sure even about that: it *might* do more harm than good. Edwin Arlington Robinson writes him about his personal problems, and he replies, "Your letter deeply touches me. There is not one among us in whom a devil does not dwell; at some time, on some point, that devil masters each of us."

Something has been said elsewhere of T.R.'s attitude toward protocol. When Prince Henry of Prussia visited Washington, Roosevelt told the German ambassador curtly that "no person living precedes the President of the United States in the White House."

Yet it took him a long time to get used to being served first at meals or to have ladies rise in his presence. He changed "Executive Mansion" to "The White House," and objected violently to being called "Your Excellency," partly because he had no right to the address and partly because he did not value something he had to share with a host of third-rate European flunkies. In Europe, on the other hand, he seemed perfectly indifferent to protocol; at the funeral of King Edward VII, he astonished the peppery French representative, jealous for the honor of republics, by his complete indifference to where he was placed.

There was one thing, however, of which there was never any doubt: T.R. would permit nobody to treat him disrespectfully. The man whom all the world called "Teddy" never heard that form of address from any man with whom he stood face to face. "No one of my family, for instance, has ever used it, and if it is used by anyone it is a sure sign he does not know me."

This dignity was not altogether derived from his high office, for it enveloped him even when his associates were rough cowboys in the West. Sometimes his sense of propriety was even fussy. He was not pleased when the papers announced that Kermit had "thrown" him, and as late as 1912 he thought it would be "a rather cheap thing" to appear in motion pictures with the Boy Scouts. He is also said to have objected to Rollo Ogden's "Letter to Theodore Roosevelt" in the March, 1905, *Atlantic;* when the publishers sustained the objection, the editor, Bliss Perry, promptly offered his resignation, which was not accepted.

But Roosevelt always kept a sense of proportion in his dignities and resentments, never allowing a sense of wounded *amour-propre* to bar his way to the attainment of a higher good. He even seems to have grown less sensitive as he grew older; in police commissioner days he was inclined to resent the sale of whistles representing his teeth, but by 1912 he could afford to be amused by a handbill circulated during the Republican convention which invited the public to assemble in Grant Park and see Colonel Roosevelt walk on the waters of Lake Michigan.

After his return from the Spanish War, he was very angry at Secretary of War Alger for refusing him a Medal of Honor, but when in 1907 the United States Medal of Honor Club offered him membership, he refused it "literally because the honor is too great for me. . . . I should be more proud than I can say to have earned it myself. As a matter of fact, I was recommended for it by my superior officers in the Santiago campaign, but I was not awarded it; and frankly, looking back at it now, I feel that the board which declined to award it took exactly the right position." His report on his South American discoveries is a very modest one, and it was in spite of his recommendation that the Rio da Dúvida was re-named Rio Roosevelt or Rio Teodoro. He knew the value of loyalty, too, whether it was loyalty to him or to another. Before the 1904 conventions, a Georgia Negro who owed his place to Senator Hanna was up for reappointment. It was reported to Roosevelt that he had said he admired T.R. and would support him for re-election against anybody but Hanna, but that if it came to a choice between Roosevelt and Hanna, Hanna must have his support.

I like Lyons [said the President], and had expected to reappoint him, but this settles the matter. A man who is loyal to his friends, and who will be so frank, when his own fortunes are in the balance, as to be unwilling to profit through any misunderstanding of his position, has the stuff in him of which good public servants are made. I wish you would say to Lyons for me that I shall lose no time in putting his reappointment beyond question.

XV. His Finest Hour

Roosevelt's real modesty is shown even more clearly in his need of appreciation and understanding. This is not, in the usual sense, a craving for popularity; it is rather a desire to be reassured as to his worth. Even his intolerance connects here; as Owen Wister says, "he hated so to have you not think as he did, if he cared for you." Popularity for its own sake he scorns. "I am not a college freshman, nor that would-be popular fox-hunting hero in Soapy Sponge." "I don't care a rap for 'popularity' as such," he writes Lady Delamere; "it is valuable as furnishing a man in public life an instrument for the accomplishment of something worth doing, but mere popularity as an end in and of itself has never seemed to me to amount to much." He is extravagantly praised in 1905 when he helps end the Russo-Japanese War, but he does not allow it to affect him much. "If I had not brought about peace I should have been laughed at and condemned." When he gets back from Africa he goes to the Scribner bookstore on Fifth Avenue and a great crowd gathers and cheers him wildly. "It is a kind of hysteria," he says. "They will soon be throwing rotten eggs at me."

The quiet appreciation and understanding of intelligent, discriminating people was something quite different, however. His classmates at Harvard remembered that even as an undergraduate T.R. would say that he wanted the esteem of his fellow men, and he did not get over wanting it when he was a world figure. "No man that I have known liked personal approval more than Roosevelt," wrote Lawrence Abbott.

When it was not forthcoming, he was hurt. "Why," he once asked Dr. Lambert wistfully, "why is it that I arouse so much animosity?" Sometimes it seemed to him that his enemies misrepresented him to such an extent that it must be virtually impossible for anybody to believe in him.

He was proud to give the Romanes Lecture because Gladstone, Huxley, Morley, and Bryce had given it before him. He was delighted when Merriam named a deer after him though he had just criticized him for his tendency to overmultiply species, and when Maurice Francis Egan praised him in a poem he valued all the kind things said "just as much as if they were true." He even loved places because they loved him. "Chicago looks at me through the perspective of space which is almost as satisfactory as looking through the perspective of time." There is also a charming reference to Michigan, which "for some reason which I do not understand . . . has always been particularly friendly to me."

When a man is under constant fire [he writes W. R. Nelson], and begins to feel, now and then, as if he did not have very many friends, and as if the forces against him were perfectly overwhelming, then, even though he is prepared to battle absolutely alone to the end, he is profoundly appreciative of the support of those whose support is best worth having.

He was touched, too, when the people of Berkeley, California, turned out in considerable numbers to hear his lectures on *Realizable Ideals*:

It had not occurred to me that people would come in numbers sufficient to fill every corner of the theatre. You have me both very grateful and a little embarrassed. You have made me feel more than a little humble; because each time I saw the audience I was afraid that they would go away feeling that they had not received just what they had a right to expect; because, friends, after all, the message I have to give to you is so very simple, and its worth depends so purely upon the spirit in which I give it and you take it.

Roosevelt's hunger for appreciation was such a marked element in his character that it sometimes became a source of weakness. Iglehart reports one occasion when a fusillade of fulsome compliments was showered upon him, ending with, "Your fame is secure for the centuries to come." Iglehart expected a witty answer. But T.R. simply replied, "It is lovely in you to say such nice things." It was Bishop's opinion, too, that because T.R. always tended to take people at their face value he was liable to be taken in by flatterers.

The need for reassurance shows again in T.R.'s incessant stock-taking. It is true that when Henry Fairfield Osborn remarked that the African detachment must have given him a chance to view himself and his career in clearer perspective, he raised his hands before his face "as if to shut out the inner vision." "I never want to look at or think about myself," he said. Nevertheless, he keeps himself perpetually on trial; he is never at ease in Zion. "There is not an action I have taken . . . and not a motive which has actuated me, which I would not be delighted to explain in full to you. . . ." He takes stock of his work as police commissioner, as secretary of the navy, as governor of New York. He evaluates his first year and a quarter in the White House, his first administration as a whole, his first five years, and his entire administration. He evaluates himself in various crises in foreign relations and in his conduct of foreign affairs in general. He may be off duty, but the inner monitor is still on guard, as when he greets visitors informally at Oyster Bay: "Well, boys! I don't look a little bit like the President of the United States, do I?" And even when he is frolicking with the children: "Of course I had not the heart to refuse; but really it seems, to put it mildly, rather odd for a stout, elderly President to be bouncing over hayricks in a wild effort to get to goal before an active midget of a competitor, aged nine years."

Having established this strain in Roosevelt's temperament, we are in a better position to understand how much he must have suffered during his later years from the feeling that his leadership had been repudiated and even, at times, that he had become a hated figure. T.R. felt that he was a back number by the time he left the presidency, and when Ray Stannard Baker suggested that he might be needed again later on, he rejected the idea on the ground that "revolutions don't go backwards." "Don't go," he said to Mark Sullivan in 1910. "The time will come when only a few friends like you will come out to see me here." Of course, if he had won in 1912, life would have started for him all over again. But he lost, and not only that but he found old friends passing him by with cold greetings. When he went to the Harvard Club in Boston only one man, General Hallowell, came up to speak to him. "By George! we were like a pair of Airedale pups in a convention of tomcats!"

I have about reached the conclusion that the feeling in this country is thoroughly hostile to me [he wrote J. C. O'Laughlin], and that my advocacy does damage to, instead of helping, a cause or an individual. I have nothing whatever to complain of in this. For a dozen years I held a great place in the confidence and good will of the American people and I was able to do many things which I most fervently believed ought to be done. . . . I believe that my usefulness in public life is about at an end.

During the war his unpopular opinions and his attitude toward the administration increased his feeling of isolation. By 1915 he does not think that his followers are more than five per cent of the American people, perhaps only one or two per cent. In February, 1916, he dares to believe that he has an appreciable minority with him once more, but in 1917 he is a nuisance, an elderly male Cassandra; his day is done; he belonged to the period of the Spanish War and the decade following. When Julian Street published his little book, *The Most Interesting American*, in 1916 (first serialized in *Collier's Weekly*), T.R. told Mark Sullivan, the editor of *Collier's*, "that this was the nicest thing that had ever happened to him, that it came at a time when he greatly needed it, and that he owed it to me. The words," Sullivan continues, "might have passed as a casual exaggeration of thanks, but something in his voice caused me to look closely at him. The emotion in his face was a measure, not of the service I had done, but of his own low spirits, his estimate of his place in the world. The incident was very touching."

It was not that Roosevelt was idle during his later years. There was a fortnight in 1913 during which he had to decline 171 invitations to banquets, rallies, etc., and one does not gather that this was in any way exceptional. In the spring of 1917 he was receiving between four and five thousand letters a week. It was only that what he did—which was all he had a chance to do—seemed to him utterly trifling.

I am busy writing [he tells Mrs. Kermit Roosevelt early in 1915]. I would have a very easy time were it not for the immense mass of fool things I have to do—for the most part merely answering idiotic letters where the character of the writer forces me to be moderately civil, or holding dreary interviews on utterly unimportant or preposterous subjects with people whom I can't very well refuse to see. Not a half of the work I actually do is to any good point; and yet I can't avoid the useless work.

Of course he is not complaining about it:

Most of the time we two old people pass out here alone, with walks in the winter woods, and books, and blazing log fires, and for me an occasional ride or afternoon's chopping; and we are very happy; I doubt if I have ever passed, not merely a more contented, but a happier, two and a half months. My dear, I hope you and Kermit may have the like privilege of growing old peacefully together, after having faced your life works without flinching.

He takes the same point of view when writing to Kermit: "From 1898 to 1910 everything went my way and I had a great career, and I have no complaint because, during the last five years, things have gone the other way." Nevertheless, you can see what it meant to him. When Grace Vanderbilt asked him whether she should put him or the mayor of New York at her right when both were her dinner guests, he voted for the mayor: "A live dog is better than a dead lion any day." Invalided in the Roosevelt Hospital, he invited the August Belmonts to come to see him. "I will make my time suit yours," he wrote, "because time is the only thing I have, and I have all there is of it."

In view of these considerations, Roosevelt's almost hysterical attempts to get to France, in spite of his conviction that he "would not last" there ("I am too old. I should crack") may have meant more than simply that he could not bear to stay out of the fight and not to contribute personally to the defeat of the enemy. May it not also have been that he did not want to come back? He had never been quite sane on the subject of death in battle. Here was his one opportunity to end his career on a note of glorious climax.

That climax was not to be. But there had already been a climax in South America, and that ordeal Roosevelt had come through like gold that has been thrice-refined. It was madness to go to South America, and it cost him his life, but what he accomplished there is a tale of painful and inspiring heroism which is not nearly so well known as it deserves to be.

For all his dominating personality, Roosevelt had always been an amazingly unselfish man toward those around him. All his anger was for impersonal things; in the business of everyday living there was no irritation in him. In the White House he would answer the telephone and humbly take messages for his children from their playmates; if a hunting companion dropped a glove, he would pick it up and restore it to him. In Cuba, in the West, and in Africa there was no question of his having any comfort that his companions lacked; he must always be the last, not the first, to be considered because he himself would have it so. He hated to be waited on, and when he was sick all his anxiety was for the trouble he was causing his nurses, whom he deluged with extravagant praise. It is an amazing thing that a man who lauded the military virtues as T.R. did should have come closer than one pacifist in a thousand to taking upon himself the role of Him who thought it no degradation to wash his disciples' feet.

The South American story has been told several times, best of all by Kermit in *The Happy Hunting Grounds.* The expedition was harassed by both illness and disaster. One man was drowned; another went berserk and killed a companion. At one time there was grave danger of Indian attack; for forty-seven days the travelers never met another human being. One third of their food was gone with only one sixth of the journey completed. They had no clothes except what they wore, which would be drenched daily by the heavy tropical rains and then steamed dry on their backs by the blazing sun which followed. If the day ended with shower instead of sun, they would lie wet all night.

Already weak after many days of fever, Roosevelt injured his bad leg by rushing into the water to save a pair of canoes from being smashed against the rocks. His wound became infected and failed to heal. He developed dysentery and "a veritable plague of deep abscesses."

When he was sickest he lay in the bottom of the boat in the blazing sun like a man upon a gridiron. Often George Cherrie said good night to him thinking he could not possibly live till morning, and greeted him again when the sun rose confident that he could not last through the day.

Once, fearing that his incapacity would slow down the able-bodied members of the party to such an extent that they must all perish for his sake, Roosevelt seriously considered putting an end to himself, thus forcing them to move on more rapidly without him. Reflection convinced him that, since Kermit would certainly insist upon bringing his body out, his death would only exacerbate their difficulties, not relieve them.

His son has preserved the record of one unforgettable night:

The fever was high and father was out of his head. Doctor Cajazeira, who was one of the three Brazilians with us, divided with me the watch during the night. The scene is vivid before me. The black rushing river with the great trees towering high above along the bank; the sodden earth under foot; for a few moments the stars would be shining, and then the sky would cloud over and the rain would fall in torrents, shutting out sky and trees and river. Father first began with poetry; over and over again he repeated, "In Xanadu did Kubla Khan a stately pleasure dome decree," then he started talking at random, but gradually he centered down to the question of supplies, which was, of course, occupying every one's mind. Part of the time he knew that I was there, and he would then ask me if I thought Cherrie had had enough to eat to keep going. Then he would forget my presence, and keep saying to himself: "I can't work now, so I don't need much food, but he and Cherrie have worked all day with the canoes, they must have part of mine." Then he would again realize my presence and question me as to just how much Cherrie had had. How good faithful Cajazeira waked I do not know, but when his watch was due I felt him tap me on the shoulder, and crawled into my soggy hammock to sleep the sleep of the dead.

When he got back to America, on the train from New York City to Oyster Bay, he was told that a number of his fellow townsmen were on board, having come down to the city to greet him. Almost too weak to stand, he dragged himself through the train and spoke to every one of them, ending in the baggage car, where he sank down upon a trunk and asked for a glass of water. When it was brought, he heard a little dog who was part of the baggage whine for it. He rose from his seat and carried the water over to where the dog was tied. There he drank half the contents of the glass and gave the little animal the rest.

XVI. "Prepare Me a Paper"

Elihu Root called Theodore Roosevelt "the most advisable man I ever knew," and John Hay spoke of the "amiability and open-mindedness" with which he accepted advice, contrary to "the general idea of his brusque and arbitrary character." "If he was convinced of your sincerity," said Albert J. Beveridge, "you could say anything to him you liked. You could even criticize him personally." And Senator Hale, a political opponent, said he could not imagine how the idea that Roosevelt acted impulsively, or without advice, ever got abroad.

E. A. Van Valkenburg says T.R. never delivered a speech without first submitting it to a group of his friends, "who often cut out long passages." He often kept a rough draft of an important message in his drawer long before the time came to send it in, so that he could get advice about it from those whose judgments he valued whenever he might see them. His Romanes Lecture was submitted in advance to Henry Fairfield Osborn, who, as he afterwards said, "blue-penciled the best part of it." In 1905 T.R. sent one of his speeches to Root, asking to have it back as soon as possible "after you have re-written it in the good old style that obtained when you were in the Cabinet." He once even submitted a speech on railroad matters to a brakeman!

"Prepare me a paper on the subject" was a frequent request. When Senator James E. Watson objected that a message to Congress lacked force, T.R. said, "You write one." Watson did, and T.R.

accepted it and sent it in with a few alterations. The famous Osawatomie speech was drafted by Gifford Pinchot, who had a hand, he tells us, in many speeches; there had already been a draft of this one by another hand, which T.R. rejected.

Of course Roosevelt took ideas from books also. The influence of Herbert Croly's *The Promise of American Life* upon the Progressive movement is well known. He was also influenced by George W. Alger's *Moral Overstrain* and James Bradley Thayer's *Legal Essays*. In 1910 he wrote Professor John W. Burgess, at Columbia, "Your teaching was one of the formative influences in my life. You impressed me more than you will ever know." When, in 1906, he read in *The Outlook* an article about overworked railway employees he at once brought it to the attention of the members of the Interstate Commerce Commission and asked them what legislation was needed.

It is an interesting sidelight on Roosevelt's undeserved reputation for rashness and impulsiveness in international affairs that he should have been unwilling even to make a personal contribution to the fund for the relief of Russian Jews in 1903 without first getting the advice of Hay, Root, and Cortelyou, who decided against it. When he joined the *Outlook* staff as contributing editor he offered to submit his first articles to Lyman Abbott for suggestions and corrections.

To be sure, he did not always take advice. Sometimes he would not even discuss it, as when he told Oscar Straus that he had made up his mind on the recall of judicial decisions and that therefore there was simply no use talking about it. These cases were the exceptions, however. Of course, he would not go against his convictions, but he was always ready to consider fresh evidence and to reconsider both views and actions in its light. "I have had to do with a number of Presidents," wrote William Howard Taft, "and with a good many chiefs, and I am well within the truth when I say that I never met a man who, upon proper presentation, would reverse himself as willingly and with as little trace of obstinacy or unreasonableness as Mr. Roosevelt." He respected people who stood by their convictions even when they disagreed with his, and he despised those who yielded to him simply because he occupied the advantageous position.

In 1908 T.R. read a message to a group of government officials for criticism. All were yes men except Justice Edward D. White, who told him that in some respects it was the worst state paper he had ever heard and, in response to his demand, particularized. Though the Whites thought they had ruined themselves with the President, T.R. grabbed Mrs. White's hands in a receiving line the very next time he encountered her: "Mrs. White, do you know your husband gave me the worst abuse the other evening that I have received since I've been President! And the worst of it was he was absolutely right, *absolutely right!*"

FOUR

The World of the Family

I. "The Happiest Home Life"

Probably Roosevelt is nowhere else quite so charming as in his family relations; it is no accident that his *Letters to His Children* should have been far and away his best-selling book. No more domestically inclined man ever lived, and this statement applies both to the home into which he was born and the home—or homes—which he established. His own considered statement is "I have had the happiest home life of any man I have ever known," and John Hay's fine sonnet to him called Heaven itself

A home not all unlike your home on earth.

"There is nothing in the world—" he tells Lee—"no possible success, military or political which is worth weighing in the balance for one moment against the happiness that comes to those fortunate enough to make a real love match—a match in which lover and sweetheart will never be lost in husband and wife."

Every reader of Roosevelt's *Autobiography* must remember his tribute to his father: "My father, Theodore Roosevelt, was the best man I ever knew." "I do not think there is a fellow in College," he writes home from Harvard, "who has a family that love him as much as you all do me, and I am *sure* that there is no one who has a Father who is also his best and most intimate friend, as you are mine." After his father's death we find such statements as "I never met any man who was like him, or who was his equal" and "I can conscientiously say that I have done nothing of which I do not think father would approve if he were alive." He began his work as president on his father's birthday. "I have realized it as I signed various papers all day long. . . . I feel as if my father's hand were on my shoulder, and as if there were a special blessing over the life I am to lead here." All the years of his mature life, a painting of his father looked down upon him in his study at Sagamore. His mother, too, he loved deeply, and all his life his letters to his sisters breathed the warmest and most intimate affection.

We know so little about Roosevelt's first wife, Alice Lee, that, in comparison with Edith Carow, there does not seem to be much to say about her. Gamaliel Bradford granted T.R. "profound human affections" but doubted that "the passion of being in love" ever took hold of him "as a devastating spiritual experience." But Bradford was wrong about this. Roosevelt himself speaks of four months of torture during his courtship of Alice Lee; night after night, he says, he did not even go to bed. At one period friends went so far as to fear for his sanity; he was lost one night in the woods; he even ordered a set of dueling pistols! "She is just the sweetest, prettiest, sunniest little darling that ever lived," he wrote after he had won her, "and with all her laughing, teasing ways, she is as loving and tender as she can be. I don't think that any man was ever so happy as I have been."

And then she married him, and bore him a daughter, and died. "Theodore is in a dazed, stunned state," wrote Cutler to Sewall. "He does not know what he does or says." And he himself thanks Andrew D. White for his letter of sympathy: "I shall come back to my work at once; there is now nothing left for me except to try to so live as not to dishonor the memory of those I loved who have gone before me." Alice Lee is not mentioned in Roosevelt's *Autobiography*, nor did he speak of her to her daughter, though, with a touch of morbidness rare in the Roosevelt ménage, she was taught to pray for "my mother who is in heaven."

For all that, Edith Carow was the love of his life. They knew each other as children, and when "Teedie" was in Europe with his family he was always homesick when he saw her picture or had a letter from her. Her love for him seems to have been lifelong, but he was deflected from her when Alice Lee swept across his path in Boston. Perhaps there had been a boy-and-girl quarrel. Someone said of President McKinley that he was in danger because he had a man of destiny behind him. One is tempted to feel the same way about Alice Lee. Roosevelt would not have been Roosevelt without Edith Carow. In intelligence and character she was her husband's equal; in tact and judgment she was his superior. And he knew it. She burned all his letters after he died, but we have abundant testimony to his feeling for her in the letters he wrote to others. "Mother is too cunning and pretty and darling for anything and looks so young." These are his favorite epithets for her, and he uses them again and again. "I do not think my eyes are blinded by affection when I say that she has combined to a degree I have never seen in any other woman the power of being the best of wives and mothers, the wisest manager of the household, and at the same time the ideal great lady and mistress of the White House." The longer he is away from her the more homesick he gets, and when she herself gets back after a journey she makes the house "feel like a home again, instead of like a temporary dwelling place." She had an operation shortly before the Barnes libel suit began. "I have been so absorbed in her," her husband wrote his sister, "that this libel suit has bothered me very little." "We now have lovely log fires in the evening," he writes Mrs. Kermit Roosevelt in the fall of 1915; "and we sit and read, and she looks so pretty and charming that now and then I have to get up and make love to her—which is rather absurd on the part of a gouty old man!"

He thought quite as highly of her in her nondomestic aspects. "She is better read, and her value of literary merit is better than mine. I have a tremendous admiration for her judgment. She is not only cultured but scholarly."

The New York *Times* once reported that T.R. lived in a man's house. So he did so far as the décor was concerned; probably every visitor to Sagamore Hill wonders how Mrs. Roosevelt managed to live with all those dead animals! But that man's house was ruled by a woman—and the man in it too. In domestic affairs her authority was absolute and unquestioned; T.R. never dreamed of making a decision about one of the children, for example, without consulting her.

She is not generally thought to have had much influence upon affairs of state, but this, I am convinced, is a mistake. For one thing, she sorted the President's mail and read the newspapers for him. James Amos says that T.R. always discussed important matters with her and that she frequently disagreed with him. "She was very much shrewder than the President in her judgment of men." She did not like Stimson, and Taft heard from Alice that she was once angry with Root for saying he was glad T.R. had hurt himself in what Root regarded as one of the insane junketings in Rock Creek Park. She is said to have suggested Garfield for the Cabinet, and Owen Wister reports her saying that if she had been consulted she would never have permitted T.R. to make his election night announcement in 1904 that he would not run again. T.R. himself told Stoddard that every time he had gone against her judgment he had paid for it.

She knew all his weaknesses as well as the bitterest of his enemies can have known them, but they made no difference whatever to her love. Mrs. Storer says that when she was planning to take the children from Washington to Oyster Bay, she said, "For Heaven's sake, don't put it into Theodore's head to go too; I should have another child to take care of." And T.R. himself says that his wife regards him as a "frail invalid needing constant attention" and also that she feels he is "just the biggest of her children." Once she absentmindedly kissed him good-by after having kissed the children, and added, "Now remember to be good while I'm away!"

When he talked wildly or indiscreetly, she could always stop him with "Theodore!" to which he would unfailingly reply, "Why, Ee-die, I was only going to say—" Even the children, it seems, took a hand in disciplining him, especially Ethel, being the only girl except Alice, who was often away from home and not much of a hand for discipline anyway. Mrs. Roosevelt loved to tease her husband and then pet him lovingly to make up for it. Once when he had made a remark about little Quentin which seemed to her uncalled for, she compared him to the father guinea pig who devoured his children! "She was perfectly delighted over the comparison and laughed and looked as pretty as possible over the vivid likeness between myself and the depraved father guinea pig in question." This kind of thing even seemed to have a therapeutic value for her:

Last night she had a headache and came down to dinner in a pink dressing gown, feeling very woebegone, but she quite waked up in her delight at my having misunderstood some story and then trying to find out about it by questions, which she said to Aunt Emily, with pitying glances, made her understand how Kermit inherited *his* habit of asking questions! This seemed to be the turning point in her evening and she brightened up and got over her headache, every now and then making a sudden little assault upon me, just as I have seen a bird ruffle up its feathers and give a sudden peck; then she would feel heart-smitten lest she had been too severe, and pet me to make up.

Once, on a public occasion, it is comforting to learn, she was wrong and he was right:

When the Sylph landed at Norfolk for the dinner we were met by General Grant to convoy us to the house. I was just finishing dressing and Mother went out into the cabin and sat down to receive him. In a minute or two I came out and began to hunt for my hat. Mother sat very sweet and pretty, looking at my efforts with a tolerance that gradually changed to impatience. Finally she arose to get her own cloak and then I found that she had been sitting gracefully but firmly on the hat itself—it was a crush hat and it had been flattened until it looked like a wrinkled pie. Mothr did not see what she had done so I speechlessly thrust the hat toward her; but still she did not understand and took it as an inexplicable jest of mine, merely saying "yes, dear," and with patient dignity turned and went out of the door with General Grant.

For Roosevelt as for Mark Twain part of the fun was to pretend that he lived under an intolerable domestic tyranny. Once, in cutting down some trees at Oyster Bay, he chopped down the telephone wires without even noticing what he had done. When Mrs. Roosevelt began to laugh at him, he tried to turn the tables by pointing out that she had not done her duty as forester by marking the trees he was to cut, "but I will . . . not hold you up to scorn before your children if you will let the subject drop once for all." Jusserand, who was present, reminded him that nobody except himself had said a word.

"Ah! But you don't know my wife. She has a language all her own. The telephone will never ring now that my wife will not begin to chuckle to herself, and if the cursed thing ever gets out of order . . . she will tell the servant to see if the wires are still up or if the trees are down. No, my dear Mr. Ambassador, people think I have a good-natured wife, but she has a humor which is more tyrannical than half the tempestuous women of Shakespeare."

Once, when she and Edward Bok exchanged glances while he was holding forth, T.R. exclaimed, "Now look at that—just look at that! There's that woman . . . and that Dutchman over there signaling to each other. I suppose that means 'Let him talk on; he's harming no one!' By Jove, I'm going to keep on talking." He seems really distressed, however, when he forgets an appointment with her and then recollects it too late to go: "She never says a word. I do all the talking when I explain. She just looks at me with that indulgent smile that she has. The most maddening instrument I know of, because it really says nothing and yet it is the most eloquent thing I have ever seen." More broadly, he tells Dr. Richards of Archie: "The dear boy gets all his good qualities from me, and all his bad qualities from his mother. You see his mother is of old New England stock, and the disapprobation of her Puritan ancestors is sometimes a part of Archie's make-up."

All this is good clean fun. What is dead earnest is the advice he sends Ted Jr. from Africa, shortly before his marriage:

Greatly though I loved Mother I was at times thoughtless and selfish, and if Mother had been a mere unhealthy Patient Griselda, I might have grown set in selfish and inconsiderate ways. Mother, always tender, gentle and considerate, and always loving, yet when necessary pointed out where I was thoughtless and therefore inconsiderate and selfish, instead of submitting to it. Had she not done this it would in the end have made her life very much harder, and mine very much less happy. It is the girl who has the hardest time in marriage; a man, even a good and loving man, is often thoughtless; and the wisest and most loving wife is she who will, with gentleness and tenderness, prevent his letting thoughtlessness "set" into selfishness.

The reason Mrs. Roosevelt's power was so effective was that she knew its limits and never transgressed them. Like her husband in politics, she had the good sense not to ask for something she knew she could not get. He did not consult her about going to the Spanish War, though she was very ill at the time, and he had been much afraid that the declaration of war would come before she began to mend. Archie Butt reports him as saying, "You know what my wife and children mean to me; and yet I made up my mind that I would not allow even a death to stand in my way; that it was my chance to cut my little notch on the stick that stands as a measuring rod in every family. I know now that I would have turned from my wife's deathbed to have answered that call." Possibly this has not been reported with verbal accuracy, but I feel reasonably sure that nothing could have kept Roosevelt home.

I do not know, either, whether Mrs. Roosevelt, in her heart, approved his going, but she did not try to hold him back, either then or later when he went to Africa, where no considerations of duty were involved. She knew that he was Theodore Roosevelt, not merely Edith Carow's husband, and that, whether he was right or wrong, he must be free to live a man's life. Very likely she would have loved him less if he had been built on a less painfully heroic scale, for there was a good deal of the Spartan in her too. But Kermit told Archie Butt that he thought his father's going to Africa had broken her heart, and she herself afterwards said that his departure was a dreadful day. "I have never known but one like it; that day when Archie's fate was in doubt and we did not know whether he would live or not." She also told G. H. Putnam that, though she did not doubt Theodore's ability to handle the lions, she was not so sure about the fevers. And Roosevelt himself speaks of her "Roman-matron-like attitude of heroically bidding me to my death when I sail in a well-equipped steamer for an entirely comfortable and mild little hunting trip." He missed her even more than he had thought he would, yet he tells his sister—and himself—that "I am sure I did the wise thing from every standpoint in doing just what I did." For all that, he thinks he will never leave her again. He does, of course, in the mad, heroic South American adventure whence he brought back his death, and he would have gone away again to France, at the very end, if Woodrow Wilson had not prevented it.

II. Christmas Every Day

Marriage—the kind of marriage Roosevelt believed in—means children (and ultimately grandchildren) as well as wife, and Roosevelt's relations with these persons are of absorbing interest also. He was charming to children in general, waved to them on the street, took off his hat to little girls, and made it an event when children were presented to him. In Europe royal children adored him and romped with him; in a small town in Kansas, on one of his trips, he opened his pew in church to ask some little girls to sit with him, because "I liked the little girls so much," and regretted that he had nothing but flowers to give them. He would never break an engagement with his own children or others, even when he had to drag himself away from official business to keep it.

Many persons are willing to give money to those from whom they can receive no return; few will give themselves; Roosevelt was one of these. Edward Bok made a permanently beautiful record [1] of T.R.'s kindness to his son Curtis after a serious illness. Champ Clark once visited him to tell him a fact to his political advantage, taking his young son with him. When the boy became interested in examining a great stuffed eagle in the President's room, T.R. deserted the father and his important concerns to devote himself to the boy, to whom he delivered a lecture on eagles and taxidermy. Another child, Cornelius Vanderbilt, Jr., was once invited to lunch alone with him in the Lincoln study at the White House. Vanderbilt could not remember what T.R. said but he never forgot "the passionate quality of his voice, the fiery pantomime of his odd, expressive face, and . . . [his] sad, whimsical smile." When T.R. came to breakfast at the home of Thomas A. Robbins, he ran upstairs with the little boy of the house and stretched himself out on the floor with his electric train, quite forgetting the company downstairs. And a woman still alive has remembered all her life the love in his voice as he came bounding up the stairs to see her where she lay carsick on the bed after the journey to Oyster Bay, and bending over her, cried, "Oh, you darling thing!" But the best story of all concerns not the children of his friends but a little Hungarian boy whom he found, one day, lost and weeping near Gramercy Park, and for whom he kept a whole table of important luncheon guests waiting for half an hour while he personally comforted the child and personally escorted him to the police station in Twenty-second Street, where he had a general alarm sent out for his parents.

If he would do such things for strangers, one can imagine what he would do for his own children. Actually there were no limits. No other children's parents known to her, says Mrs. Longworth, took so active a part in their play. He once refused an invitation from President McKinley in order to rush home and play with them. Outdoors the play could get pretty rough, or even dangerous sometimes, as when he let them down by ropes over the rocks in Rock Creek Park. And even indoors— "I play bear with the children almost every night, and some child is invariably fearfully damaged

[1] *The Americanization of Edward Bok,* Chapter XXV.

in the play; but this does not seem to affect the ardor of their enjoyment." Sometimes they wore him out, and sometimes he wore them out. Sometimes, of course, their demands were a burden, yet he grieves to lose their small-childishness and suffers a pang when they no longer need him to romp with them. "The other night before the Diplomatic dinner, having about fifteen minutes to spare, I went into the nursery, where the two small persons in pink tommies instantly raced for the bed and threw themselves on it with ecstatic conviction that a romp was going to begin. I did not have the heart to disappoint them, and the result was that my shirt got so mussed that I had to change it." Sometimes it was not a shirt that got mussed but childish serenity, to such an extent that the children could not sleep, and so, in the course of time, an edict went forth from the fount of authority that instead of romping in bed with his children, the President must play bear *before* dinner! It is interesting to note that, though he wanted the boys to be manly and the girls brave, T.R. had no silly ideas about hurrying them out of their childhood. They took rag dolls to bed with them as long as they cared to do so; at one time one of them slept with fourteen china animals! Even the boys kissed him good night after they were grown up.

With a father like Roosevelt it was, in a manner of speaking, Christmas every day, but Christmas and other holidays were, nonetheless, days of special ecstasy. "I wonder whether there ever can come in life a thrill of greater exaltation and rapture than that which comes to one between the ages of say six and fourteen, when the library door is thrown open and you walk in to see all the gifts, like a materialized fairy land, arrayed on your special table?" For several years he employed the Pain's Fireworks people to put on a forty-five minute fireworks show near his house on July 4.

But the children learned to give as well as take:

Today is Edith's birthday, and the children have been too cunning in celebrating it. Ethel had hemstitched a little handkerchief herself and she had taken her gift and the gifts of all the other children into her room and neatly wrapped them up in white paper and tied with ribbons. They were for the most part taken downstairs and put at her plate at breakfast time. Then at lunch in marched Kermit and Ethel with a cake, burning forty-two candles, and each candle with a piece of paper tied to it purporting to show the animal or inanimate object from which the candle came. All the dogs and horses—Renown, Bleistein, Yagenka, Algonquin, Sailor Boy, Brier, Hector, etc., as well as Tom Quartz, the cat, and the extraordinarily-named hens—such as Baron Speckle and Fierce, and finally even the boats and that pomegranate which Edith gave Kermit and which has always been known as Santiago, had each his or her or its tag on a special candle.

Once, too, there was a great affair at the Y.M.C.A.

Last night Mother and I went to the Young Men's Christian Association to see a circus, gotten up by the boys themselves. Quentin appeared in it as a small clown, being, I think, the youngest boy that did appear. He had charge of an elephant, which consisted of two other boys and was really very funny. The whole play was a great success and I would not have missed it for anything; and I am sure that the nice fathers and mothers, all of whom were there looking on, were glad to have the proud father and mother who happened to be in the White House present also. I thoroughly believe in the Y.M.C.A. institutions. Quentin was all painted up, with a mask and an Eddie Foy hat and the regular clown dress. He was much exhausted by excitement and triumph, and when I left for church this morning he was still sleeping the sleep of the just.

Discipline in the Roosevelt household was both Spartan and infinitely indulgent; cowardice and meanness were simply not tolerated, but no reasonable pleasures were interfered with. Archie Butt "never saw less restraint than at the President's table. Every child has something to say, and when one makes a remark it is certain to bring forth a volley of denials or contemptuous rebuttals from others. In fact, there was nothing studied or formal, and every member came in for a little fun before the dinner was over." "Father," writes Kermit, "had ever made it a practice to talk to us as if we were contemporaries. He would never order or even tell us to follow a certain line; instead, he discussed it with us, and let us draw our own conclusions." When the children were away he wrote to them in the same spirit, discussing even affairs of state, long before most people would have thought them capable of understanding such things. On Sunday church and Sunday School were a matter of course; there was no discussion about that. These things past, they were free to spend the rest of the day in accordance with their own ideas of fitness.

When they were small they made the White House such a playground as the oldest inhabitant of Washington had never seen nor the youngest imagined. Roosevelt believed in spontaneity in children's play, wanted it to express the child's own tastes and interests; the "child-mind" was an "academic synthesis" which held no interest for him. They rode bicycles and roller skates all over the house, brought the pony up in the elevator, and crawled between floors and ceilings. Once the President and Quentin made faces at each other in public, the boy in a streetcar, his father in a carriage. And once, when the pranks of this youngest boy and his "gang" were disturbing the clerks at their work, T.R. actually caused a message to be wigwagged to them from the War Department Building, ordering that their "attack on this building must immediately cease" and that they themselves "must report without delay to me for you know what"!

Animal stories from the White House years are legion. The most charming, perhaps, concerns an incident which occurred when the President was alone, but which he promptly reported in a letter to Ethel:

Today as I was marching to church, with Sloane some 25 yards behind, I suddenly saw two terriers racing to attack a kitten which was walking down the sidewalk. I bounced forward with my umbrella, and after some active work put to flight the dogs while Sloane captured the kitten, which was a friendly, helpless little thing, evidently too well accustomed to being taken care of to know how to shift for itself. I inquired of all the bystanders and of people on the neighboring porches to know if they knew who owned it; but as they all disclaimed with many grins any knowledge of it, I marched ahead with it in my arms for about half a block. Then I saw a nice colored woman and little colored girl looking out of the window of a small house with on the door a dressmaker's advertisement, and I turned and walked up the steps and asked if they did not want the kitten. They said they did, and the little girl welcomed it lovingly; so I felt I had gotten it a home and continued toward church.

T.R.'s range of toleration was probably somewhat wider than Mrs. Roosevelt's. He would cut the icing off his cake and give it to the children when she was looking the other way, and when she left the White House for a day or two, they always had the idea that "they could impose all their least desirable friends on pagan old father."

Last evening about nine we heard a noise in the nursery. I went in and there were the two little boys, in the firelight, sitting up in bed, chuckling and trying in turn to repeat poems to one another. I was received on terms of frank friendship, as a boon companion who happened to have strolled in, and in my turn repeated the concluding cantos of the Saga of King Olaf.

Once, when he was off on a picnic with his children and another little girl, they wanted to go in the water but had no bathing suits with them. Though some of the children at least had bathed naked at Oyster Bay when they were small, he seems not to have considered this a possible solution on this particular occasion. On the other hand, he did not like to refuse them. He solved his problem triumphantly by permitting them to go in *with their clothes!* "I wish you could have seen the more than Roman-matron-like austerity with which Edith and Laura received me when I headed the bedraggled procession back to them. The children were all given hot ginger and sent to bed on their return home, and on the part of both mothers there was evident a most sincere regret that it was not possible to give *me* hot ginger and send me to bed!"

For all that, there was a line that must never be crossed, or, as T.R. thought of it, you must bring your children up so that they would never want to cross it. Roosevelt loved but he did not coddle; he is as frank about the shortcomings of his children as he is about those of his political opponents; he was never one of those foolish lovers who embrace even vices when they appear in those they love. One evening he discovered that Quentin and his playmates had put spitballs on the portraits in the White House. He immediately dragged the boy out of bed and made him remove all the spitballs then and there; the next day the culprits were haled before him:

I explained to them that they had acted like boors; that it would have been a disgrace to have behaved so in any gentleman's house, but that it was a double disgrace in the house of the Nation; that Quentin could have no friends to see him, and the other three could not come inside the White House, until I felt that a sufficient time had elapsed to serve as a punishment. They were four very sheepish small boys when I got through with them!

James Amos was allowed to paddle the children when they needed it, and according to Ira Smith, the White House chief of mails, T.R. once looked on approvingly while a member of his staff gave Ethel a spanking. "If one of my boys was a bully," he says, "I'd try to thrash it out of him. If he would not defend himself against a bully, I'd thrash him until I had some degree of manhood in him. He'd require but one thrashing." And Mrs. Storer tells the delightful story of how when she opposed the boys' playing football because of the dangers involved, T.R. "glared" at her and answered "through his clenched teeth," "I would rather one of them should die than have them grow up weaklings." Which Ted and Kermit, having overheard, pondered solemnly, and appeared before him next day: "Father, we have consulted together as to which of us must die, and we have decided that it shall be the baby."

Yet (except in one area) he was never inclined to ask of anybody more than he could give. He accepted the twin facts that most men's best is not very good, and that even with perfectly sincere intentions most men are not capable of doing their best except intermittently. Ted's period of irresponsibility at Harvard angered him because it seemed so unnecessary. "If Archie, through sheer inability, failed in mathematics, I should be very sorry but I should not in the least hold it against him; but where Ted gets on probation because he has been such an utter goose as pointlessly to cut his recitations I am not only much irritated but I also become apprehensive as to how Ted will do in after life."

T.R. had his failures in discipline also. He is reported to have said that he could be president of the United States or he could look after Alice but that he could not do both. Once when he was asked whether he had really said this he laughed, and replied that if he had not said it, then he ought to have said it. Even with Alice he could assert himself, however; he could also be fussy. At the inauguration in 1905 she "stood in the front of the box and gesticulated exuberant greetings to the friends I recognized in the crowd until Father rather firmly told me to sit down." Since she was doing exactly what he was doing himself she could not quite see the justice of this. He also once telegraphed her to forbid her serving tea with Ethel Barrymore at five dollars a head for the benefit of the New York Orthopedic Hospital—"I cannot consent to such use of your name"—but fortunately the message arrived too late.[2]

If T.R. was anywhere cruel to his children, it was what might be called his "complex" on the subject of manliness that impelled him. Indeed, he even wanted girls to be manly. Mrs. Langdon Warner, who went out as a child with him and his children, afterwards reported:

He was always perfectly just and fair. He had no favorites and as few rules possible. On these walks we would race and wade and climb. We children, however, were expected, within reason, to protect ourselves. If there was a slip in climbing a tree because both hands were not used, home we went. . . . If we waded in a brook and fell, home we went again. In this way we learned how to take care of ourselves, and we never regarded the punishment which was the consequence of our clumsiness unfair.

Alice, too, was compelled to learn to dive whether she wanted to or not:

I can see Father treading water a few feet away from the float, upon the edge of which I crouched trembling, saying, "Dive, Alice; now, dive!" in a voice of increasing sternness. I would quaver, "Yes, Father!" and plop in after minutes of hesitation, terror of him finally overcoming my terror of the water. The family used to say that after a diving lesson my tears made a perceptible rise in the tide.

Ted, however, was pushed so hard intellectually that he came to "kind of a nervous breakdown," and his frightened father vowed, "Hereafter I shall never press Ted either in body or mind. The fact is that the little fellow, who is peculiarly dear to me, had bidden fair to be all the things I would like to have been and wasn't, and it has been a great temptation to push him." But his great triumph as a pedagogue was teaching Ted the letter "H." He decided to concentrate upon this letter at the outset, and he concentrated, apparently, with such ferocity that long after Ted had mastered all the

---

[2] On June 13, 1904, he had his secretary write to a certain count in care of the Austro-Hungarian embassy, expressing the President's desire that he cease sending mesages to Alice.

other letters, "H" was still an opaque mystery to him. "As I look back," wrote Mrs. Roosevelt, thirty years afterwards, "you fared worst, because Father tried to 'toughen' you, but happily was too busy to exert the same pressure on the others!"

It would seem, however, that the pressure must have been heaviest when it came to war and patriotism. Having preached intervention in 1898, he felt the obligation to go himself; having preached intervention in 1917, he felt it incumbent upon his sons to go, though he was sure that some or all of them might be wounded or even killed. "When I preach I do like to see my own family bearing out my preaching by their practice." And he writes to Kermit in the British Army, "You have an obligation to England, to America, to yourself, and to me." They seem to have agreed with him absolutely, though I often wonder what would have happened if one of them had turned out to be a conscientious objector! "It is dreadful to have those we love best go to the war; but it would be even worse if they did not go." Worse for whom? And at what point does the imposition of even our moral principles upon others become a violation of the integrity of their personalities, which is the essence of immorality?

T.R. had already met one minor test. Before the 1912 conventions, and of course before his father's bolt, Ted Jr. had expressed the idea that if the Democrats nominated Wilson he might support him against Taft. Roosevelt was quite reasonable about it—he had not, of course, yet developed his own later intense dislike for Wilson—and he conceded that "of course, that is your own affair," but he asked his son not to take any public stand which might lead to the impression that, though he was nominally supporting Taft, T.R. was actually against him. How much tenser he was in wartime may be inferred from Sonya Levien's report that when Archie took a few days off from his military duties for marriage and a honeymoon he worried about it. "I am afraid Archie has something of the slacker about him, to think of stopping for a honeymoon at this time!" She adds that shortly before Quentin's death, he mused, "My boys—I am afraid I shall never see them whole again. They are all doing this for my sake."

Coupled with his love for the boy, the most remarkable of all his children, it is no wonder, then, that Quentin's death nearly killed him. Mrs. Roosevelt herself told Lucius Swift that his keeping up the fight afterwards was a constant effort. He made an impressive appearance at a political convention immediately after receiving the news, and he dictated his letters to Josephine Stricker in a voice choked with emotion and with the tears rolling down his cheeks. But Bishop told Christian Reisner that he would break down if Quentin were mentioned to him, and once they found him weeping in the stable with his arms around the pony's neck. When he was asked to send a message to France he refused. "I have no message for France; I have already given her the best I had."

The only aspect of T.R.'s domestic affairs of which I have not spoken is his relations with his daughters-in-law and their children. I think not many girls can ever have received such a letter from a prospective father-in-law as Eleanor Alexander received from T.R. after he learned that she was to marry Ted. What a wealth of affection he poured out upon her, and he had not even met her! "Somehow, I always felt, right from the beginning, that Eleanor was one of those very very rare girls who are like Mother." Happily she never disappointed him, and when she came back from war service in France she stopped at the Roosevelt Hospital to see him before she even went home to her children. When she was carrying her first child, it was on his mind as ceaselessly as it can possibly have been upon her own, and when the baby came he called her "the dearest small soul you ever saw, and my heart is like water before her." Both the other girls and their children were welcomed in the same way, and so was Flora Whitney, to whom Quentin was engaged but whom he did not live to marry. "I wish I had a very big house and could make *all* my daughters in law live with me *all* the time!" It might have been hard on their children, since Ted Jr. complained that both his father's and his mother's sense of discipline went to pieces completely with their grandchildren, whom they allowed to do all sorts of things which their own children had never been permitted to do! One day Mrs. Roosevelt came out on the veranda at Sagamore and found that T.R. had taken Ethel's baby out of her coop. "Now, Theodore!" she cried. "Do you know what you've done? Now somebody will have to hold that baby the rest of the afternoon." "All right!" replied T.R. "I'll hold her!" And so he did, making her a third party of all his conferences.

FIVE

The World of Spiritual Values

I. Faith and Practice

William James did not particularly admire Theodore Roosevelt; he ought at least to have recognized him as a fellow pragmatist. Morison speaks rightly of his "operational approach to existence," and T.R. understood himself much better than he has been understood by any of those who have pictured him as a roaring lion going about seeking whom he might devour when he spoke of his "Greek horror of extremes." It was this element in him which caused him to see a man like La Follette as a fanatic, while La Follette regarded him as a temporizer; each was quite correct from his own point of view. Temperamentally T.R. took up an empiric attitude toward existence; he was always for the "best possible."

It has always been realized that Roosevelt had a good deal of the child in him; since the child and the woman lie very close together, it may seem surprising that his feminine element has been so generally ignored. Women are always the great empiricists, and it was not only in his empiricism that T.R. resembled them. Perhaps the manly, outdoor exterior has got in the way here, but there is no doubt that many of T.R.'s most important decisions were based on intuition, which is generally considered to be stronger in women than in men. Like a woman's, his world was highly personalized, and he always showed a tendency to judge people by their attitude toward him. Like a woman, again, he could sense the presence of hostility even when it had not been expressed, and sometimes he shied from people who had only good will toward him. What could be more feminine than what Charles Willis Thompson records his saying about an uncongenial newspaperman? "I felt creepy as soon as I saw him. I knew right away that he didn't have the Oyster Bay atmosphere and couldn't get it."

Above all, Roosevelt's pragmatism and empiricism show up in his religious life. He definitely considered himself a Christian. "As

181

a Christian statesman," so we read in one of the *Ladies' Home Journal* "President" articles, "he cannot take the Pagan view of marriage." But he thought of himself as a Christian man also. When John Willis, who initiated him into Western modes of roughing it, claimed to have made a man of him, he replied, "Yes, John made a man out of me, but I made a Christian out of John." He had a sense of fellowship with "good 'church people'" everywhere he went, just as he was repelled by dissipated people.

Yet it is hard to pin him down to a creed. Emlen Roosevelt says that as a young man on hunting trips he would lie about in the woods and talk about God and religion in a perfectly natural way. Arthur Lee, on the other hand, never heard him speak of such things, and he himself told John J. Leary that he thought a man's religion too private a thing to talk about. Professor Morison was impressed by the absence from his letters of "speculation on the larger questions of existence." Roosevelt frequently disclaims orthodoxy also, "although I try to avoid that species of intensely offensive spiritual pride which takes the form of sniggering conceit in being heterodox." When he met the Kaiser he was impressed by their harmony in fundamental moral and religious matters, but he could not share his Majesty's interest in dogmatic theology.

Roosevelt is more specific on what he does not believe than on what he does. "I am mighty weak on the Lutheran and Calvinistic doctrines of salvation by faith, myself, and though I have no patience with much of the Roman Catholic theory of church government, including the infallibility of the Pope, the confessional, and a celibate clergy, I do believe in the gospel of works as put down in the Epistle of James." Taft called him a Unitarian. Owen Wister declares that he once described himself as a Manichee, agreed with Wister that "one world at a time" was enough, and approved his quotation of Omar's

> O Thou, who Man of baser Earth didst make,
> And ev'n with Paradise devise the Snake:
> For all the Sin wherewith the Face of Man
> Is blacken'd—Man's forgiveness give—and take!

Of all the persons who came in close touch with Roosevelt, the one best qualified to judge him on his religious side was Lyman Abbott.

He was very slow to give expression to any religious experience [says Abbott]. . . . But there is no doubt in my own mind of his faith in God. But he would not define the term "God.". . . I do not know Mr. Roosevelt's doctrine of Christ. I can simply say that he demanded the concrete as I do and certainly personified God. He did not endeavor to explain the Godward side of Jesus but was attracted to and imitated the manward side of service.

Of the basic necessity of religion, and of the social values of religion, T.R. had never had the slightest doubts:

In the pioneer days of the West we found it an unfailing rule that after a community had existed for a certain length of time either a church was built or else the community began to go down-hill. In those old communities in the Eastern States which have gone backward, it is noticeable that the retrogression has been both marked by and accentuated by a rapid decline in church membership and work; the two facts being so interrelated that each stands to the other partly as a cause and partly as an effect.

He differentiated between good and bad religions and refused to accept a definition which made religion wholly "supra-natural" or unfounded in reason. Being what he was, he naturally preferred a religion of a somewhat extroverted type. "The religious man who is most useful is not he whose sole care is to save his own soul, but the man whose religion bids him strive to advance decency and clean living and to make the world a better place for his fellows to live in. . . ." He disliked sanctimoniousness as leading to hypocrisy and inspiring, by way of reaction, prejudice against all religion, and he mistrusted the type of religionist who confuses his own will with the will of God. His sense of reverence was outraged by a bishop who compared George Washington to one of the saints; he also thought it sacrilegious to carry the motto "In God We Trust" upon our coins, and was himself assailed as irreligious when he tried to take it off. He found the Book of Judges quite free of moral implications, and criticized the religion of the American frontiersman as "a creed that made much of the Old Testament, and laid slight stress on pity, truth, or mercy." He also objected to Mormonism as an Old Testament religion. There is a curious passage in his Fifth Annual Message to Congress, however, which might be said to imply not so much an Old Testament conception of God as a pagan conception:

The people of this country continue to enjoy great prosperity. Undoubtedly there will be ebb and flow in such prosperity, and this ebb and flow will be felt more or less by all members of the community, both by the deserving and the undeserving. Against the wrath of the Lord the wisdom of man cannot avail.

He observed all the conventional religious exercises and taught them to his children. He joined the church, by his own desire, when he was sixteen, attended faithfully and enthusiastically, and always partook of the sacrament. Because there was no Dutch Reformed congregation near his home in New York, he attended the Madison Square Presbyterian Church in his youth. At Oyster Bay the entire family attended Mrs. Roosevelt's church, the Episcopalian; in Washington, the President went to a little Reformed church alone. In New York he taught a mission Sunday-School class as early as 1876; for three-and-a-half years, at Harvard, he taught at Christ Church, only to be dismissed at last because he was not an Episcopalian. He afterwards felt that he had taught Sunday School in imitation of his father and that such work was not for him, but since he himself says that he had the only class at Christ Church where attendance was at all regular, this opinion would not seem to have been shared. On Sabbath-keeping he was not rigid in theory, but he himself never hunted nor played games on Sunday, and never transacted business on Sunday when it could be avoided, as he did not like to offend other people's religious sensibilities.

I have known a village baseball nine, which, because after church on Sunday afternoons it held games in a field a mile away, was a potent help in keeping young men out of the "blind-pig" saloons. It is only very backward church organizations that now object to music. But many good people still put dancing under a ban. I believe that dancing, like all other healthy and proper pastimes, should be encouraged in the parish-house; and this because I dread the professional dance-hall, where liquor can be obtained and where foolish girls go with foolish or vicious young men, while there are no older men or women to look after them.

T.R. was also a Mason, though he never went beyond the third degree.

When as a public figure Roosevelt found it necessary to comment on religious matters he always spoke as an insider. This is particularly clear in his comments on various aspects of the missionary movement, though even here his emphasis is this-worldly. "Our Christian missions have for their object not only the saving of souls, but the imparting of a life that makes possible the kingdom of God on the earth." He was once concerned over a decline in the number of young men going into the ministry; he recognized the danger of permitting workingmen to drift away from the church; and he was much interested in the functioning of the chaplains in the Army.

He read and recommended such religious books as *From Epicurus to Christ*, by William DeWitt Hyde; Father John A. Zahm's *Evolution and Dogma;* and *The Old Testament in the Light of Today*, by William Frederic Badè. Opposing both materialism and mediaevalism, he championed the scientist's right to freedom of investigation, but recognized that science cannot explain everything and that there are superstitions in science as well as in religion. In his view, the evolutionary hypothesis no more made it necessary to abandon the religious attitude toward life than did the Copernican astronomy. "The tracing of an unbroken line of descent from the protozoan to Plato does not in any way really explain Plato's consciousness." You can prove that our wills are not free; you can also prove that motion does not exist. "The chief point to me about William James," he wrote Edith Wharton, "was that although a master of physical science he declined to take the position that most of his fellows took, namely, that physical science can explain everything."

Roosevelt always set his face steadfastly against discrimination for or against any American on account of his religious creed. When he spoke at the American Mission at Khartoum in 1910, he declared, "I wish I could make every member of a Christian church feel that just in so far as he spends his time in quarrelling with other Christians of other churches he is helping to discredit Christianity in the eyes of the world. Avoid as you would the plague those who seek to embroil you in conflict, one Christian sect with another." Specifically he felt that the Christianizing of Japan had been held back by divisions among Christians.

He himself had trouble with some of the marginal groups, however. His attitude toward Quakers will be considered when we consider his attitude toward war and peace. In the early days he was bitterly opposed to the Mormons, but he changed his mind about them when they abandoned polygamy. In a campaign speech of 1896 he injudiciously placed those who believed in free silver in the same class with those who believe "in spirit rapping, or the faith-cure, or Buddhism, or pilgrimages to Lourdes, or the foot of a graveyard rabbit." In this same connection there is an amusing sentence in a letter to Benjamin Ide Wheeler about Mexican affairs: "I had already known that Madero was too soft fibred to hold on. He is, among other things, a convinced spiritualist." There is a 1906 letter to Ethel, however, in which he is much more sympathetic toward what we now call extrasensory perception. "I am not in the least surprised about mental telepathy; there is much in it and in kindred things which are real and which at present we do not understand. The only trouble is that it usually gets mixed up with all kinds of fakes." He himself carried all through Africa a religious medal which had been given to him by a Dominican nun.

Roosevelt made a special point of having both Catholics and Jews in his Cabinet, and he looked forward confidently to the Catholic and Jewish presidents he was sure the United States would have in time to come. One of the most delightful of all Roosevelt stories is the tale of what he did as police commissioner when a German anti-Semitic fanatic appeared in New York.

A great many of the Jews became alarmed and incensed about his speaking here, and called upon me to prevent it. Of course I told them I could not—that the right of free speech must be maintained, and that unless he incited to riot, he would be allowed to speak against the Jews, just as we should let Jews speak against Christians. On thinking it over, however, it occurred to me that there was one way in which I could undo much of the mischief he was trying to do, and I directed that so far as possible the policemen detailed to protect him at his meetings should themselves be Jews. This was done, and Herr Ahlwardt delivered his violent harangues against the men of Hebrew faith, owing his safety to the fact that he was scrupulously protected by men of the very race which he was denouncing.

T.R. did not believe that Protestants were essentially more tolerant than Catholics, yet he thought the Protestant movement had
prepared the way for toleration, and he thought that American
Catholics and American Protestants were much closer to each other
than either group to their spiritual ancestors. He refused to "idolize
or idealize" such leaders of the past as Luther and Calvin, but he
also insisted on giving them their due for what they had accomplished for mankind. He praised Cromwell for making an effort to
achieve religious toleration but blamed him because his ideal of
toleration stopped short this side of the Catholic Church.

In 1892, with the French Canadians swarming into New England,
Roosevelt foresaw French-Catholic dominance in some quarters.
He was not exuberant about this, though he fully believed that the
future would set things "right" again. He did not, I think, foresee
the future power of the Catholic Church in America because he did
not foresee the extent to which she would succeed in Americanizing
herself. As late as 1909 he told Archie Butt that the Roman Church
was too Latin, too out of line with our dominant tradition to flourish
greatly save through immigration. That Americanization would
nevertheless have greatly pleased him. He admired Cardinal Gibbons and Archbishop Ireland because he thought they were doing
their utmost to bring it about, and he disliked Cardinal O'Connell
because he thought he was not. Nevertheless, he consistently rejected
the arguments of those who argued that the presence of such eccle-
siastics as Cardinal O'Connell made it impossible for non-Catholics
to work with the Church:

To meet intolerance and bigotry by equal intolerance and bigotry is
simply to follow the deplorable example of the French, who have
finally produced a brand of anti-religious bigotry quite as noxious as ever
was any religious bigotry, and who pin their faith to statesmen and
scientists whose hard, intolerant, dogmatic materialism is as repulsive
as any theological intolerance could possibly be.

In 1912 he was told that the Catholic hierarchy was opposing the
Bull Moose movement. "From information that has come to me," he
replied, "I think that this is very possibly true, but whether it is or
is not my course will not be altered thereby. I will not do injustice to
any Catholic merely because certain Catholics may do or have done
injustice to me."

In his Assembly days, T.R. found many "tough citizens" among the Catholic members of the legislature, but there were others who were among his stanchest friends and allies. As police commissioner he was reproached for keeping "a lot of 'drunken Roman Catholics' on the force." He replied, "As far as I can, I will turn them out because they are drunkards, not because they are Roman Catholics; and at the same time I will turn out the drunken Protestants." Once when he was hesitating between two evenly qualified appointees to a public office, one a Protestant and the other a Catholic, he was advised that he must appoint the Protestant, since the town was controlled by an organization which would resent a Catholic holding such a position. That settled it, and he promptly appointed the Catholic. He took a Catholic priest, Father Zahm, with him to South America, and he may have been influenced in the "race suicide" matter by Father Doyle, the distinguished temperance reformer and editor of *The Catholic World.* He visited Catholic missions in Africa, stood sponsor to a Catholic child in Santa Fe, and took a "particular interest" in seeing "a strong Catholic element" developed at Harvard. It was he who persuaded the father and brother of John LaFarge, later editor of *America,* to permit the boy to study for the priesthood; God, he said, had sent him "certain lights and certain graces" which must not be ignored. At the end of his life, the outrages suffered by priests and nuns in Mexico was one item in T.R.'s indictment of Wilson's Mexican policy. Only, I think, in criticizing Pope Benedict XV for not taking a pro-Ally stand during World War I was Roosevelt unfair to the Church.

In the Philippines both Roosevelt and Taft were very careful not to offend Catholic susceptibilities and, more importantly, not to treat Catholics unjustly. "I am very strongly of the opinion that the uplifting of the people in these tropic islands must come chiefly through making them better Catholics and better citizens." He showed admirable patience, and kept his patience admirably under fire from both Catholic and Protestant extremists, in getting the problems raised by the disposal of the friars' lands settled amicably, and, on the part of the United States, generously.

Roosevelt was never unmindful of the political importance of religious prejudices in the United States, and he balanced religious groups against each other as he balanced, say, capital and labor.

But he balanced them, as he understood it, for the good of the whole, and there is no evidence that he ever sacrificed principle to expediency. In 1906 he was hopeful of winning a portion of the Catholic vote in New York, hitherto largely Democratic, for Hughes, whom he urged not to address any Protestant group unless he addressed a Catholic group at about the same time. In the campaign of 1908 he was anxious to have Debs's attack on Taft circulated in Catholic papers so as to make Catholics aware that their enemies were abusing Taft for his fairness toward the Church in the Philippines.

The unfortunate Vatican incident of 1910 did not, of course, involve any religious prejudice on Roosevelt's part; on the contrary, it developed out of his refusal to subscribe to such prejudice. Nor was St. Pope Pius X personally involved in it, for the initiative seems to have been taken by the ultramontane Spanish Cardinal Merry del Val. The papal nuncio at Vienna appeared afterwards in his official ecclesiastical aspect at a reception honoring T.R. in that city.

The contretemps would never have occurred except for the presence in Rome of a Protestant bigot with the delightfully Dickensian name of Ezra Tipple, whose notion of conducting a Protestant mission was to blast the Pope publicly as "the Whore of Babylon." There had already been an "incident" in connection with Vice-President Fairbanks's visit, and when Roosevelt applied for an audience he was told that he could be received only on condition that he was not planning to visit the Methodists, to which he replied that he could accept no conditions which would in any way limit his freedom of action but that he still hoped to have the privilege of being received by His Holiness. (He was to take up a similar position in England when it was suggested to him that he should not see the advocates of Irish home rule.) The condition was not accepted, and Roosevelt was not presented. Meanwhile, the Tipple group having violated the conditions under which he had arranged to meet the Methodists, he himself canceled this engagement. In later years Roosevelt thought that American Catholics had punished him for his failure to meet the Pope, but he never believed that he could have done other than as he did; neither did he in any way change his attitude toward the Church.

Yet there was one time in his life when Roosevelt did stand face to face with the Holy Father. This was in 1869, when, as a boy of eleven, he was in Rome with his family. Corinne Roosevelt Robinson tells the story beautifully, and it testifies eloquently to the reverence in the child's soul, which never died out of the man's:

Word passed that the Pope was coming. "Teedie" whispered to the little group of American children that he didn't believe in popes—that no real American would; and we all felt it was due to the stars and stripes that we should share his attitude of distant disapproval. But then, as is often the case, the miracle happened, for the crowd parted, and to our excited, childish eyes something very much like a scene in a story-book took place. The Pope, who was in his sedan-chair carried by bearers in beautiful costumes, his benign face framed in white hair and the close cap which he wore, caught sight of the group of eager little children craning their necks to see him pass; and he smiled and put out one fragile, delicate hand toward us, and lo! the late scoffer who, in spite of the ardent Americanism that burned in his eleven-year-old soul, had as much reverence as militant patriotism in his nature, fell upon his knees and kissed the delicate hand, which for a brief moment was laid upon his fair curling hair. Whenever I think of Rome this memory comes back to me, and in a way it was so true to the character of my brother.

II. The Hope and Menace of the Future

Christianity is neither a pessimistic nor an optimistic religion as those terms are generally understood, but it influences very importantly the courage or the lack of it with which its devotees face life. If I were required to call Roosevelt either optimist or pessimist, I should call him an optimist. But neither label could be pasted on without a number of important qualifications.

He made a religion of duty; he also made something of a religion of enjoying himself. At eighteen he says that he "literally never spent an unhappy day, unless by my own fault!" No other boy ever had such a good time in college; no president ever enjoyed the White House more, and no ex-president ever enjoyed himself more either! "I don't see how any man could have had a happier life than I have had during my fifty years, and certainly I don't know of any President who has had as happy a time, or who went out of office as pleased and interested as I now feel."

But he was never unmindful of problems and dangers. This

might be a pretty good world; it might be getting better than it used to be; it might even be that "at no period of the world's history has there been so much happiness generally diffused among mankind as now." For all that, it was not good enough. The comfortable nineteenth-century idea of automatic progress he repudiated altogether. "It is a rather irritating delusion . . . that somehow or other we are all necessarily going to move forward in the long run no matter what the temporary checks may be." But that does not mean that you are going to blow out the gas to see how dark it is. He did not like Henry Adams's novel, *Democracy:* "It had a superficial and rotten cleverness, but it was essentially false, essentially mean and base, and it is amusing to read it now [1905] and see how completely events have given it the lie." He liked *The Degradation of the Democratic Dogma* even less and wondered whether the author's mind was unhinged! "You are a great historian," he told Guglielmo Ferrero, "but you are too skeptical and pessimistic." In the last analysis, he even manages to suck comfort out of our ignorance of the future, which is so great that "the prophets of dire evil are generally as much mistaken as the prophets of the Millennium." Actually we did not know enough about the future to be sure how great any given danger might be. "The things we dread do not occur, and evils which no human being had foreseen or could have foreseen loom portentous."

Of course, it was easier for Roosevelt to keep gnawing doubts at bay during the years of his power than it afterwards became. Whatever the future might hold, he himself was doing his utmost to make things come out right; his family life was serenely and triumphantly happy; what more did he need to know? "He hadn't," so H. G. Wells reported it in 1906, "an effectual disproof of any pessimistic interpretation of the future. If one chose to say America must presently lose the impetus of her ascent, that she and all mankind must culminate and pass, he could not conclusively deny that possibility. Only he chose to live as if it were not so." He spoke of *The Time Machine* and became gesticulatory about it. "Suppose, after all, that should prove to be right. . . . *That doesn't matter now.* The effort's real. It's worth going on with. . . . It's worth it— even then."

The time came, however, when he was no longer the leader, when the control of affairs was in the hands of those whom, rightly or wrongly, he believed to be doing everything ignobly. He had expected "a certain greyness in the afternoon of life," but this was something much worse than that. It had nothing to do with what people thought about him personally; it was a question of their response to a simple issue of right and wrong. He tried to comfort himself by remembering that such things go in cycles; a people cannot always capture the heroic mood. But by 1916 he is pretty well convinced that the American people themselves are as bad as Wilson, and the intellectuals worst of all, that the Republicans are very little better than the Democrats, and the English "woodenheaded fools" because they have let Wilson take them in.

Even then he does not despair. "The mass of the people are all right," even when what they support is all wrong. At bottom most men are honest and religious, and most women are virtuous. "I hold that the average American is a decent, self-respecting man, with large capacities for good service to himself, his country and the world if a right appeal can be made to him and a right response evoked." The United States is so big that it takes a long time for the people to find anything out. "But once they do find it out, they act right because their emotions are right."

For all that, there was a melancholy side to T.R.'s soul, and it reveals itself even in what seem superficially to be expressions of the opposite character. It shows in his furious energy, his determination to cram his days more full than they can hold, as if life would otherwise be intolerable. "You see things too darkly," wrote Henry Cabot Lodge in 1903, adding that "everybody thinks you are one of the most sanguine of men, *I* . . . know better." James Bryce once remarked that Roosevelt "wouldn't always look at a thing." Lewis Einstein thought that his "buoyant exuberance and the confidence which impressed people were only veils hiding the doubt, the depression often gnawing his soul." And Owen Wister speaks impressively of "the wistfulness [which] blurred his eyes—the misty perplexity and pain, which Sargent has caught so well. This look was the sign of frequent conflict between what he knew, and his wish not to know it, his determination to grasp his optimism tight, lest it escape him in the many darknesses that rose around him all along his way."

This leads us to the one aspect of Roosevelt's religion which seems to me more Stoic than Christian; I mean his attitude toward death. "Death is always and under all circumstances a tragedy, for if it is not, then it means that life itself has become one." But it is not the worst of evils, for the failure to live worthily is that. When Henry J. Stimson's father died in 1917, he wrote his consolation,

and yet my dear fellow, your father, like myself, had come to the age when one is within range of the rifle pits; and when we have reached that age, death is not a thing which should excite deep feeling of regret or sorrow for the man himself. . . . I hope my own sons would miss me; but I certainly don't want them to miss me too much.

Roosevelt would surely have agreed with Henry van Dyke that

You never can begin to live
Until you dare to die,

though he never talked much of death, James Amos says, until the last year of his life. He had always faced it unflinchingly, for all that. We have already seen that he was ready to embrace it in South America if it meant deliverance for the other members of his party. He once told O. K. Davis that he had always taken a bottle of morphine with him on such expeditions. "I always meant that, if at any time death became inevitable, I would have it over with at once, without going through a long-drawn-out agony from which death was the only relief."

In Roosevelt's letters of consolation there is little that is distinctively Christian. "May the unseen and unknown powers be with you always" to Nicholas Murray Butler in 1903 is about as close as he comes. It is true that after his father's death, in 1878, he thinks he has only "gone before." "I can feel his presence sometimes when I am sitting alone in the evening." But this is early and not very characteristic. Nor is he very serious when he writes Endicott Peabody, "I do hope that the future life will offer the chance to talk with one's friends. The present life does not." His usual note is the one he strikes when his sister loses her son, "It is dreadful to have the young, whom we love in our innermost hearts, die. There is nothing in the world to say that will be of comfort." When John Muir's wife goes, he suggests neither God nor mankind but nature.

Again and again, T.R. speaks of death as "blackness," "darkness." "We have got but one life here, and what comes after it we cannot with certainty tell." "I have no desire before my time has come to go out into the everlasting darkness." "We must face our fate and go down into the darkness."

In the light of these utterances, I should not say that Theodore Roosevelt disbelieved in immortality, but I see no evidence that the hope of it was a living and comforting force in his life.

III. Mysticism

One other question has been raised about T.R.'s religion.

The harshest thing Gamaliel Bradford had to say about Roosevelt in his incisive portrait of him (and it should be remembered that Bradford admired T.R. very much) was on this very matter.

Whole books have been written about Roosevelt's religion. To me they simply prove that he did not have any. He had a profound sense of conduct in this world, of morals. . . . Now to me religion is the love of God, the need of God, the longing for God, and the constant sense of another world than this. I cannot find God insistent or palpable anywhere in the writings or the life of Theodore Roosevelt. He had no need of him and no longing, because he really had no need of anything but his own immensely sufficient self. And the abundant, crowding, magnificent presence of this world left no room for another.

What Bradford is saying essentially is that Roosevelt was not a mystic. Mysticism is an important element in religion, but it is not the only element, and when you pay it more than its due, or attempt to equate it with religion itself, you run into no less serious difficulties than when you do the same thing with dogma or with ritual. If all persons who lack a developed mystical awareness are to be denied religion, some of the most famous Christians in history are going to be left out.

Roosevelt's religious experience evidently had its limitations; whether he deserves, therefore, to have it said of him that he had no religion may best be left to the readers of the foregoing pages to determine. But was Bradford right even about the mystical element? There was much less emphasis upon the mystical approach to religion during Roosevelt's formative years than there is today. Nevertheless, I do not believe that this capacity was lacking in him, though no doubt both its development and its expression were in-hibited by his ever-present practical emphasis. It crops out in his nature writing and in his sensitiveness to great pictures and great poetry. Look at William Samuel Johnson's poem, "Prayer for Peace," which he quotes at the beginning of *America and the World War*. It is considerably more metaphysical in tone than anything most persons would expect from T. R. The ruins and cliffs in the Navajo desert looked to him like something vaster than the works of man,

as if some magic city, built by warlocks and sorcerers, had been wrecked by the wrath of the older gods. Evil dwelt in the silent places; from battlement to lonely battlement fiends' voices might have raved; in the utter desolation of each empty valley the squat blind tower might have stood, and giants lolled at length to see the death of a soul at bay.

And if this be dismissed as too romantic or too "Gothick," there will still be the lovely passage on Saint-Gaudens, which has already been quoted in another connection:

In the figure on the Adams grave, and in the figure called "Silence" there was nothing to hamper the play of the artist's thought, and he produced two striking creations of pure imagination. The strange, shrouded, sitting woman, the draped woman who stands, impress the beholder with thoughts he cannot fathom, with the weird awe of un-earthly things; of that horizon ever surrounding mankind, where the shadowy and the unreal veil from view whatever there is beyond, whether of splendor or of gloom.

SIX

The World of Public Affairs

I. Following His Star

In spite of his many other interests and activities, Theodore
Roosevelt was primarily a political leader and administrator. It was
here that his activities found their most important theater, and it
was here that all his most striking qualities were outstandingly
manifested.

He never made any bones about the fact that he liked being
president. He cared nothing about place or position; what he did
enjoy was power and the sense of leadership. He went into politics,
he said, because he wanted to belong to the governing class, and he
valued power because it enabled him to do the things that needed
to be done. One of his most cogent criticisms of Wilson is that he
followed public opinion instead of leading it. It was not so with
Roosevelt. "I did not divine how the people were going to think; I
simply made up my mind what they ought to think." In 1904 he
passionately desired to be elected because it hurt his pride to think
that till now he had been president by accident.

One would suppose that political ambition must have seized upon
him early in life, but there is remarkably little evidence of this. To
be sure, we have George Haven Putnam's statement "that from
the very beginning of his political work he kept before him the
idea of becoming President," and Booker T. Washington's statement
that T.R. told him he would like to be president long before his
name was mentioned as that of a candidate, but all this is pretty
vague. One or two friends in the West paid him the compliment of
suggesting that he might be president someday; it has even been
suggested that he may have gone west in the hope of rising to
political power there. This is pure conjecture, though there is an
amusing letter from Medora, in May, 1885, which states, "I do not
expect to return to politics for many years, if at all," and then adds,

196

"When does the State Convention take place? . . . I suppose I shall go." The presidency was in Lodge's mind for him in 1899, but the prospective candidate writes his sister that Cabot is a "dear old goose" who will only succeed in making him ridiculous. "I am not looking beyond the Governorship," he tells one correspondent. And again: "There is no more chance of my being made President than of my being made Czar of Russia."

Lincoln Steffens has an interesting and characteristically highly colored story about his having asked T.R. in police commissioner days whether he was working for the presidency. According to Steffens, Roosevelt made a scene, bitterly upbraiding him for putting such ideas into his head and declaring that no friend would do such a thing. But the reason he gave was not that he was not interested—"I must be wanting to be president. Every young man does"—but that if he allowed himself to entertain such notions it would interfere with his doing his very best at the job in hand and therefore defeat him.

Whether this incident occurred or not, the line of procedure indicated is quite in harmony with Roosevelt's practice. He sounds almost too good to be true when he writes Franklin K. Lane in 1911, "I am always credited with far more political sagacity than I possess; really, I act purely on public grounds and then that proves often to be good policy too." Whatever else T.R. may have lacked, it was not political sagacity. But it is equally clear that he often chose to disregard considerations of what most people considered political sagacity for the sake of higher considerations. The Civil Service commissioner determined that come what might he would enforce the law. "I am perfectly willing to be turned out—or legislated out—but while in I mean business." It was the same way as police commissioner with Sunday closing. "There is no use in looking ahead," writes the governor of New York, "as regards one's personal interests, though there is every use in shaping one's career so as to conduct it along firmly settled great principles and policies."

Essentially he behaved the same way in the White House, often repelling, alienating, repudiating influential individuals and groups. He did it deliberately, for he had made up his mind that, however much he wanted to be president, he wanted even more to be his own man. Even Pringle, who certainly cannot be called a Roosevelt idolater, can find no sign even in his most private letters "that he was thinking of political preferment." Nor did he change after he had left the White House. Assuming that he had his eye upon a return to public life, he played his cards very badly between 1910 and 1912, alienating support by advocating measures for which public opinion was not ready. When the *Lusitania* was sunk during the Barnes libel trial, with men of German ancestry on the jury, he publicly denounced it as murder, fully expecting that his statement would cost him the verdict, though to the honor of the jurymen it did not.

Roosevelt even professed indifference to fame.

I am not in the least concerned as to whether I will have any place in history, and, indeed, I do not remember ever thinking about it. . . . I want to be a straight and decent man and do good service. . . . While I live it will be a great satisfaction if I can feel this, and I should like my descendants to know it; and I should like to feel that those who know me and care for me, and whom I value, will also feel it. But aside from this it does not seem to me that after a man is dead it matters very much whether it is a little longer or a little shorter before the inevitable oblivion, steadily flooding the sands of time, effaces the scratches on the sand which we call history. As the ages roll by in the life of this globe, small indeed does the difference seem between the few weeks' remembrance of the average hard-working, clean-living citizen, and the few years, or few hundreds of years, or few thousands of years, before the memory of the mighty fades into the dim gray of time and then vanishes into the blackness of eternity.

That this is the whole truth I greatly doubt. But there are no indications that T.R. was much preoccupied with thought of fame. It was at best a chameleon's dish for a man of his lusty appetite.

The nomination for the vice-presidency in 1900 is crucial for the study of T.R.'s political ambitions; so, too, are his renunciation of a third term in 1908 and the campaign of 1912. The usual view is that Roosevelt was made vice-president because Senator Platt wanted to get him out of New York, but both Platt and Roosevelt emphatically denied this. As T.R. wrote William Roscoe Thayer as late as 1915:

It is an entire error to say that I was assured by Senator Platt that I need expect nothing further from the Republicans of New York State and therefore accepted the Vice-Presidential nomination. On the contrary,

I beat Senator Platt to his knees; I received from him openly the promise that I should be renominated as Governor of New York and forced him to put forward Woodruff for the Vice-Presidency; and when it became evident that I would have to take the Vice-Presidency because of popular feeling outside of New York) I was nominated and seconded from outside states and not from New York, because I would not permit the Platt machine even to go through the form of forcing me into the Vice-Presidency. If you care to turn to my Autobiography, pages 331–333,[1] you will see the account of the incident.

It is certain, however, that T.R. declared again and again that he would not accept the vice-presidency, and that the only one of his friends who urged him to accept it was Lodge, who saw this office, despite all appearances, as a step toward the White House. However the movement may have begun, it soon became clear that Roosevelt was the choice of the convention, and that the choice was inspired by genuine enthusiasm and faith in his future. If he intended to go on in politics at all, it would have been very difficult to refuse such a call.

Then, of course, the impossible happened, and Mark Hanna's "damned cowboy" found himself in the White House. "When I saw the runner," T.R. told J. J. Leary many years later, "I instinctively knew he had bad news, the worst news in the world." Is such a reaction as this literally possible for an ambitious man? Was this really what Roosevelt felt? or was it only what he thought he ought to feel? While it still appeared that McKinley might recover, Lodge, who knew T.R.'s character if anybody did, wrote, "It wrung my heart to think of your coming to the great place through an assassination, for I knew how terribly that idea must be haunting you and how it must weigh upon you." Later T.R. himself wrote, "It is a dreadful thing to come into the Presidency this way; but it would be a far worse thing to be morbid about it." It may be that for Roosevelt there was no difference between the two questions I have asked. He had had long practice in feeling what he ought to feel and doing what he ought to do.

Then, on election night in 1904, Roosevelt burned his political bridges behind him, by issuing an announcement concluding, "The wise custom which limits the President to two terms regards the

[1] Macmillan edition.

substance and not the form, and under no circumstances will I be a candidate for or accept another nomination." Early in December he explained his motives in a letter to John St. Loe Strachey in London:

As regards a third term: in the first place, it is a time-hallowed custom dating from George Washington, and one should not affront the feelings of good people who have grown to regard a custom as essential to the good of the country. In the next place, you must remember that the President has much more power than a Prime Minister for the time that he is in, and that is legitimate objection to his being in too long. Finally, you must remember that after a man has been in such a position as President for seven or eight years, he has inevitably contracted such animosities and caused such discontents, and above all, has inevitably delivered his "special message" so many times, as to become in the eyes of the public stale; and a new man with his principles can often do more than he himself in bringing these principles to fruition.

Politically this was an inexpedient act; by removing the President as a factor in the 1908 campaign it lessened his influence in the party and with Congress, with which his relations were very bad by the end of his term. For this reason he must have regretted it, and he admitted, too, that there were reasons when he regretted his self-abnegation for its own sake, but this, as he once wrote Nicholas Murray Butler, was only the old Adam in him. Basically he continued to believe that his decision had been the right one, and the permanent chairman of the 1908 convention, Lodge, labored loyally as his representative to prevent the convention from being stampeded in his behalf. By 1910, however, Roosevelt was busy explaining that he had meant it was a third *consecutive* term that he would not consider. He could not have used this word in 1904, for such a statement would at once have been interpreted as a bid for 1912. It is only, a president in office whose self-perpetuating tendencies could endanger the Republic; an ex-president has no control over party machinery and is therefore no menace. This is all logical enough, but I find no evidence that it was in T.R.'s mind in 1904 or even in 1908.

I have related elsewhere how Roosevelt was brought to the barricades in 1912. The crucial test is the question whether Roosevelt was willing to accept a compromise candidate in 1912. There are those who feel that he would not have done this under any circumstances, and there are words of his own which seem to support this view. But he was on record as pledged to support any candidate except Taft, provided that what he regarded as the fraudulent roll of the convention had been purged, and it is difficult to see how he could have gone back on his pledge. It is also true that because this moral issue was not faced, he rejected at least one proposition that might well have prevented Taft's nomination on the first ballot and perhaps altogether. Senator James E. Watson declared that at one point Frank Kellogg persuaded T.R. to accept Governor Hadley of Missouri as a compromise candidate but that the Pinchots and others caused him to change his mind.[2] He may also well have feared that if he eliminated himself he would strengthen the hand of the La Follette forces, a consummation which, for both selfish and unselfish reasons, he must have been eager to prevent.

Roosevelt was not the first Progressive; neither was he the last, for he abandoned the party before some of his followers were willing to grant that the cause had been lost. "I am just finishing a hopeless campaign," he wrote to the governor-general of Australia, in November, 1914, "in which I had to take part because I was not willing to see men flying the flag of righteousness go down without my sharing their fate." Up to this time he had been saying that the Progressive party was here to stay and that union with other parties was possible only if they were willing to accept the Progressive platform. Two days later he admitted to Lyman Abbott that

[2] There is an unpublished, undated telegram of T.R.'s to James M. Pierce, of Des Moines: "As a matter of fact no offer was made to me by anyone authorized to speak for the Taft people on behalf of any third candidate. Various propositions were informally made to me under circumstances that did not convince me that those making them were acting in good faith or had the power to carry out their promises, and generally with assurances that if I would accept I would myself be nominated." To these he had replied that he was not primarily interested in candidates or in candidature but in purging the roll. "Friends of Senator Cummins and Governor Hadley came to me at the same time, each assuring me that at that very moment the Taft men, or some of them, were willing to nominate Mr. Cummins and Mr. Hadley, the friends of each being of course ignorant that the identical proposition held out to them was at the same time being held out to friends of the others. . . ." On July 10, 1913, T.R. wrote Hadley, "I never heard that preposterous story about our having had a quarrel during the Republican National Convention, and my assailing you with abusive language. If you think it wise to deny them [sic], send me a copy of any paper in which they are asserted and I will do so, although really I should not think it was necessary."

the Progressive party might die just as the Free Soil party had died, though he was still sure that the movement would go on. Actually he had for some time been sounding more confident than he felt. He even told Arthur D. Hill that he had seen the handwriting on the wall ever since the 1912 failure to elect any considerable number of congressmen, senators, and state officers. In 1913 he had written Quentin that his fellow Progressives were driving him nearly mad. "I have to remember, in order to keep myself fairly good-tempered, that even although the wild asses of the desert are mainly in our ranks, our opponents have a fairly exclusive monopoly of the swine." But he never admitted that he himself had at any time acted un-wisely. "There is no repentance in my soul," he told Henry L. Nest in 1915; "and I am not in the least responsible for the present conditions. The men who are responsible for the present conditions are those who in the interest of Mr. Taft stole the Republican National Convention in 1912; and if they wish success in 1916 they will not try to put on others the blame for their own misconduct in 1912."

That Roosevelt wanted to be nominated and elected in 1916 there is no question. Such a triumph over Wilson would have been ir-resistible on the score of drama alone, and in his eyes greater things than drama were involved. "How I wish I were President at this moment!" he had exclaimed in 1915. And he told Leary that he had not wanted to run in 1912 but circumstances compelled him. In 1920 he would be too old. "1916 was my high twelve."

The scars and passions of 1912 made an active campaign in 1916 impossible, and he made it clear that he would not modify any of the things he stood for. The convention was given to understand that if they nominated any candidate who was not sound on what T.R. considered "Americanism," he and his supporters would repeat 1912. Once he even said that between a Democratic Wilson and a Republican pseudo Wilson, he would support the original.

After Hughes had been nominated, Dean Lewis hurried to Saga-more Hill, where he found T.R. and Mrs. Roosevelt sitting on the porch. "I have never seen him more serene. There was not a trace of disappointment. We had not been with him ten minutes before our own overstrained nerves were relaxed." Mrs. Roosevelt at least was not pretending. She had so little desire to return to the

White House that she had almost found it in her heart to wish her husband back in Africa during the 1912 campaign.

The danger hung over her as long as he lived. In 1918, when Edward Bok proposed his heading the Boy Scouts, T.R. said he thought Mrs. Roosevelt might like it. "She would figure it would keep me out of mischief in 1920." "I doubt if I ever go back into public place," he wrote Rider Haggard from the hospital, a month before he died. "I have had to go into too much and too bitter truth telling." But he would have taken it if it had come without effort and upon his own terms; he even told his sister he must reserve his strength for it. And James M. Beck told J. Hampton Moore that when he went to Sagamore Hill to consult Roosevelt about running for governor of New York, the Colonel advised against it. "I don't want you to run for Governor because in all probability I will be the next President. If I am I want you to be Secretary of State."

II. Playing It By Ear

Roosevelt had no elaborate theory of government; here, as elsewhere, he manifested his temperamental inclination to play it (as the saying is) "by ear." He was as much the pragmatist in government as in philosophy. "I usually found," he says, "that my interest in any given side of a question of justice was aroused by some concrete case." It follows that even such a basic question as whether the state shall exercise more power or less power tends to become, for him, not a question of principle but a question of expediency. "I am for popular rights and where they can best be obtained by the exercise of State rights I am a good States'-rights man; and where they can best be obtained by the exercise of the power of the nation I am a nationalist." He admits frankly that he was criticized for interfering with Congress. "There really is not any answer I can make to this," he replies, "except to say that if I had not interfered we would not have had any rate bill, or any beef-packers' bill, or any pure-food bill, or any consular reform bill, or the Panama Canal, or the Employers' Liability Bill." These things were good; why, then, question the method by which they were brought about? And how did Roosevelt know they were good? He knew. He felt it so. It is Protestant individualism in government, the same kind of Protestant individualism which the great evangelist embodied when, being asked, "How do you know that the Bible is inspired?" he replied, "Because it inspires me."

When Roosevelt could not get what he wanted through the regular channels, as when the Senate refused to approve a treaty for the collection of customs in Santo Domingo, he went outside and got it by executive agreement. Cabinet members whose judgment he valued were consulted individually, but the Cabinet as such had very little to say. It was not consulted about Panama or about Venezuela or about sending the fleet around the world. If he "took" Panama on his own responsibility, he got the canal built by issuing executive orders whose legality was extremely doubtful and by assuming authority which many were disposed to deny him. Taft was of the opinion that he "demoralized" his whole administration by dealing directly with any subordinate whom he chose to consult—bureau chiefs, head clerks, or whoever else had the information he needed—without bothering to channel his inquiries through responsible heads. He also bypassed his own ambassadors and the ambassadors of other powers whenever it was convenient. The British refused his request to make his friend Spring Rice their ambassador to the United States, but they had no choice about sending him over for consultation in 1905, since T. R. simply announced that he could not deal with the regular ambassador, Sir Mortimer Durand! Count Witte himself made the statement that, finding him somewhat intractable during the Russo-Japanese peace negotiations, Roosevelt thereafter ignored him and addressed his communications directly to the Czar!

Even those who object to Roosevelt's improvisations most strongly admit that he was often justified by his results. "I have been watching Roosevelt and his friends with a very deep interest," wrote Brooks Adams. ". . . He cannot state his case and he does not appreciate his ignorance enough to have the instinct to learn. . . . Still I believe him to be perfectly sincere and, in substance, perfectly right. . . . He is like a man trying to solve problems in celestial mathematics without the calculus."

Roosevelt was about as far from having the legal mind as it is possible for a man in public life to be, and when he found the law protecting the criminal he was always inclined to be a little impatient with it. He simplifies monstrously: "I feel we are certainly justified in morals, and therefore justified in law." He also had a tendency to go into a rather fuzzy legal mysticism in his appeals to such abstractions as "international eminent domain," and to cite "common" laws of whose existence nobody except himself seemed to be aware. What he really meant was that he was playing it by ear again, appealing from the letter to the spirit, resting his case upon the moral sense of mankind. "In a democracy like ours," he says, "a public servant must continually keep in mind not only what the letter of the law permits, but how far he can arouse and guide public sentiment so that it will justify him." This sounds like the rankest demagoguery; it was not that as Roosevelt applied it. But when there is a doubt as to whether he has strict legal authority for what he wishes to do, or thinks should be done, he generally takes a chance. When a legal argument can be made either way, he will make his decision on the basis of need. He is also clear that in times of crisis risks must be taken, and when he feels that he is ethically right he takes them, "even though there may be some technical or red tape difficulty."[3]

Some expressions of this tendency are distinctly amusing. Once, having asked and taken Senator Spooner's advice on a legal matter, Roosevelt told him he wished he had him in the Cabinet. "What I need is a great constitutional lawyer right at my side every minute." Spooner pointed out that he already had two—Taft and Root. "I know it," said T.R., "but they don't agree with me." Once he even kept a man in jail, though he had no legal right to do so:

Knox's position was that as the act committed by the man had been declared by the court not to be criminal, I could not keep him in prison. My position was that as he was undoubtedly a scoundrel and a swindler and morally a criminal, I certainly would not let him out of

[3] It is interesting to note that Roosevelt's own nomination for governor of New York rested upon a somewhat shaky legal basis. The question was whether he was a resident of New York State or of Washington, D.C. The nomination went through because the lawyers pointed out that the question of eligibility could only be tested by proceedings in *quo warranto*, brought by the attorney general. If T.R. were elected governor, the attorney general would probably be a Republican, and thus could be trusted not to raise the question!

prison; and that as for saying that I could not keep him in, why, he *was* in, and that was all there was about it. I think Knox had the best of the argument as regards the law, but I had the final say-so as to the facts and the man stayed in for nearly a year longer.

Roosevelt was quite aware that his enemies considered him an enemy of the Constitution. When Charles J. Bonaparte, as secretary of the navy, brought the wrath of the nation down upon his head by suggesting that "Old Ironsides" might be used for target practice, one newspaper editor attacked the suggestion as presumably inspired by T.R., "the good creature evidently thinking," chortled the President, "that my violent hostility to the Constitution is extended to anything which bears the hated title!"

He did not, of course, himself share this view. He did know that he was "a broad constructionist in constitutional matters," but that simply meant that he was with Marshall, not with Taney, and he did not consider that a reproach. He regarded the Constitution "as the greatest document ever devised by the wit of man to aid a people in exercising every power necessary for its own betterment, and not as a straight-jacket cunningly fashioned to strangle growth." "I did not usurp power," he says, "but I did greatly broaden the use of executive power." Like Lawrence Abbott, he must have been proud that none of his acts were ever declared unconstitutional by the courts.

Of course, this does not in itself prove that he was always right. In the specific matter with which he is most often accused of having been trigger-happy, however—the use of troops to quell public disorders—Roosevelt was more than commonly scrupulous. Once he even protected the sovereignty of the state of Nevada after her governor had declined to do so. And when in the course of a strike at the Treadwell Mine in southeastern Alaska strikers stole dynamite, and the governor of Alaska requested troops, he granted the request with extreme reluctance. "I do want to be sure that every resource of the civil power has been exhausted before an appeal is made to the military arm."

He came closest to going beyond his powers in connection with the great coal strike of 1902, but he had shown the patience of a saint in trying to negotiate with impossible people; the threat of intervention was the last card he had to play; and while I believe he would have played it, it is clear that he was greatly relieved when he did not have to.

The trouble with this particular coal strike [he wrote his sister, Mrs. Cowles], was that the conditions were absolutely peculiar, because we dealt with a necessity of life. . . . I could no more see misery and death come to the great masses of the people in our large cities and sit by idly, because under ordinary conditions a strike is not subject to interference by the President, than I could sit by idly and see one man kill another without interference because there is no statutory duty imposed upon the President to interfere in such cases. Great though the questions involved were as between capital and labor, and vital though I deemed it that violence should be stamped out and the right of the non-union man or of anyone else to work without hindrance established, yet everything had to give way to the prime necessity of saving the people as a whole from a fearful calamity—or rather, had to be postponed to thus saving them.

This is quite in line with T.R.'s usual feelings as to the respective claims of law and human need; it is also in harmony with the conviction of One greater than T.R. that "the sabbath was made for man, and not man for the sabbath." If he must act in the coal strike, he wrote Winthrop Murray Crane, he would act without advice, reluctantly, knowing that he was setting an evil precedent, "rather than expose our people to the suffering and chaos which would otherwise come."

Of course, it is quite possible to agree with T.R. about the coal strike and still to reject, as Taft did, his tendency to magnify the Executive at the expense of the other two branches of the government, and set him up as a kind of "universal providence" to "set all things right." Taft's own theory was quite different. "The President can exercise no power which cannot be fairly and reasonably traced to some specific grant of power or justly implied and included with such express grant as proper and necessary to its exercise." Even when he shared Roosevelt's impatience with what was wrong he still deplored his lack of "the most sensitive consideration of the methods by which . . . progress might safely be attained" and his blindness to the ultimate results of such "short cuts" as his impatience sometimes led him to take.

III. Between Scylla and Charybdis

It must not be assumed, however, that Roosevelt had no political faith. He did believe in feeling your way as you go, but he did not on that account ignore guideposts.

In 1906 T.R. called himself Jeffersonian in his "genuine faith in democracy and popular government" and Hamiltonian in his conviction of "the need of the exercise of broad powers by the National Government." He is still calling himself a "strong Hamiltonian" in 1918. He knew that democratic institutions cannot be used successfully except by people who are ready for them. For one thing, they involve "the right of the foolish to take part just like any one else in doing the work, and it is not always easy to suffer fools gladly." But, however foolish the people may be, he believed that they were more often right than those to whom they had delegated authority, and at the same time he believed that the Federal Union, as established by the Constitution, is the only kind of government under which, in a country as large as ours, freedom could possibly be preserved. Despite his own aptitude for leadership, he never believed that a people could be saved by a leader; if they were to be saved, they must save themselves. And, though he worked through the Republican party for all but four years of his life, the party was never more than a means toward an end. "I find it very, very hard," he says, "to work in any way as a party man."

All Roosevelt's faith in the individual and in individual initiative as the source of progress was on the side of laissez faire, letting men stand or fall by themselves. But though he had had good laissez-faire training at Harvard, he realized that, in the present stage of our development, this ideal could not be literally applied, for it would give a fair chance in life to comparatively few people; he was driven, therefore, to championing governmental interference in order to secure justice and equality of opportunity. The purpose of such interference, however, must always be not to abolish the chances of competition but to make them more even.

This meant an increase in the powers of the federal government and consequently of the Executive. He did not accept the theory of government by checks and balances, and the doctrine of a "neutral ground" between state and federal authority was only, in his eyes, a device to provide escape for wrongdoers. In the interest of efficiency in government he wanted wide powers of removal for the President, which point of view sometimes brought the wrath of his old comrades, the Civil Service reformers, down upon his head. One of the reasons he believed reform could not come through the Democratic party was that he saw it tied to the outmoded principle of states' rights.

In the days of absolute monarchy, Roosevelt admitted, the people needed to be protected against their government, but now that the source of power lies in the electorate, the extension of authority must cease to be a menace. As the American party system has developed, with many elections offering only a choice between evils, this has turned out a somewhat academic distinction. Roosevelt is upon somewhat firmer ground when he points out that the limitation of the Executive's term under our system of government makes a "strong" head less dangerous for us than it would be under a monarchy, but he quite failed to foresee such abuses of power as the stubborn and successful determination of one of his successors to hold on to the presidency until death snatched it from him, to say nothing of such cruel and ruthless exercise of power as the forcible and completely unnecessary removal of Japanese and Japanese-Americans from their homes on the Pacific coast after the United States entered World War II.

Roosevelt's belief in moderation was also something close to being a political principle. It is true that in some moods he could speak of himself as a radical, but he always had to make his own definition of the word. "Lincoln was a radical compared to Buchanan and Fillmore; he was a conservative compared to John Brown and Wendell Phillips; and he was right in both positions." One of the best of his homely figures alludes to this: "If a room is fetid and the windows are bolted I am perfectly contented to knock out the windows, but I would not knock a hole into the drain-pipe." "I have found out," he says, "that in this life we don't generally get exactly what we want; and I am well pleased to get anything near what I want." And again, more specifically, "The Senate is not exactly crazy to do what I desire, and frequently I can help a cause best by keeping fairly quiet about it in public."

In speech after speech he balances extreme against extreme with such Euphuistic precision that his severer critics saw him committed to a middle-of-the-roadism so incorrigible that it negatived action altogether. Mr. Dooley expressed this point of view with incomparable humor: "'Th' thrusts are heejous monsthers built up be th' enlightened intherprize iv th' men that have done so much to advance progress in our beloved country,' he says. 'On wan hand I wud stamp thim unther fut; on th' other hand, not so fast.'" La Follette states the same thing more seriously: "His most savage assault upon special interests was invariably offset with an equally drastic attack upon those who were seeking to reform abuses. These were indiscriminately classed as demagogues and dangerous persons." The implied criticism is just when, and if, truth and wisdom lie at the extremity. When they lie in the middle, the criticism is not just. T.R. did not believe that extremists were always in advance of their age. Sometimes, he thought, they were merely off to one side.

IV. Morals and Money

But perhaps Roosevelt's essential moderation is seen most clearly in connection with his attitude toward the problem of capital and labor. On its moral side, this interested him as deeply as any domestic affairs he had to deal with during his administration, but it is a complicated matter, and it needs to be considered against the whole background of his attitude toward finance in general. T.R., as we have seen, proclaimed himself incompetent in a number of areas. But only in connection with finance does he give the impression that he rejoices in his incompetence.

Economics, he says frankly, is a subject about which he knows nothing. Because of his ignorance in this area, he had more trouble with currency problems than with anything else he was required to deal with as president. In 1915 Wilson's financial policy seemed reasonable to him, but he may be mistaken, he says, "for I know mighty little about Finance." He even felt the handicap of his ignorance in speaking for the Liberty Loan, as well he might in view of his cavalier statement that "the bonds are issued in such a way that the farmer and the wage-worker have exactly the same chance as the banker to purchase and hold as many or as few as they wish."

Roosevelt's own financial affairs were managed for him by Douglas Robinson and other relatives, upon whose advice he was almost childishly dependent in such crises as the tax mixup of 1898 which almost prevented him from becoming governor of New York. Household finances were completely in charge of Mrs. Roosevelt, who not only paid all the bills but put into her husband's pocket such money as she thought he would need. When he went off on a trip, she gave the money to cover it not to T.R. but to James Amos. When she was ill, Ethel took over the checkbook. When he was on his European tour, Lawrence Abbott managed everything. "I don't want the $100 very badly at the moment—" T.R. writes Douglas Robinson late in 1897—"or at least I shan't after January 1st. For this week I am getting along on a counterfeit dollar bill and two lead nickels." He never carried much money; once he even had to walk back to the White House for lack of streetcar fare. Roosevelt realized that his ignorance in this area made him incompetent to deal with one whole side of governmental business, but he found comfort in reminding himself that "Abraham Lincoln knew mighty little about currency or the tariff, and he would have made a fool of himself if he had tried to take the lead as regards them."

The question arises: Was T.R. really the financial moron he considered himself, or was his difficulty only lack of interest? It was Bill Sewall's opinion that "he would have made good at pretty nearly anything, except, perhaps as a money-maker, and he would have made good at that, too, if he had ever cared to put his mind to it."

I cannot say that Roosevelt had the New Testament attitude toward wealth, for he recognizes frankly that we are living in a social order in which all human values are dependent upon a certain measure of economic security. But, though he was born and bred in a prosperous city home and had, on his father's side, a thoroughly mercantile background,[4] he may certainly be said to represent

[4] The elder Theodore Roosevelt left an estate of about $800,000, of which his son's share was approximately one-fourth. Howard K. Beale says ("Theodore Roosevelt's Ancestry," p. 201), "To protest, as Theodore always did, that the family was other than very wealthy was to carry modesty to the point of telling less than the whole story." According to the New York *Times* (Jan. 15 and Nov. 2, 1919), T.R.'s own estate came to $810,607.33. There was $85,000 in life insurance.

the distrust felt by an earlier, still predominantly agricultural, America for men of wealth. He did not find the type of man who generally succeeds in making a great deal of money very interesting; neither did he think him fit to govern a country. In general he did not like such men personally, and he liked their sons even less. In the Barnes libel suit, he identified Clarence Mackay as "the son of the great Nevada miner, and . . . a New York business man of wealth," but when he was asked if Mackay were not president of the Postal Telegraph Company, he answered, "I do not know." Again, he did not know that James Stillman represented Rockefeller's interests in the City Bank. "I have heard some association of the name of Rockefeller and Stillman, but I am not familiar with the New York business relationships . . . ; I have never gone into them at all."

Roosevelt made a high grade in mathematics in his Harvard entrance examinations, but in college he found his mathematics course difficult. Since he organized a Finance Club, the outgrowth of a Harvard course in the financial history of the United States and devoted to a study of the currency system of other nations, his later indifference would not seem to have been as yet fully developed. On the other hand, it is hard to see how any young man could have managed his personal finances much more incompetently than T.R. did up to his marriage to Edith Carow. Of course, it was primarily bad luck that wiped out a large part of his investment in the Western cattle venture. But it is also true that most people of good judgment did not share Roosevelt's faith in the venture. On one occasion he handed over a $14,000 check to Merrifield and Sylvane without a contract and with no security except their word (which, however, in this instance, proved to be quite enough). On the other hand, when he bought a partnership in the book-publishing business of George H. Putnam, he gave him a check for $20,000, with only about half that much in the bank to cover it.

In 1887 and 1893 he feared he might have to close Sagamore Hill, and again, oddly enough, in 1900, though "the idiots of the magazines now wish to pay me very large prices for writing, on account of my temporary notoriety." In later years he tried to make Sagamore Hill pay for itself by selling hay, corn, potatoes, and apples. The expenses involved in building the North Room gave him pause in 1905, and the cost of putting in a necessary road distressed him in 1911. Though he won the Barnes libel suit in 1915, he wrote Endicott Peabody that it cost him $50,000. Perhaps that is why he told Hamlin Garland in that year that he could not take it easy but must go on driving himself because he needed money. Like Henry James, he is often inclined to overplay his poverty. One of his favorite jokes was that he always made an effort to keep on good terms with Alice, who had an inheritance from her mother, since she was the only one in the family who had any money.

His earning capacity varied considerably; for a considerable share of the time, writing was his principal source of income. In 1894 he enjoyed three days' lecturing at Chautauqua "as I was paid well." He called 1899 his first prosperous year; he celebrated by giving his wife "a really beautiful little watch," the first "handsome present" he had ever been able to give her. He handled his writing contracts in a businesslike way, but he was not greedy. He rejected Robert Collier's offer of $100,000 for his African adventures and accepted instead an offer of $50,000 from Scribners.[5] Similarly he accepted the contributing editorship of *The Outlook* at $12,000 annually, which was less than one fourth of what other magazines had offered him, and less than one eighth of what he might have had in business. At the time of his death he was earning $30,000 a year from the *Metropolitan* and the Kansas City *Star;* this, he wrote Ted and his wife, is "important until all of you take up your life in ordinary shape again."

Even at the time of the Panic of 1907, Roosevelt did not wholly lay aside his superior attitude toward economics. He does not believe, he tells Emlen Roosevelt, that a new currency law could cure the ill, but "as I am not an expert in finance," he gives no reason for this belief. He preferred to retreat to high moral grounds, which he did profess to understand, and he was at least daring when he declared that, while he did not admit that his policies had caused the panic, they might have contributed to it, but that even if this were so he did not propose to modify them. "In any great

[5] Scribners' original offer was $25,000, Collier's $50,000, and Roosevelt would have taken the Collier offer if Scribners had not met it. He also had offers from *Everybody's* and *McClure's.* In 1908 Collier offered him $60,000 to go to India and write six articles about his trip, which he refused.

movement for righteousness, where the forces of evil are strongly intrenched, it is unfortunately inevitable that some unoffending people should suffer in company with the real offenders. This is not our fault." [6] For all that, his actions in the crisis seem intelligent. He kept free of panic himself, and he certainly did not lose faith in the future of either the country or the party. As early as 1906 he had suggested important changes in our fiscal system to Congress, but he had not followed this up in any way. It is possible that with more interest in economics he might have moved toward the more stable banking system later achieved under Wilson.[7]

As has already been pointed out, Roosevelt was trained at Harvard in laissez-faire economics. In 1882 he joined the New York Free Trade Club, and as late as the campaign of 1896 he was "not prepared to say" that an international agreement to use both gold and silver in our currency would do harm. He has been much criticized for junking free trade when he decided upon a political career under Republican auspices, but the action is completely in character: he always knew that you cannot have everything in politics, and what more painless area of compromise could there have been for him than this one where his emotions were not deeply enlisted nor his intellectual grasp very strong?

These considerations are also involved in some other matters for which Roosevelt was criticized. They make it easier to believe that he really was confused about his taxes in Oyster Bay and New York City,[8] that he really was ignorant about campaign contributions in 1904, and that, though both statements were certainly false, he believed he was telling the truth when he said that the United

[6] He always took up a high moral attitude, too, toward speculating in stocks, which to him was as reprehensible as "gambling at cards or in lotteries or on the racetrack." "It would seem that the Federal Government could at least act by forbidding the use of the mails, telegraph and telephone wires for mere gambling in stocks and futures, just as it does in lottery transactions" (*Public Addresses and State Papers*, VI, 1611).

[7] It is interesting to note that Charles and Mary Beard (*The Rise of American Civilization*, I, 596), though quite cognizant of T.R.'s shortcomings in the economic area, yet called him the first president who aimed to use the powers of the government to bring about "a distribution of wealth in the interest of the golden mean," a daring heresy in his time.

[8] This matter is too complicated to summarize here. The reader will find a fair-minded account in Philip C. Jessup, *Elihu Root*, I, 198–200. But see also George E. Mowry, *The Era of Theodore Roosevelt*, pp. 178–79.

States had paid $40,000,000 "direct to the French Government" for the Panama Canal and that the records could be "readily found by anybody who honestly sought to find them."

There still remains, however, the question whether, in such cases, Roosevelt merely did not know or whether he did not wish to know. It is clear that his naïveté could on occasion be great. Thus, O. K. Davis once urged him to touch lightly on the "race suicide" theme before an audience of poor people, for whom there were economic problems involved in raising large families which T.R. himself had never had to face. "By George, O. K., that's so, and I never thought of it." And if anything could be more naïve than this, it is a sentence in a letter to Mrs. W. H. Hall: "The increasing cost of living I simply do not understand."

Roosevelt's indifference to economics shows even in his relationship to imperialism. It would be too much to say that he is completely unaware of the economic advantages involved, but he certainly does not stress them. The economic arguments against imperialism—"big business" was generally opposed to the Spanish-American War—he ignores, and there is no reason to suppose that his policies in this area would have been any different if no economic considerations had been involved either way. But it is in connection with what Pringle calls his "life-long policy of evasion on the tariff" that Roosevelt's indifference to straight economic considerations shows up most clearly in the political area. In April, 1906, he tells Lyman Abbott that there should be "radical modifications," but by June he thinks the tariff is creating "much sound and fury, relative to its real importance." By 1909, when he was out of office, there was "no real ground for dissatisfaction," and what needed to be met was not "an actual need, but a mental condition among our people, who believe there ought to be a change." He had got out, leaving the whole problem to his successor, though, as Blum has clearly shown, in 1905 he had very skillfully used the threat of tariff revision to force Cannon and other stalwarts to give him such things as railway rate legislation, which he wanted much more. His last message to Congress said not that the time had come to revise the tariff but to "prepare" for a revision of the tariff. In view of the important part which tariff legislation played in wrecking Taft, this may seem less kind than clever on T.R.'s part, but, as Baker has shown in detail, Roosevelt managed to involve himself as deeply in Payne-Aldrich controversies as even the unfortunate Winona speech involved Taft; if he ever was disingenuous, it was when he discussed Taft's tariff and reciprocity policies. By 1910 he had convinced himself that it would have been "wicked folly" to have touched the tariff during his term, and during the 1912 campaign he contributed to *The Saturday Evening Post* [9] an article on the tariff called, "The Deceitful Red Herring." If he had been elected, he would very likely have disappointed those Progressives who had created the insurgent movement largely because of their desire for tariff revision.[10] The truth is that T.R. never swerved significantly from the point of view which he expressed to William Roscoe Thayer when he said, "My dear boy, the tariff is only a question of expediency." And nobody ever surpassed T.R. in ignoring expediency.[11]

V. Class Conflict and the Public Welfare

The capital-labor conflict was entirely different, for though it rested upon an economic basis, it involved important moral and human considerations. T.R.'s whole policy in this area was based upon his desire to avoid a class war. He was oppressed by the thought that all the republics of ancient and mediaeval times had failed because their people had divided themselves into opposing camps. As he puts it in an unpublished letter of November 10, 1904, to Philander C. Knox:

It would be a dreadful calamity if we saw this country divided into two parties, one containing the bulk of the property owners and con-

[9] Vol. CLXXXV, Oct. 26, 1912, pp. 3–4.

[10] Progressives who met in Chicago to endorse La Follette in October, 1911, avoided taking a stand on the tariff; so did the Republican governors who asked T.R. to run. Baker cites these facts without appearing to realize that they tend to make T.R.'s own position seem somewhat less anomalous.

[11] Roosevelt expressed his opinions concerning Woodrow Wilson so very freely that it is interesting, in the present connection, to note Wilson's considered judgment of him. According to Joseph P. Tumulty (*Woodrow Wilson As I Know Him*, p. 125), the President said of his predecessor "that he had done a great service in rousing the country from its lethargy, and in that work he had rendered admirable and lasting service, but beyond that he had failed, for he had not, during his administration, attacked two of the major problems: the tariff and the currency, which he, Wilson, considered to be the heart and centre of the whole movement for lasting and permanent reform in America."

servative people, the other the bulk of the wage-workers and the less prosperous generally, each party insisting upon demanding much that was wrong, and each party sullen and angered by real and fancied grievances. The friends of property, of order, of law, must never show weakness in the face of violence or wrong or injustice, but on the other hand they must realize that the surest way to provoke an explosion of wrong and injustice is to be shortsighted, narrow-minded, greedy and arrogant, and to fail to show in actual work that here in this republic it is peculiarly incumbent upon the man with whom things have prospered to be in a certain sense the keeper of the brother with whom life has gone hard.

There was nothing in T.R.'s background to give him any special understanding of, or sympathy with, the laboring man. He admitted his early ignorance freely, and Hurwitz's detailed study was dedicated to demonstrating a reactionary stand on many labor issues during his early career. Yet he turned against the economic barons surprisingly early. In 1883 he called "the wealthy criminal class" the "most dangerous of all dangerous classes" and wished that he could "pass a bill of attainder on Jay Gould and all of Jay Gould's associates." This was seven years before Jacob A. Riis published *How the Other Half Lives*, to which Pringle gave important credit for Roosevelt's awakening on this issue. T.R. was wholly convinced that capitalism could not survive without correcting its abuses, and accused the National Association of Manufacturers of inviting revolution. "One of the most efficient methods of averting the consequences of a dangerous agitation, which is eighty per cent wrong, is to remedy the twenty per cent of evil as to which the agitation is well founded." The coal magnates were very indignant in 1902 when they learned that he had asked the attorney general to determine whether the Sherman Act could be invoked against them, but it is a mistake to suppose that they made their protest because they objected to government interference with business. On the contrary, they wanted the attorney general to proceed against the miners' union, and they wanted the President to use force against the miners instead of negotiating with them. J. P. Morgan was not Jay Gould, and the help he gave Roosevelt—and the nation—in settling the coal strike was of incalculable value, but this did not mean that he and the President thereafter saw eye to eye in capital-labor matters. As T.R. wrote Brooks Adams in 1903:

The Morgan-Hill people and their sympathizers have shown a literally astounding lack of insight and forethought in failing to recognize that supine acquiescence on my part in what they were doing would have inevitably meant state ownership, or rather national ownership, of the railroads of the United States in a short term of years. It is merely to state an axiom to say that the public must exercise some control over the great highways and avenues of commerce. I want this control to be the minimum necessary to secure from them efficient public service.

T.R. certainly considered himself the friend of labor. "I will do everything in my power for the wageworkers of the country *except to do what is wrong.*" In 1910 he quoted approvingly Lincoln's famous statement that "Labor is prior to, and independent of, capital. Capital is only the fruit of labor, and could never have existed if labor had not first existed. Labor is the superior of capital, and deserves much higher consideration." "It is hypocritical baseness," he cries, "to speak of a girl who works in a factory where the dangerous machinery is unprotected as having the 'right' freely to contract to expose herself to dangers to life and limb."

But he did not want the tyranny of labor either. As he saw it, trades-unionism had grown up to combat the exactions of capital and, not unnaturally, had inherited many of its vices. "The eighth commandment reads: 'Thou shalt not steal.' It does not read: 'Thou shalt not steal from the rich man.' It does not read: 'Thou shalt not steal from the poor man.' It reads simply and plainly: 'Thou shalt not steal.'" When Wilson surrendered to the Railroad Brotherhood and Congress passed the Adamson Act, he was indignant. He himself had long before told the Brotherhood how much he prized their approval, but "if ever in a moment of passion or folly you turn against the law and try to pull down the law, then I will stand against you." Toward the close of the war he saw Wilson "bidding for bolshevist support in both labor and farm circles," and he knew that that was the way madness lies.

And the immense number of sloppy minded people, like good Willard Straight, tend to think, in spite of seeing what bolshevism has done for Russia, that Wilson can organize the I.W.W. & the Townley Non-partisan League, and the Henry Ford pacifists, and the Hearst and New Republic gutter-, and parlor-, bolshevists, into a wonderful, semi-reform, semi-socialist, wholly materialist, and utterly hypocritical and sham sentimental, movement—which will make every one happy without anyone's hereafter having to serve or suffer or strive.

So he insisted, without variableness or shadow of turning, from the beginning of his career until the end, that public order must be maintained at all times, by force if necessary, against any group that seeks to overthrow it. No man and no party in America stands above the law. The law must be enforced by lawful means, and if you have any sense you will not content yourself with quelling the disturbance and failing to scrutinize the causes which produced it. Nevertheless, once the issue has arisen, it must be met squarely. Murder is murder, and murder is not debatable. Whether it is the Buffalo dock strike, or the Chicago teamsters strike, or the race riots in East St. Louis, or the dynamiting of the Los Angeles *Times*, or the Mooney case, or the killing of Governor Steunenberger, there is never any question where he stands. If the laboring man wishes to join a union, that is his right, and nobody must be permitted to interfere with it. But if he wishes not to join a union, that is his right also, and nobody must interfere with that either. Nor can there be any toleration for restrictions which seek "to reduce the work of the high-grade man to the level of the low-grade man." When William A. Miller was dismissed from the Government Printing Office because his union had dropped him for suggesting timesaving improvements in binding methods, Roosevelt ordered him reinstated. "I am President of the United States, and my business is to see fair play among all men, capitalists or wage-workers, whether they conduct private business as individuals or as members of organizations."

This middle-of-the-roadism on capital-labor problems shows, too, in Roosevelt's attitude toward socialism, already several times referred to. As early as 1908 he says that there is nothing in the word that ought to frighten anyone. What extreme socialists advocate could never work, and would take us back to the Stone Age if it did, but what many people who call themselves socialists are asking for is reasonable enough. The moralist in Roosevelt revolted at what he considered the sexual looseness often associated with socialism; the religionist balked at its materialism; its class consciousness offended him both as a humanitarian and as a nationalist. Yet he was quite clear that "the growth in the complexity of community life means the partial substitution of collectivism for individualism, not to destroy, but to save individualism."

In 1915, replying to a letter from Reginald Wright Kauffman, in which the latter had signed himself an ex-socialist, T.R. wrote, "I am a near-Socialist! That is, I want to adopt the many excellent things in the Socialist propaganda without adopting the things that seem to be evil." And he signed himself, "Your rationalist-individualist and rational-Socialist friend." Even though this was post-1912, it was largely semantic entertainment and intellectual pyrotechnics. It was in 1912, as all the world knows, that Roosevelt deserted, for the time being, the middle of the road. He had come out for an inheritance tax as early as 1906, at which time he also told Lyman Abbott that he believed in a progressive income tax but thought it would be difficult to establish and administer. It is also true, as Mowry has recently and effectively argued,[11a] that his messages and speeches of 1907 and 1908 were more "Progressive" than has generally been recognized. But it was his championship of the recall of judicial decisions, the intiative, the referendum, the recall, and other heresies that rendered impossible a nomination which was already unlikely enough. In passing he even threw out wilder suggestions, like that contained in a private letter of 1914 to Raymond Robins, in which he says, "I do not see why we should not have for every man a two years' hard, manual, industrial service, that is, universal and obligatory industrial service for a limited time, just as many nations have found it necessary to have such universal obligatory military service for a limited time."

Woodrow Wilson, then, was quite correct in seeing a new paternalism, breaking in some aspects with historic American individualism in the Progressive movement. For all that, moderation was not wholly dead, and if Roosevelt had been elected in 1912, I make no doubt his administration would have been a good deal less radical than his campaign. Even during the campaign, he accused Lodge, who broke with him on the constitutional issues, of overstressing the importance of initiative, referendum, and recall as much as they were being overstressed by those who hoped for salvation through them. In T.R.'s eyes they were not instruments of salvation, though he did hope that they might, under some circumstances, be useful tools. He even admitted that in unwise hands they

[11a] George E. Mowry, *The Era of Theodore Roosevelt*, pp. 222–24.

might be dangerous, and here, as in his determined attempt to build up the powers of the Executive, he seems less scrupulous about protecting the American people, not from himself but from those who might come after him, than prudence would seem to require. By 1916, however, Theodore was himself again, denying that he had ever been greatly interested in any of these radical devices. And by May, 1918, the Russian revolution had inspired a distinct chilliness toward all leftish experimentation.

There is some difference of opinion as to T.R.'s interest in welfare legislation. He clearly did not believe that much could be done about child labor except through state action. Both Upton Sinclair and Dr. Harvey W. Wiley felt that T.R. was somewhat lukewarm about packing-house and pure-food legislation. Personal elements entered here; Wiley and Roosevelt were clearly antipathetic spirits, and Sinclair's brand of sensationalism always repelled him.[12] After the revelations of Samuel Merwin and Charles Edward Russell, Roosevelt did nothing more than send Garfield to Chicago, and Garfield made a report favorable to the packers. This need not have been, as Filler says, because the administration was then "on excellent terms with William Lorimer, the Republican boss of Cook County and a beef-trust champion," but whatever the reason, Roosevelt had not got to the bottom of the problem, nor did he do so until after *The Jungle* had appeared. Indeed, he did not fully swing into action until after he had read the proofs of three forthcoming articles in *The World's Work*. Nor did he threaten to release the devastating Neill-Reynolds report until it appeared that the House would not pass the Beveridge legislation without some such action on the President's part.

Another important test of political liberalism is provided by one's attitude toward free speech. There is not much point in becoming agitated over such statements as the one made by T.R. before the Spanish-American War, that it would give him pleasure to put the editors of the *World* and the *Evening Post* in jail as soon as hostilities began. Nobody supposes that he would have done

---

[12] In an unpublished letter to J. H. Cort, May 1, 1908, Roosevelt declares that, though *The Jungle* "did in loose and declamatory style call attention to a few real evils," on the whole it was "absurdly false." "As regards most of his statements that I have had the chance to examine, I should say that it would not be accurate to describe them as imaginary, but as sheer inventions with no basis in truth whatsoever."

it. I am less sure about his feeling that Thorstein Veblen ought to be in jail—or, as he once says, ought to be shot—in 1918, and I have no doubt at all that he really believed in 1888 that anarchists ought to be shot down upon the first attempt to put their principles into practice. But here we have passed from freedom of speech to freedom of action. Once he moved to have an anarchist paper excluded from the mails: "The preaching of murder and arson is certainly as immoral as the circulation of obscene and lascivious literature. . . . No law should require the Postmaster General to become an accessory to murder by circulating literature of this kind."

In 1902 a clerk in the War Department and an employee of the Brooklyn Navy Yard were discharged for having expressed opinions of which the President disapproved, and once he wanted a Library of Congress employee dismissed for having written him an insulting letter. At the very end of his life he supported a movement to bar James Harvey Robinson's *Mediaeval and Modern Times* from the schools because the chapter on "The Origin of the War of 1914" was "an outrageous piece of German propaganda." (Actually it makes Germany primarily responsible for the war.)

In spite of such errors, however, Roosevelt in his final phase had little choice about becoming the champion of freedom of speech even in wartime, for he was himself the outstanding critic of the government. It is shocking to remember that Americans once seriously considered making criticism of the President itself a criminal act. Whatever his motives, Theodore Roosevelt rendered magnificent service in opposing this proposal; if it were enacted into law, he declared, he would at once proceed to test its legality, and no sane person can doubt that he would have done so. His whole course of action during World War I helped to establish the principle that even in wartime the President of the United States is a human being and not a sacred cow. Even *The Nation,* which did not love him, conceded, "It is largely to Mr. Roosevelt that we owe our ability to discuss peace terms and to criticize at all." [13]

Moreover, it was not only for those who agreed with him that T.R.

---

[13] During the war he turned over to the Department of Justice a letter from a correspondent who had accused Wilson and the leaders of both houses of being "traitors to our country, who have succumbed to British gold." While insisting on "proper criticism by the people of their public servants," T.R. finds this "seditious and treasonable."

advocated freedom of speech during wartime. In 1914 it was inaccurately reported in the newspapers that a rich man had declared that he would drop from his will a $10,000,000 bequest to Harvard University unless she dismissed Professor Hugo Münsterberg, distinguished professor of psychology, who had become one of the leading spokesmen for the German cause in the United States. Münsterberg promptly offered his resignation, which, to her everlasting honor, Harvard refused to accept. To his, Roosevelt praised the university's decision both publicly and privately. "Harvard," he wrote Münsterberg, "cannot afford to sell the right of free speech for ten million dollars or any other sum." As late as September, 1917, he vigorously opposed the exclusion of Tom Watson's antiwar paper, *The Jeffersonian*, from the mails. "To say that a man's position is wrong is not in the least equivalent to saying that his paper should be kept out of the mails because he takes that position."

VI. The Game of Politics

Little has been said so far of T.R.'s handling of the political machinery or of the game of politics. No more than with other public men were the conditions under which he worked of his own choosing. He was always thwarted on the one hand by the fools who will not do what needs to be done and on the other by the even more exasperating fools who want to do so much that they accomplish nothing. "In a wearyingly large number of cases . . . one has to accept the best possible, when it is far short of the best."

Compromise means adjustment, and this at once raises the moral issue. "In public life I have never done anything that was not absolutely right," so T.R. wrote Ted and Eleanor in the last years of his life, "but I have learned by bitter experience that this is useless unless I also walk with the utmost wariness." He rejected Lecky's idea that politics are a handicap to the statesman. When it comes to a question of principle there is nothing to do but stand by your guns. On questions of policy, on the other hand—"and most questions, from the tariff to municipal ownership of public utilities and the franchise tax, are primarily questions of policy"—you have to reach a working agreement with others. He himself thought that he had compromised considerably less than Lincoln did. In the Barnes libel suit he was quizzed on this point in some detail:

"Then you do not attack anything unless there is a feeling against it, is that what you mean to say?"

"I attack—I attack iniquities, I attack wrongdoing, I try to choose the time for an attack when I can get the bulk of the people to accept the principles for which I stand. I believe you can only accomplish reforms of a permanent character when you can educate the people up to the point of standing by them."

"You stand by righteousness, do you not?"

"I do."

"With due regard to opportunism?"

"I stand by righteousness, always."

"With due regard to opportunism?"

"No, sir; not when it comes to righteousness."

"Does not your last answer state that?"

"It does not, sir. I say I believe emphatically that you must have a due regard for opportunism in the choice of the time and methods for making the attack. But you must stand for righteousness, whether you are going to be supported or not."

Roosevelt may be said to have made up his mind to function as a party man as early as 1884, when he decided to support Blaine, whose nomination he had fought in the convention, instead of bolting the ticket with the mugwumps and supporting Cleveland. Certainly he functioned so as governor of New York. He has been criticized in this capacity for his soft-pedaling of the canal frauds and for contenting himself with refusing to continue Louis Payn as insurance commissioner, but acceptng another Platt-approved appointee, Francis J. Hendricks, instead of investigating and expos- ing the whole noxious insurance corruption, as Hughes was to do, and some of these criticisms may well have substance. But Roose- velt did not have a free hand; Gosnell has shown conclusively that, under the setup governing their operations in New York State, both Platt and the governor operated within a narrow range of choice. "The powers of removal that the governor did possess were carefully hedged about by many restrictions and were not sufficient to en- able him to really direct the course of his administration."

How good a politician was Roosevelt? Some good judges place him very high. Cleveland called him "the most perfectly equipped and the most effective politician thus far seen in the Presidency." James Bryce said that he had "never seen a more eager, high-minded and efficient set of public servants than the men doing the work of the American Government" during his administration. It is John Morton Blum's judgment that Roosevelt "accomplished more in remodeling administrative structures than had all his predecessors since Lincoln."

Certainly he made some bad appointments. Lincoln Steffens once queried him about some of them. According to Steffens's account, T.R. ranked them in order of badness, beginning with his making the brother of a senator's mistress a district attorney. Steffens once printed a very indiscreet story in which he said the President had had to "bribe" legislators. He was called before the Cabinet, where he was accused of "criminal libel" against the President. But when he demurely inquired whether in the event of his being tried he could call the President himself as a witness to prove that he got the facts from him, T.R. broke in, declaring that the thought of criminal charges was absurd. "This is a difference between two writers about the use of words."

When Steffens himself first proposed making a journalistic investigation of the workings of the federal government, Roosevelt was unwilling to cooperate, saying that such conduct on his part would make it more difficult for him to work with government officers and get the work of government done. Early in 1906, however, he changed his mind, not only giving Steffens his blessing but directing all employees and officials to tell him what he wanted to know, not incompatible with the public interest, and promising them protection for themselves should any question arise. It is interesting, and probably significant, that the series Steffens was able to turn out was not sensational enough to please his editor and was never published.

During the struggle over railroad rate legislation, T.R. never explained why he suddenly abandoned Senator Tillman and the other Democrats who were trying to get his bill through and, calling the newspaper correspondents to the White House, announced that he was willing to accept the Allison Amendment. Filler believes that T.R. here put a brake on public sentiment which, without him, would have secured more drastic control of the railroads, quoting Samuel Untermyer's judgment that the Hepburn Act "saved us from Government ownership of the Railroads." Well, government ownership was exactly what T.R. wished to avoid, and it may be that that is why he acted as he did. But his treatment of his associates was still pretty rough.

He was rough, too, in eliminating Hanna, as we have seen, but he was anything but that in his approaches to "Uncle Joe" Cannon, the czar of the House of Representatives. "I think Mr. Roosevelt talked over with me virtually every serious recommendation before he made it," said Cannon, "and he requested me to sound out the leaders in the House, for he did not want to recommend legislation simply to write messages." There are letters to Cannon which, I confess, make me gag slightly. "I do not usually feel inclined to try to influence your judgment in matters of home legislation, for my experience has been that your judgment is rather more apt to be sound than mine in such matters." And again, "Now, Uncle Joe, stand by me if you can."

Another Illinois senator, William Lorimer, once tolerated, T.R. publicly repudiated after the Chicago *Tribune* had shown reason to believe that he had bought his seat. Taft complained that it was not fair that Lorimer should be condemned without having been tried and convicted, and accused T.R. of inconsistency in that, having blasted Lorimer, he went to Cincinnati, and, at the Longworth home, fraternized with "Boss" Cox, who was quite as bad.

Many of Roosevelt's politically expedient acts were much less spectacular than those already cited. He could postpone his decision about Brownsville until after an election, and he could audaciously order a full-scale postal scandal investigation just before one. Sometimes the politically reckless thing turned out for him expedient. Sometimes extravagant language paved the way for milder demands; sometimes he used the language for educational purposes. Once at least we know that he asked for four battleships because he wanted two. When a vote was needed to pass a ship subsidy bill, a congressman is said to have been routed out with the message, "If Dixon votes with us, he shall have his patronage, and if he does not he shall not."

Yet, though he may have enjoyed playing the game of politics, this was not what Roosevelt did best. He was too impatient to be a really distinguished practitioner in this area, too spectacular, and too honest. He was not politic, for example, when he announced in

1904 that he would not accept another term. As Hermann Hagedorn expresses it, his second term "was not rich in legislative accomplishment, for the Senate was consistently hostile, and gradually
even the House turned against him, accusing him of overwhelming
ambition and dictatorial methods." By the end of the term, Congress
and the President was frankly at each other's throats. In December
T.R. called Speaker Cannon out of his chair to the White House,
demanding to see him before a committee report was presented. In
January, for the first time since the days of Andrew Jackson, Congress voted to lay a President's message upon the table. On the
morning of Taft's inauguration, T.R. sent Congress his 421st message, and the newspapers headlined

ROOSEVELT SENDS STINGING REBUKE FOR FINALE

He was anything but politic in 1910 and in 1912 also, as we have
already seen. If he attracted conservative support by his policy on
the trusts, he drove it all away again with the constitutional changes
he advocated.

VII. American Minorities

What Roosevelt was really interested in was not the technicalities
of government but the welfare of human beings. This meant the
welfare of the individual, and it meant too the welfare of various
groups, sometimes conflicting, or seeming to conflict, with those of
others, and as regards the larger groups called nations, it frequently
involved those problems of war and peace in which Roosevelt was
so deeply interested, and in connection with which there has
been so much controversy.

Though Roosevelt used the term "race" loosely, and not quite
consistently, he was well aware that all racist theories rest upon a
very shaky ethnic foundation. He made fun of those who use
"Aryan" and "Teuton" with reverential admiration. "Anglo-Saxon"
he thought absurd except as applied to the Anglo-Saxon period in
English history; he even regretted using the term "Scotch-Irish" in
The Winning of the West. For himself, "common heirship in the
things of the spirit makes a closer bond than common heirship in the
things of the body," and he would not permit the old stock to tyran-
nize over the new in America. "I think my whole public life has

been an emphatic protest against the Peabodys and Van Renssalaers arrogating to themselves any superiority over the Caseys and Schwarzmeisters."

Yet he knew that race—or what passes as such—is a power in the world. "Race questions stand by themselves." He even doubted that racial feeling was basically more tolerant now than it had been in earlier days.

He had no idea that all peoples were alike. It is true, as Beale has emphatically pointed out, that he never commits himself to the view that there are races and nations which are incapable of civilization. It is also true that when he encounters a highly developed individual who belongs to an undeveloped race he treats him just as he would treat an equally developed American or white man. But he never forgot that there were developed and undeveloped races, and he had no sympathy with those who would legislate for earth as if it were heaven. Consequently, he has nothing but scorn for those who would "give self-government to a number of individuals who regard themselves overdressed when they wear breech-clouts." Consequently, again, he can permit himself to speak of "Morocco, Turkey, and the barbarous countries generally" or refer to the "difference between the barbarism of a Moor and the barbarism of a Tartar."

Roosevelt is quite capable of using the word "foreigner" as a term of reproach when he is angry at somebody: Southern and Central Americans, for example, are always "dagoes" when they behave badly or happen to annoy him. All through the war he cited China as a horrible example of what the United States might become: to be "Chinafied" would be the worst fate that could befall us. The terms he uses do not show much knowledge of Chinese civilization, while to attribute the condition of Chinese coolies to China's military weakness was, of course, a fantastic oversimplification. Roosevelt was immensely concerned over California's assault on Japanese sensibilities—and this was immensely to his credit, both as a statesman and as a man—but he showed no concern whatever over the earlier Chinese exclusion act, partly perhaps because Japan was in a much better position to create international difficulties but also, one must believe, because he admired Japan and despised China. Even here, however, it should be noted that individual Chinese were always treated with the same courtesy as Japanese, and that he insisted strenuously that every consideration be shown to Chinese merchants and scholars.

Israel Zangwill dedicated *The Melting Pot* to Roosevelt, but in the early days he had some very curious views concerning the varying susceptibility of races to amalgamation. Nothing could read much more strangely today than this 1898 statement:

My own experience is that practically the Scandinavians and Protestant Germans mix completely with the native Americans as soon as English becomes their home language; they then become indistinguishable from them, intermarrying freely. On the other hand the Irish are kept apart by their religion, at least to a large extent; though curiously enough the religion does not seem to have the same effect upon the French when once they have learned to speak English.

Roosevelt's attitudes toward various racial groups in the United States and elsewhere were necessarily involved in a number of his acts and policies as president. The domestic front may be surveyed first.

Indians Roosevelt met as an historian before he was called upon to deal with them as a government official. As an historian, he was unsympathetic, reacting forcefully against what he considered the sentimental attitude of Helen Hunt Jackson and other writers. "To most of the land on which we found them they had no stronger claim than that of having butchered the original occupants." He was repelled by Indian cruelties, and he could see no sense in leaving a vast continent as an exclusive hunting preserve for "scattered savage tribes" who led "meaningless, squalid, ferocious lives." Nevertheless, he admits freely that many wrongs were done to Indians by white men, among them some which cannot be pardoned.

In Dakota Roosevelt met Indians personally. "I suppose I should be ashamed to say that I take the Western view of the Indian," he declared in New York in 1886. "I don't go so far as to think that the only good Indians are the dead Indians, but I believe nine out of ten are, and I shouldn't like to inquire too closely into the case of the tenth." In *Ranch Life and the Hunting Trail*, published two years later, he is more sympathetic, for here we find him differentiating between tribe and tribe and between individual and individual. He ultimately developed considerable faith in the Indian capacity for advancement, and, with the aid of Mary Austin, Natalie Curtis, and others, he came to value Indian art and Indian music. As president he recommended that Indians should be treated as individuals, with the aim of absorbing them into American life.

T.R.'s attitude toward Jews as a religious group is considered elsewhere. His attitude toward them in other aspects is nearly as good, but not quite. Early in his career he administered a tongue-lashing to a group of fellow club members who were planning to blackball a Jew who had applied for membership. He sympathized with Dreyfus. Early, again, I find a reference to "Jew bankers," à la Henry and Brooks Adams; later, there is a fling at the pro-German and pacifist Jews who surround Wilson, though T.R. immediately adds that most Jews are loyal. In 1902 he tried without avail to help persecuted Jews in Rumania; in 1903 he cleverly engineered a protest against the Russian massacre at Kishinev, without involving the United States in diplomatic difficulties. At the end of the Russo-Japanese War, he took advantage of the good will then prevalent by making a personal appeal to Count Witte to attempt to remove the Russian ban on travel by American Jews. He once protested to Arthur Train the use of a Jewish villain in one of his stories.

Much more serious problems arose in connection with "that most-sinned against of races—the colored." "I feel as hopeless as you do about the black problem of our own nation," T.R. writes General Taylor in 1900. But once more there is no sentimentalizing, "The white man," he wrote Warrington Dawson, "does not do his full duty with the negro; and in no way do white men fall short of their duty more than in the case of those very foolish white men who refuse to face facts and refuse to see that the average negro is on a different and far lower strata than is the case with the white man." This point of view he maintains quite consistently. Even in the Spanish War, he felt that, while the colored troops had done well, they showed disadvantages as compared to the whites, and that they needed very careful leading.

Roosevelt had nothing but contempt for those Southerners who "shriek in public about miscegenation, but . . . leer as they talk to me privately of the colored mistresses and colored children of white men whom they know." But he also expressed his concurrence in the views of Robert Strange that social intermingling of the

races, not being a matter of civil privilege and therefore not subject
to the regulation of civil law, must be left to the people of each
community to settle for themselves; that it was as much in the
interest of Negroes as of whites that racial purity should be maintained; and that Negroes should be encouraged to seek the finest
education which they are capable of assimilating and thus become
leaders among their own people.

Whatever present-day Negroes may think of some of these judgments, they should, in justice to Roosevelt, consider what he tried
to do for their race. His first act in a national convention was to
support the nomination of a Negro, ex-Congressman John R. Lynch,
as temporary chairman of the convention of 1884. In 1903 he backed
up Judge T. G. Jones, who had sentenced a number of white men
to the penitentiary for violation of the federal peonage law. In
1904 he insisted upon having some Negroes on the Louisiana delegation, and moved to have an exhibition of their achievements
included in the Jamestown Exhibition. In 1908 he ordered the
Department of Justice to take legal action, if necessary, to force the
Nashville, Chattanooga, & St. Louis Railway Company to comply
with the order to provide colored passengers with accommodations
equal to those provided for whites, and when the Ben Greet Players
appeared on the White House lawn, he directed that the seats in
the section for Negroes must be just as desirable as those in the
white section. In 1911 he urged the University of North Carolina
Press to publish a book by the only colored officer then in the
United States Army.

He always showed special concern for the educated Negro and,
realizing that few posts were open to him, tried to give him his
fair share of government appointments. He appointed Negroes to
responsible positions in New York, Chicago, and Boston, being the
first president so to act. In the South he was more conservative.
He himself said that he had reduced the number of Negro appointees in the South, and had "gone as far in refusing to appoint
them as I could short of joining with those who wish to take the
position that under no circumstances must any colored man ever
get hold of an official position." Yet he appointed William D. Crum
collector of customs at the Port of Charleston, and when the Senate
refused to confirm Crum, he kept him in office by interim appoint-

ments, despite all Southern protests. Toward the end of his life, when both men appeared at a meeting to honor the overthrow of czarist tyranny, he clashed publicly and sensationally with Samuel Gompers over the current race riots in East St. Louis, Illinois. "Not for a moment shall I acquiesce in any apology for the murder of women and children in our own country."

Once a Negro who had been introduced into Sagamore Hill by T.R.'s faithful attendant, James Amos, himself a Negro, stole some jewelry. On this basis a friend generalized about the untrustworthiness of Negroes, but Roosevelt would have none of it:

It is as emphatically unjust to the race to speak of the criminal's misdeed as a reflection upon the race while ignoring the record and standing of the colored man under whom he served, and of the colored man who arrested him, as it would be to speak of the ordinary white criminal's record as a reflection upon the white race. . . . The whole affair emphasizes the need for treating each man on his merits without regard to the color of his skin, and the injustice of holding a race accountable for the misdeeds of an individual.

Roosevelt's attempt to treat Negroes justly involved him in a number of celebrated controversies. I have already referred to the appointment of William D. Crum in South Carolina. Decidedly more amusing was the case of Mrs. Minnie M. Cox, Negro postmistress of Indianola, Mississippi, who, after having long given satisfactory service, was forced to resign under duress, whereupon Roosevelt closed the post office and forced the people of Indianola to go thirty miles to the next town for their mail. Ultimately they hired a Negro to pick it up for them! Much better known, however, is the storm precipitated immediately after T.R. came into the White House, when he invited Booker T. Washington, whom he regarded as the most distinguished man in the South, to dine with him. Roosevelt afterwards had doubts as to the wisdom of this invitation; he even feared he might have hurt Negroes instead of helping them; but he had no doubts about its propriety. "I never thought much about it at the time," he wrote in 1904. "It seemed to me so natural and so proper."

Two of T.R.'s decisions, however, caused much displeasure among American Negroes. One was his 1912 decision not to admit Negroes into the councils of the Progressive party in the South (which drove

Booker T. Washington himself into the Republican camp); the other came in connection with the famous Brownsville incident.

The 1912 decision was purely a matter of political strategy. As Roosevelt expressed it to Bradley Gilman:

For over forty-five years we have tried in these States to build up a Republican Party in which the negro should be a big element, and the result has been disastrous from every standpoint. The effort has accomplished literally nothing of good. . . . It has made the Republican Party in most Southern States a negligible quantity. . . . It has kept the Southern white men in all the districts in which there is any appreciable number of negroes united within the Democratic Party. . . . It has not succeeded in giving the negro any influence whatever in government.

In reply to a question from the gallery at the Progressive Convention, he explained (as O. K. Davis reports it)

that, by the building-up of another political party in the South, acting on the same principles on which the Democratic Party acted, there would be developed a demand all through those States for the negro vote, and that both parties would be contending for it, just as they do in the North. In that way, he predicted, the negro would come into his political rights.

The record of the Brownsville investigations, largely inspired by Senator Joseph B. Foraker, fill half a dozen large volumes, but what happened (or was believed to have happened) can be stated briefly. On the night of August 13, 1906, fifteen to twenty members of three all-Negro companies of United States soldiers, who had been stationed at Fort Brown since about the first of August, and who had already had some friction with the townspeople, shot up the town of Brownsville. One man was killed and two wounded. Some shots, fired into houses, narrowly missed women and children.

T.R. wanted the guilty men. When he found them shielded, as he conceived it, by a conspiracy of silence, he discharged without honor nearly all the members of the three companies involved. Six Medal of Honor soldiers were concerned and thirteen who had been awarded certificates of bravery for merit.

The duty of the Army, the President argued, is to protect, not murder, Americans.

Unless that duty is well performed, the Army becomes a mere dangerous mob; and if conduct such as that of the murderers in question is not, where possible, punished, and, where this is not possible, unless the chance of its repetition is guarded against in the most thoroughgoing fashion, it would be better that the entire Army should be disbanded.

He denied that he had "punished" the offenders.

The punishment meet for mutineers and murders such as those guilty of the Brownsville assault is death; and a punishment only less severe ought to be meted out to those who have aided and abetted mutiny and murder and treason by refusing to help in their detection. I would that it were possible for me to have punished the guilty men. I regret most keenly that I have not been able to do so.

Whether T.R. was right or wrong about Brownsville, it is silly to argue that race prejudice was involved. He would have acted in exactly the same way if the offenders had been white men. And surely no intelligent Negro and no true friend of Negroes will argue that Negroes should have larger license to commit crimes than other men.

The President has been accused of violating traditional Anglo-Saxon notions of justice in dismissing these men without trial and running the risk of punishing the innocent rather than letting the guilty go free. It does not seem unreasonable to suppose that some of those accused of having entered into a conspiracy of silence were simply ignorant. Senator Foraker offered a more radical objection. He did not believe that the soldiers had done the job at all. The argument, which is based upon the kind of bullets found in the streets and the condition of the soldiers' guns after the firing, is very complicated, and T.R. found it unconvincing:

The only motive suggested as possibly influencing any one else was a desire to get rid of the colored troops, so strong that it impelled the citizens of Brownsville to shoot up their own houses, to kill one of their own number, to assault their own police, wounding the lieutenant, who had been an officer for twenty years—all with the purpose of discrediting the negro troops. The suggestion is on its face so ludicrously impossible that it is difficult to treat it as honestly made.

Concerning First Sergeant Mingo Saunders, whose unhappy plight particularly caught the imagination of the newspapers, Roosevelt declares investigation had shown that "in spite of his reputation for personal courage, [he] was as thoroughly dangerous, unprincipled and unworthy a soldier as ever wore the United States uniform, and that under no conceivable circumstances should he ever be allowed again in the army."

A Negro friend of Bradley Gilman's told him that the investigation had been badly bungled. "An unknown negro detective, say from New York, thrown into that camp and mingling with the soldiers, would have had the secret out of them in twenty-four hours." Such crafty methods of working did not occur to T.R. and might very likely not have appealed to him if they had. James Amos, who is certainly generally a reliable witness, tells a story, nowhere else recorded, which, if accurately reported, considerably changes the picture. Amos says that T.R.

got some of the accused troopers to call at the White House. They tried to hold out at first, but under Mr. Roosevelt's questioning they broke down and admitted the guilt of their companies. The President never used this confession in justification of his act. The soldiers had not made it willingly, but only under the influence of his dominating personality and while it completely satisfied his mind he never felt at liberty to use it, though he might have hushed the whole controversy by doing so.

Foraker did show, however, that some of Roosevelt's early statements about what happened at Brownsville were overdefinite and exaggerated, and there was a certain ebbing of truculence in his later statements. Owen Wister says Roosevelt admitted to him that at one point he had been badly advised by the War Department. Amos makes a special point of his thoughtfulness in moving the troops out of Texas, for their own protection, before they were discharged. The majority of the Senate committee sustained Roosevelt's action, but the controversy outlasted his administration. After the Senate fight had begun, he directed Taft, as secretary of war, to accept applications for re-enlistment from soldiers who could make a reasonable case for their innocence, but only eleven men were finally re-enlisted. On January 27, 1909, a little more than a month before he went out of office, T.R. wrote Senator Aldrich:

I have no question . . . that the bulk of Company B . . . are guilty to a degree that should rightly bar them from ever again reentering the American army. I am strongly inclined to believe, however, that the bulk of the members of Companies C and D had no such guilty knowledge as would make it necessary permanently to debar them from reentry to the service.

Roosevelt did not, I think, regard Brownsville as one of his successes. He omitted all mention of the controversy from his *Autobiography*.

VIII. Americans and Others

The foreign countries toward which it seems profitable to consider Roosevelt's attitude are four: England, Germany, Russia, and Japan.

His early attitude toward England, the result of traditional American patriotic enthusiasm, and probably influenced by resentment of her attitude during the American Civil War, was inclined to be hostile. England's friendliness during the Spanish-American War began to induce a change of heart, though as late a 1901 he can remark that England is the one nation whose violation of the Monroe Doctrine would ultimately redound to our interest: "She could take the Philippines and Porto Rico, but they would be a very poor offset for the loss of Canada."

T.R. was against England on the Irish Home Rule issue; he resented not getting any help from her in the Russo-Japanese peace negotiations; and he seriously suspected her good intentions in the Morocco crisis of 1906. When the Kaiser told him in 1910 that he himself adored England, T.R. replied that that was a stronger statement than he himself would make. Nevertheless, he was pretty well convinced by 1900 that "it is for the good of the world that the English-speaking race in all its branches should hold as much of the world's surface as possible," and that should disaster overtake the British Empire it would mean war for the United States in five years.

Roosevelt's pro-British feeling in World War I needs no recalling; his friends and his enemies agree that he was one of the important forces toward bringing America into the war. In his correspondence with Lord Grey and others he is frank in speaking of England's violation of America's neutral rights, but he puts his whole plea on the basis of British self-interest. For her own sake, and the sake of the cause she represents, Britain must not antagonize America or run the risk of cutting off supplies vital to her interests. Once he even suggested naïvely that, if the Allies have to put themselves in the wrong, "I wish it could be a French and not a British ship that took the action"! He did not have much sympathy with British leaders in power after the war; he even challenged Kipling's exaggerated statement of America's debt to the British Navy. "I think the English are a pretty thick-headed lot," he wrote Harriet Gaylord, at the end of 1918. For all that, he was for close cooperation between Britain and America after the war, and virtually his last message to the American people was to urge an all-inclusive arbitration treaty with Britain.

The most startling thing about Roosevelt's relations with England, however (as Tyler Dennett and others have shown since his death), was that, in 1905, by personal diplomacy and negotiations conducted over Elihu Root's head, he created an unofficial alliance in the Far East not only with Britain but with her ally, Japan. When T.R. told Finley Peter Dunne that he was with him "heart and soul, in laughing away such folly as 'the Anglo-Saxon Alliance business,'" he was therefore telling the truth only in a strictly technical sense. At no time was there a formal alliance. T.R. knew perfectly well that the Senate would never have ratified any treaty looking toward that end. He must also have known that American public opinion would not have tolerated what he actually did, had the facts become known. In his own mind his act was a move toward preserving white supremacy; he probably even thought of it as an influence for peace in the Orient. But it committed the American people, without their consent, to a course of action full of danger to themselves and their country.

It is hard to see how any American president could have served Japan's interests more diligently than Roosevelt did. In the nineties, it is true, he had mistrusted the Nipponese, but when they accepted our domination in Hawaii, he apparently concluded that they posed no real threat to our interests. In welcoming the Oriental representatives to the Jamestown Exposition in 1907 he singled out "in particular . . . the representative of the mighty island empire of Japan; that empire, which, in learning from the West, has shown that it had so much, so very much, to teach the West in return."

The full story of T.R.'s fight to protect the Japanese in California and to prevent that state from disturbing Japanese-American relations by adverse legislation regarding segregation in the schools and the ownership of land is told in his letters and in Thomas A. Bailey's *Theodore Roosevelt and Japanese-American Relations.* "The infernal fools in California, and especially in San Francisco, insult the Japanese recklessly, and in the event of war it will be the Nation as a whole which will pay the consequences." Roosevelt did not want Oriental immigration into the United States, but he did want a gentleman's agreement with Japan which would make it possible for her to regulate Japanese immigration from her side.

To achieve his ends Roosevelt went far beyond the line of duty—and probably beyond his constitutional rights—to say nothing of running the risk of being snubbed personally, by intervening with both the governor of California and the mayor of San Francisco. At one time the San Francisco School Board, and their mayor with them, made a pilgrimage to the White House! Roosevelt himself told Baron Kaneko that nothing in his administration had given him more trouble than California's anti-Japanese policy; he told Bishop Lawrence he would make "any sacrifice" to prevent war with Japan.

There were those who thought that to prevent war with Japan Roosevelt had come close to declaring war on California! On December 5, 1906, the San Francisco *Chronicle* called the hero of San Juan "an unpatriotic President who united with aliens to break down the civilization of his own countrymen"! As in the Brownsville case, he permitted himself some exaggeration and inexactitude in his description of the case, and as usual he was very patient and tactful in the actual negotiations.

Through all these negotiations Roosevelt frankly admitted the possibility of war with Japan, for he believed that the Japanese had the same proportion of jingo fools as the United States. Characteristically he used the crisis to encourage the development of his universal panacea for peace, a strong Navy. Yet he refused to lose his head. Even in 1907, when all Europe expected war between the United States and Japan, he was calm. "War between the United States and Japan," he wrote Bishop Harris, "is to my mind unthinkable, for it could come only as the result of such folly and wickedness as to stamp all who were responsible for it, no matter in which country they dwelt, with eternal infamy." Not even the Kaiser's warning that the Japanese were infiltrating Mexico with hostile designs against the United States alarmed him. Finally, he deliberately gambled on peace by sending the fleet around the world, issuing especially careful directions as to how American sailors should conduct themselves in Tokyo. He admitted that he did not know what the effect of this action would be: there was one chance in ten that it might make for war; the other nine, he thought, were in favor of peace.

Roosevelt also approved of Japan extending herself in Manchuria and in Korea. This, he thought, would act as a check upon Russia and become a force for peace and stability in the Orient. The attitude of the United States concerning Korea was communicated to the Japanese premier by Secretary of War Taft in Tokyo on July 27, 1905. Apparently Taft took the initiative, but T.R. promptly cabled, "Wish you would state to Katsura that I confirm every word you have said." Roosevelt has been criticized for the inconsistency between this friendliness toward Japanese expansionism and his indignation when Germany invaded Belgium. The inconsistency is more apparent than real. He habitually distinguished between developed and undeveloped countries. Rightly or wrongly, he believed that the Koreans had demonstrated their inability to govern themselves, and that by developing Manchuria the Japanese would aid the spread of civilization. Germany, in Belgium, only destroyed it.

Baron Kaneko later claimed that in 1905 Roosevelt suggested to him that Japan proclaim "a Japanese Monroe Doctrine" for Asia, promising to "support her with my power" if she did. However this may be, he continued to be deeply interested in Japanese-American relations clear into Wilson's administration. Seven months before he died, he wrote a long article defending Japan's course in World War I and combating those who sought to build up ill will between her and the United States.

Russia was no problem for the United States in T.R.'s time, but he saw more clearly than most men that she might someday become one. He recognized that traditionally she was our friend, but he believed that this situation had begun to change for the worse as early as the time of the Spanish-American War. At the beginning of his presidency, he saw her as menacing Anglo-American interests in the Far East, and in 1904 he asked the Navy for a plan of action "in case it became necessary for our Asiatic squadron to bottle up the Vladivostock Russian squadron." This does not mean that T.R. expected war with Russia in 1904; indeed, he states specifically that he did not. "I shall certainly not fight unless we have ample reasons, and *unless I can show our people that we have such cause.*" But to suggest the possibility even to deny it was startling in 1904.

In the Russo-Japanese War, Roosevelt's sympathies were with Japan, but he wanted each power to continue in the Far East as a check upon the other. Apparently, however, he liked the Russians less after his experiences as mediator. "They are utterly insincere and treacherous; they have no conception of truth, no willingness to look facts in the face, no regard for others of any sort or kind, no knowledge of their own strength or weakness; and they are helplessly unable to meet emergencies." Also, he feared they might be disposed to "try another throw" with Japan for supremacy in Asia.

Yet he never doubted that Russia was a great nation. "Undoubtedly the future is hers unless she mars it from within." As early as 1896 and 1897 he talked prophetically about her. Someday she would experience a "red terror" compared to which the French Revolution would seem pale. Someday she might crush Germany for good and all. "If she ever does take possession of Northern China and drill the Northern Chinese to serve as her Army she will indeed be a formidable power."

By 1914 he was inclined to be hopeful that Russia might escape the red terror; he thought liberal ideas gaining. Russia was not going to turn to Asia. "Down at bottom . . . the Russian is just about like you or like me." He hoped, too, that Russia's war experiences might liberalize her. When the March Revolution occurred in 1917, he sent a message through Count Ilya Tolstoy, in which he spoke to the Russian people "as a fellow democrat and a fellow radical, when I urge them, for the sake of the ultimate welfare of the mass of the people of Russia, to see that their striking victory is used with such moderation and wisdom as to prevent all possibility of reaction." It was not to be. Roosevelt lived to see the fall of Kerensky, and Lenin was in power when he died.

IX. President and Kaiser

The story of Roosevelt's relations with Germany involve both his attitude toward a people and his relations with a man, Kaiser

Wilhelm II. In both connections I find more wavering on Roosevelt's part than often appears elsewhere.

In his *Autobiography* T.R. tells us that his stay in Germany as a child gave him a feeling for the German people which made it impossible for him ever to think of them as foreigners. And even in the middle of World War I he wrote Professor Münsterberg that the German Club of Milwaukee was the club in which he felt most at home.

Yet in 1889 he would welcome a spat with Germany, and in this connection he declared absurdly that "the burning of New York and a few other seacoast cities would be a good object lesson." In 1897 he is almost as bad. "I must say," he writes Commander B. H. McCalla, "I would like to take the 'tuck' out of the Kaiser's people."

But two years later, "The German is of our blood, our principles and our ideas." He not only wishes Germany well wherever her interests do not conflict with those of the English-speaking peoples but he wishes that she would ally herself with these peoples against the rest of the world. If she were wise, she would strike down Russia.

By 1900 he is worried about her seizing southern Brazil, but he would also like an agreement with her to work together in China. In 1901 he feels, contradictorily, that Germany must be kept out of the Western Hemisphere and that it would be a fine thing if she and the United States could work together in South America. In 1906 he likes and respects Germany but does not believe that she reciprocates the feeling. In 1907 he thinks her more warlike than either Britain or America. In 1908 he believes that she has been more successful than other nations in counteracting the evils that come in with modern luxury; he also sounds her out on an arbitration treaty. At the very end of his term he told Knox that he did not think her dangerous to the United States.

The war, of course, made a great change, but it did not represent a clean break with the past. "I have a very genuine respect and admiration for the Germans," T.R. wrote Kipling in November, 1914, "and I alienate them with great reluctance." He condemned Germany for her violation of Belgium; he would, he insists, have condemned any other power in exactly the same way. And in *Fear God and Take Your Own Part*, he praised Germany even while demanding action against her. "I am myself partly of German blood." "No nation is always right. . . . Since this country became a nation, there have been occasions when it has so acted as to deserve the condemnation of mankind." "I shall stand by Germany in the future on any occasion when its conduct permits me to do so. We must not be vindictive, or prone to remember injuries; we need forgiveness, and we must be ready to grant forgiveness." [14]

When Roosevelt was president, the world generally regarded him and the Kaiser as having a good deal in common temperamentally. In his early days, mistrusting Germany, T.R. had mistrusted the Kaiser also, but after 1900 he came both to respect him more and to fear him less. The Kaiser, on his part, always professed the warmest feelings both for Roosevelt and for his country, and his stock with T.R. was considerably heightened by the fact that he, alone among monarchs, "stood by me like a trump" during the Russo-Japanese negotiations. At one time England thought the President under the Kaiser's influence.

Even in the Russo-Japanese matter, however, Roosevelt privately told James Ford Rhodes that that Kaiser was "a regular fuss-cat," and he spent a good deal of time, and wrote a good many letters, explaining that, though he liked the Kaiser and admired him, he thought him much too "jumpy" to be a safe ally. "The Kaiser has had another fit and is now convinced that France is trying to engineer a congress of the nations, in which Germany will be left out." "I wish to Heaven our excellent friend, the Kaiser, was not so jumpy and did not have so many pipe dreams." Even so, he was sure that jumpiness was the worst England or anybody else could have to fear from Wilhelm; he had no evil purpose. In 1907, when Carnegie got hold of a crazy story that Germany was building up her fleet against America, Roosevelt took the initiative in a private letter to the Emperor—"I have entire confidence in your genuine friendship to my country"—to which his Majesty replied cordially, and heatedly, that "all Mr. Carnegie has heard in London are foul and filthy lies." When, in 1908, to the consternation of the Foreign Office, the Kaiser gave a wildly alarmist interview to the American journalist,

[14] On May 6, 1917, T.R. appealed to the Secretary of State to grant the request of Dr. Karl Buenz to be allowed to return to Germany. What Dr. Buenz did, he argued, was done as a representative of Germany, in accordance with the international code, and while the United States was still at peace with her.

William Bayard Hale, Roosevelt persuaded the New York *Times* to kill the story in the interest of international amity, but though his faith in the Kaiser's good judgment was lessened, he still did not "for a moment believe" that what he had said "indicated a settled purpose." [15]

One of the great controversies concerning Roosevelt concerns the role he played in 1902 when Germany, Britain, and Italy, moving to collect their just debts from Venezuela, established a "peaceful blockade" of that country—and collided with the Monroe Doctrine. Germany's attitude does not seem to have been any more aggressive than England's; it is not quite clear why Roosevelt should have feared her more. According to T.R.'s own story, communicated many years afterwards to William Roscoe Thayer, and printed by him in his *Life of John Hay,* the President forced the Kaiser to accept arbitration by sending him word that, unless he agreed to do so within ten days, the American fleet would be ordered to the Venezuela coast. This matter has been debated by everybody who has written in detail about Roosevelt's conduct of foreign relations, and in recent years the weight of scholarly opinion has tended toward rejecting Roosevelt's account. Recently, however, Howard K. Beale has made a very strong case for it. If there was an international crisis, it came and went without the public ever having learned that it existed and without leaving ill feelings on either side. There was no bluster, and negotiations were so conducted that no question of face-saving could arise. T.R. must have used considerable tact in throwing American weight into the situation, perhaps less threateningly than he suggested to Thayer at a time when both of them were completely out of sympathy with anything German. The absence of contemporary documentary evidence, which has been cited against Roosevelt, would be quite in harmony with this hypothesis, and in harmony too with his usual methods in handling delicate matters.

In 1906, at the Kaiser's request, Roosevelt interested himself in the Algeciras conference which was called to settle the German-

[15] In 1905 T.R. did not want to write to the Kaiser at President Eliot's request because "he is all the time asking me to do things. Sometimes I can do as he requests and sometimes I can not. But I do not want to put myself under obligations to him." Two years later he wrote Carnegie, "He is a big man and I have the heartiest admiration for him."

French crisis in Morocco. American interests not being involved, the President was reluctant to intervene, but finally agreed to do so in the interest of peace. But, though the Kaiser accepted the outcome with every token of gratitude and satisfaction, American influence at Algeciras was far more pro-French than pro-German; Pringle even sees the conference as contributing to the policy of "encirclement" that became so important a cause of World War I. I am not supposing that the Kaiser was a wholly disinterested party at Algeciras, nor do I imagine that he was actuated solely by a devotion to world peace, but there was no justification for Roosevelt's contemptuous ascription of his fears to "pipe dreams." There was a very real menace to Germany, and there was a very real menace to peace. Once more the particular crisis was bridged over, and Roosevelt's tact contributed to the bridging. "In the United States," writes Allan Nevins, "Roosevelt made a tactful effort to cloak the German defeat, and at a meeting of German-American veterans on March 12th, in a speech which both Sternberg and Jusserand had previously read, he gave warm praise to the Kaiser for the triumph of Germany's commendable aims at Algeciras."

Roosevelt and the Kaiser met at Berlin when Roosevelt visited there in 1910, and was entertained at the Palace, and again in London, at the funeral of King Edward VII. In Berlin the Kaiser not only attended T.R.'s lecture but put the Army through its paces for him. Afterwards he gave him a whole series of photographs of the event, which are still kept at Sagamore Hill, each inscribed by the Kaiser and signed on the back with humorously indiscreet captions.[16] One writer about Roosevelt, Earl Looker, has declared that from this time Roosevelt knew that war was inevitable and that he returned to America to prepare his country for it.

There is some slight, independent evidence to support this view, but it nearly all comes indirectly. E. E. Garrison says that T.R. told him and a group of men at the Harvard Club of the Kaiser's love of and plans for his war machine shortly after his return to New York. Hermann Hagedorn reports that, a year after his Berlin visit, T.R. told Mrs. Cowles that if Germany should ever conquer England and make herself supreme in Europe, she would be almost

[16] Four of these pictures, with their captions, were published in *Life*, XXVIII, March 20, 1950, pp. 18–19.

certain to try her strength against America next. And Marshall Stimson's "Chapter from an Unpublished Autobiography" tells how, after T.R. had spoken on preparedness in San Francisco, Stimson accused him of warmongering. He replied, "At the invitation of Kaiser Wilhelm, I attended the spring maneuvers of the German army. If you had heard and seen what I saw when I was in Germany you would feel just as I do." In 1915 T.R. wrote Booth Tarkington, "what I saw in Germany five years ago very thoroughly opened my eyes."

The principal argument against Looker's view is that there is nothing in the letters T.R. wrote in 1910 and subsequently to support it. Even more cogently, he did *not* return to America to prepare us for war or for any international problems whatever. Instead he moved gradually into the Progressive campaign, with Armageddon on the domestic front.

It seems clear, however, that T.R. was somewhat disappointed in the Kaiser when at last they stood face to face. He said so, in so many words, to Taft, when he visited him at Beverley, in June, 1910, adding that he had found him "vain as a peacock." Will Irwin, too, quotes him as saying that he found the Kaiser's point of view "very sordid." It is clear that he thought him less well read than he had expected and vain of his knowledge in the very fields where there was least justification for vanity. Only in military history and technique was he, in Roosevelt's view, well informed. But Roosevelt also told Taft that he did not think the Kaiser wanted war with England, and in his long 1911 letter to G. O. Trevelyan, recounting the history of his European trip, while stipulating that "there were many points in international morality" upon which he and the Kaiser did not agree, he takes pains to report his confidence that Wilhelm "never postulates to himself such an idea as the conquest of England." Indeed, he even lists among their points of cordial agreement their common "cordial dislike of sham and of pretense, and therefore . . . cordial dislike of the kind of washy movement for international peace with which Carnegie's name has become so closely associated." Furthermore, it was not until the war in Europe was nearly over that T.R. came to believe that the Kaiser had been personally responsible for it.[17]

[17] As late as April 26, 1918, T.R. refused to write a piece about the Kaiser for *The Outlook*. "I wouldn't be willing to do so. My criticism of him is on his

Practically every book on T.R. tells how, when the Kaiser wanted to talk to him but announced that he had only forty-five minutes to spare, Roosevelt replied that he would be very glad to see him but could only give him twenty minutes. This story appears in a number of different forms. Mrs. Robinson tells it practically as I have given it here, except that it is twenty-five minutes instead of twenty. In Thayer's biography the twenty-minute limit is imposed by Roosevelt's having an appointment with Mrs. Humphry Ward. But the most authoritative account seems to be that of Henry White, which is given in Allan Nevins' biography of White as follows:

Roosevelt paid a courtesy call on the Kaiser at Buckingham Palace, but, relieved to find him out, left a card on which he had written that he was looking forward to seeing him at a state reception. Just as White and T.R. were re-entering their car, the Kaiser drove up, exclaiming how sorry he would have been to miss his guest, and how lucky he was to have arrived in time. "I have an hour to spare and we can have a good talk together." Roosevelt replied that he had many things to do and could not spare so much as an hour. "How much time can you give me?" asked the Kaiser, to which Roosevelt, after consulting his watch, replied, "I'll give you twenty minutes." "All right," replied the Kaiser, "I'm very glad to get that much of your time. Let's go off and have a talk together."

Kaiser Wilhelm II is said to have been much hurt by T.R.'s pronounced anti-German stand in World War I. From his own point of view he was quite justified. Though I do not doubt that he was "jumpy," he seems to have been far more consistent in his attitude toward Roosevelt than Roosevelt was toward him. There is no reason to doubt the sincerity of his admiration. It survived the Venezuela incident and the Algeciras conference. At the time of the Japanese war scare in 1907 he sent word through his ambassador that if war came Germany would furnish the United States with a base of supplies. Whatever the Kaiser's motives and tactics in the European power game may have been, there is no evidence that he was unfriendly toward Roosevelt or Roosevelt's America at any time.

---

public actions." The month before he had gagged at Hal Reid's title, *The Beast of Berlin*. He had also refused to allow Wilfred Grenfell to make any public allusion to the pictures the Kaiser had given him in 1910. Wilhelm, he added, was right about Carnegie, who had hurt, not helped, the peace cause.

SEVEN

The World of War and Peace

I. Praise of Battle

Perhaps no other controversy about Roosevelt is quite so impassioned as the controversy over his attitude toward war and peace. The views range all the way from those who see him as one of the most dangerous militarists we have had in America to the 1909 statement of so good a pacifist as Washington Gladden that "no man has ever done so much to promote peace on earth." Perhaps it might be useful, for once, to look at the evidence, so far as possible without prepossessions.

If we want wild statements in praise of war, and in favor of warlike action in particular emergencies, we shall find no difficulty in getting them, especially from the early T.R. When he wrote his book on the War of 1812, he thought we ought to have fought France as well as England. He wished, too, that we had taken Canada in Thomas Hart Benton's time, though he is careful to add: "Of course no one would wish to see . . . any . . . settled communities now added to our domain by force." Yet in 1893 he wanted ultimately to drive every European power off this continent, and in 1895 he was all ready to fight England over Venezuela. "The clamor of the peace faction has convinced me that this country needs a war." In 1896 he declares again, "If it wasn't wrong I should say that personally I would rather welcome a foreign war." Even when there was no accommodating crisis at hand, he could still feel belligerent. In 1885 Charles G. Washburn met him in Chicago on his way to his ranch in Dakota. "He would like above all things now to go to war with some one," wrote Washburn. "He has just walked out of the hotel with his rifle on his shoulder. . . . I urged him to give up his frontier life, but he is charmed with it and wants to be killing something all the time."

As everybody knows, he did his utmost to get this country into the Spanish-American War. "I am a bit of a jingo," he writes on November 4, 1897—"I wish we would turn Spain out of Cuba before Congress meets." On November 15 he admitted that McKinley had preserved both peace and the nation's honor, but this apparently did not lessen his conviction of the necessity for intervention. His letter to his naval chief, Secretary Long, after the sinking of the *Maine,* is surprisingly moderate in its tone. He hopes no other battleship will be sent to replace it. "In point of force it is either too great or too small." But in a private letter of the same date, he declares, "The *Maine* was sunk by an act of dirty treachery," and wishes McKinley would order the fleet to Havana. On March 21 he pulls out all the stops in a letter to Brooks Adams: "The blood of the Cubans, the blood of women and children who have perished by the hundred thousand in hideous misery, lies at our door; and the blood of the murdered men of the *Maine* calls not for indemnity but for the full measure of atonement which can only come by driving the Spaniard from the New World." This is the same position that he takes up in his *Autobiography.* Before the final break came, he must have known that Spain was ready to yield without fighting, but I am sure he would have been very much disappointed with such a diplomatic victory, for by this time he had fully convinced himself that a nice little war would be good for the American character. In 1899 he says that he is glad the Spanish War came when it did as it saved him from an unwholesome sedentary life! In later years he was to say that San Juan Hill had given him the most glamorous memory of his life.

Some of his utterances about war in the abstract are even worse than what I have already quoted:

The victories of peace are great; but the victories of war are greater. No merchant, no banker, no railroad magnate, no inventor of improved industrial processes, can do for any nation what can be done for it by its great fighting men. No triumph of peace can equal the armed triumph over malice domestic or foreign levy. No qualities called out by a purely peaceful life stand on a level with those stern and virile virtues which move the men of stout heart and strong hand who uphold the honor of their flag in battle.

This dates from 1897, the same year in which T.R. thought that the Russian might be "the one man with enough barbarous blood in him to be the hope of a world that is growing effete" and in which he got himself into hot water with a bellicose address at the Naval War College in which he declared, among other things, that "the diplomat is the servant, not the master of the soldier." But it was five years earlier that, in a literary essay, he had written, I think, the worst thing he ever said about war. It is interesting that these words were set down before he himself had had any experience of battle.

Every man who has in him any real power of joy in battle knows that he feels it when the wolf begins to rise in his heart; he does not shrink from blood and sweat, or deem that they mar the fight; he revels in them, in the toil, the pain and the danger, as but setting off the triumph.

It was from the Confederate Bullochs, not from the Roosevelt side of the house, that T.R. derived his military inheritance; his father and his five brothers and their cousin, James Roosevelt, of Hyde Park, were all of military age at the time of Civil War, but none participated in it. In early youth, T.R. himself seems to have been quite indifferent to military glory. It may be that the military seed took root when he began "making" his body, among other reasons because, after a humiliating experience with bullies, he wished to be able to defend himself; forever after, in any event, great battles and the literature in which they are celebrated held a romantic glamour for him, as the *Hero Tales from American History*, written in collaboration with Lodge, would alone prove.

Roosevelt's zeal for personal military service is further evidence of his attitude toward war. Though the only war in which he fought was a small one, the limitation was not voluntary on his part. "We had always quite simply taken it for granted," writes Mrs. Longworth, "that if there should be a war, Father would be in it." Let the remotest chance of trouble appear on the horizon, and he would be busy writing letters, getting permissions, and making plans to participate in any conflict that might materialize. He did this even in 1912 when he was mildly afraid of war with Japan, a war of which he disapproved and which he had done his utmost to prevent. He did it when there was danger with Mexico, just after he had got out of the South American jungle. Even when everything was quiet, he could not get this matter off his mind. He mentioned it to the governor of Wyoming in 1902; with supreme irrelevance he even touched on it in his Christmas letter to the Kaiser, the last year he was in the White House: "But if—what I most earnestly hope may never occur—there should be a big war in which the United States was engaged, while I am still in bodily vigor, I should endeavor to get permission to raise a division of mounted rifles."

"The truth is," said William Howard Taft of his estranged friend in 1911, "he believes in war and wishes to be a Napoleon and to die on the battlefield. He has the spirit of the old berserkers." This is a curious mixture of truth and error. Napoleon neither died on the battlefield nor wished to do so, and whatever else may be said of T.R., he was never seduced by the Napoleonic ideal. That he had a sickly longing to die in battle cannot, however, be gainsaid.

This was far from being a World War I attitude exclusively. As early as 1912, Jack Leary told T.R. he had always believed it was his ambition to die in battle. "By Jove," he replied, "how did you know that?" And Leary recalled an incident of the Spanish War when, finding a hopelessly wounded man in his regiment propped up against a wall, instead of commiserating him, T.R. shook his hand and said, "Well, old man, isn't this splendid!" In his essay on "The Cuban Dead" he grows positively lyrical over this horror.

In 1918 he faced death not for himself but for his sons, which was very much harder. It would be ridiculous to suggest that he wanted them to die in battle; for the one who did, no father could have grieved more. But even here there are utterances whose fevered intensity makes me squirm. "I hope and pray that they'll all come back, but before God, I'd rather none came back than one, able to go, had stayed at home." After Quentin's death, he wrote Ted and Eleanor:

There is no use pretending that we do not bitterly mourn. . . . But he had his crowded hour, of a life that was not only glorious but very happy; he had got his man; he had rendered service; he had a fortnight or three weeks when he stood on a crest of life which can not even be seen by sordid and torpid souls who know neither strife nor honor nor love, and who live forever in a gray fog at the lowest level.

He is probably fortifying himself against further possible disaster when he drives horror into Mrs. Roosevelt's heart by declaring that if the war lasts long enough none of the boys will come back, and there is fanaticism as well as heroism in the hoarse cry, "Haven't I bully boys? One dead and two in the hospital!" When he thought he himself was dying in hospital early in 1918, he whispered to his sister, "I am so glad that it is not one of my boys who is dying here, for *they* can die for their country."

One of his Kansas City *Star* editorials describes sympathetically the bitterness of the men who were taken into the Army in World War I but not permitted to do any fighting. It is clear that he feels sorry for those who were cheated out of this experience. He is not thinking of it as a disagreeable duty; it is a privilege of manhood. And one thinks of John Morton Blum's saying that "the awful suspicion ever lingered that he cared as much for fighting as for right."

Roosevelt's attitude toward pacifists and conscientious objectors is relevant here. In peacetime they generally crossed him by opposing military preparedness, which he sincerely regarded as the only possible form of peace insurance; from his own point of view, then, he opposed pacifism because he wished to keep the peace. "In this country," he tells Henry Ford, "pacifism has been the enemy of morality for over fifty years." Such activities as the peace ship annoyed him not only because they were useless and silly but because, drawing people's minds away from more rational methods of preventing war, they were vicious as well.

Even the Society of Friends came under Roosevelt's fire.[1] In this book on Benton, T.R. declared bluntly that "in the long run, a Quaker may be quite as undesirable a citizen as a duellist," and no

---

[1] It is not always recognized that there was a Quaker strain in T.R.'s own family. "Theodore's Grandmother Roosevelt brought a long line of Quaker ancestry to the Roosevelt household. Her Luckens and Teisen ancestors had been Mennonites in Germany but became Friends before or soon after migrating to Pennsylvania, while her Croasdale, Hathernthwaite, McVaugh, and Potts forebears had been Friends whose names appeared in the annals of Friends' Meetings in America, as well as in England before their migration to this country." (Beale, "Theodore Roosevelt's Ancestry," pp. 198–99.) Roosevelt could claim this Quaker kinship when it pleased him to do so. During the campaign of 1904 he wrote G. M. Philips, principal of State Normal School, West Chester, Pennsylvania (Oct. 21, 1904), acknowledging a message from the president of Haverford College, "I wish you would tell him for me that I myself am of Quaker ancestry, and that one of my ancestors . . . was a prominent Friend early in the seventeenth century in Pennsylvania." (George Fox was not in full activity until the second half of the seventeenth century,

statement except his reference to Thomas Paine as "a filthy little atheist" returned to haunt him more often in later years. In 1900 he apologized for it at least twice, once in a letter to William Walton, in which, while bravely and honestly declaring that he has not altered his convictions, he concedes that "were I now to rewrite the sentence, I should certainly so phrase it that it could not be construed as offensive to the Society of Friends, a body whose social virtues and civic righteousness justly command universal respect." Speaking to a Quaker audience at Plainfield, Indiana, he was even more conciliatory. It was his usual custom to say the worst that could be said about any group to the group itself; here he goes so far in the other direction as almost to raise the question of a divided mind. When he quoted the passage from the *Benton* in his Stafford Little Lecture at Princeton in 1917, he did "rewrite the sentence," substituting "professional pacifist" for "Quaker." During World War I, however, he generally took a different line, praising warmly those Quakers who supported the war, as he had already lauded Quaker soldiers in the Union Army during the Civil War.

By this time, however, Roosevelt was much more concerned about conscientious objectors than about Quakers as such. He devoted a whole chapter to them in *The Foes of Our Own Household,* and regardless of what one's own views may be, I think one must grant that he is nowhere more superficial and evasive. None of his complaints get down to fundamentals; none ever really face up to any of the fundamental problems involved in the conflict between the conscience of the individual Christian and the state. Again and again he begs the question or draws red herrings across the trail: Most conscientious objectors are slackers or pro-Germans. There are "persons whose conscience makes them do what is bad." If the

---

and William Penn did not visit Pennsylvania until 1682.) On March 9, 1905, T.R. wrote a letter to Dr. Jesse C. Green in Friends' language, or a reasonable reproduction thereof:

Friend,

I was glad to hear from thee. One of my forebears was a member of the Society of Friends, and dwell't at or near West Chester two hundred years ago. His name was David Potts, I think.

Wishing thee well, I am

Very truly

Theodore Roosevelt

conscientious objector is sincere, he must refuse to interfere with a white slaver who is kidnapping his daughter. And so on.

It is all wrong to permit conscientious objectors to remain in camp or military posts or to go back to their homes. They should be treated in one of three ways: First, demand of them military service, except the actual use of weapons with intent to kill, and if they refuse to render this service treat them as criminals and imprison them at hard labor; second, put them in labor battalions and send them to France behind the lines, where association with soldiers might have a missionary effect on them and cause them to forget their present base creed and rise to worthy levels in an atmosphere of self-sacrifice and of service and struggle for great ideals; third, if both of the above procedures are regarded as too drastic, intern them with alien enemies and send them permanently out of the country as soon as possible.

I do not know whether T.R. would have liked to deport Andrew Carnegie also, but in 1905 he wrote Whitelaw Reid that Carnegie's kind of "utterly stupid condemnation of war" nearly always resulted "from a combination of defective physical courage, of unmanly shrinking from pain and effort, and of hopelessly twisted ideals." In 1913 he produced a four-and-a-half-page tirade against Norman Angell's book, *The Great Illusion*: "What fathomless contempt one does have for such a writer!" At the beginning of 1917 there is an almost hysterical letter to Harriet Boyd Hawes, who had sent him a copy of *Current Events* containing a reference to this "needless and stupid war." "No respectable school in the United States should, after this, ever permit *Current Events* to be admitted within its precincts, and the editor . . . and the writer of the article are wholly unfit to be citizens of a nation which claims kinship with Washington and Lincoln."

II. Reservations and Qualifications

Despite his dislike of pacifists, Roosevelt strenuously objected to being considered an "advocate of bloodshed." "I very earnestly desire peace." Elsewhere he says more sharply, "Nobody wants war who has any sense." In 1914 he wrote Morris Jastrow to deny he had ever held the view that war was essential to national development. He dissented from H. S. Chamberlain's glorification of the Third Punic War; he had no sympathy with Carlyle's *Frederick the*

Great; he was not willing to go along with Benjamin Kidd in stressing the importance of strife in social evolution. Nor did he see his own America as blameless. Not only did "manifest destiny" lead to an "easy international morality"; he was even willing to grant that the United States had sometimes been a menace to the nations of the southland.

T.R. had no minute or exact knowledge of the technical or professional side of military life and very little interest in it. He had much more feeling for the Navy than for the Army. He more than doubled the fleet during his presidency, and whenever there was a cloud upon the international horizon, or he was disappointed in the failure of a move toward arbitration or disarmament, the first thing he thought about was building up the Navy. By 1906, on the other hand, he claimed to have reduced the Army by twenty-five per cent, thus achieving what he regarded as about the proper size. For all his insistence that every man should rush to the colors in wartime, he had very little sympathy with those who make the Army a peacetime career; when his son Ted showed signs of considering it, he argued against it vigorously, objecting to the regimentation involved, and seeing the professional Army as primarily a refuge for those who are not capable of carrying the burdens of an independently directed civil life. In the Spanish War he expected his men to fight bravely, but his notions of discipline, both for them and for himself, were unconventional, to say the least of it. Once at least he bitterly criticized the Marine Corps and expressed the idea that they should be absorbed into the regular Army. Like most presidents, he had his conflicts over pension bills and sometimes found himself at odds with the G.A.R.

How good a commander T.R. was in the one war in which he actually participated I find it somewhat difficult to determine. In the technical sense he seems to have been greatly inferior to Wood. What he was was a boundless inspiration. He exposed his men mercilessly (and himself along with them), asked the impossible of them and frequently got it, and his casualty lists were very high. "I have spent their blood like water . . . when there seemed an object and have flung them straight against entrenchments and kept them hour after hour, dropping under rifle and shrapnel fire." Once he threatened to shoot retreating troops. Once he himself, strolling about in a place where no sane American could be supposed to be, was himself nearly shot by one of his own troops. Being as they were daredevils of his own stamp, his men only loved him the more for these things. But they caused Newton D. Baker, nearly twenty years later, to doubt his competence as a commander. Baker was not willing, as reported by Alvin Johnson, "to risk a repetition of the San Juan Hill affair, with the commander rushing his men into a situation from which only luck extricated them." Long before that time, the San Juan tactics had led an enthusiastic Texan into a campaign oration which culminated on a curious note: "My fellow citizens, vote for my Colonel! vote for my Colonel! *and he will lead you, as he led us, like sheep to the slaughter!*"

Apart from the actual fighting, however, nothing could have surpassed T.R.'s interest in his men and his care for their welfare. He shared their hardships, spent his own money on their comforts, and smashed military regulations, when necessary, to protect their health. "In the campaign against Santiago," writes a member of another regiment, "he was digging trenches with a pick, like his men. He sleeps in a miserable tent and chews hardtack like the rest." Perhaps the famous round robin in which he was importantly involved, and which he is generally supposed to have given to the press, did not really get the soldiers removed out of the yellow fever territory and shipped to Montauk Point, after the fighting was over, for there are those who argue that this decision had already been made. There is no question, however, that its release was an outrageous breach of military discipline and that Roosevelt was actuated by a sincere desire to save his comrades' lives.

From the fall of 1914 to the end of his life Roosevelt was out for universal military training and service. He wanted it to start in the schools when the boy was about sixteen; this should be followed by six months' (he afterwards upped it to nine months') actual army service. Ultimately he thought we might have to add industrial service; by the time he wrote *The Foes of Our Own Household* he wanted to train girls as well as boys.

But though it is true that he had made, by proxy, an investigation of the Swiss system as early as the time he was governor of New York, this had not always been his view. In 1906, in the *Ladies' Home Journal,* he had advocated not "the foreign system of forcing young men into the army" but an interest in sports and physical training which would keep the young man in a condition to be a good soldier when and if the emergency arose. In 1911 he agreed with Sir Ian Hamilton that conscription was not desirable on military grounds. Even in 1916 he admitted that universal military training was not "of prime military consequence, but of prime consequence to us socially and industrially." In *The Great Adventure*, on the other hand, he argues that if we had had it the war would have been over in ninety days. During his last years he was also busy explaining why he had not advocated it while he was president. Sometimes he thinks he did, and it is true that in one message to Congress he had spoken favorably of the Swiss system, but he did not follow this up in any way, which it would, indeed, have been quite useless to do. Sometimes, however, he admits that he himself was not awake to the need at this time. "We have all of us had to change our views because of what has occurred during the last thirteen months," he wrote in 1915. "A year and a quarter ago I would not have dreamed of advocating universal military service for the United States."

Roosevelt's own best-known statement on war and peace is "If I must choose between righteousness and peace I choose righteousness," or, more elaborately, "Peace is normally the handmaiden of righteousness; but when peace and righteousnes conflict then a great and upright people can never for a moment hesitate to follow the path which leads toward righteousness, even though that path also leads to war."

Logically the principal objection to these statements is that they quite evade the question as to whether war itself—the war method of settling controversies between nations—is or is not righteous. Righteousness involves two things. The end sought must be worthy. And it must be served by means which are not in themselves immoral. Until, therefore, this question has been faced and answered there can be very little gained by further discussion of the righteousness of either war or peace.

Roosevelt tries to get around the question by distinguishing between just and unjust war. "Unjust war is dreadful; a just war may be the highest duty." "I am perfectly willing that this Nation should fight any Nation if it has got to, but I would loathe to see it forced into a war in which it was wrong." There is no revolt here against war as such. Indeed, "the best and highest work" a man can perform is given in just war; hence the Medal of Honor is the "greatest distinction open to any American." In one passage, "warcraft" is actually listed with "service to his fellows" as a type of the kind of activity that makes a man's life worth living! But just war being rare, men may also render distinguished service in statemanship, art, literature, science, and philanthropy. These he puts next. In one passage T.R. goes on to the logical conclusion of this kind of reasoning and denies the moral implications of war altogether. "War is a dreadful thing, and unjust war is a crime against humanity. But it is such a crime because it is unjust, and not because it is war." Since war inevitably involves killing and destruction, this puts killing and destruction themselves in a neutral zone.

Supporting this point of view, Roosevelt engages in oversimplification freely and draws a number of false analogies. When Senator Capper proposes forbidding Americans to travel on belligerent vessels in wartime, Roosevelt compares him to a man whose wife had had her face slapped on the street advising her to stay at home. Again, he declares that, since lives are lost in industry as well as in war, those who demand the end of war must also put an end to all hazardous industry. But surely T.R. did not believe that the man whose wife has had her face slapped should shoot the aggressor, or burn down his house with his wife and children in it, and surely he must have known that even if he did these things, the consequences to society would be far less serious than those which might well follow Americans being allowed to travel on belligerent vessels. Surely he knew, too, that deaths in industry are the result of accident and that deaths in battle are the result of design. Finally, he argues that war is a necessary hazard for men as motherhood is a necessary hazard for women. It would be difficult to find a worse parallel. There is no analogy between what the soldier does and what the mother does. The mother gives life; the soldier destroys it. The two are completely antithetical types. If women refused to bear any more children, the race would end. If men refused to fight, a great many things might happen, but the death of the race would certainly not be one of them.

Roosevelt believed further that war is not always more destructive than peace. "There are kinds of peace which are highly undesirable, which are in the long run as destructive as any war." This was true of the Turkish slaughter of the Armenians. It was true of the conditions Wilson had permitted to exist in Mexico. Even wars of conquest, however wrong in the abstract, often had good results, especially when they were waged against barbarous peoples. "Every expansion of civilization makes for peace. In other words, every expansion of a great civilized power means a victory for law, order, and righteousness." It does not make any difference that we may not happen to like that kind of world. Roosevelt himself looked forward to a time when war should be no more. But that time was not yet, and to pretend that it was would postpone the day, not bring it nearer. "The only way by which remedies can be provided is by looking disagreeable facts resolutely in the face and not by lying about them." As the world stands, only a strong nation can expect to be accorded its rights, and only "the warlike power of a civilized people" can give the world peace.

Militarism as such Roosevelt professed to loathe. He admitted that it was a danger in some countries, but it was no danger in the United States. We were freer from militarism than any other great nation had ever been. "Declamation against militarism has no more serious place in an earnest and intelligent movement for righteousness in this country than declamation against the worship of Baal or Ashtaroth." In the early days at least he admitted that no foreign power was a danger to the United States. He admitted, too, that "there is something to be said . . . for the theory that this nation shall never have any interests outside its own borders." This choice however, he deliberately declined to make. He chose that we should be a world power and take the risks. Toward this decision he was impelled by his faith both in America and in American moral and political ideals, by his sincere conviction that a world in which a strong America was a vital force would be a better world to live in than one in which his country kept to herself, and by the absurdly exaggerated valuation which, as we have seen, he placed upon physical courage.

If Roosevelt himself ever killed anybody it was a Spaniard in the Spanish-American War. The first time he reports this incident he is not quite sure whether he did it or not; later he tends to state it as a highly creditable fact, and when he is fighting for the Medal of Honor which Secretary Alger denied him, he makes it one of his claims. There are times when his Western contacts seem to have made him somewhat cavalier about the value of human life. There was the marshal in Wyoming, "a gentle, kindly little fellow, very soft-spoken, and had killed a large number of men." Even more suggestive is a reference to Jack Willis as "a Donatello of the Rocky Mountains—wholly lacking, however, the morbid self-consciousness which made Hawthorne's faun go out of his head because he had killed a man." Once, too, he complained to Spring Rice that American generals during the Spanish War, like British generals during the Boer War, had to contend

with a public sentiment which screamed with anguish over the loss of a couple of thousand men in the field; a sentiment of preposterous and unreasoning mawkishness, as is instanced by the fact that the actual mortality in the two wars, taken in the aggregate, did not equal the aggregate mortality in the two countries, during the same number of years, of the women who died in childbirth; nor, as regards my own country, of the men who were killed in private quarrel.

In such passages Roosevelt seems to abandon the individualism which is elsewhere so characteristic of him; the individual counts for nothing and the state for all. He had more trouble with cruelty than with death, and it is all to his honor that he forced the retirement of Brigadier General Jacob Hurd Smith in the Philippines. "Inspector General Breckinridge happened to mention quite casually to me, with no idea he was saying anything in Smith's disfavor, that when he met him and asked him what he was doing, he responded 'shooting niggers.' Breckinridge thought this a joke. I did not." Nevertheless, he did know that hideous cruelties were being perpetrated in the Philippines, and when he accepted the war he could not avoid accepting them too. In 1904 he himself complained to Riis that Wood's critics must be under the impression "that war can be waged with rosewater." He is quite right that it cannot, and this is the very reason why, regardless of the cause for which it is being fought, it comes of itself under a moral judgment which, as we have seen, Roosevelt ignores. Writing to Wood himself he quotes approvingly from the letter of a seaman who had written that the only way to civilize the "bad" districts in the Philippines was to " 'clean them out' and then keep after them," and who went on to praise Wood for doing just this. At Jolo, he said, Wood had reported

the enemy's loss to be 1500 killed—5000 would come nearer the mark. At Lanan he reports 1000 killed, but I have friends who were with him, and who counted that number after two days' fighting, which was only one-fourth of the time actually fought.

Two years earlier T.R. had actually told Josephine Shaw Lowell that "Everything that has tended to prolong the war in the Philippines by holding out to the insurrectionists sympathy and aid has directly tended to keep alive the cruelties."

The strain of stoicism and puritanism which was an important element in Roosevelt's character also enters here. No man honored women more than he did, or sympathized with them more in the pangs of childbirth and the weary strain of child rearing, and no man was more contemptuous toward those women who shrink from such burdens. He clung to the cultivation of the military virtues as an antidote to the enervating luxury that he feared for America. "Mr. Roosevelt," wrote Francis Leupp, "does not believe in getting too far away from primitive man." This was a matter of faith with him, not preference, or at least not preference alone, for he did not believe that a race which lost its fighting edge could survive. "Unless we keep the barbarian virtues, gaining the civilized ones will be of little avail."

This explains, too, the quixotism which comes out in Roosevelt only, I think, in connection with war. In politics he never went into a fight that he did not have a fair chance of winning. In labor conflicts he took up the position that "Murder is murder. It is not rendered one whit better by the allegation that it is committed on behalf of a 'cause.' " When it comes to war, both these positions are abandoned. It is better to be defeated in war than it is not to have fought. "As has been well and finely said, a beaten nation is not necessarily a disgraced nation; but the nation or man is disgraced if the obligation to defend right is shirked." It was also to be said that "in war there is no substitute for victory," but in such passages as these Roosevelt seems not to know it. Instead, he seems to be taking up the position that nations fight wars not to win them but to develop their characters. And as a matter of fact he once said that he thought India had developed the British character and that the Philippines would develop the American character. In 1896, when he was urging intervention "on behalf of the wretched Cubans," he added, "It would be a splendid thing for the Navy, too"!

He goes further yet when he develops a theoretical situation worthy of a latter-day "horror" film. If an American city should be held for ransom by a foreign foe, we ought, he says, to permit its destruction, not pay the ransom! When General McAndrew declared at a Boston meeting that the truth about the agonies of war should be told, so that when a crisis came people would not mistake frenzy for patriotism, Roosevelt applauded, but quickly added that, even if we were unprepared for war, the American people would always "go to war at the drop of a hat if . . . the national honor or the national interest was seriously jeopardized." There is a remarkable letter to Spring Rice in which he develops the notion that, with international law as fluid as it is, two nations may each be right from its own point of view. "If I were a German I should want the German race to expand." He even blames the Kaiser for his moderation toward Russia. On the other hand, it is perfectly right for England to oppose Germany. In such an utterance, war seems to get itself confused with a chess game, and nationalism loses all contact with human values.

III. Keeping The Peace

Roosevelt knew that he was regarded in many quarters as a firebrand, and there was nothing of which he was more proud than that during his seven and one-half years in the White House "not an American soldier or sailor was killed in action with any foreign power." It seems that Richard Watson Gilder once had the nerve to tell him that he hoped he would not get us into war. "What, a war?" cried T.R. "With me cooped up here in the White House!" Pringle has justly pointed out that "on the one occasion when he believed war with a major power possible, with Japan between 1906 and 1908, he made valiant efforts to prevent it."

To prevent war, Roosevelt used a combination of firmness, fearlessness, and courtesy. To his way of thinking, the courtesy was quite as important as the other two. As he tells Maurice Francis Egan, "I do want to make the little nations feel that we are just as respectful to them as to any other, and just as careful of their rights as of those of the big nations." When discourtesy existed, it was promptly acknowledged and atoned for:

Please send a note at once to the French Government stating that we deeply regret the action of the immigration officials toward the French engineers at Porto Rico. A careful and thorough investigation has been made and it is evident that a grave injustice was perpetrated, and this we wish to acknowledge in the fullest manner. All of the officers concerned in the arrest have been reprimanded, and the regulations so changed that no outrage of this character can hereafter occur.

Everybody who had a part in the Roosevelt administration was made to understand the President's attitude clearly. "Neither civil nor military officials of the United States will be allowed to make public statements disrespectful or offensive to foreign nations, or to their fellow Americans of any given origin." There is an interesting 1908 letter to Captain A. C. Dillingham:

I thank you for your interesting article. It would be an entirely improper article to publish, however, because it is always improper publicly to write about war with a certain opponent as a "probable enemy." The War Board, and naval officers in confidential communications must continually consider and carefully go over questions of conflict with every possible enemy, but to make public statements about any of them as a probable enemy is to help by just so much to turn the probable enemy into a certain enemy.

T.R.'s peace record in the Western Hemisphere is in many aspects impressive. Ardent though he was for the Spanish-American War he always set his face against annexing Cuba. It is true that our withdrawal from that island after the war was not complete, and that we retained the right to intervene "for the preservation of Cuban independence, for the maintenance of a government adequate for the protection of life, property and individual liberty." In 1906 T.R. had to do just that, but though he moved with the greatest reluctance, foreign observers now very generally concluded that the United States would retain possession. It was Theodore Roosevelt himself who made this impossible. "I will not even consider the plan of a protectorate." And when Albert J. Beveridge wrote that "Tom, Dick, and Harry" thought it nonsense "to keep on setting up one Cuban Government after another," T.R. replied tartly that this showed "that even the most ignorant have their limitations, and that it is not safe to follow the advice even of those who know nothing about the subject." His peaceful intervention in Santo Domingo, where the United States took over the customhouse, paid off the country's creditors, and administered her financial affairs, was similarly wise and forbearing; since it obviated the necessity of (and forestalled the excuse for) intervention by any other power, it was obviously a service to peace. When Joseph Bucklin Bishop expressed the hope that T.R. was not planning to annex Santo Domingo, the President replied:

I have been hoping and praying for three months that the Santo Domingans would behave so that I would not have to act in any way. I want to do nothing but what a policeman has to do in Santo Domingo. As for annexing the island, I have about the same desire to annex it as a gorged boa constrictor might have to swallow a porcupine the wrong end to. Is that strong enough?

In 1906 the United States prevented war between Guatemala and Salvador, incidentally improving our relations with Mexico by securing her cooperation. In 1907 the United States and Mexico, again acting together, failed to settle differences between Nicaragua and Honduras, but the Central American Peace Conference resulted in the signing of some important treaties.

It was different with the Philippines, though I think that even those who totally disagree with T.R. on the necessity of Philippine conquest must grant that he was wholly sincere in his view "that nobody wished the Philippines, but that the force of events rendered it impossible to avoid doing our duty there." Our duty, as he saw it, was to govern the Filipinos for their own good, not our own, and to withdraw, with no strings attached to our withdrawal, as soon as they were able to stand on their own feet. "To turn the islands over to Aguinaldo and his followers," he wrote President Eliot in 1900, "would have been in my judgment not merely a mistake, but the kind of preposterous mistake which from the national standpoint is as bad as any crime and which would have resulted in infinitely greater misery and bloodshed than any crime." In 1904 he wrote the same correspondent a very long letter which he finally decided not to send in which he explained in detail why he did not think it wise to promise the Filipinos their independence. "They certainly will not be fit for independence in the next half dozen or dozen years, probably not in the next score or two score years." It did not take quite so long as that. At the time of the Japanese war scare of 1907, he saw the Philippines as our Achilles heel and was ready to give them up. "I wish to God we were out of the Philippines," he once said to David Starr Jordan. He finally came out for Filipino independence in an article on "The Navy as Peace-maker," in the New York *Times*, November 22, 1914, on the some-what qualified ground that neither the American people nor the administration were ready to face up to the responsibilities involved in holding them. On January 11, 1917, he wrote Brander Matthews, "I wish we could make Porto Rico independent, or give it to Cuba."

IV. Arbitration

Though Roosevelt felt as early as 1896 that Eliot, Schurz, and others, including "the futile sentimentalists of the international arbitration type" were "producing a flabby, timid type of character, which eats away the great fighting features of our race," his services to the cause of arbitration were far from being inconsiderable. It was his own view that he saved the Hague Tribunal from being an "empty farce" by getting the Venezuela dispute and a point at issue between Mexico and the United States submitted to it, and this view is far from indefensible.

In 1904 Roosevelt and Hay negotiated arbitration treaties with many nations, but a dispute with the Senate as to whether the documents in question were "treaties" or "agreements" almost pre-vented ratification, the President taking the view that the modifica-tions asked for would result in making the settlement of disputes harder instead of easier. He could see nothing but "solemn farce" in "ratifying an arbitration treaty that says nothing whatever but that under certain conditions we shall again go through the matter of considering whether or not we will have another arbitration treaty."

In 1905 Roosevelt expected the next Hague Conference to frame

a general arbitration treaty. He did not believe that it was possible
to agree to arbitrate everything, and for that reason he thought
it important to define clearly what could be arbitrated and what
could not. What the United States hoped primarily to accomplish
was to limit the size of battleships. In the summer of 1906 T.R.
had enough hope that this proposal would be accepted so that he
told Carnegie he would like to go to the conference himself and
negotiate directly with the Kaiser and the other parties involved.
But both England and Germany were cold to the American suggestion, and by the third week of the conference T.R. was so
completely disillusioned that he had even stopped following its
proceedings closely. In November, 1907, he told Carnegie that he
would recommend to Congress an increase in the size of the Navy.
Whether more would have been accomplished if Roosevelt had
attended the conference or if he had pushed negotiations personally,
as he did at Portsmouth and at Algeciras, we shall never know.

When T.R. made his African-European trip of 1909–1910, Carnegie appealed to him to intercede directly with both the German
and the British government for peace. Though Roosevelt had some
doubts as to the wisdom of this procedure, he agreed to do what
he could. But fate was not kind. The German press got wind of
the matter and played it up unfairly before Roosevelt reached
Berlin, and the death of King Edward VII placed the visit to
London in an entirely unexpected light. There was some frank
talk between T.R. and the Kaiser, nevertheless, and the Nobel
Prize speech at Christiania came out for disarmament, arbitration
between all civilized nations, the development of the Hague Tribunal, and the union of the great powers in a League of Peace,
"not only to keep the peace among themselves, but to prevent, by
force if necessary, its being broken by others." T.R. concluded that
"the ruler or statesman who should bring about such a combination
would have earned his place in history for all time and his title
to the gratitude of all mankind." The Kaiser was not a dull man;
he must certainly have known who was being addressed.

In 1911 Roosevelt opposed Taft's arbitration treaties. I am not
sure that he was right; even *The Outlook* was against him. But his
opposition implied no coldness toward peace, for he sincerely
believed that these treaties, imposing obligations upon this country

which it would not have been possible for her to carry out, would cause trouble rather than prevent it. He told Carnegie that he had hesitated long before writing his article against the treaties

just because I hated to do anything that might seem distasteful to you. I finally came to the conclusion that it would be weakness on my part not to write it, and that I had better write it before the terms of the treaty were irrevocably decided upon, because I believe that the treaty can be put into, and adopted in, such form as will make it really beneficial.

Though Roosevelt admitted to Münsterberg in 1914 that he could conceive of circumstances under which a treaty should be broken, he was generally scrupulous in the extreme about discharging even obligations which had been assumed unwisely; thus he maintained in 1913 (*The Outlook* was again on the other side) that we were bound by the Treaty of 1908 with Great Britain to arbitrate the question of Panama Canal tolls. When he visited Taft at Beverly he expressed doubt that the next disarmament conference would accomplish anything of importance. In December, 1911, he refused to attend the New York Citizens' Peace Banquet, at which Taft was to speak, "because I am not hungry." This was interpreted as a direct slap at the President. But this time Carnegie himself had warned Taft "that the function was of dubious standing and that it would be wiser not to go." And even Pringle, who supports Taft and opposes Roosevelt in this dispute, admits that the Taft treaties were impracticable, while the banquet itself was "a fearful fiasco," whose memory "must have lingered, like the echo of a nightmare, in Taft's mind for years."

The Progressive platform of 1912 advocated "international agreement limiting the size of naval forces, and, pending such agreement, the maintenance of a policy of building two battleships a year." Jane Addams had great difficulty swallowing the battleships.

The Alaskan boundary dispute must have at least a passing glance in connection with Roosevelt's record on peace and arbitration, for he has been accused here of truculence and of setting up a fake arbitration tribunal and then so "rigging" it that Canada could not possibly win.

It is true that there were elements of danger in this situation. It is true that the President announced beforehand that if the negotiations failed he would occupy the disputed territory and run the line on his own "hook." It is true that the American negotiators —Root, Lodge, and ex-Senator George Turner—were far from being "eminent jurists," and that the anti-Canadian views of the last two were well known. But it is also true that the Canadian claim was altogether inadmissable, and that the tribunal was not an arbitral tribunal at all—the Senate refused to ratify the treaty until the word "arbitral" had been deleted from the preamble—but a device to enable Canada to back down without losing face. Lord Alverstone, the sole English member, who cast the deciding vote, always insisted that he voted with the Americans not merely to secure a peaceful settlement but because no other vote would have been reasonable. Roosevelt had tried to get two Supreme Court justices to serve on the tribunal and had failed to do so; this was probably fortunate. As he afterwards pointed out, jurists would have felt obliged to decide the question strictly upon its merits; on this basis Canada could have secured no concessions, and very likely no agreement would have been reached. There is also some reason to believe that the appointment of two senators as negotiators was helpful in getting the resultant treaty through the Senate. Lord Charnwood says frankly, "I do not want to be dogmatic, but I think it perhaps significant that I began to study this point with feelings of intense indignation against Roosevelt, and that I end with the absolute conviction that he did both a very able and most right and friendly thing."

V. Peace in the Orient

T.R.'s great triumph as arbitrator came when he negotiated an end to the Russo-Japanese War. For this he received the Nobel Prize for Peace. It is generally assumed that he did not intervene until both belligerents had requested him to do so. Actually he had offered his good offices at the very beginning and had been repelled. Roosevelt trusted Japan far more than he trusted Russia in the Orient but he was not hopelessly biased in her favor. He always remembered that the Japanese were an Oriental people, and he pretended to no complete understanding of their psychology. The world would be safer, and American interests in the Far East would be safer, if an equilibrium of forces could be preserved.

By January, 1905, the Russian position was so bad that Roosevelt again fruitlessly urged the Czar's government to make peace. Actual intervention did not come until June, however, having been suggested by Japan, and if the reader would understand the endless tact and patience which the President displayed, there is simply no substitute for reading through the step-by-step record of the negotiations as it is preserved in the fourth volume of his *Letters*. "To be polite and sympathetic in explaining for the hundredth time something perfectly obvious," he wrote Jusserand, "when what I really want to do is to give utterance to whoops of rage and jump up and knock their heads together—well, all I can hope is that the self-repression will be ultimately helpful for my character."

His tact did not include truckling, and when Cassini protested that the President was seeing too much of the Japanese minister, he replied that he considered the suggestion impertinent and did not care to have it repeated. He appealed direct to the Czar when he felt that such appeals might be helpful, and he turned to the Kaiser to help him with the Czar. At a crucial stage, he skillfully invoked the Japanese sense of pride and honor, that the negotiations should not be permitted to founder for failure to secure a money indemnity.

Roosevelt's detractors do their best to avoid being impressed by his services in this contingency and to play down the disinterestedness of his motives. Neither Russia nor Japan was in a position to continue fighting longer, it is urged; therefore, peace must have come even if the President had never entered the picture, and the negotiations were all shadowboxing. Obviously neither nation would have ended the war out of consideration for Roosevelt if she had not wished to do so, but this does not detract from Roosevelt's skill or tact. We have known wars to drag on simply because nobody had sense enough to know how to end them.

It is also true that in making peace Roosevelt was considering the interests of his own country as well as those of the combatants, but it has yet to be shown that self-interest caused him to treat either Russia or Japan unfairly. "As I told you at the time," he wrote Senator Hale, "while my main motive in striving to bring about peace . . . was the disinterested one of putting an end to the bloodshed, I was also influenced by the desirability of preventing Japan from driving Russia completely out of East Asia." For this, too, he has been criticized, notably by Mark Twain, who believed that by saving Russia's neck in 1905 T.R. had simply prolonged the reign of czarist tyranny. As a matter of fact, if he had been considering American self-interest and nothing but American self-interest, the thing for Roosevelt to do would probably have been to let both combatants come as close to bleeding themselves white as their own common sense would permit. The Uinted States had nothing to lose and much to gain from such a course. There was only one argument against it: it would have been wrong.

We know that these considerations occurred to Roosevelt. In later years his physician, Dr. Alexander Lambert, who was with him in Colorado when he was recalled to Washington, told Henry L. Stoddard that Roosevelt undertook the negotiations with real reluctance for the very reasons here outlined. "My duty is to secure peace and I am going back to get it. We'll have to let the future take care of itself." Archie Butt, too, recorded Roosevelt's telling him afterwards that, since the treaty was not wholly satisfactory to Japan, she would ultimately try to regain her prestige in a war aimed at the Philippines. He had delayed this war for five years by sending the fleet around the world. When it came, we would win, "but it will be one of the most disastrous conflicts the world has ever seen." If these statements represent T.R.'s views with any exactitude, then there is all the more reason for saying that in the Russo-Japanese negotiations T.R. tore his allegiance away from *Realpolitik* and gave it to peace. In 1911 he wrote Baron Takahira that, though the peace was unpopular both in Russia and in Japan, and had aroused considerable feeling against him, he did not care about this, "for I am sure I did what was right."

VI. "I Took Panama"

In Panama, on the other hand, there was no negotiating. The building of the Panama Canal, consequently, though generally considered the greatest achievement of the Roosevelt administration, has also occasioned some of the severest criticism ever directed against him. Officially even the United States government has now lent itself to what might be called the anti-Roosevelt view. To compensate Colombia for the secession of Panama and soothe her wounded feelings, Wilson's State Department negotiated a treaty under which she was to receive our "sincere regret" and $25,000,000, but it was not until 1921, under a Republican administration, and with the approval of T.R.'s closest friend, Henry Cabot Lodge, that this (modified) treaty was approved by the Senate.

Roosevelt himself never admitted that any apology needed to be made for what either he or his country had done in Panama. Everything done was "in accordance with the highest principles of national, international, and private morality." His opponents in Colombia were so untrustworthy that negotiating with them was like trying to nail currant jelly to the wall. Exercising "the undoubted ethical right of international domain," he wrought and achieved greatly. The landing of our troops at Panama at the time of the revolt not only prevented a corrupt and tyrannical government from reconquering a liberty-loving people; it also prevented an orgy of bloodshed. Finally, since French interests were involved, it may even be credited with having headed off the intervention of a European power, an act which might well have had the most serious consequences not only for Colombia but for the United States also.

The fact that Americans—and Republicans—repudiated T.R.'s Panama Policy in 1921 does not prove that he was wrong, for the reversal was determined by practical considerations and the desire to secure Colombian oil. Neither, of course, does the fact that Roosevelt accomplished his aims prove that he was right. When he himself dismissed the matter with "I took the Canal Zone," he was in one of his prima donna moods, and he no more did justice to himself than prima donnas often do in their published interviews. "I took the Canal Zone and let Congress debate and while the debate goes on the Canal does too." "And now instead of discussing the Canal before it was built, which would have been harmful, they merely discuss me—a discussion which I regard with benign interest."

The story of the American negotiations with Colombia and their failure, of the Panama revolt and the part of the United States therein, deserves, and has received, whole books of its own. The negotiations involved payments both to Colombia and to the French company which had previously attempted to build a canal and abandoned the job. The Hay-Herran Treaty with Colombia was ratified by the United States Senate on March 17, 1903. On August

19, after long and exasperating negotiations, Colombia turned it down.

Roosevelt and Hay have been described as highhanded in bringing undue pressure to bear upon a weaker state. It has been argued that the treaty finally negotiated was not the treaty the Colombian Senate expected to receive, and that Herran himself had signed it with great reluctance. At one point, Hay warned Colombia of consequences which "every friend of Colombia would regret" if the treaty were not ratified; surely he would never have permitted himself such indecorous language in dealing with a major power. There is one shocking statement in Roosevelt's own Message to Congress, January 4, 1904, where he says of Colombia, "In our anxiety to be fair we had gone to the very verge in yielding to a weak nation's demands which that nation was helplessly unable to enforce from us against our will." Now, Roosevelt had always maintained that a state which cannot enforce its rights cannot expect to receive them in this world, but it had never been assumed that the United States was conducting its own foreign policy on this basis.

Despite this indiscreet statement, T.R.'s answer, no doubt, would be that he was not doing anything of the kind. President Marroquín was a corrupt usurper for whom Roosevelt had no respect, and he was probably right in his assumption that the Colombian Senate was merely rubber-stamping Marroquín's actions and trying to hold up both the United States and the French company for all that they were worth.

After the revolt, the United States recognized the new de facto government in Panama hardly more than an hour after having been informed that it existed, and United States troops prevented Colombian forces from effecting reconquest. There has been a great deal of acrimonious discussion as to whether or not Roosevelt and his government were involved in the rebellion, all of which is a little silly, both because it is clear as day that officially they were not (even the New York *World* failed to uncover any incriminating evidence) and because we have Roosevelt's own statement as to what he would have done if the revolt had not occurred. "If they had not revolted, I should have recommended Congress to take possession of the isthmus by force of arms; and, as you will see, I had actually written the first draft of my Message to this effect."

Furthermore, there was no need for becoming involved in the revolt, for the President was perfectly familiar with the activities of both Philippe Bunau-Varilla and William Nelson Cromwell. Officially these people had never been given the green light; unofficially they must have known that, once Panama had seceded, the United States would recognize the *fait accompli.*

I take it for granted from what has since occurred [so the President wrote Silas McBee, on January 6, 1904], that in October . . . [Bunau-Varilla] was advising the revolution, and doubtless was assuring them that the Washington Government was bound to interfere. He would have been a very dull man indeed had he been unable to forecast such interference, judging simply by what we had done the year before, and the year before that, and the year before that. . . . In the published article in the Paris paper, Le Matin, of Sept-2d, he forecasts our action two months later, although as far as I know he never saw any one connected with the Department until about the middle of October.

Many years later Roosevelt told William Roscoe Thayer, "I had only to sit still and profit by their plot—if it succeeded." It would be impossible to sum up the situation with more succinct accuracy.[2]

Roosevelt's course in Panama occasioned one of Elihu Root's famous *bon mots,* that it was a pity so great an achievement should be tainted with the least show of legality. T.R., however, welcomed

[2] Apparently Roosevelt felt some genuine admiration for Bunau-Varilla. On July 7, 1914, he wrote him: "One of the rather contemptible features of a number of our worthy compatriots is that they are eager to take advantage of the deeds of the man of action when action is necessary and then eager to discredit him when the action is once over. You, my dear Sir, are a fighting man. . . . You rendered incalculable service to France, and as an incident thereto, to my country." On March 13, 1915, he added, "You were fortunate enough to be not only interested in, but an ardent worker for, a great cause. You had the fine zeal and enthusiasm for the accomplishment of the work which men of the right get to feel when they are committed to enterprises of such a nature; a zeal and enthusiasm wholly disinterested so far as any material reward for the man himself is concerned." But he apparently did not think that Cromwell was connected with the revolt that occurred at all. On July 9, 1914, he wrote Julius Chambers: "I have no proof in the matter, but my understanding was that Cromwell had been interested in getting up, or helping, a revolution through certain people on the Isthmus, and that the revolution which took place and with which Bunau-Varilla was connected, went off first, which accounted for Cromwell's anger with Bunau-Varilla. I had become satisfied as soon as I investigated the matter that there were at least a dozen revolutionary movements under way on the Isthmus, and, if one did not come off, the others would."

legal sanction, as when John Bassett Moore reminded him of our rights under an 1846 treaty with New Granada and Oscar Straus brought up the point about the treaty "running with the land" and thus binding us to protect the isthmus. But to cite this treaty as justification for our using troops to prevent Colombia from putting down a revolt or regaining the isthmus was absurd; no country surely ever made a treaty with another power to protect it against itself. We had often intervened in Panama before, but all interventions except one had been at Colombia's request. The truth is that by this time Roosevelt was not acting under treaties; he was acting under the assumed right of the United States to keep order in the Western Hemisphere. He could have supported Colombia instead of Panama had he chosen to do so but that would have meant blood. Moreover, it would not have been in the American interest. He could have stayed out altogether, but that too would have meant blood. God being assumed to be the God of Peace, there was, for once, no conflict between His and our interests.

Roosevelt built the Panama Canal by vigorous frontier methods. He followed his star and his own faith in his intuitive righteous judgment. "I feel we are certainly justified in morals," he says, "and therefore justified in law." In his feeling that the end result was beneficent—for America and for the world—he was probably right. But he was wrong when he declared that the canal could have been built in no other way. If he and Hay had been more patient, an agreement might yet have been reached with Colombia, or if this had failed, we could have built the canal across Nicaragua, which, until recently, the President himself had favored. Then Colombia would have got nothing (which even a moralist-president might reasonably have considered an adequate punishment for her sins) and there would have been no heritage or wise or foolish bad feeling against the United States in Central America. To be sure, the French company would have got nothing either, and Bunau-Varilla would have got nothing. But that ought not to have worried Roosevelt greatly, for Bunau-Varilla was not a moralist.[3]

[3] Nobody has ever discovered who got the $40,000,000 supposed to have been paid to the French government, but this does not involve Roosevelt directly. A scandal was once started, directed against his brother-in-law, Douglas Robinson, and Taft's brother Charles, but this has never been substantiated; both the opposition newspapers and the Democratic National Committee declined to use it.

VII. The Demon of Interventionism

There was only one Panama in the Roosevelt administration, but there were a number of exigencies when action of one kind or another was considered. Roosevelt refused Lodge's request that he send a warship to Newfoundland in 1905 when the Newfoundland fishermen were refusing bait licenses to the fishermen of Gloucester. But he did send warships to Turkey in 1903 and 1904, and it was touch and go for a time with China as the result of the boycott agitation. Between 1905 and 1908, also, there was grave danger of serious trouble with that "villainous little monkey," Castro, in Venezuela, and it may well be that Root deserves more credit than Roosevelt for having prevented this.

The President was continually being pressured by this, that, or another group to intervene in one way or another in behalf of various peoples and causes in different parts of the world. In 1906 he sternly rebuked Curtis Guild, Jr., apparently for nothing worse than having signed a petition in behalf of the people in the Congo Free State:

If I had absolute power and if this country were prepared to embark on a long career of disinterested violence on behalf of all sufferers outside its limits, I should gladly go into these various cases; though even then I should have to take them up one at a time, as to comply at once with all the requests of all the enthusiasts would mean immediate war with considerably over half the globe. But, of course, no one contemplates our going to war over any of these matters, and there is not the slightest obligation on the Nation to interfere as regards any one of them, and we have not the slightest right to interfere under any form of law . . . it is a little difficult to construct a theory upon which I should take action in one particular case and in none of the others.

But Roosevelt's talk is not always as soothing as this. In 1903 he wrote John Hay that he wished "to go to the very limit I think our people will stand" with Russia over Manchuria. If only he could be sure that France and Germany would not intervene, he would not mind "extremes." In 1905 he tells Trevelyan that "if I could get the people to back me," he would be tempted "to go into a crusade against the Turk" over the Armenians. "But," he quickly adds, "as this is of course a sheer impossibility I simply dare not give expression to my sympathy and indignation, lest harm and not good should result." In 1908 he expressed himself more elaborately to Sir Harry Johnston, with special regard to the Western Hemisphere:

I do not think we shall intervene in Haiti. Of course we ought to, but this people of ours simply does not understand how things are outside our own boundaries. Of course I do not desire to act unless I can get the bulk of our people to understand the situation and to back up the action. . . . In Panama, Cuba, Santo Domingo and Porto Rico it needed months or years of preparation before we could get our people to see things straight. . . . We ought to have intervened in Venezuela again and again during the past seven years. We ought to have interfered in Central America and Haiti. In all three places we ought now be doing something of the same kind that we are doing in Cuba, Santo Domingo or Panama, according to the exigencies of the case. But the American people simply were not alive to the situation.

How seriously to take these things I really do not know. Some of them, like Roosevelt's fiery denunciation of individuals, may well come under the heading of relieving his feelings. I doubt that this explanation will cover all cases.

On July 24, 1905, Roosevelt wrote Spring Rice that as soon as the Russo-Japanese War began, "I notified Germany and France in the most polite and discreet fashion that in the event of a combination against Japan to try to do what Russia, Germany and France did to her in 1894, I should promptly side with Japan and proceed to whatever length was necessary on her behalf." Again, the German diplomat, Hermann von Eckardstein, has recorded that Roosevelt told him in 1910 that if, at the time of the 1906 crisis, Germany had invaded France, "we in America would not have kept quiet." "I certainly would have found myself compelled to interfere," he added.

So far as I know there is no documentary evidence to support either of these claims, but Roosevelt's taste for tactful personal diplomacy being what it was, this does not necessarily invalidate them, and his secret agreement with England and Japan in the Far East lends some color to the first. In any event, we who are living in a day when we enjoy all the benefits of interventionism, and who look back upon two world wars plus a "police action" in Korea, and forward to heaven only knows what complications as the result of multitudinous treaties to defend even those who do not wish to be defended, can hardly fail to feel that these words of T.R.'s stand out of the record in letters of fire.

VIII. The Greater Armageddon

We come finally, now, to Roosevelt's course and attitude in World War I. If the average American were asked to describe that course he would probably reply that T.R. openly condemned Germany and championed the Allies from the day the war began, and that from then until the United States went in he kept up a constant agitation for intervention. In view of his vociferous, unsparing, and unceasing condemnation of Wilson's "pacifist" policies, it is easy to understand why this view should be held. But it is wrong in almost every particular.

Roosevelt's first considered public utterance on the war was made in an article in *The Outlook* on September 23, 1914. In this article he resolutely declined to pass judgment on either side. The invasion of Belgium was wrong, "if there is any meaning to the words 'right' and 'wrong' in international matters," but he stated fairly the reasons why Germany felt it had to be done and by which she justified it, and he admitted that, at one time or another, all the great powers had acted upon the basis here outlined. "I wish it explicitly understood that I am not at this time expressing judgment one way or the other upon Germany for what she did to Belgium."

As for America, "It is certainly eminently desirable that we should remain entirely neutral, and nothing but urgent need would warrant breaking our neutrality and taking sides one way or the other." As a policy, neutrality had both advantages and disadvantages. It would help "to maintain peace in so much of the world as is not affected by the war, and to conserve our influence for good toward the re-establishment of genuine peace when the time comes." The price we pay for neutrality, on the other hand, is that we forfeit "our right to do anything on behalf of peace for the Belgians" now. Nevertheless, "it would be folly to jump into the gulf ourselves to no good purpose; and very probably nothing that we could have done would have helped Belgium. We have not the smallest responsibility for what has befallen her," though our sympathy for her is "very real." Such sympathy is entirely compatible "with full acknowledgment of the unwisdom of our uttering a single word of official protest unless we are prepared to make that protest effective; and only the clearest and most urgent National duty would ever justify us in deviating from our rule of neutrality and non-interference." He admits that there may be some question whether we are not "violating obligations which we have explicitly or implicitly assumed in the Hague treaties." But this is incidental. The prime purpose of the article is not to urge America to take up any particular position toward the war in Europe but rather to put herself into a position of military preparedness so that the equivalent of Belgium's fate could not possibly befall her.

Because of its obvious inconsistency with what Roosevelt was later to say, this article was, in the course of time, to call for considerable explaining. In his *Impressions of Theodore Roosevelt*, Lawrence F. Abbott tried to take the blame (as he conceived it) by declaring that some of what Roosevelt said was written at his request. "For this error of judgment, which was due to my desire to be loyal to the government as well as non-partisan, I am afraid Roosevelt never forgave me, although he never alluded to it in criticism or blame." But it is difficult to think of Roosevelt yielding his own better judgment to Abbott's.

Roosevelt's own most elaborate apologia for his *Outlook* article was made in a letter to John C. Klein.[4] According to this letter, Roosevelt wrote what *The Outlook* printed because he believed it. After seeing the Belgian commissioners, however, he came to feel that the administration

had deliberately deceived our people as to their duty and the facts in the case. I became convinced that Wilson had suppressed the information at its disposal as to the horrible outrages committed in Belgium. I got hold of the Hague conventions and read them through in full, and I became convinced that President Wilson had with unworthy timidity failed to act as he ought to have acted under these Conventions.

He did not hold himself blameless for writing his arrticle, T.R. continued,

[4] *Leslie's Weekly*, June 8, 1918, pp. 791 +.

but I wish to point out that this only error of any consequence which I have committed since the World War broke out was this certainly venial, and I think pardonable error, of standing by President Wilson during the first sixty days, before it became clear in my mind that the highest interest of morality, justice and patriotism demanded that I should oppose him.

But we must not rely entirely for our knowledge of Roosevelt's attitude toward the war upon the *Outlook* article and his commentary upon it. For there are other articles, statements, and letters dating from the beginning of the conflict, and I propose to run through some of the most significant of these up to the time America entered the war.

1914: On August 5, two days after Germany marched into Belgium, T.R. addressed a conference of the Progressive party in New York. In this brief address he said nothing about Belgium but rather invited his hearers to give thanks that they were living in America. Progressives, he declared, would work with any man who would help the United States to come through the crisis honorably and unharmed, and, so far as possible, work for peace and justice for all mankind.

On August 8 he wrote letters to two outstanding pro-Germans— Hugo Münsterberg and George Sylvester Viereck. He told Münsterberg that he would not be misled into a "rush against Berlin." He thought that each side might be right from its own point of view and looked forward to a league of great powers to preserve peace. To Viereck he wrote that he wished "to avoid in any way saying anything that would tend to exaggerate and inflame the war spirit on either side. I simply do not know the facts. It is a melancholy thing to see such a war."

On August 22 he wrote Arthur Lee in England that the feeling in this country was anti-German, pro-English, pro-French, pro-Belgian, and lukewarm with regard to Russia and Serbia. For himself, as an ex-president, he accepted the obligation of neutrality. He admired the Germans but disliked "the Government of Prussianized Germany for the last forty years." He thought that if he were president now he would register a protest against "the levy of the huge war contributions on Belgium."

By October 3 Roosevelt is writing Spring Rice that if he had been president he would have warned Germany, under the Hague Convention, as early as July 30–31, to respect Belgium's neutrality. "Of course I would not have made such a statement unless I was willing to back it up." The very same day he writes Münsterberg that there are no two sides to the Belgian question and that he believes a victorious Germany would be a danger to the United States. But he is still saying that he does not believe Germany's dominant motive was aggression and that all the talk about the Kaiser desiring a "blood-bath" is nonsense. He would oppose the dismemberment of Germany; for one thing, she is needed as a bulwark against Russia.

An article in the New York *Times* on November 8 is generally taken as marking the end of Roosevelt's official neutrality. On November 4 he wrote Kipling that he had not revealed his full mind about Belgium, knowing that the public was not ready for it, and his daughter Ethel that he was "utterly sick of the spineless 'neutrality' of the Administration." In December he tells James P. Robinson that he is "not in the least anti-German" but that he is "very strongly pro-Belgium" and feels "that we ought to stand fearlessly on that issue." To F. C. Selous he goes much further, "I wish I were in the war myself!" On December 2, however, in a letter to Friedrich, Freiherr von Stumm, he again refuses to choose between the German and the Allied cause; in fact, he says he thinks the chances of the war are now rather in favor of Germany. Two days later, he wrote a friendly letter to Admiral von Tirpitz, introducing Senator Beveridge, who went abroad to do some articles for *Collier's*. On December 22 he refused to sign an Anglo-American appeal which had been sent to him. "I do not believe that this is the right attitude for Americans to take. England is not my motherland any more than Germany is my fatherland." He sent a copy of the letter to Münsterberg as evidence that he was playing fair.

1915: On New Year's Day Roosevelt put his signature to the preface of *America and the World War*, a volume based on the utterances he had made so far and summing up his attitude at the beginning of the new year. Though this volume is intensely critical of President Wilson, Roosevelt does not ask military intervention on the side of the Allies. The closest he comes to it is in Chapter X:

Poor Belgium, in spite of being prepared, was almost destroyed, because great neutral nations—the United States being the chief offender [5]—have not yet reached the standard of international morality and of willingness to fight for righteousness which must be attained before they can guarantee small, well-behaved, civilized nations against cruel disaster.

He accuses Wilson of disregarding our obligations under the Hague treaties even while he is negotiating new treaties. "We should have interfered at least to the extent of the most emphatic diplomatic protest . . . and then by whatever further action was necessary" when Belgium was invaded. Yet—"It is not at this time necessary for me to state exactly what, in my judgment, ought to have been done." He still sees a crushed Germany as "a disaster to mankind" and speaks kindly of the Kaiser personally.

James Ford Rhodes met T.R., after a considerable interval, early in January. "I drew the inference," he writes, "that Mr. R. was for the Allies, though he did not say so in so many words." Even with friends, then, he was still reticent. On the 22nd, he wrote Edward Grey a long, understanding letter, in which he begged England, for her own sake, not to adopt policies that would alienate America. On February 22, in a letter to John St. Loe Strachey, he is troubled that some Englishmen still regard him as pro-German. I do not know to what he refers when he writes, "I have fought hard to make us take action against Germany." He adds, "With a great moral issue involved, neutrality does not serve righteousness."

On April 6, for the first time in any letter than I have seen, he comes out flatfootedly against Germany on any other issue than Belgium. The new issue is submarine warfare. "It is all I can do to control myself in writing." When Germany issued her warning that Americans traveling in the *Lusitania* or other ships flying the British flag, must do so at their own risk, he declared that if he

[5] It may seem odd that, though he made much of the United States failing to fulfill her obligations under The Hague Convention, T.R. never criticized the small neutrals for this same failure. As late as Nov. 20, 1917, he was writing Maurice Francis Egan about the importance of keeping the Scandinavian nations, etc., "out of the war at all costs. It is quite enough to have seen Belgium, Servia and Roumania destroyed, without asking or permitting other small nations to share their fate." If we seek to bring economic pressure to bear on them, "we must always weigh on the one side the damage we do Germany and on the other side the suffering we cause the neutral, and the antagonism we thereby justly arouse."

were in authority he would at once warn Germany that if any American lives were lost he would confiscate every German vessel in an American port, including the *Prince Eitel*. (He later told Thayer he would have given the German ambassador his papers and required him to sail on the *Lusitania*.)

The sinking of the *Lusitania* undoubtedly increased Roosevelt's war mood. "I never wished to take part in the European war," he wrote Congressman Irvine L. Lenroot in 1917, "until the sinking of the Lusitania and the other boats." Publicly, however, he did not ask for war, though he did ask for a cessation of all commerce with Germany and a vigorous assertion of our right to trade with whomever we pleased. "I do not believe that the firm assertion of our rights means war but it is well to remember that there are things worse than war."

As a matter of fact, T.R. had not yet given up hope of peace. Writing to Belle and Kermit on May 27, he says, "If I were President, this country would now be at war with Germany, unless Germany had completely backed down, which, as a matter of fact, I think she probably would have done." On June 17 he writes again to Lee. Now he is sure he would have made Germany behave from the beginning of the war, or else he would have made her fight us. But the very same letter declares, "The exasperating thing is that peace can perfectly well be kept, both with Germany and Japan, if only we will treat both of them courteously, and at the same time proceed to make ourselves really efficient for our defence." It is true that in August he wrote R. J. Cuninghame, "If our nation goes into this war, as in my judgment it ought to. . . ." (Even in April, before the *Lusitania* went down, he had written Selous, "I am very sorry that the United States is not in the struggle.") Yet at the end of May he acknowledged a letter from the Archduke Ludwig Salvator and tried to send him his South American book. "Outside of Europe," he said, "I doubt if there is any man who has felt a more poignant regret than I have over this dreadful war, for I have not only a real feeling of friendship but a genuine admiration for so many of the combatants on both sides."

1916: The preface to *Fear God and Take Your Own Part* is dated February 3. Here, partly rewritten, is what he wishes to preserve of his writing about the conflict since *America and the World War*.

He now goes considerably further than he went in the earlier book, but not even yet does he ask for a declaration of war. "Germany has waged war against us," however. She did this by sinking ships, and she did it by violating the supreme law of our land (treaty law) when she invaded Belgium. On the latter count, we missed our opportunity to act. But the former is still a live issue. "Therefore, either Germany will have to surrender on the point at issue, or this protest of ours will prove to have meant nothing, or else there must be a war."

On June 7 Roosevelt opposed a negotiated peace, and on June 19 he said that the Germans are "fighting in a cause I abhor," but he still admires their strong qualities. He does not define the grounds of his abhorrence. As late as election eve, he still saw some slight chance of avoiding war if Hughes were elected and adopted a strong policy. With Wilson there was no chance, for though Wilson would never go to war unless he was kicked into it, he was precisely the kind of weakling and blunderer who fumbles his way into war. The interesting thing about this is that Roosevelt was supporting what he regarded as the only chance to keep America out of the war. He never publicly asked for a declaration of war against Germany until after January 31, 1917.

In view of his generally belligerent tone, this is interesting indeed, and it is not the only paradox involved in T.R.'s wartime attitude. What is almost as surprising is how very little he has to say about the respective merits of the Allied and the German cause. Until submarine warfare begins, he talks about nothing but the wrongs of Belgium, and thus he oversimplifies the issues of the war enormously. Even in the fall of 1914 he was opposed to efforts to end the war without

reparation for Belgium and a guarantee against repetition of such conduct as that of Germany to Belgium. From the standpoint of humanity and taking into account the future as well as the past, it would be better that the war should continue indefinitely than that this point should not be reached.

Both in Belgium and upon the high seas Germany is inhuman; therefore, she must be opposed. He himself says again and again that he would have taken up the same attitude toward the Allies if they had violated Belgium. But, then, what would have become of democracy and all the other ideals for which the Allies were supposed to be fighting? Would Roosevelt have been willing that the United States should fight for the enthronement of autocracy in the world in order to avenge Belgium? It might almost be said that Roosevelt is opposing war itself, or illegitimate methods of waging war, rather than any particular nation. He approaches the problem quite as emotionally as he accuses the pacifists of approaching it. Only, unlike the pacifist, he hates war so much that he is willing to make war against it!

To be sure, my statement also has an element of oversimplification in it. Though Roosevelt says surprisingly little about the political principles and ideals for which the Allies were supposed to be fighting, it might no doubt be argued that he took them for granted. The clearest passage is in *Fear God and Take Your Own Part:*

> As things actually are at this moment, it is Germany which has offended against civilization and humanity—some of the offenses, of a very grave kind, being at our own expense. It is the Allies who are dedicated to the cause and are fighting for the principles set forth as fundamental in the speech of Abraham Lincoln at Gettsyburg.

Early in 1915 he wrote John Roosevelt, "It is sheer nonsense of course to argue that Germany and Austria were not the aggressors in this war."

Again, though he did not make this very clear either, Roosevelt believed that a Europe in which Germany, not Britain, was the dominant power would be an uncomfortable world for the United States.

> I am doing my best [he wrote Stewart Edward White, at the end of August, 1914], to keep neutral and am well aware that it is possible we shall be brought into trouble with England's ally, Japan, while I need hardly say that I am under no allusions [*sic*] about Russia. Nevertheless it does seem to me that neither Japan nor Russia could give a more brutal illustration of the theory that "Might makes Right" and that there is no such thing as morality in international affairs than Germany is now giving. It is pretty hard for me to keep silent about what has gone on in Belgium. . . . I would esteem it quite on the cards to see Germany and Japan cynically forget the past and join together against the United States and any other power that stood in their way.

Henry L. Stoddard says that in October, 1915, T.R. declared that our only choice was between fighting Germany now with allies or fighting her later on our own. When Joseph Medill Patterson questioned his logic, he admitted that Germany probably would not attack us at once. But she would begin to take an interest in the Caribbean; she might intervene in Cuba; sooner or later she would threaten the Panama Canal.

This, of course, is all highly theoretical matter. Even more theoretical—and more interesting—is the question of what would have happened if Roosevelt had been in the White House in 1914, as he might very well have been. In view of the *Outlook* article and the other testimony we have examined, it is evident that the actual Roosevelt of July-August, 1914, was not sufficiently clear about the issues involved to have done what he afterwards said ought to have been done at that time. This does not in itself prove, however, that Roosevelt in the White House, with his abnormally sensitive fingers on the pulse of the world's affairs and with all Wilson's information at his disposal, would not have been clear.

The fullest and most interesting report we have on what Roosevelt afterwards said would have been his procedure comes to us from Senator Simeon D. Fess of Ohio:

I should immediately have issued a proclamation citing the fact that every nation represented at the Hague Conference had declared in favor of holding strictly to the principle of the inviolabilty of neutral territory in warfare and the United States must insist on the sacred obligation being carried out in the existing emergency. There is not the slightest doubt that this pronouncement would have met with hearty approval from all the neutral powers of the world; particularly by those states contiguous to the coast of Germany—Scandinavia and Holland, which were especially concerned for their own economic interests and on whose good-will the Teutons were dependent for their food supplies in case of war. . . .

With this overwhelming moral force exerted through a "league of neutral nations" menacing the Kaiser, he not only would have hesitated to carry out his ruthless intention to invade Belgium, but more than likely he would have welcomed such a declaration of neutral rights as would prevent the entente powers from occupying Belgium and thus have safeguarded German interests in the Kiel Canal, the biggest strategic factor of the War for the country. Thus, with the only casus belli then in sight which offered an inducement for Great Britain to enter the war removed from the political arena, Parliament could not have been induced to resort to arms. The British Government would then have been compelled to tell her neighbor across the Straits of Dover that, as yet no sufficient cause for belligerent action had arisen, just as Earl Grey had already done in specifically informing St. Petersburg that a Serbian quarrel did not answer the purpose. France, in turn, could do nothing more than to notify the Czar that she, too, could not go to war for the Sarajevo affair and the question would then have reverted to Russia for further diplomatic parley, for which the Kaiser, now thoroughly alarmed by the overwhelming forces arrayed against his dynasty, had already made provision. Everyone recognized at this critical stage of the international controversy that only a little time was needed for discussion to bring about a peaceful issue to the turmoil in Europe and Roosevelt would have made "time to burn."

It might have worked. It just possibly might have worked. If it had, you and I would have a much more comfortable world to live in than we have today. And the Everlasting Boy of Sagamore Hill, who never got over thinking about war romantically, and yet was able, on occasion, to work so wisely and disinterestedly for peace, could have had all the Nobel Prizes rolled into one.

But should we ever have known what we owed him, or how much we had escaped? [6]

[6] Roosevelt died too early to get into the League of Nations fight, but there is not much doubt what his attitude toward it would have been. As we have already seen, he had himself advocated a league at Christiania. During the war, however, he would not even talk about it; the conflict itself, he said, was too pressing. "I wish that good Edward Grey would not continue to bleat with feeble amiability about securing universal peace through a League of Nations." This seems all the more significant because, as *The Foes of Our Own Household* shows, Roosevelt's interest in social progress did not die during the war period. Virtually his last message to his country concerned peace, but on a much narrower scale than that comprehended by a world league. He was ready to negotiate an all-inclusive arbitration treaty with Great Britain. As for the League itself, he refused to go along with Beveridge's out-and-out opposition to it; his position, if he had lived, would doubtless have been much more like that of Lodge; indeed, Mrs. Robinson says that the Lodge reservations were drafted in part at his bedside. Before going into a league he wanted to be quite sure that it would help peace, not hinder it, that it would not involve scrapping the Monroe Doctrine, and that it would not mean our getting into wars with which we had no concern. He did not wish to police Germany, Russia, and the Balkan States; he was not willing to give France and Italy a blanket promise to support them in their future wars; he was not ready

IX. The Man Who Sleeps at Oyster Bay

Theodore Roosevelt has been asleep at Oyster Bay for considerably more than a generation, but though it is impossible not to be
aware that he belongs to an older and, in many respects, simpler
America than the one which (for our sins) we inhabit, his personality has lost hardly any of its vividness. He himself once
remarked that Lincoln would have been forgotten if it had not
been for the Civil War. He had no Civil War, but he is not forgotten; he is the only one of our presidents commonly called "great"
who did not need a "crisis" to develop him, and even those who
deny his greatness cannot wipe out the interest of him.

"In the way of grading which we have at Oxford," said the Archbishop of York, after listening to the former President's Romanes Lecture, "we agreed to mark the lecture 'Beta Minus,' but the lecturer
'Alpha Plus.' While we felt that the lecture was not a very great
contribution to science, we were sure that the lecturer was a very
great man." It has been said that a great writer does not need to
describe great experiences but that he must have a great attitude
toward all experience, and we all know how an actress or a singer
can, on occasion, take even tawdry materials and, by infusing herself
into them, irradiate them with beauty. Roosevelt's greatness impressed friends and enemies alike; even Wilson's secretary of war,
Newton D. Baker, struggling with him when he wanted to be sent
to France, once inadvertently addressed him as "My dear Mr.
President"! One day a whole group of newspapermen sent their
papers a lengthy report on one of his speeches. To their astonishment, not a paper printed what they had sent in. Upon rereading
the speech, they all concluded that there was really nothing in it
which warranted its being given newspaper space. "It was not

---

to fight "every time a Jugo-slav wishes to slap a Czecho-slav in the face." He
was not willing to have national patriotism superseded, and he did not think
it safe for the American people to look outside themselves to their own
defense. In December, 1918, he wrote Clemenceau: "We feel that each
country must have the absolute right to determine its own economic policy,
and while we will gladly welcome any feasible scheme for a League of Nations,
we prefer that it should begin with our present allies, and be accepted only as
an addition to, and in no sense a substitute for the preparedness of our own
strength for our own defense." With these things understood, he saw no reason
why we could not "cautiously . . . try out" a league.

what Colonel Roosevelt said, but the manner of his saying it, that had affected the convention."

He was often right. He was sometimes wrong. He did not have all the answers to the riddle of human days. Sometimes, even, he seems more perplexed than other men. He was capable of being blinded by prejudice or passion so that he failed to see either men or issues clearly. H. G. Wells was haunted by "the friendly peering snarl of his face, like a man with the sun in his eyes. He sticks in my mind . . . as a very symbol of the creative will in man, its limitations, its doubtful adequacy, its valiant persistence amidst perplexities and confusions." These things sometimes led to a clouding of judgment in Roosevelt which might make him, on this issue or that, unsafe to follow, but once you know him it does not make you love him less.

"Like a man with the sun in his eyes," says Wells. He had the sun in his heart, too. He accepted the universe, as few men have ever accepted it. His ability to give himself to the duty which confronted him was without stint or limit; few among those capable of such self-assertion have embraced such self-abnegation. Even when he was wrong, he was wrong for the right reasons. His faults were due to the fact that he was a human being. A man foursquare, good to the core of him and infinitely loving, he enriched life for all who had the wonderful privilege of knowing him, and left his country and the world an example of undying inspiration.

Notes

The following annotations are largely confined to quoted matter. To annotate every *statement* in the book would have taken an impossible amount of space, since five or six authorities often lie behind one simple sentence.

Roman numerals correspond to those used to number sections in the text. Arabic numerals within parentheses indicate correspondingly-numbered sections in the bibliography which follows, where see also key to abbreviations, etc.

Unpublished letters, etc. from which quotations have been taken are named at the beginning of each section. The thousands of letters examined from which no quotations were taken have not been listed.

One: The World of Action

I. (1) *Works*, IV, 173; XXII, 64. (2) *PASP*, V, 729. (3) *Letters to Kermit*, p. 146. (7) Gilman, p. 296. Robinson, p. 50. (8) Bradford, p. 29. (9) Adams, *Education*, p. 389. Hoover, p. 231.

II. To J. B. Bishop, Jan. 30, 1903. To Philip A. Roosevelt, Dec. 19, 1918. (1) *Works*, XIX, 223; XXI, 479. (3) *Letters*, I, 458, 655; II, 1033; VI, 968; VII, 2, 26. *Letters to Kermit*, p. 89. (5) *Barnes vs. R*, I, 417. (7) Wister, p. 107. (8) Bradford, p. 24. Burroughs, p. 105. (10) Addams, etc., p. 523.

III. (1) *Works*, IV, x–xi; XXIII, 388. (3) *Letters*, V, 176. (7) Dawson, p. 145. Gilman, p. 52. Paulmier and Schauffler, pp. xiv–xv. (9) Chanler, pp. 191, 201. Howe, *Rhodes*, pp. 308–9. Thayer, II, 333.

IV. (5) *Barnes vs. R, passim.* (7) Street, p. 10. (9) Gilder, p. 483.

V. (1) *Works*, IV, 432. (7) Hagedorn, *R Family*, pp. 313–15. (9) Barrus, *Life and Letters*, II, 365. Deland, p. 269. James, *Eliot*, I, 159. (10) Levien.

VI. To Mrs. Theodore Roosevelt, Jr., July 13, 1911. (3) *Letters*, VI, 1500. (6) "The Recent Prize-Fight," *O*, XCV (1910), 550–51. "Commercialism, Hysteria and Homicide," *O*, XCIX (1911), 409–10. (7) Charnwood, p. xviii. Reisner, p. 179. (9) Butt, *Letters*, p. 37. Gwynn, I, 437. (10) Welling, p. 366.

VII. To Kermit Roosevelt, Feb. 16, 1908. (3) *Letters to Kermit*, pp. 116, 178. (7) Drinker and Mowbray, p. 450. Reisner, p. 186. Willis and Smith, pp. 19–24. (9) Foulke, *Hoosier Autob.*, pp. 117–18.

VIII. To the Grand Exalted Ruler, B.P.O.E., Mar. 3, 1907. To Sir John L. Harrington, Dec. 29, 1908. To W. T. Hornaday, Oct. 30, 1908. To David V. Houston, Aug. 7, 1916. To Hal Minot, July 27, 1879. To Elizabeth Stuart Phelps, Nov. 18, 1905. To Warburton Pike, Jan. 18, 1905. To Frederick C. Selous, Sept. 11, 1911. To Philip B. Stewart, Feb. 19, 1907. To Henry van Dyke, Oct. 24, 1907. To William Wood, Sept. 15, 1911. (1) *Works,* I, 89; II, xxxi–xxxii, 265, 413–14, 426; IV, 514; V, 14; XIV, 206–7, 505; XXI, 503, 610. *Deer Family,* pp. 75–76. (3) *Letters,* VI, 1093, 1125. (7) Willis and Smith, pp. 16, 19, 25, 27–28.

IX. To C. P. Connolly, Apr. 25, 1913. To Horace Potter, Mar. 10, 1906. To Anna Roosevelt, Nov. 1876. (1) *Works,* IV, 451. (3) *Letters,* II, 860, 1042. (8) Beers, pp. 9–10.

X. To Lawrence Godkin, Dec. 21, 1901. To Mrs. Arthur Lee, May 29, 1915. To Archie Roosevelt, Sept. 17, 1908. To Kermit Roosevelt, Sept. 27, 1908, Oct. 1, 1915. To F. C. Selous, Sept. 11, 1911. Alexander Lambert to Julius Klausner, Jr., Feb. 7, 1924 (copy in Widener). (1) *Works,* IV, 188; XXI, 507, 551; XXII, 17, 23; XXIV, 397–98. (3) *Letters,* I, 10–11, 475; III, 475; IV, 1048; V, 312; VIII, 1313. *Letters to Kermit,* p. 58. (7) Cutright, p. 197. Davis, p. 429. Hagedorn, *Boys' Life,* p. 383. Reisner, p. 125. T.R., Jr., p. 34. (8) Kermit Roosevelt. (9) Butt, *Letters,* p. 156. Griscom, p. 221. Perry, *Dana,* p. 467.

Two: The World of Thought

I. (1) *Works,* XII, 279; XXI, 27. (3) *Letters,* VIII, 1278. *Letters . . . to A. R. Cowles,* p. 16. (7) Charnwood, p. 58. Cutright, p. 239. Gilman, pp. 343–44. Hagedorn, *R Family,* p. 236. Wilhelm, pp. 82–83. (9) Jusserand, p. 222. (10) Stefansson.

II. To Kermit Roosevelt, Feb. 24, 1916. (3) *Letters,* VI, 1330; VII, 412. (7) Hagedorn, *R Family,* p. 217. Kullnick, pp. 278–79. (9) Garland, *My Friendly Contemporaries,* pp. 145–46. Thayer, II, 356.

III. To W. L. Abbott, Dec. 31, 1914. To Frank M. Chapman, June 17, 1907. To Estelle Hart, July 13, 1907. To Mr. and Mrs. Theodore Roosevelt, Jr., Aug. 15, 1918. W. Emlen Roosevelt, Record of the Roosevelt Museum. (1) *Works,* III, 162; IV, xiii–xiv, 173–74; XIV, "History as Literature," "The Origin and Evolution of Life"; XV, 349; XXII, 18. (3) *Letters,* I, 7; V, 258, 498; VIII, 1433. (7) Edward B. Clark, *The Lion Hunter,* Leaflet, The Bird Club of Long Island, N. D. Lewis, p. 384, Robinson, p. 232. (9) Grey, pp. 64–69.

IV. To Robert U. Johnson, Jan. 6, 1900. To Brander Matthews, Jan. 11, 1917. (1) *Works,* IV, ix; IX, 213; XVIII, 303. (2) *PASP,* III, 5.

(3) *Letters,* I, 95, 136; II, 1046. *Letters . . . to A. R. Cowles,* p. 116. (7) Cutright, p. 92. Davis, p. 200. Lewis, p. 389. M. L. Storer, p. 15.

V. To Mrs. Grant La Farge, June 6, 1904. To Houghton, Mifflin and Company, Jan. 23, 1907. (1) *Works,* XIV, 465. (3) *Letters,* IV, 806; VII, 427. (7) Abbott, p. 185. Leupp, p. 307. Looker, *White House Gang,* p. 107. Wood, p. 368. (9) Bok, *Twice Thirty,* p. 216. Butt, *Letters,* p. 337. Foulke, *Hoosier Autob.,* p. 130. Wharton, p. 311. Whitlock, *Journal,* p. 155. H. G. Wells, *The Future in America* (H, 1906), p. 343.

VI. To E. F. Ware, May 7, 1904. To Paul Wienand, May 7, 1913. *Works,* XX, 237, 240–41, 442; XXI, 32. (3) *Letters,* V, 488.

VII. To Gilbert Murray, Nov. 11, 1908. To George W. Smalley, May 15, 1905. (1) *Works,* VIII, 70. (3) *Letters,* V, 398. (8) Kermit Roosevelt, p. 30.

VIII. To Truxton Beale, Apr. 2, 1915. To C. C. Burlingham, June 5, 1906. To David Gray, July 20, 1908. To W. W. Jacobs, Oct. 31, 1911. To R. U. Johnson, Jan. 5, 1906. To Philander C. Knox, Dec. 5, 1902. To J. C. Shaffer, "July 27." To Cecil Spring Rice, "April 22." (1) *Works,* IV, 83; VIII, 29; XIII, 367, 388; XIV, 6, 16, 375; XV, 266. (3) *Letters,* I, 343, 370, 439–40; II, 909, 918; III, 324, 427; IV, 968, 1047, 1166; V, 24; VI, 901; VII, 27, 29, 442–44, 1426. Lodge, *Correspondence,* II, 34. (7) Robinson, p. 103. Thayer, p. 71. (8) Kermit Roosevelt, p. 29. (9) Butt, *Letters,* p. 86.

IX. To Winston Churchill, June 7, 1913. To Edna Ferber, Apr. 4, 1913. To R. W. Gilder, June 4, 1894. To David Gray, July 20, 1908. To George Harvey, Nov. 28, 1905. To John Macrae, Dec. 20, 1916. To Josephine Preston Peabody Marks, Dec. 13, 1916. To Mary N. Murfree, Oct. 24, 1907. To Edwin Arlington Robinson, Apr. 1, 1905. To Thomas Robins, Jan. 3, 1916. To Corinne Roosevelt Robinson, July 3, 1918. To Mr. and Mrs. Kermit Roosevelt, Dec. 27, 1915. To Albert Shaw, Sept. 3, 1907. To C. Alphonso Smith, Dec. 20, 1916. To Stanley Waterloo, Dec. 15, 1897. To E. J. Wheeler, Feb. 27, 1917. To J. William White, Dec. 23, 1914. To Robert S. Yard, Nov. 11, 1905. (1) *Works,* I, 13; III, 303; IX, 424; XII, 576–79; XIV, 440, 449; XV, 282, 461; XX, 41; XXI, 336. *Outlook Editorials,* p. 5. (2) *PASP,* IV, 426. (3) *Letters,* I, 126–27, 286, 309, 358, 390, 410, 620; II, 1009, 1110, 1383; III, 9, 75, 112; IV, 857; V, 709; VII, 29–30, 740; VIII, 1216. *Letters . . . to A. R. Cowles,* p. 198. (7) Robinson, p. 6. (9) Elliott, *Three Generations,* p. 347. James, *Letters,* I, 379–80, II, 273, 449. *Mark Twain in Eruption,* p. 20.

X. To Kuno Meyer, Aug. 22, 1904. To Fr. Michael O'Flanagan, June 7, 1912. (1) *Works,* V, 158–59; XIV, 283, 411–17; XV, 284; XXIV, 160.

(2) *PASP*, IV, 398. (3) *Letters*, I, 96; III, 698. (7) Abbott, pp. 189–90. (9) Rosen, I, 261.

XI. To Randolph Howard, Jan. 16, 1899. To Mrs. James T. Leavitt, Dec. 18, 1907. (1) *Works*, XV, 474. (3) *Letters to Kermit*, pp. 47–48. (7) Robinson, pp. 128, 202–3. (8) Kermit Roosevelt, p. 5.

XII. (3) *Letters*, VIII, 1156. (7) Wood, pp. 219–20, 361.

XIII. (3) *Letters*, IV, 716, 758; V, 179, 1030. (7) "Some Recent Criticism of America," *Eclectic Magazine*, N.S. XLVIII (1888), 578–90. (7) Wister, p. 319.

XIV. To Maude Adams, Oct. 24, 1907. To David Belasco, May 13, 1915. To A. R. Cowles, Sept. 29, 1897. To Ralph M. Easley, Dec. 19, 1918. To O. W. Holmes, Feb. 18, 1904. To Brander Matthews, "March 21." To David C. Montgomery and Fred Stone, Dec. 17, 1914. To Thomas C. Platt, June 12, 1899. To George C. Tyler, Feb. 6, 1912. To Bayard Veiller, Feb. 18, 1913. (1) *Works*, IX, 402–3. (3) *Letters*, V, 562. Lodge, *Correspondence*, II, 76. (6) "Commercialism, Hysteria and Homicide," *O*, XCIX (1911), 409–10. (7) Blackton. Gilman, p. 231.

XV. (1) *Works*, XXI, 487. (3) *Letters*, II, 1049; VII, 706; VIII, 1453. (7) Amos, pp. 116–17. Douglas, p. 114. Hagedorn, *R in Bad Lands*, p. 280. Iglehart, pp. 332–33. (9) Cherrie, p. 255. J. B. Scott, p. 141. (10) Curtis and Abrams, "R's Love for Music," New York *Evening Sun*, Nov. 13, 1919. Hulda Lashanska, "T.R., Music Lover," New York *Globe and Commercial Advertiser*, Mar. 13, 1919.

XVI. (1) *Works*, XII, 564; XIV, 403–4, 405–10. (2) *PASP*, IV, 699. (3) *Letters*, I, 306. (7) Genthe, p. 127. (10) Brown.

Three: The World of Human Relations

I. To "Mr. Conklin," Feb. 5, 1912. To H. E. Dike, Nov. 28, 1911. To W. T. Durbin, Sept. 9, 1903. To Kermit Roosevelt, Dec. 28, 1914. To Franklin C. Smith, Jan. 24, 1906. To Frederic A. Whiting, Jan. 21, 1913. "The Practicability of Equalizing Men and Women," Graduate dissertation, Harvard College, June 30, 1880. (1) *Works*, IV, 77; XIV, 162, 193; XV, 524, 594; XXII, 297. (2) *PASP*, IV, 402; VI, 1294, 1662, 1706–7. (3) *Letters*, II, 938; VI, 1341–42, 1519–20; VII, 475; VIII, 1269. (6) "An Achievement for Decency," *O*, CIII (1913), 116. "The Presidency," *LHJ*, Feb. 1906, p. 21; Sept. 1906, p. 17. (7) Blum, p. 106. Hagedorn, *Bugle*, pp. 91–92. Riis, p. 354. Wister, pp. 235–36. (9) Griscom, p. 222. Jessup, II, 208–9. Palmer, *With My Own Eyes*, p. 257.

II. To James E. Cassidy, Dec. 3, 1917. To F. W. Hawes, Aug. 10, 1907. To James H. Wilson, Mar. 19, 1900. (1) *Works*, XVI, 34–41. (5) *R vs. Newett*, I, 7–34. (7) Davis, p. 421. Hurwitz, p. 152. Lang, p. 308.

(9) Adams, *Letters, 1892–1918*, p. 374. (10) Dantz, "T.R. Cowboy and Ranchman." Clarence True Wilson, "Methodist Rights in Politics," *Forum*, LXXVI (1928), 668–81.

III. To Albert J. Beveridge, June 24, 1905. To King Edward VII, Apr. 25, 1906. To W. D. Foulke, Feb. 7, 1912. To John Brisben Walker, Feb. 26, 1906. (7) Dennett, p. 211. Pringle, p. 497. (9) Busbey, pp. 221–22. Dennis, pp. 487–88. Griscom, pp. 244–45. Jessup, I, 440. Kennan, II, Chapters xxv–xxvi. Tarbell, *Rockefeller*, p. 251. Villard, pp. 151, 177–82. Washington, p. 166. Willson, p. 291. (8) Root, p. 5. (10) Lyman Abbott, "T.R., A Personal Sketch," p. 523. Anon., "An Official Denial," *O*, XCIX (1911), 1048. Sinclair.

IV. To R. W. Gilder, Nov. 17, 1907. To Francis J. Heney, Nov. 7, 1914. To Brander Matthews, Jan. 5, 1912. To D. E. Thompson, Nov. 16, 1907. To Howard Townsend, June 5, 1904. (1) *Works*, XV, 353. (3) *Letters*, III, 428, 558; VI, 994–95; VIII, 983. (7) Charnwood, p. 21. Einstein, p. vi. Riis, pp. 131–32. Thayer, pp. 11, 21. (8) Thompson, *Presidents*, p. 112. (9) Badè, II, 412. Butt, *Taft and R*, II, 562. Cobb, p. 282. Foulke, *Hoosier Autob.*, p. 127. Garraty, p. 349. Gwynn, II, 191. Howe, *Rhodes*, pp. 236–37. Jeritza, pp. 19–20. Jessup, II, 202, 552. Perry, *Dana*, p. 254. Stephenson, p. 203. Straus, pp. 207–8. Sullivan, *Education of an American*, pp. 207–8. Tumulty, pp. 287–88. Wharton, p. 317. White, *Autob.*, p. 297; White, *Masks*, p. 284. (10) Levien.

V. To A. R. Cowles, Nov. 26, 1876, Sept. 2, 1880. To Mr. and Mrs. Kermit Roosevelt, June 16, 1915. (1) *Works*, XXIII, 484–85. (3) *Letters*, I, 98; II, 889; IV, 1037; VI, 1146, 1373; VII, 3, 78, 193, 775. *Letters to Kermit*, p. 149. *Letters . . . to A. R. Cowles*, p. 276. (7) Wister, p. 125. Wood, p. 19. (9) Bishop, Bonaparte, p. 187. Bowers, p. 248. Butt, *Letters*, p. 147. Cherrie, p. 254.

VI. To Mrs. Gustaf Bergstrom, May 7, 1915. To W. G. McAdoo, Aug. 26, 1913. To Marguerite McFadden, Oct. 29, 1911. To the New York Eye and Ear Infirmary, May 7, 1915. To the Postmaster, Philadelphia, Oct. 29, 1911. To Theodore Roosevelt, Jr., Dec. 25, 1917. To Charles G. Washburn, May 7, 1915. "On the Need of Commonplace Virtues," MS, 1897. (1) *Works*, XXI, 381. (2) *PASP*, VI, 1601. (3) *Letters*, IV, 950. (7) Davis, p. 208. Morgan, pp. 196–97. Reisner, p. 144. Wood, p. 102. (9) Hoover, p. 36. Thompson, *Presidents*, p. 142. (10) Egan.

VII. To Mrs. Theodore Roosevelt, Jr., Nov. 27, 1910. To A. H. Anderson, Jan. 17, 1913. To Lemuel E. Quigg, Apr. 12, 1913. (1) *Works*, XVI, 315. (3) *Letters*, I, 326, 392, 397; (7) Leary, p. 21. Wood, p. 216. (9) Howe, *Wendell*, pp. 242, 251. Whitlock, *Letters*, p. 112.

VIII. To Lyman Abbott, Aug. 23, 1904. To W. E. Chandler, Aug. 12,

1897. To Alford W. Cooley, Feb. 13, 1912. To Marchesa A. de Vitti de Marco, June 1, 1915. To J. B. Foraker, Jan. 27, 1912, Jan. 27, 1915. To Charles McCarthy, Feb. 13, 1912. To R. S. Naon, Jan. 16, 1915. To Whitelaw Reid, Oct. 19, 1906. To Theodore Roosevelt, Jr., Nov. 21, 1910. To Julian Street, June 6, 1916. To Walter W. Strong, Dec. 15, 1916. (3) *Letters*, I, 93, 122, 132, 171, 554; II, 1415; III, 53, 97, 481–82, 663; IV, 730, 888, 1190; V, 242, 341, 408, 428–29; VI, 919, 1164, 1465, 1472; VII, 31, 36, 564; VIII, 817, 948, 995, 1067, 1081, 1118, 1154, 1302, 1305, 1373. (5) *Barnes vs. R*, I, 473–74. (7) Abbott, pp. 48–49. Blum, p. 53. Hurwitz, p. 151. Pringle, p. 282. Thayer, p. 314. (9) Butt, *Letters*, p. 126. Dennett, *Hay*, pp. 408–9, 436. Nevins, *Cleveland*, p. 197. Pusey, I, 169–73, 235–49.

IX. To Alford W. Cooley, Aug. 29, 1911. To "Fisher," June 30, 1911. To Theodore Roosevelt, Jr., Dec. 7, 1911. To Benjamin Ide Wheeler, Aug. 22, 1911. (3) *Letters*, IV, 1175; VI, 1157, 1231; VII, 52, 343–44, 480, 489, 508, 531, 568. (7) Howland, p. 185. Leary, pp. 198–205. (9) Adams, *Henry Adams and His Friends*, p. 638. Butt, *Taft and R*, II, 811–13, 859–60. Hammond, II, 578. Howe, *Storey*, p. 281. Pringle, II, 813–14, 815, 841. Sullivan, *Our Times*, IV, 331–32. Mrs. Taft, pp. 383–84. (10) Needham, "Why R Opposes Taft." Washburn.

X. To J. B. Bishop, Feb. 10, 1913. To Joseph L. Bristow, June 17, 1913. To W. D. Foulke, May 22, 1917. To Kermit Roosevelt, Jan. 2, 1916. To Henry L. Stoddard, July 8, 1914. To A. D. Swann, Apr. 22, 1913. To J. William White, Sept. 3, 1915. To Woodrow Wilson, June 23, 1902. (1) *Works*, XIX, 519. (3) *Letters*, III, 277, 391; VI, 1201; VII, 569, 723, 747, 768, 790; VIII, 830, 963, 976, 1091, 1106, 1198–99. (6) Review of M. P. Follett, *The Speaker of the House of Representatives*, *AHR*, II (1896), 176–78. (7) Leary, p. 326. Pringle, pp. 545–46. Street, p. 16.

XI. (1) *Works*, XVIII, 314. (3) *Letters*, VI, 1277–78; VII, 86, 408, 412, 476.

XII. To J. B. Bishop, Oct. 22, 1903. (1) *Works*, XVIII, 8. (3) *Letters*, I, 644; VI, 644; VII, 649, 677; VIII, 1413. *Letters . . . to A. R. Cowles*, p. 301. (5) *Barnes vs. R*, I, 499, 505. (7) Einstein, pp. 107–8. Leary, p. 454. Reisner, p. 222. (9) Dunn, I, 268.

XIII. To Joseph A. Ford, Jan. 1, 1908. To J. C. O'Laughlin, June 2, 1911. To "Mr. Schaffer," 1916. (1) *Works*, XVIII, 251; XIX, 442–43, 445–46; XXII, 484. (3) *Letters*, II, 1356; IV, 1096; VI, 867, 901, 1317; VII, 64, 451. (7) Davis, Chap. xxvii. Pringle, p. 218. Reisner, p. 163.

XIV. To Samuel H. Barker, Aug. 11, 1911. To William H. Bradley, Dec. 11, 1902. To Walter Morris, Apr. 21, 1910. (1) *Works*, I, xxviii; IX,

213; XV, 506–7. (3) *Letters,* III, 392; V, 695; VII, 543; VIII, 1024. (7) Thayer, p. 224. (8) Osborn, p. 270. (9) Hagedorn, *Wood,* I, 154.

XV. To A. R. Cowles, May 17, 1917. To Lady Delamere, Sept. 22, 1910. To W. R. Nelson, Sept. 29, 1914. To J. C. O'Laughlin, 1912. To Kermit Roosevelt, May 8, 1915. To Mrs. Kermit Roosevelt, Jan. 16, 1915. To J. M. Wall, Apr. 8, 1913. (1) *Works,* XV, 630; XXI, 302. (3) *Letters,* I, 516; II, 1068; V, 1, 677; VII, 302. (7) Abbott, p. 285. Hagedorn, *R Family,* pp. 328, 364. Iglehart, p. 26. Reisner, p. 268. Washburn, p. 166. Wister, p. 116. (8) Kermit Roosevelt, pp. 433–35. (9) R. S. Baker, p. 205. E. R. Belmont, pp. 106–7. Sullivan, *Our Times,* IV, 453; V, 199.

XVI. To John W. Burgess, 1910. To Elihu Root, Sept. 25, 1907. Memorandum by Albert Shaw (Widener). (1) *Works,* VIII, xix. (7) Reisner, p. 118. Washburn, p. 118. (8) Osborn, pp. 262–65. Root, p. 5. (10) W. H. Taft, "My Predecessor," *Collier's,* XLII, Mar. 6, 1909, p. 25.

Four: The World of the Family

I. To Thomas A. Fulton, Oct. 17, 1899. To Mrs. S. B. Leavitt, Dec. 15, 1903. To C. R. Robinson, May 1, 1915. To Mrs. Kermit Roosevelt, Oct. 24, 1915. (1) *Works,* XXI, 567; XXII, 10. (3) *Letters,* I, 18, 45, 65–66, 474; II, 1079; III, 392; V, 860; VI, 891, 1241; VII, 35, 60, 110. *Letters . . . to A. R. Cowles,* p. 261. *Letters to Kermit,* pp. 17, 49, 61, 191–92. (7) Amos, p. 30. Longworth, p. 8. Robinson, pp. 206–7, 218. Sewell, p. 11. (8) Bradford, p. 29. (9) Bok, *Twice Thirty,* pp. 210, 212. Butt, *Letters,* pp. 127, 146; *Taft and R,* I, 122. Storer, p. 21. (11) Richards.

II. To Pain's Fireworks Co., 1911. To Archie Roosevelt, Feb. 9, 1908. To Kermit Roosevelt, Feb. 19, 1904. (3) *Letters,* II, 803–4; III, 97, 203, 406, 543–44, 655, 682; VI, 972, 1004; VII, 110, 133, 344; VIII, 1207, 1316. (6) "The President," *LHJ,* Jan. 1907, p. 19. (7) Abbott, p. 306. Hagedorn, *Guide,* p. 70; *R Family,* pp. 50, 379, 383. Leary, p. 178. Lewis, p. 451. Longworth, p. 37. Looker, *White House Gang,* p. 152. (8) Kermit Roosevelt, p. 14. (9) Butt, *Letters,* p. 64. Storer, p. 22. (10) Levien. Vanderbilt.

Five: The World of Spiritual Values

I. To Abbot Charles, Nov. 20, 1911. To Paul F. Dehmel, July 8, 1912. To Arthur Lee, Oct. 1, 1915. To William H. Roberts, July 8, 1905. To Sr. M. Sebastian, Oct. 31, 1911. To Edith Wharton, Jan. 5, 1912. To Benjamin Ide Wheeler, Aug. 22, 1911. (1) *Works,* XI, 10; XIV, 34–35; XV, 490; XVI, 329, 363; XVII, 315; XVIII, 381; XXI, 135, 139–40, 566. (2) *African and European Addresses,* p. 6. (3) *Letters,* I, xxvii; II, 972,

1348–49; III, 8; V, xvi; VI, 1200; VII, 211, 372–73. (6) "The President," *LHJ*, Sept. 1906, p. 17. (7) Hagedorn, *R in Bad Lands*, p. 424. McCaleb, p. 66. Reisner, p. 235. Robinson, p. 47. (8) Thompson, p. 121. (9) La Farge, p. 59.

II. To E. H. Buxton, Dec. 8, 1908. To Endicott Peabody, June 29, 1915. To H. J. Stimson, Oct. 23, 1917. (1) *Works*, XIV, 231; XXI, 163; XXIV, 557. (3) *Letters*, I, 19, 132; II, 802, 992, 1217; III, 403; V, 10; VI, 839, 961, 1139; VII, 35, 891; VIII, 1096. (7) Davis, p. 434. Einstein, p. 39. Leary, p. 5. Wister, pp. 67–68, 363. (9) H. G. Wells, *The Future in America*, pp. 349–50.

III. (1) *Works*, IV, 26; XII, 564. (8) Bradford, p. 30.

Six: The World of Political Affairs

I. To Lyman Abbott, Nov. 7, 1914. To Thomas A. Fulton, Oct. 17, 1899. To the Governor-General of Australia, Nov. 5, 1914. To Herbert S. Hadley, July 10, 1913. To Arthur D. Hill, Nov. 9, 1914. To Thomas Humphrey, Feb. 18, 1899. To Franklin K. Lane, Dec. 21, 1911. To Henry L. Nest, Apr. 10, 1915. To Gifford Pinchot, Mar. 29, 1915. To James M. Pierce, undated telegram. To Quentin Roosevelt, Sept. 29, 1913. To John St. Loe Strachey, Dec. 5, 1904. To W. R. Thayer, 1915. To Jonas S. Van Duzer, May 17, 1885. (1) *Works*, XXI, 440–43; XXIV, 460. (3) *Letters*, I, 167, 175; II, 1159, 1277; III, 150; V, 517; VIII, 1114, 1414. (7) Hagedorn, *R Family*, p. 117. Leary, pp. 2–3. Lewis, p. 426. Moore, pp. 291–92. Pringle, p. 182. (9) Bok, *Americanization*, p. 282. Garraty, p. 220. Olcott, II, 270–71. Steffens, *Autob.*, pp. 258–60. Washington, p. 168.

II. (1) *Works*, XVIII, 109; XIX, 436–37; XXII, 404; XXIV, 24. (3) *Letters*, III, 362; V, 10; VI, 910. *Letters . . . to A. R. Cowles*, pp. 253–54. (7) Bailey, p. 199. Douglas, p. 261. Lewis, pp. viii, xviii. Wood, pp. 160–61. (9) Garraty, p. 291. Goldman, p. 97.

III. To R. M. Ferguson, Feb. 20, 1906. To George C. Holt, Dec. 12, 1906. To Cameron Winston, Aug. 27, 1897. (1) *Works*, XIX, 81; XXIV, 14. (3) *Letters*, V, 216–17; VIII, 1368. (9) La Follette, pp. 487–89.

IV. To Robert Bridges, June 30, 1908, Dec. 2, 1908. To the Department of Justice, Kansas City, Mo., 1917 or 1918. To Mrs. W. H. Hall, Sept. 15, 1911. To Endicott Peabody, June 29, 1915. To Douglas Robinson, Dec. 27, 1897. To Mr. and Mrs. Theodore Roosevelt, Jr., Aug. 21, 1918. To Charles Scribner's Sons, Aug. 8, 1908. (2) *PASP*, VI, 1377. (3) *Letters*, I, 391; II, 1102, 1153; V, 218, 317, 836; VII, 153, 237, 885. Lodge, *Correspondence*, II, 335. (5) *Barnes vs. R*, I, 484, 487. (6) "Issues of 1896," *Ce*, N.S. XXIX (1895), 68–72. (7) Davis, p. 430. McCaleb, pp. 171, 180. Sewall, p. 103. Thayer, p. 295.

V. To Brooks Adams, July 18, 1903. To J. H. Cort, May 1, 1908. To
Philander C. Knox, Nov. 10, 1904. To F. S. Luther, Jan. 23, 1918. To Mr.
and Mrs. Theodore Roosevelt, Jr., Aug. 21, 29, 1918. (1) *Works,* VII,
798; VIII, 962; XVII, 428; XVIII, 212, 579; XIX, 102, 535. (3) *Letters,*
III, 515; VI, 1311, 1585; VIII, 826, 1234–35, 1389–90. (7) Hurwitz,
pp. 363–64. Wood, p. viii. (9) Bowers, p. 266. Filler, p. 162. Watson,
p. 168.

VI. To C. R. Robinson, May 1, 1899. To Mr. and Mrs. Theodore Roosevelt, Jr., Aug. 29, 1918. (1) *Works,* XV, 399. (3) *Letters,* V, 605. (5)
Barnes vs. R, I, 393–94. (7) Blum, p. 19. Charnwood, p. 104. Foulke,
p. 64. Hagedorn, *Boys' Life,* p. 279. (9) Busbey, p. 219. Filler, p. 216.
Gosnell, p. 215. Milton, p. 177. Rainsford, p. 406. Steffens, *Autob.,* pp.
577–79. Watson, p. 67.

VII. To Nelson W. Aldrich, Jan. 1, 1909. To Warrington Dawson, Oct.
21, 1911. To William H. Fleming, Aug. 20, 1906. To Bradley Gilman,
July 24, 1912. To Carl Schurz, Jan. 1, 1904. To James E. West, Oct. 12,
1908. (1) *Works,* I, 19; XIV, 65; XV, 548; XXIV, 508. (2) *PASP,* V,
1071, 1073, 1098. (3) *Letters,* I, 346; II, 1385; III, 24; IV, 1041; V, 227;
VI, 1503, 1507; VII, 787. (6) "The President," *LHJ,* Nov. 1906, p. 19.
(7) Amos, pp. 57–58, 64. Davis, pp. 229–30. Gilman, p. 251. Hagedorn,
R in Bad Lands, p. 355.

VIII. To M. C. Harris, Aug. 6, 1907. To Harriet Gaylord, Dec. 30,
1918. (1) *Works,* XXIII, 454. (2) *PASP,* VI, 1214–15. (3) *Letters,* I,
555, 647; II, 1176–77; III, 97, 122; V, 475, 528; VII, 824; VIII, 889,
1186. (6) "What the Japanese Have Stood For in World War," New York
Times, Nov. 30, 1919. (7) Beale, p. 264. (9) Pringle, I, 299.

IX. To Lawrence F. Abbott, Apr. 26, 1918. To Andrew Carnegie,
Sept. 15, 1907. To Charles W. Eliot, July 24, 1905. To Wilfred T. Gren-
fell, Feb. 17, 1915. To Commander B. H. McCalla, Dec. 28, 1897. To the
Secretary of State, May 6, 1917. To Booth Tarkington, June 29, 1915.
Marshall Stimson, "Chapter from an Unpublished Autobiography," MS,
Widener. (1) *Works,* XX, 250–54. (3) *Letters,* I, 157; II, 1050; IV, 1150,
1159; V, 18, 542, 544; VII, 394 ff.; VIII, 831, 1354–55, 1396. *Letters to
Kermit,* p. 70. (9) Howe, *Rhodes,* p. 122. Nevins, *Henry White,* pp.
279, 303–4.

Seven: The World of War and Peace

I. To Harriet Boyd Hawes, Jan. 11, 1917. To Whitelaw Reid, Nov. 13,
1905. To Mr. and Mrs. Theodore Roosevelt, Jr., Aug. 15, 1918. To P. B.
Weld, Jan. 4, 1913. Graduation dissertation, Harvard College, MS,
Widener. (1) *Works,* VIII, 29, 197; XIV, 330, 372; XXI, *The Foes of*

Our Own Household, Ch. xiii. R *in Kansas City Star,* pp. 221–22. (3)
Letters, I, 504, 510, 621, 647, 707, 773–74, 776, 798; II, 1407; VI, 1441–
42; VIII, 1022, 1153. (7) Blum, p. 141. Hagedorn, *Boys' Life,* p. 380.
Howland, p. 271. Leary, p. 240. Robinson, p. 338. (9) Gladden, pp.
388–89. Haynes, pp. 143–44. Longworth, p. 21.

II. To R. W. Gilder, May 24, 1897. To B. S. Hurlbut, Dec. 13, 1908.
To Josephine Shaw Lowell, May 9, 1902. To Endicott Peabody, Aug.
27(?), 1907. To Jacob Riis, Mar. 24, 1904. To James Brown Scott, Aug.
26, 1915. To Leonard Wood, Aug. 12, 1904. (1) *Works,* VII, xv–xvi;
XV, 287, 357; XVII, 296, 347, 472, 548; XVIII, 332; XX, 41–42, 274;
XXI, 561; XXII, 149. (3) *Letters,* I, 644, 862; II, 1089, 1100; III, 298,
558, 563; V, 17, 263, 475–76, 695, 855, 1085; VII, 901; VIII, 854, 1114.
(6) "Expansion and Peace," *Independent,* LI (1899), 3401–5. "The
President," *LHJ,* Aug. 1906, p. 17. (7) Drinker and Mowbray, p. 132.
Leupp, p. 196. (9) Alvin Johnson, p. 253.

III. To A. C. Dillingham, Nov. 17, 1908. To Maurice Francis Egan,
Oct. 25, 1906. To Brander Matthews, Jan. 11, 1907. To the Secretary of
State, Jan. 23, 1906. (3) *Letters,* II, 1396, 1415; III, 677; IV, 768; V,
560; VIII, 908. (7) Pringle, p. 280; Riis, p. 300. (9) Jordan, I, 309.
Pringle, I, 305–6.

IV. To Andrew Carnegie, May 23, 1911. (3) *Letters,* I, 356; II, 1092–
93; V, 852; VI, 63–64. (7) Charnwood, pp. 133–34. Lewis, p. 377. (9)
Pringle, II, 746, 752.

V. (3) *Letters,* V, 474; VII, 470. (7) Hagedorn, *R. Family,* pp. 225–
26. (9) Stoddard, pp. 151–52. (10) Butt, New York *Herald,* Jan. 31,
1924.

VI. To Philippe Bunau-Varilla, July 7, 1914, Mar. 13, 1915. To Julius
Chambers, July 9, 1914. To Silas McBee, Jan. 6, 1904. (1) *Works,* XXIII,
356. (2) *PASP,* II, 713. (3) *Letters,* VI, 897. (7) Pringle, p. 332. (9)
Thayer, II, 190, 328.

VII. To Curtis Guild, Jr., Apr. 2, 1906. To Sir Harry Johnston, Dec.
4, 1908. (3) *Letters,* III, 532; IV, 1175, 1284. (7) Beale, p. 447.

VIII. To Georges Clemenceau, Dec. 10, 1918. To R. J. Cuninghame,
Aug. 6, 1915. To M. F. Egan, Nov. 20, 1917. To Irvine L. Lenroot, Mar.
5, 1917. To the Archduke Ludwig Salvator, May 29, 1915. To James P.
Robinson, Aug. 22, 1914. To John Roosevelt, Mar. 3, 1915. To Mr. and
Mrs. Kermit Roosevelt, May 27, 1915. To F. C. Selous, Dec. 4, 1914,
Apr. 2, 1915. To Oscar Straus, Nov. 23, 1914. To Admiral von Tirpitz,
Dec. 4, 1914. To George Sylvester Viereck, Aug. 8, 1914. To Stewart
Edward White, Aug. 31, 1914. (1) *Works,* XX, 58, 137, 193–94, 201,

226, 251, 354. *R in Kansas City Star,* p. 229. (3) *Letters,* VII, 809–11; VIII, 821, 831, 867, 897–903, 949, 957, 1066, 1368. (7) Abbott, p. 251. Hagedorn, *Bugle,* p. 205. Wood, pp. 306–7. (9) Howe, *Rhodes,* p. 245.

IX. (7) Davis, p. 225. Pringle, p. 520. (9) Wells, *The Future in America,* p. 350.

Selected Bibliography

R indicates Roosevelt. TR indicates Theodore Roosevelt. When TR is written T.R. it indicates that the name occurs in this form in the title quoted. Thus John J. Leary's book is called *Talks with T.R.*, not "Talks with Theodore Roosevelt."

The following additional abbreviations are employed:

A	D. Appleton and Company
AC	Appleton-Century Company
AHR	*American Historical Review*
AMP	Atlantic Monthly Press
AP	Association Press
Atl	*Atlantic Monthly*
B	Broadway Publishing Co.
BM	The Bobbs-Merrill Company
Ce	The Century Company
Ce	*Century Magazine*
ColUP	Columbia University Press
D	Doubleday and Company (and its predecessors)
DM	Dodd, Mead & Company
Do	George H. Doran Company
Du	E. P. Dutton & Co.
DUP	Duke University Press
F	Farrar, Straus and Cudahy (and its predecessors)
H	Harper & Brothers
HaW	*Harper's Weekly*
HB	Harcourt, Brace and Company
HM	Houghton Mifflin Company
Ht	Henry Holt and Company
HUP	Harvard University Press
JD	The John Day Company
JHP	Johns Hopkins Press
JM	Julian Messner
K	Alfred A. Knopf
LB	Little, Brown and Company
LHJ	*Ladies' Home Journal*
Lo	Longmans, Green and Company

M   The Macmillan Company
McC   A. C. McClurg and Company
MVHR   *Mississippi Valley Historical Review*
MY   Moffat, Yard and Company
NAR   *North American Review*
O   *Outlook*
OUP   Oxford University Press
P   G. P. Putnam's Sons
PUP   Princeton University Press
R   Fleming H. Revell Company
R of Rs *American Review of Reviews*
RH   Reynal and Hitchcock
S   Charles Scribner's Sons
SAQ   *South Atlantic Quarterly*
SEP   *Saturday Evening Post*
SM   Small, Maynard and Company
SS   Simon and Schuster
St   Frederick A. Stokes Company
StUP   Stanford University Press
UCP   University of Chicago Press
UNCP   University of North Carolina Press
VP   Viking Press
W   John C. Winston Company
WW   *World's Work*
YUP   Yale University Press

There is *A Bibliography of TR*, by John Hall Wheelock (S, 1920). See also Nora E. Cordingley, "Extreme Rarities in the Published Works of TR," *Papers of the Bibliographical Society of America*, XXXIX (1945), 20–50.

(1) The best edition of *The Works of TR* is the "Memorial Edition," edited by Hermann Hagedorn, 24 vols. (S, 1923–1926). This edition is cited in the notes as *Works*.[1]

[1] The following partial analysis of the "Memorial Edition" is added to make the references in the Notes more meaningful. Volume I: "Editor's Foreword," pp. vii–xi; "Introduction," by George Bird Grinnell, pp. xiii–xxviii; *Hunting Trips of a Ranchman*, pp. 1–297; *Game-Shooting in the West*, pp. 299–347; *Good Hunting*, pp. 349–96. Volume II: "R and the Pioneer Spirit," by Stewart Edward White, pp. ix–xxvi; *The Wilderness Hunter*. Volume III: "R the Companion," by Alexander Lambert, pp. ix–xxvi; *Outdoor Pastimes of an American Hunter*. Volume IV: "The Naturalist and Book-Lover: An Appreciation," by William Beebe, pp. ix–xv; *A Book-Lover's Holidays in the Open*, pp. xvii–xxxvi, 1–336; "The Young R" by Owen Wister, pp. 339–56; *Ranch Life and*

The following items are not included in the "Memorial" or other collected edition:

American Problems (Outlook Co., 1910); *The Deer Family* (with others) (M, 1902); *Essays on Practical Politics* (P, 1888); *Life-Histories of African Game Animals*, 2 vols. (with Edmund Heller) (S, 1914); *National Strength and International Duty* (PUP, 1917); *Outlook Editorials* (Outlook Co., 1909); *Roosevelt in the Kansas City Star*, ed. Ralph Stout (HM, 1921); *Some American Game* (P, 1897); "The War with

---

the Hunting Trail, pp. 357–614. Volume V: "R in Africa," by Carl Akeley, pp. ix–xx; *African Game Trails*. Volume VI: "Introduction," by Frank M. Chapman, pp. ix–xxxviii; *Through the Brazilian Wilderness*, pp. xxxix–xlvi, 1–366; *Papers on Natural History*, pp. 367–475. Volume VII: "R: Historian and Patriot," by William S. Sims, pp. ix–xxiii; *The Naval War of 1812*. Volume VIII: "The Statesmanship of TR," by Albert J. Beveridge, pp. ix–xxxii; *Thomas Hart Benton*, pp. xxxiii–xxxvi, 1–270; *Gouverneur Morris*, pp, 271–544. Volume IX: "The 'Hero Tales,'" by Henry Cabot Lodge, pp. ix–xviii; *Hero Tales from American History* (with Henry Cabot Lodge), pp. xix–xxiv, 1–189; "R, Citizen of New York," by Julian Street, pp. 193–214; *New York*, pp. 215–435. Volume X: "R as Pioneer," by Albert Bushnell Hart, pp. ix–xxix; *The Winning of the West*, I. Volume XI: "R, Historian and Statesman," by George Haven Putnam, pp. ix–xxii; *The Winning of the West*, II. Volume XII: "R as Historian," by Hamlin Garland, pp. ix–xvii; *The Winning of the West*, III, pp. xix–xxii, 1–414; *Men of Action*, pp. 415–635. Volume XIII: "R, Soldier, Statesman, and Friend," by Leonard Wood, pp. ix–xxi; *The Rough Riders*, pp. xxiii–xxviii, 1–208; *The Fifth Corps at Santiago*, pp. 209–61; "Cromwell and R," by Viscount Lee of Fareham, pp. 265–82; *Oliver Cromwell*, pp. 283–461. Volume XIV: "TR as a Man of Letters," by Brander Matthews, pp. ix–xxiii; *Literary Essays*. Volume XV: *Citizenship, Politics, and the Elemental Virtues*: "Editor's Note," pp. ix–xi; "'Saith the Preacher!'" by William Allen White, pp. xiii–xvi; *American Ideals*, pp. xvii–xxii, 1–259; *The Strenuous Life*, pp. 261–565; *Realizable Ideals*, 567–643. Volume XVI: "Editor's Note," pp. ix–x; "TR as Political Leader," by Albert Shaw, pp. xi–xxxviii; *Campaigns and Controversies* (Essays and Addresses, 1882–1901). Volume XVII: "Editor's Note," p. ix; "R as President," by Gifford Pinchot, pp. xi–xxxiii; *State Papers as Governor and President*. Volume XVIII: "Editor's Note," p. ix; "R's Conduct of Foreign Affairs," by Elihu Root, pp. xi–xxvii; *American Problems* (Addresses as President). Volume XIX: "Editor's Note," p. ix; "The Great Progressive," by Herbert Knox Smith, pp. xi–xx; *Social Justice and Popular Rule* (Essays, Addresses, and Public Statements, 1910–1912). Volume XX: "R and the Peace of Righteousness," by John Grier Hibben, pp. ix–xiv; *America and the World War*, pp. xv–xxviii, 1–216; *Fear God and Take Your Own Part*, pp. 217–533. Volume XXI: "R and the World War," by Henry L. Stimson, pp. xi–xxiii; *The Foes of Our Own Household*, pp. xxv–xxx, 1–240; "The Inspiration of TR," by E. A. Van Valkenburg, pp. 243–51; *The Great Inspiration*, pp. 252–544; *TR's Letters to His Children*, edited by Joseph Bucklin Bishop, pp. 455–614. Volume XXII: *An Autobiography*. Volumes XXIII–XXIV: *TR and His Time, Shown in His Own Letters*, by Joseph Bucklin Bishop.

the United States, 1812–1815," in William Laird Clowes, *The Royal Navy* (Sampson Low, 1901), VI, 1–180. With George Bird Grinnell, TR edited three books for the Boone and Crocket Club, all published by Forest and Stream Publishing Company: *American Big-Game Hunting* (1893); *Hunting in Many Lands* (1895); *Trail and Camp-Fire* (1897). In addition to his signed contributions in these volumes, TR wrote "Literature of American Big-Game Hunting" in the first, part of "Head-Measurements of the Trophies at the Madison Square Garden Sportsmen's Exhibition" in the second, and "Books on Big Game" in the third. A fourth volume, edited by Grinnell, *American Big Game in Its Haunts* (1904), contains a paper by TR.

These anthologies have been drawn from TR's writings: Robert Bridges, *The R Book* (S, 1904); Donald Day, *The Hunting and Exploring Adventures of TR*, with an introduction by Elting E. Morison (Dial Press, 1955); Hermann Hagedorn, *The Americanism of TR* (HM, 1923), *The Free Citizen* (M, 1956), and *The TR Treasury* (P, 1957); Farida Wiley, *TR's America*, which is devoted to his nature writing (Devin-Adair, 1955). See also, *TR Cyclopedia*, ed. Albert Bushnell Hart and Herbert R. Ferleger (R Memorial Association, 1941).

(2) For TR's speeches, I used, besides the "Memorial Edition," *Presidential Addresses and State Papers*, "Homeward Bound Edition," 8 vols. (Review of Reviews Company, 1910). This work is cited in the Notes as *PASP*. See also, *African and European Addresses*, with introduction by Lawrence F. Abbott (P, 1910); *California Addresses* (San Francisco, Cal. Promotion Committee, 1903).

(3) The great collection of TR's letters is *The Letters of TR*, edited by Elting E. Morison and others, 8 vols. (HUP, 1951–1954). This work is cited in the Notes as *Letters*. Three very long and delightful letters from this collection have been reprinted in *Cowboys and Kings*, edited by E.E.M. (HUP, 1954). See, further, *Letters from TR to Anna Roosevelt Cowles* (S, 1924); *Letters to Kermit*, edited by Will Irwin (S, 1946); *Selections from the Correspondence of TR and Henry Cabot Lodge*, edited by Lodge, 2 vols. (S, 1925); *Betts-R Letters*, edited Charles H. Betts (Lyons, N. Y.: The Lyons Republican Co., 1912); Joseph B. Foraker, *Correspondence with President R* (No publisher, no date); "Letters of TR and Charles Dwight Willard," *Amer. Scholar*, III (1934), 465–86; R. W. G. Vail, "Your Loving Friend, T.R. Letters to H. D. Minot," *Collier's* LXXIV, Dec. 20, 1924, pp. 8–9+; George B. Utley, "TR's *The Winning of the West:* Some Unpublished Letters," *MVHR*, XXX (1944), 495–506. See, also, *Letters to His Children* in "Memorial Edition," Vol. XXI, importantly supplemented by " 'Your Father Loves You Dearly'—

T.R.," with an introductory note by TR, Jr., *Good Housekeeping*, CIV, Jan. 1937, pp. 24–27+.

(4) The only published diaries are *TR's Diaries of Boyhood and Youth* (S, 1928). TR's unpublished Spanish War diary is in the Houghton Library.

(5) Records of the two libel suits in which TR participated are in *R vs. Newett: A Transcript of the Testimony Taken at Depositions Read at Marquette, Michigan* (Privately printed, 1914) and *William Barnes against TR* (*Supreme Court of the State of New York—Appellate Division—Fourth Department*), 4 vols. (Walton, N. Y., The Reporter Co., 1917).

(6) TR's articles in newspapers and magazines are like the sands of the sea in number. A great many have been reprinted (and sometimes revised and rewritten) in his books. I had originally intended to list here all the uncollected articles that I thought of interest. Further reflection convinced me that this would take more space than could reasonably be given to it, especially since most of the articles are readily available through the periodical indexes. Where I have taken a quotation from an uncollected article, bibliographical information is given in the notes.

(7) This list contains books about TR: Lawrence F. Abbott, *Impressions of TR* (D, 1919); James E. Amos, *TR: Hero to His Valet* (JD, 1927); Thomas A. Bailey, *TR and the Japanese-American Crises* (StUP, 1934); Howard K. Beale, *TR and the Rise of America to World Power* (JHP, 1956); John W. Bennett, *R and the Republic* (B, 1908); Joseph Bucklin Bishop, *TR and His Time* (see Section 1—*Works*, Vols. XXIII–XXIV); J. Stuart Blackton, "My Neighbor TR" (MS—Widener Library); John Morton Blum, *The Republican R* (HUP, 1954); A. L. Boyce, "Contacts . . . with TR, 1904–1919" (MS—Widener Library); Robert Bridges, *TR as Author and Contributor* (pamphlet—S, 1919); M. J. Brusse, *With R through Holland* (Holland-American Line, 1911); John Burroughs, *Camping and Tramping with R* (HM, 1907); Lord Charnwood, *TR* (Atlantic Monthly Press, 1923); Albert Loren Cheney, *Personal Memoirs of the Home Life of the Late TR*, Second edition (Washington, The Cheney Publishing Co., 1920); Edward H. Cotton, *The Ideals of TR* (A, 1923), and *TR the American* (Beacon Press, 1926); Paul Russell Cutright, *TR the Naturalist* (H, 1956); Oscar King Davis, *Released for Publication: Some Inside Political History of TR and His Times, 1898–1918* (HM, 1925); Warrington Dawson, *Opportunity and TR* (No publisher given, 1923) William C. Deming, ed., *R in the Bunk House and Other Sketches* (Laramie, Wyo., The Laramie Printing Co., 1927); Tyler Dennett, *R and the Russo-Japanese War* (D, 1925); George W. Douglas,

The Many-Sided R (DM, 1907); Frederick E. Drinker and Jay Henry Mowbray, *TR, His Life and Work* (National Publishing Co., 1919).

Lewis Einstein, *R, His Mind in Action* (HM, 1930); William Dudley Foulke, *R and the Spoilsmen* (National Civil Service Reform League, 1925); Bradley Gilman, *R the Happy Warrior* (LB, 1921); Hermann Hagedorn, *The Boys' Life of TR* (H, 1922), *The Bugle That Woke America: The Saga of TR's Last Battle for His Country* (JD, 1940), *A Guide to Sagamore Hill* (TR Association, 1953), *The R Family of Sagamore Hill* (M, 1954), *R in the Bad Lands* (HM, 1921), and *R, Prophet of Unity* (S, 1924); Annie Riley Hale, *Bull Moose Trails* (Published by the Author, 1912), and *Rooseveltian Fact and Fable* (B, 1908); William Bayard Hale, *A Week in the White House with TR* (P, 1908); Murat Halstead, *The Life of TR* (Saalfield Publishing Co., 1902); Daniel Henderson, *"Great-Heart": The Life Story of TR*, Second edition (K, 1919); Howard C. Hill, *R and the Caribbean* (UCP, 1927); Harold Howland, *TR and His Times* (YUP, 1921); Howard L. Hurwitz, *TR and Labor in New York State, 1880–1900* (ColUP, 1943); Frederick C. Iglehart, *TR, The Man As I Knew Him* (Christian Herald, 1919); Max Kullnick, *From Rough Rider to President* (McC, 1911); Lincoln A. Lang, *Ranching with R* (Lippincott, 1926); John J. Leary, *Talks with T.R.* (HM, 1920); Francis E. Leupp, *The Man R: A Portrait Sketch* (A, 1904); Wm. Draper Lewis, *The Life of TR*, Introduction by William Howard Taft (W, 1919); Henry Cabot Lodge, *TR* (HM, 1919); Eugene Looker, *Colonel R, Private Citizen* (R, 1932) and *The White House Gang* (R, 1929); Walter F. McCaleb, *TR* (A. & C. Boni, 1931); J. Hampton Moore, *R and the Old Guard* (Macrae-Smith, 1925); James Morgan, *TR, the Boy and the Man* (M, 1907); George E. Mowry, *TR and the Progressive Movement* (University of Wisconsin Press, 1946); Ludwig Nissen, *Reminiscences of TR* (pamphlet—No publisher given, 1920); Gordon C. O'Gara, *TR and the Rise of the Modern Navy* (PUP, 1943); John C. O'Laughlin, *From the Jungle through Europe with R* (Boston, Chapple Publishing Co., Ltd., 1910); Hilda Paulmier and Robert Haven Schauffler, eds., *Roosevelt Day* (DM, 1932); Edmund Lester Pearson, *TR* (M, 1920); Evelene Peters, *R und der Kaiser* (Leipzig, Universitätsverlag von Robert Noske, 1936); Henry F. Pringle, *TR, A Biography* (HB, 1931); Charles A. Prouty and others, *President R's Railroad Policy* (Ginn, 1905); Christian F. Reisner, *R's Religion* (Abingdon Press, 1922); Oliver E. Remey and others, *The Attempted Assassination of Ex-President R* (Milwaukee, Progressive Publishing Co., 1912); William H. Richardson, ed., *Some R Reminiscences . . . by Members of the R Association of Jersey City* (Jersey City Printing Co., 1920), and *TR, One Day of His Life: Reconstructed from*

Contemporaneous Accounts of His Political Campaign of 1912 (Jersey City Printing Co., 1921); Jacob A. Riis, *TR the Citizen* (M, 1904); Corinne Roosevelt Robinson, *My Brother TR* (S, 1921); Theodore Roosevelt, Jr., *All in the Family* (P, 1929).

William W. Sewall, *Bill Sewall's Story of T.R.* (H, 1919); Clifford Smyth, *TR* (Funk & Wagnalls Co., 1931); Bellamy Storer, *Letter of Bellamy Storer to the President and the Members of His Cabinet, November 1906* (privately printed); Maria Longworth Storer, *TR the Child* (London, W. Straker, Ltd., 1921); Julian Street, *The Most Interesting American* (Ce, 1915); William Roscoe Thayer, *TR, An Intimate Biography* (HM, 1919); Addison C. Thomas, *R among the People* (Chicago, The L.W. Walter Co., 1910); Eugene Thwing, *The Life and Meaning of TR* (Current Literature Publishing Co., 1919); George Sylvester Viereck, *R: A Study in Ambivalence* (New York, Jackson Press, 1919); Frank B. Vrooman, *TR, Dynamic Geographer* (OUP, 1909); Charles G. Washburn, *TR, The Logic of His Career* (HM, 1916); Wayne Whipple, *The Heart of R: An Intimate Life-Story of TR* (W, 1923); Donald Wilhelm, *TR as an Undergraduate* (Luce, 1910); Jack Willis and Horace Smith, *R in the Rough* (Ives Washburn, 1931); Owen Wister, *R, The Story of a Friendship* (M, 1930); Frederick S. Wood, ed., *Roosevelt As We Knew Him* (W, 1927); J. A. Zahm, *Through South America's Southland, with an Account of the R Scientific Expedition to South America* (A, 1916).

Carleton Putnam's *TR: The Formative Years* (S, 1958), the first volume of what promises to be a magnificent four-volume biography of TR, did not appear until after my book had been completed. In my final revision, I have used three or four items of information but have taken no quotations from it.

Charles Hanson Towne collected a large number of poetic tributes to TR in *R as the Poets Saw Him* (S, 1923). But the most significant poetic monument thus far is Russell J. Wilbur, *TR: A Verse Sequence in Sonnets and Quartorzains* (HM, 1919).

There are three important collections of cartoons: Raymond Gros, ed. *T.R. in Cartoon* (Saalfield, 1910); John T. McCutcheon, *T.R. in Cartoons* (McClurg, 1910); Albert Shaw, ed., *A Cartoon History of R's Career* (Review of Reviews, 1910).

(8) The following books have sections devoted to TR: Daniel Aaron, *Men of Good Hope, A Study of American Progressives* (OUP, 1951); Lyman Abbott, *Silhouettes of My Contemporaries* (D, 1922); Henry A. Beers, *Four Americans* (YUP, 1919); Joseph Bucklin Bishop, *Notes and Anecdotes of Many Years* (S, 1925); Gamaliel Bradford, *The Quick and*

the Dead (HM, 1931); John Burroughs, *Under the Maples* (HM, 1921); James Lea Cate and Eugene N. Anderson, *Medieval and Historiographical Essays in Honor of James Westfall Thompson* (UCP, 1938); Julius Henry Cohen, *They Builded Better Than They Knew* (JM, 1946); Calvin Coolidge, *The Price of Freedom* (S, 1924); W. H. Crook, *Memories of the White House*, ed. Henry Rood (LB, 1911); Mike Donovan, *The R That I Know . . . and Other Memories of Famous Fighting Men* (B. W. Dodge & Co., 1909); Charles Macomb Flandrau, *Loquacities* (A, 1931); Frank Harris, *Contemporary Portraits*, Fourth Series (Brentano's, 1923); William C. Hudson, *Random Recollections of an Old Political Reporter* (Cupples & Leon Co., 1911); James Huneker, *Variations* (S, 1921); William T. Hutchinson, ed., *The Marcus W. Jernegan Essays in American Historiography* (UCP, 1937); Stephanie Lauzanne, *Great Men and Great Days* (A, 1921); Frederick H. Law, *Modern Great Americans* (Ce, 1926); Peter R. Levin, *Seven by Chance: The Accidental Presidents* (F, 1948); Henry Cabot Lodge, *A Frontier Town and Other Essays* (S, 1906); Isaac F. Marcosson, *Adventures in Interviewing* (John Lane, 1919); Brander Matthews, *The Tocsin of Revolt and Other Essays* (S, 1922); H. L. Mencken, *Prejudices*, Second Series (K, 1920); Charles Edward Merriam, *Four American Party Leaders* (M, 1926); Bennett Milton, *The Presidents and Civil Disorder* (The Brookings Institution, 1941); William Dana Orcutt, *Celebrities off Parade* (Willett, Clark, 1935); Henry Fairfield Osborn, *Impressions of Great Naturalists* (C, 1928); James Ford Rhodes, *The McKinley and Roosevelt Administrations, 1897–1909* (M, 1922); Kermit Roosevelt, *The Happy Hunting-Grounds* (S, 1920); Elihu Root, *Men and Policies* (HUP, 1924); Stuart P. Sherman, *Americans* (S, 1922); Frederic J. Stimson, *My United States* (S, 1931); Charles Willis Thompson, *Party Leaders of the Time* (G. W. Dillingham Co., 1906), and *Presidents I've Known and Two Near Presidents* (BM, 1929); Dixon Wecter, *The Hero in America* (S, 1941); John S. Wise, *Recollections of Thirteen Presidents* (D, 1906).

(9) The following books, devoted mainly to other subjects, contain references to TR: Charles D. Abbott, *Howard Pyle: A Chronicle* (H, 1925); Jack Abernathy, *"Catch 'Em Alive Jack," The Life and Adventures of an American Pioneer* (AP, 1936), and *In Camp with TR* (Oklahoma City, Times-Journal Publishing Co., 1933); Sam Hanna Acheson, *Joe Bailey, The Last Democrat* (M, 1932); Henry Adams, *The Education of Henry Adams* (HM, 1918), *Letters, 1892–1918*, ed. Worthington C. Ford (HM, 1938), and *Henry Adams and His Friends*, ed. Harold Cater (HM, 1947); Jane Addams, *The Second Twenty Years at Hull-House* (M, 1930); Cyrus Adler, *Jacob H. Schiff, His Life and Letters*,

2 vols. (D, 1929); DeAlva S. Alexander, *Four Famous New Yorkers* (Ht, 1923); Eugene N. Anderson, *The First Moroccan Crisis, 1904–1906* (UCP, 1930); Isabel Anderson, *Presidents and Pies* (HM, 1920); William Frederic Badè, *The Life and Letters of John Muir,* 2 vols. (HM, 1924); Ray Stannard Baker, *American Chronicle* (S, 1945); Richard C. Baker, *The Tariff under R and Taft* (Hastings, Neb., Democrat Printing Co., 1941); James W. Barrett, *Joseph Pulitzer and His World* (Vanguard, 1941); David S. Barry, *Forty Years in Washington* (LB, 1924); Clara Barrus, *John Burroughs, Boy and Man* (D, 1920), and *The Life and Letters of John Burroughs,* 2 vols. (HM, 1925); Hamilton Basso, *Mainstream* (RH, 1943); Emily Bax, *Miss Bax of the Embassy* (HM, 1939); Charles A. Beard and Mary Beard, *The Rise of American Civilization,* 2 vols. (M, 1928); Norman Beasley, *Frank Knox, American* (D, 1936); Thomas Beer, *Hanna* (K, 1929); Eleanor Robson Belmont, *The Fabric of Memory* (F, 1957); Poultney Bigelow, *Seventy Summers,* 2 vols. (Edward Arnold, 1925); J. B. Bishop, *Charles Joseph Bonaparte, His Life and Public Services* (S, 1922); J. B. Bishop and Farnham Bishop, *Goethals, Genius of the Panama Canal* (H, 1930); David Bispham, *A Quaker Singer's Recollections* (M, 1920); Edward Bok, *The Americanization of Edward Bok* (S, 1922), and *Twice Thirty* (S, 1925); Herbert W. Bowen, *Recollections Diplomatic and Undiplomatic* (New York, Grafton Press, 1926); Claude G. Bowers, *Beveridge and the Progressive Era* (HM, 1932); Gamaliel Bradford, *Journal,* ed. Van Wyck Brooks (HM, 1933); George Brett, *Forty Years-Forty Millions, the Career of Frank A. Munsey* (F, 1935); John Ely Briggs, *William Peters Hepburn* (State Historical Society of Iowa, 1919); Ira V. Brown, *Lyman Abbott, Christian Evolutionist* (HUP, 1953); David Bryn-Jones, *Frank B. Kellogg: A Biography* (P, 1937); Roger Burlingame, *Of Making Many Books* (S, 1946); Anna Robeson Burr, *Weir Mitchell, His Life and Letters* (Duffield, 1930); L. White Busbey, *Uncle Joe Cannon* (Ht, 1927); Nicholas Murray Butler, *Across the Busy Years,* 2 vols. (S, 1940); Archie Butt, *Letters,* ed. Lawrence F. Abbott (D, 1924), and *Taft and Roosevelt,* 2 vols. (D, 1930).

John Chamberlain, *Farewell to Reform* (Liveright, 1932); Walter Chambers, *Samuel Seabury, A Challenge* (Ce, 1932); Mrs. Winthrop Chanler, *Roman Spring* (LB, 1934); Frank M. Chapman, *Autobiography of a Bird-Lover* (AC, 1933); George K. Cherrie, *Dark Trails* (P, 1930); Champ Clark, *My Quarter Century of American Politics,* 2 vols. (H, 1920); Irvin S. Cobb, *Exit Laughing* (BM, 1941); Louis A. Coolidge, *An Old-Fashioned Senator: Orville H. Platt of Connecticut* (P, 1910); Lewis Corey, *The House of Morgan* (New York, G. Howard Watt, 1930); Royal

Cortissoz, *The Life of Whitelaw Reid*, 2 vols. (S, 1921); James M. Cox, *Journey through My Years* (SS, 1946); Shelby M. Cullom, *Fifty Years of Public Service* (McC, 1911); Natalie Curtis, *The Indian Book* (H, 1907); Josephus Daniels, *Editor in Politics* (UNCP, 1941); Loyal Davis, *J. B. Murphy, Stormy Petrel of Surgery* (P, 1938); Charles G. Dawes, *A Journal of the McKinley Years,* ed. Bascom N. Timmons (R.R. Donnelley, 1950); Margaret Deland, *Golden Yesterdays* (H, 1941); Tyler Dennett, *John Hay: From Poetry to Politics* (DM, 1933); Alfred L. P. Dennis, *Adventures in American Diplomacy, 1896–1906* (Du, 1928); Chauncey M. Depew, *My Memories of Eighty Years* (S, 1922); Benjamin P. De Witt, *The Progressive Movement* (M, 1915); Robert J. Donovan, *The Assassins* (H, 1955); George H. Doran, *Chronicles of Barabbas, 1884–1934* (HB, 1935); John Drew, *My Years on the Stage* (Du, 1922); Arthur W. Dunn, *From Harrison to Harding,* 2 vols. (P, 1922), and *Gridiron Nights* (St, 1915).

Maurice Francis Egan, *Recollections of a Happy Life* (Do, 1924); Maud Howe Elliott, *Sicily in Shadow and in Sun* (LB, 1910), and *Three Generations* (LB, 1923); W. W. Ellsworth, *A Golden Age of Authors* (HM, 1919); Robert D. Evans, *An Admiral's Log* (A, 1910); Edwin A. Falk, *Fighting Bob Evans* (Cape & Smith, 1931); Louis Filler, *Crusaders for American Liberalism* (HB, 1939); Russell H. Fitzgibbon, *Cuba and the United States, 1900–1935* (Menasha, Wis., George Banta Publishing Co., 1935); Charles R. Flint, *Memories of an Active Life* (P, 1923); Joseph B. Foraker, *Notes of Busy Life,* 2 vols. (Stewart & Kidd, 1917); Julia B. Foraker, *I Would Live It Again: Memories of a Vivid Life* (H, 1932); William Dudley Foulke, *Fighting the Spoilsmen* (P, 1919), *A Hoosier Autobiography* (OUP, 1922), and *Lucius B. Swift, A Biography* (BM, 1930); Mrs. Daniel Chester French, *Memories of a Sculptor's Wife* (HM, 1928); Hamlin Garland, *Companions on the Trail* (M, 1931), *A Daughter of the Middle Border* (M, 1921), *My Friendly Contemporaries* (M, 1932), and *Roadside Meetings* (M, 1930); John A. Garraty, *Henry Cabot Lodge: A Biography* (K, 1953); E. E. Garrison, *Roosevelt, Wilson and the Federal Reserve Law* (Boston, The Christopher Publishing House, 1931); Arnold Genthe, *As I Remember* (RH, 1936); Herbert Adams Gibbons, *John Wanamaker,* 2 vols. (H, 1926); Rosamond Gilder, ed., *Letters of Richard Watson Gilder* (HM, 1916); Frederick H. Gillet, *George Frisbie Hoar* (HM, 1934); Washington Gladden, *Recollections* (HM, 1909); Elsie Glück, *John Mitchell, Miner* (JD, 1929); Eric F. Goldman, *Charles J. Bonaparte, Patrician Reformer: His Earlier Career* (JHP, 1943); Samuel Gompers, *Seventy Years of Life and Labor,* 2 vols. (Du, 1925); Marie D. Gorgas and Burton J. Hendrick, *William Crawford*

Gorgas, His Life and Work (D, 1935); Harold F. Gosnell, *Boss Platt and His New York Machine* (UCP, 1924); Robert Grant, *Fourscore* (HM, 1934); Viscount Grey, of Fallodon, *Fallodon Papers* (HM, 1926); Solomon B. Griffin, *People and Politics, Observed by a Massachusetts Editor* (LB, 1923), and W. *Murray Crane* (LB, 1926); Lloyd C. Griscom, *Diplomatically Speaking* (LB, 1940); Stephen Gwynn, ed., *The Letters and Friendships of Sir Cecil Spring Rice*, 2 vols. (HM, 1929).

Hermann Hagedorn, *Edwin Arlington Robinson, A Biography* (M, 1938), and *Leonard Wood: A Biography*, 2 vols. (H, 1931); Sir H. Rider Haggard, *The Days of My Life*, 2 vols. (Lo, 1926); John Hays Hammond, *Autobiography*, 2 vols. (F, 1935); Norman Hapgood, *The Changing Years: Reminiscences* (F, 1930); George Harvey, *Henry Clay Frick, The Man* (S, 1928); John Hay, *Letters and Extracts from His Diary*, 3 vols. (Washington, Privately printed, 1908); George H. Haynes, *The Life of Charles G. Washburn* (HM, 1931); Will H. Hays, *Memoirs* (D, 1955); Charles Downer Hazen, ed., *The Letters of William Roscoe Thayer* (HM, 1926); Burton J. Hendrick, *The Life of Andrew Carnegie*, 2 vols. (D, 1932); George F. Hoar, *Autobiography of Seventy Years*, 2 vols. (S, 1903); Henry F. Holthusen, *James W. Wadsworth, Jr.: A Biographical Sketch* (P, 1926); Irwin Hood ("Ike") Hoover, *Forty-Two Years in the White House* (HM, 1934); Esme Howard, *Theatre of Life* (LB, 1936); L. O. Howard, *Fighting the Insects* (M, 1933); M. A. DeWolfe Howe, *Barrett Wendell and His Letters* (AMP, 1924), *George von Lengerke Meyer, His Life and Public Services* (DM, 1920), *James Ford Rhodes, American Historian* (A, 1929), *John Jay Chapman and His Letters* (HM, 1937), and *Portrait of an Independent: Moorfield Storey* (HM, 1932); Mildred Howells, ed., *Life in Letters of William Dean Howells*, 2 vols. (D, 1928); Henry James, *Letters*, ed. Percy Lubbock, 2 vols. (S, 1920); Henry James, *Charles W. Eliot*, 2 vols (HM, 1930); Maria Jeritza, *Sunlight and Song* (A, 1924); Philip C. Jessup, *Elihu Root*, 2 vols. (DM, 1938); Alvin Johnson, *Pioneer's Progress* (VP, 1952); Claudius O. Johnson, *Borah of Idaho* (Lo, 1936); Clifton Johnson, *John Burroughs Talks* (HM, 1922); Robert Underwood Johnson, *Remembered Yesterdays* (LB, 1923); Walter Johnson, ed., *Selected Letters of William Allen White* (Ht, 1947), and *William Allen White's America* (Ht, 1947); Willis F. Johnson, *George Harvey, "A Passionate Patriot"* (HM, 1929); Alex Johnston, *The Life and Letters of Sir Harry Johnston* (Jonathan Cape, 1929); Sir Harry H. Johnston, *The Story of My Life* (BM, 1923); David Starr Jordan, *The Days of a Man*, 2 vols. (World Book Co., 1922); J. J. Jusserand, *What Me Befell* (HM, 1934); Otto H. Kahn, *Of Many Things* (Boni & Liveright, 1926); Richard Kearton, *A Naturalist's Pil-*

grimage (HM, 1926); George Kennan, *E. H. Harriman, A Biography* (HM, 1922); Grant C. Knight, *The Strenuous Age in American Literature* (UNCP, 1954); H. H. Kohlsaat, *From McKinley to Harding: Personal Recollections of Our Presidents* (S, 1923).

John LaFarge, *The Manner Is Ordinary* (HB, 1954); Robert M. La Follette, *La Follette's Autobiography: A Personal Narrative of Political Experiences* (Madison, Wis., The Robert M. La Follette Co., 1913); Franklin K. Lane, *Letters,* ed. Anna W. Lane and Louise Herrick Wall (HM, 1922); William Lawrence, *Henry Cabot Lodge, A Biographical Sketch* (HM, 1925), and *Memories of a Happy Life* (HM, 1926); John D. Long, *America of Yesterday,* ed. Lawrence S. Mayo (AMP, 1923); Alice Roosevelt Longworth, *Crowded Hours* (S, 1933); W. H. Mallock, *Memoirs of Life and Literature* (H, 1920); E.S. Martin, *The Life of Joseph Hodges Choate,* 2 vols. (S, 1921); William G. McAdoo, *Crowded Years* (HM, 1931); John T. McCutcheon, *Drawn from Memory* (BM, 1950), and *In Africa* (BM, 1910); James McGurrin, *Bourke Cockran* (S, 1948); Leo E. Miller, *In the Wilds of South America* (S, 1918); Edward P. Mitchell, *Memoirs of an Editor* (S, 1924); Elting E. Morison, *Admiral Sims and the Modern American Navy* (HM, 1942); John, Viscount Morley, *Recollections,* 2 vols. (M, 1917); T. Bentley Mott, *Myron T. Herrick, Friend of France* (D, 1929), and *Twenty Years as Military Attaché* (OUP, 1937); Charles M. Mount, *John Singer Sargent* (Norton, 1955); Maud Nathan, *Once Upon a Time and Today* (P, 1933); Allan Nevins, *Grover Cleveland, A Study in Courage* (DM, 1933), *Henry White: Thirty Years of American Diplomacy* (H, 1930), *John D. Rockefeller,* 2 vols. (S, 1940), and *Letters of Grover Cleveland* (HM, 1933); Charles S. Olcott, *The Life of William McKinley,* 2 vols. (HM, 1916).

Albert Bigelow Paine, *Mark Twain: A Biography,* 3 vols. (H, 1912); Frederick Palmer, *Newton D. Baker: America at War,* 2 vols. (DM, 1931), and *With My Own Eyes* (BM, 1933); George H. Parker, *The World Expands* (HUP, 1946); Samuel W. Pennypacker, *The Autobiography of a Pennsylvanian* (W, 1918); Bliss Perry, *And Gladly Teach* (HM, 1935), *Life and Letters of Henry Lee Higginson* (AMP, 1921), and *Richard Henry Dana, 1851–1931* (HM, 1933); Gifford Pinchot, *Breaking New Ground* (HB, 1947); Thomas C. Platt, *Autobiography,* ed. Louis J. Lang (New York, B.W. Dodge, 1910); Henry F. Pringle, *The Life and Times of William Howard Taft,* 2 vols. (F, 1939); Merlo J. Pusey, *Charles Evans Hughes,* 2 vols. (M, 1951); George H. Putnam, *Memories of a Publisher, 1865–1915* (P, 1915); W.S. Rainsford, *The Story of a Varied Life* (D, 1922); C.C. Regier, *The Era of the Muckrakers* (UNCP, 1932); Agnes Repplier, *J. William White, M.D.* (HM,

1919); Emma Repplier, *Agnes Repplier, A Memoir* (Dorrance, 1957); Leon B. Richardson, *William E. Chandler, Republican* (DM, 1940); Mary Roberts Rinehart, *My Story* (F, 1931); Presley Marion Rixey *et al.*, *The Life Story of Presley Marion Rixey* (Strassburg, Va., Shenandoah Publishing House, Inc., 1930); Theodore Roosevelt, Jr., *Average Americans* (S, 1919); Baron Rosen, *Forty Years of Diplomacy*, 2 vols. (K, 1922); Victor Rosewater, *Back Stage in 1912* (Dorrance, 1932); Otto A. Rothert, *The Story of a Poet: Madison Cawein* (Louisville, Ky., John P. Morton & Co., 1921); Hugh Lenox Scott, *Some Memories of a Soldier* (Ce, 1928); James Brown Scott, *Robert Bacon, Life and Letters* (D, 1923); Don C. Seitz, *Joseph Pulitzer, His Life and Letters* (SS, 1929); George W. Smalley, *Anglo-American Memories*, Second Series (P, 1912); Ira R.T. Smith and Joe Alex Morris, *"Dear Mr. President": The Story of Fifty Years in the White House Mail Room* (JM, 1949); Lincoln Steffens, *Autobiography* (HB, 1931) and *Letters*, 2 vols. (HB, 1938); Nathaniel W. Stephenson, *Nelson W. Aldrich* (S, 1930); William R. Stewart, *The Philanthropic Work of Josephine Shaw Lowell* (M, 1911); Henry L. Stimson and McGeorge Bundy, *On Active Service in Peace and War* (H, 1948); Henry L. Stoddard, *It Costs To Be President* (H, 1938); George Stewart Stokes, *Agnes Repplier, Lady of Letters* (Univ. of Pennsylvania Press, 1949); Maria Longworth Storer, *In Memoriam Bellamy Storer, with Personal Remembrances of President McKinley, President Roosevelt and John Ireland, Archbishop of St. Paul* (Privately printed, 1923); Amy Strachey, *St. Loe Strachey, His Life and His Paper* (Brewer and Warren, n.d.); John St. Loe Strachey, *The Adventure of Living* (P, 1922); Oscar S. Straus, *Under Four Administrations: From Cleveland to Taft* (HM, 1922); Mark Sullivan, *The Education of an American* (D, 1938), and *Our Times*, Vols. I–VI (S, 1926–1935); Sir Percy Sykes, *Sir Mortimer Durand, A Biography* (Cassell, 1926); Horace Dutton Taft, *Memories and Opinions* (M, 1942); Mrs. William Howard Taft, *Recollections of Full Years* (DM, 1914); Ida M. Tarbell, *All in the Day's Work* (M, 1939), and *The Life of Elbert H. Gary: The Story of Steel* (A, 1925); William Roscoe Thayer, *The Life of John Hay*, 2 vols. (HM, 1915); Janet Penrose Trevelyan, *The Life of Mrs. Humphry Ward* (Constable, 1923); Joseph P. Tumulty, *Woodrow Wilson As I Know Him* (D, 1921); Mark Twain, *Autobiography*, ed. A.B. Paine, 2 vols. (H, 1924), and *Mark Twain in Eruption*, ed. Bernard DeVoto (H, 1940); Oswald Garrison Villard, *Fighting Years* (HB, 1939); Charles Wagner, *My Impressions of America* (McClure, Phillips, 1906); Louise Ware, *Jacob A. Riis* (AC, 1938); Booker T. Washington, *My Larger Education* (D, 1911); James E. Watson, *As I Knew Them* (BM, 1936); Richard

Welling, *As the Twig Is Bent* (P, 1942); M.R. Werner, *Julius Rosenwald* (H, 1939); Edith Wharton, *A Backward Glance* (AC, 1934); William Allen White, *Autobiography* (M, 1946), and *Masks in a Pageant* (M, 1928); Brand Whitlock, *Journal*, ed. Allan Nevins (AC, 1936), and *Letters*, ed. A.N. (AC, 1936); Harvey W. Wiley, *An Autobiography* (BM, 1930); John K. Winkler, *William Randolph Hearst, A New Appraisal* (Hastings House, 1955); Count Witte, *Memories*, ed. Abraham Yarmolinsky (D, 1921); Simon Wolf, *The Presidents I Have Known from 1860 to 1918* (Washington, D.C., Byron S. Adams, 1918); Linnie Marsh Wolfe, *Son of the Wilderness: The Life of John Muir* (K, 1947).

(10) This final section contains a list of magazine articles about TR: Lyman Abbott, "TR: A Personal Sketch," *O*, LXXV (1904), 523–26, and "TR as I See Him," *O*, CII (1912), 301–5; Jane Addams and others, "TR, Social Worker: A Symposium," *Survey*, XLI (1919), 523–31; Carl Akeley, "The R I Knew," *Woman's Magazine*, Nov. 1919, pp. 9, 63; J.C. Alves de Lima, "Reminiscences of R in Brazil," *Brazilian American*, V, Feb. 1927, pp. 7+; Orland K. Armstrong, "He Tracked Bear for R," N.Y. *Herald-Tribune*, Jan. 3, 1932, pp. 4–5+; Thomas A. Bailey, "TR and the Alaska Boundary Settlement," *Can. Hist. R.*, XVIII (1937), 123–30; Howard K. Beale, "TR's Ancestry, A Study in Heredity," *New York Genealogical and Biographical Record*, LXXXV (1954), 196–205; Dan Beard, "Masonic Recollections of R," *New York Masonic Outlook*, III (1926), 43; Nelson M. Blake, "Ambassadors at the Court of TR," *MVHR*, XLII (1955), 179–206; Samuel G. Blythe, "Having a Bully Time: The Minor Activities of a Major President," *SEP*, CLXXXI, Jan. 30, 1909, pp. 3+; Charles J. Bonaparte, "Experiences of a Cabinet Officer under R," *Ce*, N.S LVII (1910), 752–58; Herbert W. Bowen, "R and Venezuela," *NAR*, CCX (1919), 414–17; Glenn Brown, "R and the Fine Arts," *American Architect*, CXVI (1919), 709–19, 739–59, and "A Tribute to TR," *American Mag. of Art*, X (1919), 216; Russell Buchanan, "TR and American Neutrality, 1914–1917," *AHR*, XLIII (1938), 775–90; William G. Burgin, "The Political Theory of TR," *SAQ*, XXII (1923), 97–114; Travers D. Carman, "Campaigning with TR," *O*, CXXI (1919), 181–82; Leander T. Chamberlain, "A Chapter of National Dishonor," *NAR*, CXCV (1912), 145–74; Edward B. Clark, "The Lion Hunter as a Bird Lover," *SEP*, Mar. 1, 1919, pp. 15+, and "Real Naturalists on Nature Faking," *Everybody's*, XVII (1907), 423–27; Mrs. Ralph Stuart Clinton, "As a Girl Saw TR," *LHJ*, XXXVI, Oct. 1919, pp. 174, 177; John Corbin, "R in His Writing," *Sat. R. of Lit.*, III (1927), 590–91; Royal Cortissoz, "R and the Fine Arts," N.Y. *Tribune*, June 1, 1919; Whitney R. Cross, "Ideas in Politics: The Conservation Policies of the

Two Roosevelts," *Jour. History of Ideas*, XIV (1953), 421–38; Natalie Curtis, "Mr. R and Indian Music," *O*, CXXI (1919), 399–400, and "TR in Hopi-Land," *O*, CXXIII (1919), 87+.

William T. Dantz, "TR, Cowboy and Ranchman," *HaW*, XLVIII (1904), 1212+; Frederick M. Davenport, "President R in the Yellowstone," *O*, CXLII (1926), 27+; Charles Dawbarn, "TR, The Man and President: The Impressions of a Visitor to Oyster Bay," *Pall Mall Mag.*, Jan. 1909, pp. 66–71; Tyler Dennett, "Could T.R. Have Stopped the War?" *WW*, XLIX (1925), 392–99; John Dewey, "TR," *Dial*, LXVI (1919), 115–16; Henry C. Dwight, "A Little Journey with TR," *O*, CXXXVIII (1924), 286–88; Maurice F. Egan, "TR in Retrospect," *Atl*, CXXIII (1919), 676–85; Guglielmo Ferrero, "TR: A Characterization," *SAQ*, IX (1910), 286–88; John A. Ferris, "When R Came to Dakota," *Wide World*, March 1921, pp. 435–40; George Fitch, " 'Seeing R'," *American Mag.*, LXVI (1908), 228–36; Ambrose Flack, "TR and My Green-Gold Fountain Pen," *New Yorker*, XXIV, May 22, 1948, pp. 90+, and "The President's Advice," *SEP*, CCXXI, Apr. 12, 1949, pp. 24+; W. Robert Foran, "With R in Africa," *Field and Stream*, Oct. 1912, pp. 591–95; James Earle Fraser, "The R I Knew," *Designer*, Oct. 1919, p. 7; Hamlin Garland, "My Neighbor, TR," *Everybody's*, XLI, Oct. 1919, pp. 9–16, 94; John A. Garraty, ed., "TR on the Telephone," *Amer. Heritage*, Vol. IX, No. 1, Dec. 1957, pp. 99–108; Edwin A. Grosvenor, "A Phi Beta Kappa Interview with TR," *Phi Beta Kappa Key*, III (1919), 544–45; Curtis Guild, Jr., "TR at Harvard," *Harv. Grad. Mag.*, X (1901), 177–83; Hermann Hagedorn, "Conversation at Dusk along the Little Missouri," *O*, CXXIII (1919), 137–43; Luella J. Hall, "A Partnership in Peace-Making: TR and William II," *Pacific Hist. R.*, XIII (1944), 390–411; *Journal of Am. Hist.*, XIII (1919), 297–350—TR Memorial Number; Viscount Kentaro Kaneko, "R on Japan," *Asia*, XXXII (1932), 538–41; George Kennan, "The Psychology of Mr. R," *NAR*, CCIII (1916), 790–94.

J. Laurence Laughlin, "R at Harvard," *R of R's*, LXX (1924), 391–98; Francis E. Leupp, "R the Politician," *Atl*, CIX (1912), 843–52, and "Taft and R: A Composite Study," *Atl*, CVI (1910), 648–53; Sonya Levien, "The Great Friend," *Woman's Home Companion*, XLVI, Oct. 1919, pp. 7+; Seward W. Livermore, "The Venezuela Crisis of 1902–1903," *AHR*, LI (1946), 452–71; James C. Malin, "R and the Elections of 1884 and 1888," *MVHR*, XIV (1927), 25–38; C. Hart Merriam, "R the Naturalist," *Science*, N.S. LXXV (1932), 181–83; Victor H. Metcalf, "Personal Recollections of TR," *U. of Cal. Chronicle*, XXI (1919), 139–44; Robert J. Mooney, "Boxing and Wrestling with R in the White House," *O*, CXXXV (1923), 310–12; William McK. Mooney, "Boxing Lessons from TR,'

Leslie's Ill'd Weekly, CXXXIII (1921), 548–49; George E. Mowry, "TR and the Election of 1910," *MVHR*, XXV (1939), 523–34; Laurence O. Murray, "Greatness of TR, Told by His Former Assistant," Elmira *Sunday Telegram*, Oct. 4, 1925; *Natural History*, Jan. 1919–R Memorial Number: Douglas O. Naylor, "Col. R as His Guide Remembers Him," New York *Times*, Jan. 6, 1929; Henry B. Needham, "R on the Progressive Fight," *SEP*, CLXXXVI, Oct. 25, 1913, pp. 3–4+, "Where R Stands Today," *SEP*, CLXXXIII, Apr. 22, 1911, pp. 3+, "Why R Opposes Taft," *SEP*, CLXXXIV, May 4, 1912, pp. 3+; Allan Nevins, "If Roosevelt Looks Back at Roosevelt," *N.Y. Times Mag.*, Oct. 22, 1933, pp. 4+; Russel B. Nye, "TR as Historian," *Nassau County Hist. Jour.*, III, Fall-Winter 1940, pp. 3–7; Vincent O'Sullivan, "TR," *New Witness*, Jan. 17, 1919, pp. 234-36; Thomas Nelson Page, "President R from the Standpoint of a Southern Democrat," *Metropolitan*, March 1905, pp. 671–81; Frederick Palmer, "The T.R. Who Lives in the Memory," *N.Y. Times Mag.*, Jan. 1, 1939, pp. 6+; Henry F. Pringle, "TR and the South," *Virginia Quar. R.*, IX (1933), 14–25; George H. Putnam, "TR, Boy and Man," *R of R's*, LIX (1919), 153–55; John H. Richards, "R's Talks with His Physician," ed. Hermann Hagedorn, *SEP*, CXCV, Dec. 9, 1922, pp. 40+; Donald Richberg, "We Thought It Was Armageddon," *Survey*, LXI (1929), 723–25+; J. Fred Rippy, "The Initiation of the Customs Receivership in the Dominican Republic," *Hispanic-Amer. Hist. R.*, XVII (1937), 419–57; Margaret Roberts, "In the Bad Lands, When I Knew T.R.," *McCall's*, Oct. 1919; Corinne Roosevelt Robinson, "Recollections of My Brother as a Mason," *N.Y. Masonic Outlook*, III (1926), 41–43; Theodore Roosevelt, Jr., "A Boy's Book Rambles," *Bookman*, LX (1925), 687–91; Earle D. Ross, "R and Agriculture," *MVHR*, XIV (1927), 287–300.

Homer Saint-Gaudens, "R and Our Coin Designs," *Ce*, XCIX (1920), 721–36; William S. Sims, "R and the Navy," *McClure's*, LIV, Nov. 1922, pp. 32–41, Dec. 1922, pp. 56+, and "TR at Work," LIV (1923), pp. 61+; Upton Sinclair, "Good Bye, Teddy," *New Appeal*, Feb. 8, 1919; V. Stefansson, "Colonel R as Explorer," *R of R's*, LIX (1919), 165–66; M. E. Stone, Jr., "TR—Please Answer," *Metropolitan*, XXXIV (1911), 415–27, 543–54, 723–32, XXXV (1911), 265–78, 487–500; Julian Street, "On the Jump with R," *Collier's*, LVII, June 10, 1916, pp. 5–6+, and "The Convention and the Colonel," *Collier's*, LVII, July 1, 1916, pp. 5–7+; Josephine Stricker, "R a Hero to the Private Secretary," *N.Y. Tribune Magazine and Review*, Oct. 5, 12, 1919, and "R at Closest Range," *Delineator*, XCV, Sept. 1919, pp. 13+; Simeon Strunsky, "TR and the Prelude to 1914," *Foreign Affairs*, IV (1925), 144–53; Frederic E. Sturdevant, Untitled series of articles by an eyewitness of R's tour in

Egypt and Europe, San Francisco *Chronicle*, Jan. 12, 19, 26, Feb. 2, 9, 1919; William H. Taft, "My Predecessor," *Collier's*, XLII, March 6, 1909, p. 25; André Tardieu, "Three Visits to Mr. R," *Independent*, LXIV (1908), 860–63; William Roscoe Thayer, "Bowen vs. R," *NAR*, CCX (1919), 418–20; Charles Willis Thompson, "R Ten Years After," *Commonweal*, IX (1929), 308–10; James A. Tinsley, "R, Foraker, and the Brownsville Affray," *Jour. of Negro Hist.*, XLI (1956), 43–65; W.P. Trent, "TR as a Historian," *Forum*, (1896), 566–76; Cornelius Vanderbilt, Jr., "A Farewell to Fifth Avenue," *Redbook Magazine*, LXII, Feb. 1934, pp. 17+, Mar. 1934, pp. 36+; Louis Viereck, "R's German Days," *Success*, Oct. 1905; Albert T. Vollweiler, "R's Ranch Life in North Dakota," *Quar. J. of the Univ. of N.D.*, IX (1918), 31–49; Charles G. Washburn, "R and the 1912 Campaign," *Mass. Hist. Soc. Proceedings*, LIX (1925–1926), 303–12, and "TR," *Harv. Grad. Mag.*, XXVII (1919), 451–81; Richard L. Watson, Jr., "TR and Herbert Hoover," *SAQ*, LIII (1954), 109–29; Carl J. Weber, "Poet and President," *New Eng. Q.*, XVI (1943), 615–26; Richard Welling, "My Classmate, T.R.," *American Legion Monthly*, VI, Jan. 1929, pp. 9+, and "TR at Harvard; Some Personal Reminiscences," *O*, CXXVI (1920), 366–69; H. J. Whigham, "The Colonel As We Saw Him," *Metropolitan*, XLIX, March 1919, pp. 5, 7–8; Jack K. Williams, "R, Wilson, and the Progressive Movement," *SAQ*, LIV (1955), 207–20; Leonard Wood, "The Man Who Sleeps at Oyster Bay," *LHJ*, XXXVI, Oct. 1919, pp. 12–13+.